The Lessons

The Lessons

How to Understand Spiritual Principles, Spiritual Activities, and Rising Emotions

REVEREND SANDRA CASEY-MARTUS
CARLA R. MANCARI

The Lessons: How to Understand Spiritual Principles, Spiritual Activities, and Rising Emotions

Copyright © 2008 Sandra Casey-Martus and Carla R. Mancari. All rights reserved. No part of this book may be reproduced or retransmitted in any form or by any means without the written permission of the publisher.

Published by Wheatmark™
610 East Delano Street, Suite 104
Tucson, Arizona 85705 U.S.A.
www.wheatmark.com

International Standard Book Number: 978-1-58736-977-3
Library of Congress Control Number: 2007937850

Dedicated to
The Holy Spirit in the name of Jesus Christ
The Inspiration for this work

I sought you Lord in all the
noise of this world, in every part.
I sought you Lord until . . .
I found you in the silence of
my Heart.

CONTENTS

THESE ARE NOT chapter headings, but a list of lesson topics (teaching statements) of The Lessons. It is suggested Part I (1-15) be read and studied in the order it is arranged. Part II (16 – 207) topics (listed alphabetically) and Part III may be read and studied in any order. An asterisk indicates a lesson with a student's story.

EDITORS' FOREWORD xv
PREFACE xvii
ACKNOWLEDGMENTS xix
INTRODUCTION 1
INTRODUCTION BY SANDY 2

Part I
Lessons: 1 – 15

LESSON: 1 — SPIRITUAL WALK - JOURNEY 7
LESSON: 2 — AN INVITATION 7
LESSON: 3 — STRAIGHT GATE AND NARROW WAY 8
LESSON: 4 — SPIRITUAL HEART CENTER 9
LESSON: 5 — AWARENESS – CONSCIOUSNESS* 10
LESSON: 6 — CONDITIONING 14
LESSON: 7 — ATTACHMENT 15
LESSON: 8 — ATTRACTION 17
LESSON: 9 — ATTENTION* 19
LESSON: 10 — FORGIVENESS 21
LESSON: 11 — PURIFICATION PROCESS 22
LESSON: 12 — DETERMINED PURPOSE 24
LESSON: 13 — THE CHRIST CENTERED PRAYER* 24
LESSON: 14 — POWER PRAYER* 27
LESSON: 15 — HAND-TO-HEART PRAYER 30

Part II
Lessons: 16 – 207

LESSON: 16 — ACCEPT - ALLOW - RESPECT 35
LESSON: 17 — ACCEPTANCE 35
LESSON: 18 — ADVERSITY 36
LESSON: 19 — ALONENESS 37
LESSON: 20 — ANALYZING 37
LESSON: 21 — ANGER 38
LESSON: 22 — ANOINTING 39

LESSON: 23 — AVOIDANCE	39
LESSON: 24 — BAPTISM	40
LESSON: 25 — BELOVED	41
LESSON: 26 — BIRTH - DEATH	41
LESSON: 27 — BODY*	42
LESSON: 28 — BREATH	45
LESSON: 29 — CAN'T	45
LESSON: 30 — CELIBACY*	46
LESSON: 31 — CHARITY	48
LESSON: 32 — CHANGE - CONVERSION	48
LESSON: 33 — CHOICES AND DECISIONS*	50
LESSON: 34 — COMMITMENT	52
LESSON: 35 — COMPANY	52
LESSON: 36 — COMPARING	53
LESSON: 37 — COMPASSION	54
LESSON: 38 — COMPLACENCY	55
LESSON: 39 — CONCENTRATION	55
LESSON: 40 — CONFIDENCE	57
LESSON: 41 — CONSCIENCE	58
LESSON: 42 — CONSCIOUSNESS - RECOGNITION	58
LESSON: 43 — CONSENT	59
LESSON: 44 — CONTEMPLATIVE	60
LESSON: 45 — CONTRADICTIONS	61
LESSON: 46 — COURAGE	62
LESSON: 47 — CREATION	62
LESSON: 48 — CRISIS - SPIRITUAL	63
LESSON: 49 — DESIRES AND TEMPTATIONS*	64
LESSON: 50 — DETACHMENT*	66
LESSON: 51 — DIALOGUE - INTERNAL	68
LESSON: 52 — DISCERNMENT	69
LESSON: 53 — DISCIPLESHIP*	69
LESSON: 54 — DOUBTS	71
LESSON: 55 — DRAMA*	73
LESSON: 56 — DREAMS	74
LESSON: 57 — DRIFTING*	75
LESSON: 58 — EGO	78
LESSON: 59 — ENLIGHTENMENT*	78
LESSON: 60 — ENOUGH IS ENOUGH!*	79
LESSON: 61 — EUCHARIST*	81
LESSON: 62 — EVIL	82
LESSON: 63 — EXPANSIVE CONSCIOUSNESS*	82
LESSON: 64 — EXPECTATIONS*	84
LESSON: 65 — EXPERIENCES - SPIRITUAL	86
LESSON: 66 — FAITH	87
LESSON: 67 — FAITHFULNESS*	87
LESSON: 68 — FALL - GRAND FALL	89
LESSON: 69 — FEAR	91
LESSON: 70 — FLEXIBILITY	92
LESSON: 71 — FOCUS	93

LESSON: 72 — FOOD	93
LESSON: 73 — FREE - TOTALLY	95
LESSON: 74 — FREEDOM	96
LESSON: 75 — FRUSTRATION	96
LESSON: 76 — GIFTS	98
LESSON: 77 — GRACE	99
LESSON: 78 — GRATITUDE - EXPRESSED - SINCERE	99
LESSON: 79 — GRIEF*	101
LESSON: 80 — HABIT	102
LESSON: 81 — HEALING	103
LESSON: 82 — HEALTH - SPIRITUAL	104
LESSON: 83 — HOPE	105
LESSON: 84 — HOLY INSTANT	105
LESSON: 85 — HOLY SPIRIT	106
LESSON: 86 — HUGS	107
LESSON: 87 — HUMILITY - A HUMBLE SPIRIT*	108
LESSON: 88 — HUMOR	110
LESSON: 89 — IMAGININGS	111
LESSON: 90 — IMITATING	112
LESSON: 91 — IMPATIENCE	112
LESSON: 92 — IMPERSONAL	113
LESSON: 93 — INNER - OUTER*	114
LESSON: 94 — INSIGHTS AND REALIZATIONS	115
LESSON: 95 — INSPIRATION	116
LESSON: 96 — JESUS - PRE-EXISTENCE - PERSONAL - IMPERSONAL*	116
LESSON: 97 — JOY	118
LESSON: 98 — JUDGING	119
LESSON: 99 — KINGDOM	119
LESSON: 100 — LANGUAGE	120
LESSON: 101 — LAYERS	121
LESSON: 102 — LAZARUS RISING	123
LESSON: 103 — LESSONS - MISTAKES - ERRORS	125
LESSON: 104 — LISTENING	126
LESSON: 105 — LONELINESS	127
LESSON: 106 — LONGING	128
LESSON: 107 — LOVE (GOD'S)	130
LESSON: 108 — LOVING - DIVINE	131
LESSON: 109 — MARRIAGE	132
LESSON: 110 — MEMORY - RECALL	133
LESSON: 111 — MIND	133
LESSON: 112 — MOTHER MARY - SPIRIT OF MARY	134
LESSON: 113 — MOTIVATION	135
LESSON: 114 — NEGATIVITY	136
LESSON: 115 — "NO."	136
LESSON: 116 — OBEDIENCE*	137
LESSON: 117 — OPPOSITES	139
LESSON: 118 — OVERCOMING	140
LESSON: 119 — PATIENCE	141
LESSON: 120 — PENANCE	142

LESSON: 121	PENTECOST	142
LESSON: 122	PERSECUTION AND CRUCIFIXION	143
LESSON: 123	PERSON	144
LESSON: 124	PERSONALITY	144
LESSON: 125	PIERCING	145
LESSON: 126	POSITION	146
LESSON: 127	POWER - ABUSIVE	147
LESSON: 128	PRACTICAL LIVING	148
LESSON: 129	PRAISE AND BLAME*	148
LESSON: 130	PRAYER METHOD - SILENT	150
LESSON: 131	PRAYING - PRAYERS	150
LESSON: 132	PREPAREDNESS - READINESS - WILLINGNESS*	153
LESSON: 133	PRESENCE	154
LESSON: 134	PRESENT	155
LESSON: 135	PRIDE	156
LESSON: 136	PROGRESS	157
LESSON: 137	QUESTIONS	157
LESSON: 138	QUIET	158
LESSON: 139	QUITTING	158
LESSON: 140	RECOGNITION - JESUS' PRESENCE	159
LESSON: 141	RECONCILIATION - ATONEMENT - SALVATION*	159
LESSON: 142	REFERENCE	162
LESSON: 143	REFLECTION	163
LESSON: 144	REGRESSION- SPIRITUAL	163
LESSON: 145	REJECTING REALITY	164
LESSON: 146	RELATIONSHIPS	164
LESSON: 147	REMORSE	165
LESSON: 148	RESURRECTION - ASCENSION	166
LESSON: 149	RETREAT CENTER	167
LESSON: 150	SACRED AND SECRET	168
LESSON: 151	SENSES	169
LESSON: 152	SENSITIVITY	169
LESSON: 153	SERIOUS	171
LESSON: 154	SERVANT I - THE CHRIST*	171
LESSON: 155	SERVANT II - INDIVIDUAL TYPES	173
LESSON: 156	SEXUAL ENERGY	175
LESSON: 157	SIGN OF THE CROSS	175
LESSON: 158	SILENCE - OUTER AND INNER	176
LESSON: 159	SIN	177
LESSON: 160	SITTING	178
LESSON: 161	SLEEP	178
LESSON: 162	SOUL	179
LESSON: 163	SOUL PAIN	180
LESSON: 164	SOUNDS	180
LESSON: 165	SPIRITUAL DIRECTORS	181
LESSON: 166	STRANGER	183
LESSON: 167	SUFFERING	184
LESSON: 168	SUPPLY*	185
LESSON: 169	SURRENDER	187

LESSON: 170	SYMBOLS AND RITUALS	188
LESSON: 171	TEACHER - TYPES	188
LESSON: 172	TEACHER PRINCIPLES	189
LESSON: 173	TEARS - CRYING	190
LESSON: 174	THOUGHTS - EMOTIONS - FEELINGS	191
LESSON: 175	TIME	191
LESSON: 176	TOOLS	192
LESSON: 177	TRANSITION	193
LESSON: 178	TRUST I: THE CHRIST*	193
LESSON: 179	TRUST II: TRUST IN A CHRIST CENTERED TEACHER*	195
LESSON: 180	TRUST III: TRUST REQUIRED OF A STUDENT	197
LESSON: 181	TRUTH	198
LESSON: 182	TRYING	199
LESSON: 183	TWO WORLDS	200
LESSON: 184	UNFORGETTABLE	201
LESSON: 185	VALUING AND APPRECIATING*	201
LESSON: 186	VANITY	203
LESSON: 187	VIRGINAL CONCEPTION*	204
LESSON: 188	VOCABULARY	205
LESSON: 189	VOICES - COMMENTS AND THOUGHTS - INTERNAL*	206
LESSON: 190	VOID*	208
LESSON: 191	VULNERABLE*	209
LESSON: 192	WAKING UP	210
LESSON: 193	WALKING ALONE	211
LESSON: 194	WALKING IN PLACE	211
LESSON: 195	WASTE	212
LESSON: 196	WHEN THE STUDENT IS READY	213
LESSON: 197	"WHY, GOD?"	213
LESSON: 198	WILL-FREE	214
LESSON: 199	WITHDRAW	215
LESSON: 200	WISDOM*	216
LESSON: 201	WITNESS	217
LESSON: 202	THE "WORD"	217
LESSON: 203	WORDS - WRITTEN - SPOKEN	218
LESSON: 204	WORSHIP	219
LESSON: 205	X-MAS - CHRISTMAS	219
LESSON: 206	YIELDING	220
LESSON: 207	ZONE — SPIRITUAL	221

Part III
Exercises
Major Points
"Now What?"
Conclusion

EXERCISES	225
MAJOR POINTS	228
"NOW WHAT?"	229
CONCLUSION - A CERTAINTY	230

EDITORS' FOREWORD

DO NOT RUSH through this book. Forge ahead slowly, and contemplatively, and we believe you will be rewarded.

In an effort to learn and practice silent prayer, with Carla as our teacher, we were introduced to and asked to edit this work. The truths found in this work are enlightening and evocative. The student is blessed.

Along the way, through Sandy's stories, we have also come to know Sandy. She brings a down-to-earth, fresh-faced dimension to the very rewarding path that Carla would have us follow.

This is a work that has been sorely needed, as we know of no work of this magnitude, which teaches meditation and spiritual principles with an in depth, distinctive quality of inspiring guidance.

The student and teacher have had a unique association for over thirteen years. Although the connection between the student and teacher is a strong, private, and sacred one, nothing is held back. All is shared and freely given.

By slowly working through each Lesson, one feels a great sense of peace through truth and the realization that Christ is truly in our innermost being. No matter what areas of our outer selves demand attention, The Lessons define and ameliorate these symptoms, turning us inward again and again toward Jesus.

This work defines, guides, and teaches spiritual principles and truths most difficult to comprehend. It is of immense self-help value.

Gloria McCabe, B.A., Editor
Ellen S. Coyle, B.S, MEd., Editor

PREFACE

THIS WORK WAS developed over a period of 14 years. It is the result of a voluntary, ongoing, committed student - teacher metaphysical - spiritual relationship.

The relationship began in a barn during the dead of winter at a retreat center and continued with periodic visits, phone calls, and the use of the internet via email.

The Lessons were the written answers from the Spiritual Heart Center to the student's questions. The more serious the student became the more extensive the Lessons. The format of numbering each lesson was helpful as a learning tool and reference. When emailing or phoning for further explanation, the student could easily identify the topic in question. Numbering was also helpful when putting down and picking up lessons at a later time for study again.

The student kept and collected the lessons. As the student progressed, she found it was helpful to return and reference lessons periodically. As the student attained stages of enlightenment and began teaching, she was increasingly aware of the value The Lessons would have for Christian truth seekers.

Thus, what appears here are The Lessons and an occasional annotated story by the student written to flesh out a particular lesson teaching. The reader may attain a taste of how a student had worked with and/or struggled with a particular lesson, as she or he reads through the student's story.

The intent of this work is to present a definitive, concise Christian reference/work book to enhance and facilitate the understanding of spiritual principles. The goal for all being the realization of a permanent abiding awareness of the Holy Spirit in the name of Jesus Christ.

The Bible Scripture verses quoted, within The Lessons, are from the King James Version.

ACKNOWLEDGMENTS

THIS PRESENTATION WAS a joint effort. One particular student in the beginning, and many students since, made these translations of truth possible.

We are eternally indebted to all of the many teachers who have appeared in our lives on our spiritual journey.

Our appreciation to Gloria McCabe, Ellen S. Coyle, and Carol Hoffman who reviewed and patiently edited the manuscript. They gave, generously, of their time and effort without reward.

We are grateful to you, who seek truth and pray this work may help you on your spiritual walk, during your spiritual journey.

To the Creator of us all, we marvel at the guidance attended and the mind, heart, and soul realizations allowed through the Holy Spirit in the name of Jesus Christ.

INTRODUCTION

Whether you are just beginning your Christian Spiritual walk or have traveled it for a lifetime, you have the opportunity to read and study Christ Centered Spiritual Principles, as they relate to this world of opposites and beyond.

The Lessons were written from the Spiritual Heart Center. They were specifically written in response to Sandy's questions and needs. The Lessons lay the ground work upon which the Contemplative Invitation Teaching for the Christ Centered Prayer rests. Many have benefited from these teachings over the years. The Lessons are applicable to you, who are seeking the truth of your being.

The Lessons may assist you to understand, realize and recognize inner truth. You may begin to grasp the subtleties of the rising vibrating energies within an aware-awakened consciousness.

The Christian Spiritual walk is a journey to the reality of your true Being. As a Christian, Jesus Christ is your inner Guide, Teacher, and Master. You are an inner pilgrim journeying into the unknown to the known presence of God Oneness.

You, who are searching for truth, seeking to understand spiritual principles, spiritual activities, and rising emotions may benefit from the study of The Lessons. They may assist you in your daily prayer practice, and also find application in daily life.

You are encouraged to engage in a silent inner prayer practice. The three Christ Centered Prayer Practices, often referred to in The Lessons, are the silent Christ Centered Prayer, Power Prayer, and Hand to Heart Prayer. The Christ Centered Prayer method was revealed by Jesus Christ. It has been proven easy to learn, and is an effective spiritual practice supporting all phases of one's spiritual life journey.

The Lessons, prayer practices and soul explanations may take you on the ride of your life. Life's meanings may expand and the reality of your being may more fully reveal itself. When you understand the inner workings of consciousness, you may naturally and spontaneously enjoy a better connection with others. For the followers of Jesus Christ, it is from within the Spiritual Heart Center that the Holy Spirit reveals truth in the name of Jesus Christ. The Spiritual Heart Center is where mystical mysteries are resolved, and understanding and wisdom (in due time) are realized. "Straight *is* the gate, and narrow *is* the way" to the known awareness of reality. It awaits you through the practice of the Christ Centered Prayer (Lesson: 13).

Expansive awareness is all-inclusive. It excludes no thing, no one. With the least bit of intentional, devotional turning toward Jesus Christ, you may awaken from the conscious, personal sense state to an awareness of the impersonal oneness of God.

Within the Spiritual Heart Center the Holy Spirit in the name of Jesus Christ, reveals truth. It is here Christ Consciousness vibrates within the light of awareness of God, and penetrates all mysteries of life. The Spiritual Heart Center is the inner most Sacred place of your being. It is your Holy of Holies. You may begin your spiritual walk by turning within and may discover all that you seek. These treasures, once realized, may support, encourage, and perpetuate your progress on the spiritual path.

Life, awakened in awareness, is one in God. It is with your God Source you come to identify. You are about to enter the Spiritual Heart Center Zone. Come walk with Sandy and me through The Lessons.

INTRODUCTION BY SANDY

IN THIS WORK I am the student. My participation is one of questioning. My passion is deep and the stakes are high. After all I am dealing with the "ultimate" questions of life, death, meaning, purpose, place and real identity. Who? What? When? Where? Why? The answers to my questions fill these pages in raw honesty in the form of lessons. This manuscript is an ongoing dialogue and teaching between me and my teacher. As I formed the questions the answers began to inform, and reform me!

I attribute initiation into this spiritual walk to God and report my free response and consent. I was not coerced, threatened, nor for that matter promised a "rose garden." I was simply and directly invited into conversation with God. I agreed. These conversations, often facilitated by a wise teacher, helped me understand and decipher God's language and intent. When I found myself drifting or confused it was necessary, and indeed, a grace filled occasion to have one compassionate teacher to visit, email, or listen to on the other end of the phone.

There is only one thing I enjoy more than being a teacher and that is being a student! I recognize the direct relationship that exists between the student's desire and the teacher's response. When desire to learn and desire to teach meet in conversation, knowledge is exchanged in mutual satisfaction. Teaching and learning join. Gratitude is a mutual response. I know this from personal experience having spent a long time on both sides of the educative exchange.

Initially I was drawn to the utter mystery of God's presence in a well-carved church, at the age of eight with a simple invitation from a friend, "Would you like to go with me to church on Sunday?" My life's vocation began with a child's unselfconscious, "yes." An alluring world of silence, incense, whispers, bells; candles, icons, statues, dimmed lights, hardwood floors, rich red velvet curtains, stained glass windows all intrigued me, and held me captive. I intuited a yet unknown, unseen presence whom I wanted to know intimately and personally. Nothing ever has been the same since uttering that first "fiat." I never looked back and never regretted that consent.

My initiation into the sacred mysteries has been deeply Christian. My childhood conversations were with Jesus (of Nazareth). Gradually, they matured to include silent prayers on the Christ (of Faith). I prayed a lot, read a lot, visited lots of churches in secret, and lived what I would describe as an "intensely private" religious life. Running parallel to an otherwise "normal" suburban nuclear family childhood, was a relentless desire to deepen my relationship with God even more.

As long as I can consciously remember I have had a deep longing for God. I wanted it all — the knowledge of God and God. Throughout the 59 years of my life, to date, I have had many competent and wise teachers — many shapes, sizes, ages, personalities, and genders! Their patience, wisdom, and willingness to share information have informed my own teaching. Over the years parents, relatives, children, friends, pastors, priests, monks, nuns, neighbors, cats, ocean, sky, wind, sea, and space have mentored, prepared, and readied me for the experience of God's divine indwelling.

There is an old saying, "When the student is ready, the teacher appears." For me, *that* teacher appeared in a small barn during a contemplative prayer retreat in Colorado over thirteen years ago.

I had studied and spent over 20 years practicing various forms of contemplative prayer (East and West), and my new teacher suggested I select and stay with one Christian method. My response was initially hesitant and defensive. The ensuing comment, "Fine, perhaps you are not ready," immediately challenged my competitive nature. The result was ironic and shortly after that conversation I did, in fact, become exclusively a Christ Centered Prayer practitioner. My Christian spiritual walk was invigorated and renewed. It was to be the straight gate and narrow way — a journey into the heart of God.

This work is the manifestation of an on-going, student - teacher relationship of over thirteen years. The journey has not been without its detours, bumps, occasional dramas and disasters, as well as peak moments of delight and refreshment. I regret nothing, would change nothing, and I am grateful for it all.

As you read through these Lessons, please note they record one particular soul with one unique constellation of circumstances, resources, and challenges. My spiritual walk is certainly not exhaustive given the myriad of possibilities for any given human life's quest. I suspect some of the themes are universal and it is my prayer that these may resonate with you, the reader, in a helpful and illuminating way.

To know someone has crossed a similar threshold, walked the territory and survived, can be encouraging. I certainly am not "finished" with my walk, and I offer these pages as a study guide on your walk. Our God wants nothing more than to share the eternal Divine life and love with all.

Student
Reverend Sandra Casey-Martus

PART I
Lessons: 1 – 15

The Lessons are in the original format. As a learning tool and reference, you will find the numbering of each teaching statement (not paragraphs within the topics of the Lessons) is helpful. Numbering is also helpful when putting down and picking up a lesson at a later time for study again.

Each Lesson is a teaching that may benefit a beginner, advanced, and awakened student on a spiritual walk. If you find any teaching is difficult to understand, set it aside and continue with your Christ Centered Prayer practice (Lesson: 13). As your awareness expands, your understanding will evolve. Trust the Christ.

All the Lessons are as applied to the Contemplative Invitation Teaching.

LESSON: 1 — SPIRITUAL WALK - JOURNEY

The Spiritual walk - journey is a Christ Centered inner awakening to the reality of your true being. God; Christ the Son; and Holy Spirit; the Comforter is a living presence within a devotional heart. It is a journey that awakens you to the awareness and oneness of where you are, and have never left.

1. Your spiritual journey is by the Grace of God in awareness and the prompting of the Holy Spirit in the name of Jesus Christ. It is an inward pilgrimage of the unknown to the known presence of God.

2. On your Spiritual journey, you have scripture, prayers, sacraments, and a silent prayer practice to assist you. Realizations may manifest in your individual conscious expression of the known indwelling God presence.

3. Your God presence is all-inclusive. You may awaken from the personal sense state to the impersonal presence of God. "At that day ye shall know that I *am* in my Father, and ye in me, and I in you" (John 14: 20).

4. As a follower of Jesus Christ, you may walk a spiritual path and journey to the recognition and acceptance of Jesus Christ as your Guide and Master. You are carefully and painstakingly taken on a spiritual journey some thought possible only through arduous practices and by living a Christian monastic life.

5. Your Christ Centered walk may begin when there is the least bit of intentional, devotional turning toward Jesus Christ. In that moment, Jesus fulfills a living promise that allows the Holy Spirit, in His name, to teach and awaken you, who sleeps, "Where for he saith, Awake thou that sleepest, and arise from the dead, and Christ shall give thee light" (Ephesians 5: 14).

6. In your fully realized state of being, you come to know the Oneness of God's existence. The Holy Spirit in the name of Jesus Christ transforms the normal mundane sleeper to the most magnificent, natural and normal being. Natural, because you are more comfortable with your physical normality.

7. Through the relationship of the normal, personal, physical humanity of Jesus and the teaching of the Holy Spirit in the name of Jesus Christ, it is your God source you may identify. Jesus is the way, the truth, and the life. He guides you through Himself, and yourself, to your God reality. "Jesus saith unto him, 'I am the way, the truth, and the life: no man cometh unto the Father, but by me'" (John 14: 6).

8. The mind takes you on an outer journey through attraction of appearances in false concepts. Jesus Christ takes you on an inner journey through the aware reality of your being. "For through him both of us have access in one Spirit unto the Father" (Ephesians 2: 18).

+ +

LESSON: 2 — AN INVITATION

As it is written in Scripture, Jesus is constantly issuing an invitation to follow Him every moment of your life. It is an invitation to share the gifts and nature of God. "And he saith unto them, Follow me, and I will make you fishers of men" (Matthew 4: 19).

1. The invitation is never withdrawn. It is an open-ended invitation that allows you to follow in your own time and at your own pace. Jesus invites and then patiently awaits your arrival.

2. Jesus never pushes. He invites, and is available. It is an invitation, you need not know the way. Follow Jesus and He will show you the way. When you are ready, the inner door opens wide. Step inside.

3. Jesus has instructed you to follow His example, His way, and His teachings. He has left a trail to

follow. It is not difficult to find. It awaits your foot steps. "For even hereunto were ye called: because Christ also suffered for us, leaving us an example, that ye should follow his steps:" (I Peter 2: 21).

4. You are invited to return to your reality — your home. The way home lies within your Being. The candies of this world are bitter sweet. They are not lasting nor can they ever fill you as the Christ can.

5. Accept the invitation, and through the activity of the Holy Spirit in the name of Jesus Christ the way home will be a light one. "Come unto me, all ye that labour and are heavy laden, and I will give you rest" (Matthew 11: 28).

6. Jesus promises to lead. Accept His invitation to "Follow Me." You are being invited to share all that God has, all that God is. Accept the invitation, and be guided through a straight gate and narrow way to a spiritual feast of the truth in the Oneness of the Christ Consciousness. Follow Jesus.

+ +

LESSON: 3 — STRAIGHT GATE AND NARROW WAY

STRAIGHT IS THE gate and narrow is the way between the resting mind and the Sacred Spiritual Heart Center. It is the way that directly leads to the awareness of the Christ Consciousness. "Then said Jesus unto them again, Verily, verily, I say unto you, I am the door of the sheep" (John 10: 7).

1. As a Christian truth seeker, straight is the gate and narrow is the way that Jesus instructs you to follow, "Because strait *is* the gate, and narrow *is* the way, which leadeth unto life, and few there be that find it" (Matthew 7: 14).

2. It may be the most difficult to find; however, once found, it is the most attainable with the help and guidance of Jesus Christ. "That thy way may be known upon earth, thy saving health among all nations" (Psalm 67: 2).

3. When you intentionally begin the silent Christ Centered Prayer practice (Lesson: 13), you are taking the straight gate and narrow way; *you* have found it.

4. If it is difficult for you to learn how to follow the straight gate and narrow way, be in constant remembrance, "I can do nothing on my own . . ." (John 5: 30). A realized conscious awareness of this one Scripture teaching would take you to the straight gate and narrow way. It would bring you into a humble spirit and help maintain a silent prayer practice.

5. With the practice of the silent Christ Centered Prayer, you may gradually awaken to insights, revelations, and realizations of reality. "Thy way, O God, *is* in sanctuary: who *is* so great a God as *our* God?" (Psalm 77: 13).

6. Be patient with your silent prayer practice. The Christ of your being is not asking you to hurry. You are in a hurry when you first realize there is a silent prayer practice that points in the direction that takes you directly to the straight gate and narrow way. With a determined purpose, allow the purification process to gradually give rest to a restless mind.

7. Accept the unconditional Loving of God is not rushing you. It waits patiently and understands the straight gate and narrow way may be a difficult one for you. Place your total dependence and trust in Jesus Christ.

8. The straight gate and narrow way doesn't accept a half hearted attempt. It is the way that asks all that you are and all that you can be. Trust the bumps on the way will smooth out, as you wear them down. Every moment you practice the Christ Centered Prayer, may help to smooth out a rough spot.

9. There is no room on the way for experimentation or compromise. There is never an allowance for wavering from the known truth. It requires your full attention, devotion, obedience, and the earnest sincerity of your determination. However, it allows for time out and rest as it moves you on either slowly, or

rapidly, according to your devotional determination. At times, Jesus walks slowly, allowing you to catch up and at other times, He stops to wait for you. "In all thy ways acknowledge him, and he shall direct thy paths" (Proverb 3: 6).

10. Keep in mind, as you practice the silent Christ Centered Prayer, the straight gate and narrow way (and you are on it) takes you directly to one place — the realized Christ Consciousness. Have confidence that, "God *is* my strength *and* power: and he maketh my way perfect" (II Samuel 22: 33).

11. The straight gate and narrow way has no bends or slants. It goes in only one direction at all times, from the resting mind to the Sacred Spiritual Heart Center, and looking back, or around, may cause stumbling or possibly falling onto another way. A way that may appear easier to travel because the gate is wide and the way broad. Be not deceived, "Enter ye in at the strait gate: for wide *is* the gate, and broad *is* the way, that leadeth to destruction, and many there be which go in thereat:" (Matthew 7: 13).

12. The straight gate and narrow way takes you home to the awareness of the Christ Consciousness within the Spiritual Heart Center and, because you have done all in His name, Jesus awaits your arrival.

++++++++++++++++++++++++++

LESSON: 4 — SPIRITUAL HEART CENTER

For followers of Jesus Christ, the heart is a symbol of the Sacred Hearts of Jesus and of Blessed Mother Mary. It is in the area of the Spiritual Heart Center that the teachings of the Holy Spirit in the name of Jesus Christ manifest.

1. There exists a spiritual center, at the center of the chest between the breast, referred to as the Spiritual Heart Center and, "Now he which establisheth us with you in Christ, and hath anointed us, *is* God; Who hath also sealed us, and given the earnest of the Spirit in our hearts" (II Corinthians I: 21 - 22).

2. Within the Spiritual Heart Center is where the Christ Consciousness is; the prodigal child's (your) home. It is where the Father awaits your arrival and offers the feast of greater awareness of your being. "And because you are children, God hath sent the Spirit of his Son into our hearts, crying, Abba! Father!" (Galatians 4: 6).

3. As you are aware of the Spiritual Heart Center, you may come to realize the awareness of the Christ Consciousness where a purer, finer vibrating energy may be realized. "I call to remembrance my song in the night: I commune with mine own heart: and my spirit made diligent search" (Psalm 77: 6).

4. As a follower of Jesus Christ on this earth plane, your footsteps have but one purpose — to take you to the awareness of the Christ Consciousness and the Oneness of your God being. The Spiritual Heart Center is the access door (Jesus) to your reality. "For with the heart man believeth unto righteousness; and with the mouth confession is made unto salvation." (Romans 10: 10).

5. It is the Christ in "Christ-ian," through the Spiritual Heart Center, where you may seek to realize your Oneness existence. Your heart, soul, and mind devoted to the love of your God will guide your footsteps into an expanded Spiritual Heart Center. "Jesus said unto him, Thou shalt love the Lord thy God with all thy heart, and with all thy soul, and with all thy mind" (Matthew 22: 37).

6. Within the Spiritual Heart Center, the Holy Spirit reveals truth that is manifested through the Christ Consciousness and translated with a purified mind. "But that on the good ground are they, which in an honest and good heart, having heard the word, keep *it*, and bring forth fruit with patience" (Luke 8: 15).

7. It is here all mystical mysteries are resolved and knowledge, understanding, and wisdom is realized. It is here you may realize your uniqueness — the Word made flesh. "Blessed *are* the pure in heart: for they shall see God" (Matthew 5: 8).

8. The Christ Centered Prayer practice, may guide you directly to the straight gate and narrow way within the awareness of the Spiritual Heart Center, the Christ Consciousness, and the reality of your being. Trust Jesus is guiding and leading the way. "LET not your heart be troubled: ye believe in God, believe also in me" (John 14: 1).

9. With a realized awareness of the expanded Spiritual Heart Center, your form may be filled with the light of awareness of the Christ and graced with the unconditional Love of God. "And ye shall seek me, and find *me* when ye shall search for me with all your heart" (Jeremiah 29: 13).

10. Within the Spiritual Heart Center, you are taken on a mystical walk and journey through the Sacred Scriptures on a path traveled by Jesus Christ. It is within the Spiritual Heart Center you may realize the Christ Consciousness, expansiveness of awareness, and beyond.

+ +

LESSON: 5 — AWARENESS – CONSCIOUSNESS

AWARENESS IS CALM, silent, subtle, changeless, and without opposites. In the light of awareness consciousness, individual conscious expressions, mind, and the mind contents (senses, sensations) vibrate as manifestations.

1. Awareness is the light in all that occurs. It is like the calm depths of an ocean. On an ocean's surface appears the individual waves pounding the earth's sands. However, in each wave exists its source, the calm waters of the depths of the ocean. You cannot separate the calm depths of an ocean's waters from its individual surface waves nor can you separate the light of awareness from consciousness. The light of awareness is in all states of vibratory energy. Awareness has no edges. Therefore, nothing, no one, is ever lost in the universe. Whether you are awakened, or not, *awareness exists.*

2. With the light of awareness, consciousness' vibratory energy is expressed, much like the ocean waves, as individual conscious mind and body. You falsely perceive you are a separate personal being. The illusionary return way is in reverse — from the outer most extreme perception to the most inner depth of your being. It is the straight gate and narrow way. One way perceived out, and one way perceived back — from the one to the many, from the many to the one. All occurring in conscious awareness and beyond to being pure awareness.

3. As you go beyond the mind and body consciousness to the realization of being expansive awareness, your conscious mind and body is sustained by the light of awareness. As you again become conscious of the mind and body, the consciousness of a separate personal "I" rises. What you may realize is that it is awareness that makes consciousness possible. The fact that you may go beyond consciousness, tells you that you are not consciousness. You are not that which changes. You are not that which comes and goes. You are that which is permanent, changeless, real. You are pure expansive awareness.

4. In expansive awareness reality, there is no inner, outer, going out, nor coming back. There is no duality in awareness. The different speeds/frequencies of the energy vibration give a false sense of descending or ascending. There is just the awakening to the realizing that you actually never went anywhere. You are where you began. You are seeking what you already are. Until you are awakened, you are a sleep walker in a relative world of imaginary separate beings. When you are aware of your God essence, you are aware of all individuals as yourself. The natural state of your being is love, love of self, love of all your individual manifested selves.

5. When consciousness and its contents vibrate, you are aware of consciousness, and its contents. You cannot however, be cognizant of awareness — itself, yourself. You can be aware of being conscious, but you cannot be conscious of awareness.

6. When watching a movie, you are only conscious of the contents appearing on the movie screen. The screen is the field of awareness. The contents are the appearances. You are conscious of the appearances. When the projected images are turned off, the screen remains blank for the next projection. That is the way awareness exists. It allows the appearances of images and contents that are constantly changing, while it remains unchanged.

7. With the light of awareness, consciousness with its contents, is constantly appearing. Look out of a window. What do you see? Mountains, trees, houses, animals? Where are they appearing? All are appearing in the light of day. The light of day is the one thing you take for granted and never consider. You don't say, "Ah! What a beautiful morning in the light of day." You don't say, "Ah! What a beautiful view of the mountains in the light of day." The light is not given any thought. Your attention is on the images not that which allows the images to appear.

8. It is the rising sense of mind within consciousness that creates a separate false sense of a self conscious "I, me, my, mine" which in turn attaches its personal sense of being to everything the mind creates. Thus, the dreamer and the dream are created and perpetuated in the false belief that they are a reality. All that the conscious mind creates deteriorates and dies. That which cannot last is not real. That which you *are* is permanent, real — pure awareness. "*Thou* fool, that which thou sowest is not quickened, except it die" (I Corinthians 15: 36).

9. Awareness must be realized. As you go beyond the conscious mind of a personal being and awake to your reality of Being, the mind is not able to make logic of what is rationally illogical. To attempt to understand the awareness reality of your Being with the rising conscious mind, is an exercise in futility. The mind cannot grasp that which is beyond it.

10. You can never fall out of awareness and you cannot be conscious of awareness. Awareness is beyond the conscious mind. There is no "I" in awareness, no self-reflection, nor any self-identity. In awareness, there are no opposites, no separate false sense of a personal being. There is the expansiveness of be - ing.

11. During a silent Christ Centered Prayer practice (Lesson: 13), you are instructed to become aware of the Spiritual Heart Center. If you are practicing with a determined purpose, you may wake up to your reality. You are not in transition from consciousness to awareness. Consciousness and its contents fade and you are what you are — awareness, empty and full, nothing and everything.

12. As consciousness vibrates within awareness, it is at its finest, purest state, and is referred to as Spiritual Consciousness or (for followers of Jesus Christ), the Christ Consciousness. It is the Christ Consciousness Jesus referred to as the Father.

13. There is one Christ Consciousness expressing as the rising individual (not separate) expressions of consciousness. Waking up in awareness of the Christ Consciousness removes the illusionary sense of many separate minds. "*There is* one body, and one Spirit, even as ye are called in one hope of your calling; One Lord, one faith, one baptism, One God and Father of all, who *is* above all and through all and in you all" (Ephesians 4: 4 - 6).

14. Within the Christ Consciousness, there are infinite "individual" expressions of consciousness. It is like a pot of boiling water. There are many individual bubbles vibrating from within the contents of the pot, the water. As with the bubbles in the water, you are an individual but never separate or apart from your God-source. Bubbles rise in water and individual expressions of consciousness rise in Christ Consciousness within Awareness (the pot). Neither are apart from their source.

15. It is the light of awareness that gives rise to consciousness' vibrating energy. It is within consciousness mind rises, and within mind a conscious sense of a physical body rises. The speed of the vibrating energy determines the various conscious manifestations. The mind and its contents, thoughts, ideas, feelings with the senses, and sensations create a "sense" of a separate self identity. Attachment to and identification with the sense of a separate self leads to a mistaken false "personal" separate sense self. To

attach and identify with this separate sense of self is the first step in the creation of the illusionary separate false self.

16. On this earth plane, the body as an expression of consciousness' mind energy vibrates at a slower speed. The slower vibrating energy frequency enables the body to appear and it is sensed as a solid form. As you falsely identify with the mind, you falsely identify with a physical body separate from other beings. The false sense of a separate mind and body is the easiest vibratory energy to get attached to. The false sense of a separate personal body to defend, in fear of harm or dying, may cause a perceptual gap difficult to venture beyond.

17. Because of your false sense of being separate, rather than an individual expression of the Christ Consciousness, other individual expressions of the Christ Consciousness become difficult to understand. Ignorance of the oneness (within awareness of Be-ing) causes a lack of communication, manifested evils, and wars on this plane to occur. You may spend a great deal of time and effort in attempting to understand and adjust to the various individual expressions of consciousness.

18. You are constantly mixing, changing, and experiencing the different individual expressed manifestations of consciousness. Conscious mind personalities have the ability for change/progress. Nothing on this earth plane is set in concrete. There is no un-manifested consciousness. Realize the light of awareness in the Christ Consciousness, and a sense of separation fades. "That they all may be one; as thou, Father, *art* in me, and I am in thee, that they also may be one in us: that the world may believe that thou hast sent me" (John 17: 21).

19. Whatever is within your individual expression of consciousness will eventually rise and manifest — that includes change/progress. You are never fixed at any individual expression of consciousness. There is constant possibility of the realization of oneness. Awakening to the awareness of the truth of your being is always available. "Jesus answered him, The first of all the commandments *is*, Hear, O Israel; The Lord our God, is one Lord:" (Mark 12: 29).

20. Truth may be realized with the practice of the silent Christ Centered Prayer. A silent prayer practice creates space and the awareness of the silence which allows the rising of consciousness' contents. When seeking to realize the Christ Consciousness, you respect all manifesting individual expressions of the Christ Consciousness, as you would respect your own. "And the second *is* like unto it, Thou shalt love thy neighbor as thyself" (Matthew 22: 39).

21. As you sojourn through this world of life and death you may have, through thought, word, and deed, misused (polluted) the purest of energy. This misuse of your Christ Consciousness' pure vibrating energy must be restored to its original purity. It is your responsibility to acknowledge this and consent to its restoration. The silent Christ Centered Prayer practice, may purify the vibrating energy bringing an understanding of truth teaching with the least amount of time and effort. "Let this mind be in you, which was also in Christ Jesus" (Philippians 2:5).

22. When the awareness of the Christ Consciousness is realized, you maintain and live out from the awareness, realized consciousness. To do otherwise, is to insult your spiritual integrity. You are always accountable for holding fast to that which you are fully aware and live your life accordingly. Whether you are living the life of a recluse, or in this world of activity, you are who or what you are — fully aware, and you are responsible for staying awake.

23. You don't have the luxury of dabbling in other individual expressions of consciousness. This could cause slippage and a return to a former expression of consciousness. Much like a detour, or mini fall, it may hold you for a time in a place previously traveled. For example, one individual may believe in God, another may not. You must accept, allow, and respect the individual's expression of consciousness while vigilantly honoring your own realized aware expression of consciousness.

24. It isn't wise nor prudent to intentionally move from a realized expression of consciousness to a previous expression of consciousness. You constantly maintain the expressed realized aware conscious-

ness. Once you have shattered self-identification with the separate false sense of mind and body, you have traveled beyond the false concepts which have held you captive. There is never a need to re-travel a road well worn. The awareness of what has already been realized in consciousness is ever present. Going beyond realized pure awareness may occur instantly, when least expected (Lesson: 190).

25. It is the ignorance of reality that creates distortions. Practice the silent Christ Centered Prayer method and you may awaken with the realization you are not the body, not the mind, nor consciousness. Yours is a greater reality. You are more, don't settle for less. Venture beyond the sense of body, mind, and consciousness. You are working with the perception of a separate false personal sense to the impersonal realized be-ing of pure expansive awareness. Your silent Christ Centered Prayer practice, with a determined purpose, may assist you in the waking up process.

26. You have created the dreamer and the dream. Neither of which is the reality of who or what you are. You have identified with the dreamer and the dream — wake up and dream no more. Realize the one pure expansiveness of awareness of your God being. Realizing your reality allows you to recognize the illusionary world of opposites and dissolves the false ties of self-identification to an imaginary life. "Lay not up for yourselves treasures up on earth, where moth and rust doth corrupt and where thieves break through and steal" (Matthew 6: 19).

....

STUDENT'S STORY:

Working and moving backwards from the understandable yet mistaken attachment to a separate individual false sense of self (called 'Sandy'), and its corresponding feelings of alienation and suffering to being one aware, is true freedom and eternal life. That truth, for me, is awareness of oneness, Be-ing. The subsequent realization of consciousness rising in awareness clarifies the long quoted "unity in diversity," "trinity," or "three in one" so commonly referred to in our traditions as mystery. I agree mystery is mysterious, but it is not unreal. Granted, it cannot be "grasped" by the mind because the experience transcends the mind. As we know, mind, senses, reason, will, intellect, and memory all rise within conscious awareness but they are not "Awareness."

This truth has been further clarified as Christ Consciousness rising within awareness and it reveals Jesus. That truth for me has been an awareness of participation in Christ Consciousness.

In Christ there is no darkness, no separation, no alienation, no suffering, and no death. There is simply the Christ, the Word of God, the Holy One of God in whom there is no other. The realization of this one, truth, life, and light came quite unexpectedly during a silent prayer period with my teacher. I experienced myself moving from my usual separate personal sense of being "Sandy" into a realization of oneness in Christ and then dissolving through this oneness to the realization of pure Being — expansive awareness.

In a very real way all must awaken from the identification with an individual personal separate sense of being to the oneness of the awareness of the Christ Consciousness where Jesus Christ is one in His Father. This is to know the Father as Jesus knows the Father. Jesus is the way and the way to the Father is through Him. This is no longer a platitude for me but a direct realization. Sandy to Jesus and through Jesus to the Father Consciousness, to pure expansive awareness. It is the journey home spoken of from all ages.

This realization unfolded during a silent prayer session. I experienced becoming smaller and smaller as an individual personal sense of Sandy until "I" ultimately disappeared dissolving completely. Gone. What remained had no object of perception, no personal separate sense, just oneness of being pure expansive awareness, pure Be-ing without being aware "of" anything or anyone. This realization is by grace in the Trinity spoken of by Jesus in the Gospel of John. Words are difficult to convey this realization. Awareness is reality.

It has also taken over a year to begin to assimilate and articulate in words how the realization has led to an understanding and wisdom, wisdom I continue to grow into. Awareness is the light in "enlightenment." It is the light, I might add, that has never been extinguished nor can it be. It is the light of pure awareness that shines in the darkness and the darkness cannot overcome it. It is the "light" in Jesus' "I AM" statement so often quoted in the gospel of John. It is the light come into the world. The light in Jesus, reveals His light to everyone who has eyes to see and hearts to love. It is the light of pure expansive awareness that is permanent, unfading, and eternal. Moving out from awareness, the pre-existent "Word" spontaneously rises within Christ Consciousness and through it all things are made. "All things were made by him; and without him was not any thing made that was made" (John I: 3).

The Prodigal Son made a return journey from enmeshment in the world of illusion and so do we. We move from a sense of separation and the separate sense of self to the realization of oneness. This is the journey from ignorance, alienation and suffering, to awareness, and ultimately, from death to life. We come to realize that this "Word" of life and light exists within us. It is us, from all eternity, and it is the greatest gift the Father can give the Son who shares all with us through the power of the Holy Spirit. To realize this gift gives glory, worship, and honor to God through the Holy Spirit in the Name of Jesus Christ.

+ +

LESSON: 6 — CONDITIONING

CONDITIONING IS USUALLY accomplished with labels, names, identity - given to persons, objects, feeling, thoughts, emotions through sense impressions, and repetition.

1. As an aware conscious being, you have a mind, thoughts, senses: hear, taste, touch, see, and smell which have a natural power to receive impressions through the body organs.

2. The thoughts and sense impressions are stamped with the conditioning of the culture or society you live in.

3. You are conditioned in thought, word, and deed from the moment you enter this world of opposites (Lesson: 17). Conditioning is constantly being taught or passed on through parents, friends, peers, authority figures, environment, and culture.

4. Your moral judgment is based on the conditioning of what is considered to be right or wrong, according to an established culture and/or religion.

5. Because shapes and forms of objects are constructed for use, you are conditioned to think and see the shapes and forms' functional use rather than knowing their essence.

6. For example: a block of wood cut from a tree then carved into a chair or table is always seen and thought of as a chair or table. When actually, it still remains the wood (tree - seed) and if it were burned, it would be ashes. The chair or table is only a functional concept of its reality.

7. When using the sense of seeing and thinking, you see and think "chair, "table." You are not aware of purely seeing. You are seeing a concept; thus, you are not knowing or being pure awareness. If you are not an aware being, you are believing in the conditioned sense impressions.

8. Conditioning creates useful functional concepts as a chair or table for the purpose of communication and the identifying of objects and individual beings. However, it also may create false concepts of thought patterns and sense impressions.

9. False concepts are created when you accept the appearance of the concept of anything or individual as its reality. Conditioning may create a false sense of a self separate and apart from the reality of your being.

10. From the time of birth, your sense of a mind and physical body is given a name. The repetition

of hearing your mind and body addressed with the given name, you come to identify with it as who you are. You are taught the use of I, Me, My, and Mine which becomes personal attachments to the name. All are concepts, none of which are the reality of who or what you are.

11. The entire packaging of conditioning of the mind, thoughts, and physical body are sense impressions that lead you to falsely identify as a separate personal being but, you are not a separate personal being.

12. The Christ Centered Prayer practice may help to reveal your true nature in awareness through the Holy Spirit in the Name of Jesus Christ.

+ +

LESSON: 7 — ATTACHMENT

ATTACHMENT IS WHAT binds you to this world and limits freedom of being. The belief a "you" exists as a separate person allows attachment to come into existence. In reality, there isn't any time when you are not one with your God. "For in him we live, and move, and have our being; as certain also of your own poets have said, For we too are his offspring" (Acts 17: 28).

1. The moment you think "I, Me, My, Mine," attachment rises and it is the attachment that causes the suffering. It is the personal conditioning of "I, Me, My, Mine" that creates a personal sense of a separate self. You are never separate, you are an individual expression of consciousness, but never separate nor apart from your God-source. "That they should seek the Lord, if haply they might feel after him, and find him, though he be not far from every one of us" (Acts 17: 27).

2. To be attached to a separate false sense of a personal self is to suffer. When you are attached to a separate false sense of a personal self, you experience a lonely separate existence. You are always seeking another to fulfill your every need and happiness. It is an imaginary sense of your reality. You are an impersonal spiritual aware being, one with the Father, Son, Holy Spirit — The Holy Trinity. "At that day ye shall know that I *am* in my Father, and ye in me, and I in you" (John 14: 20).

3. It is the false belief in a personal sense that causes an unreal experience of an imaginary drift — a false sense move in consciousness of a separate false sense of self. The personal sense of being is a disruptive force on a spiritual path. As you live out from this personal sense of self, you take everything personally. You are defensive, over sensitive, and seldom listen to what is actually being said or seen. You are wanting to constantly please everyone and constantly seeking approval. It is not possible.

4. There is only the God of your being to work for and to please. When doing this, you are a perfect expression of your God-Self. "While I live will I praise the LORD: I will sing praises unto my God while I have any being" (Psalm 146: 2).

5. The false concept of a personal self, who doesn't exist, keeps you on the edge of a life perpetuating the false concept. As a false concept of a personal self, you believe you must protect it at all times, at all cost. There is no personal self to protect. The God of your being can never be harmed and It protects Itself (you) at all times.

6. As memory thoughts rise, and you attach painful emotions to them, suffering occurs. It is always yours to hold or withhold. The power is given to you from within. Attachment of any kind is the misuse of energy, thus it weakens your strength on the spiritual path. Thoughts are constantly rising; you must decide how best they may serve you.

7. When there is the sense of a false concept of a personal self, emotions are easily attached to rising thoughts. Attaching emotions to rising thoughts is a conditioning process of impressions. Thoughts are vibrating energy rising as thinking, no more - no less.

8. Thoughts in and of themselves, have no emotions attached to them. You attach the descriptive judgment of good, bad, hurtful, or pleasure to them according to your conditioned memory experiences. You attach, and you give the attached emotions the power to please or to hurt you.

9. Usually, you are most attached to thoughts or emotions that may give you pleasure. Attaching to pleasure can be a subtle pull in its direction. Interestingly, you seldom, if ever, complain about the emotions that give pleasure; however, it is the same energy rising. The difference is for you to make — pleasure or pain. For example, a farmer had two horses that he could not tell apart. A friend suggested he measure them and then perhaps he would be able to know the difference between them. He did and, sure enough, the black one was four inches taller than the white one.

10. Like the farmer, your vibrating energy within consciousness sees no differences. Actually, one thought is no different from another. Vibrating energy is vibrating energy, *you* create the difference.

11. In your God reality, there are never any differences, never any opposites. Like the farmer, senses are always just seeing, hearing, etcetera. The emotional differences you attach to rising thoughts are based in your conditioned memory experiences.

12. Attaching different emotions, hate, anger, joy, or love to rising thoughts that rise one moment and fall the next, is to attach yourself falsely to that which cannot sustain itself. How can an immortal God identify with a passing temporary thought existence?

13. It may, for a time, be difficult not being attached or responding to emotions as thoughts rise. You have been conditioned to respond to the thoughts and attaching emotions to them.

14. You do continue to experience rising thoughts and emotions. The change is that you are no longer attached to them. You come to live out from a deeper compassionate nature, in an unconditional loving for yourself and for all individual expressions of consciousness.

15. Yes, living out from your God-source requires an adjustment in your thought patterns. It requires patience, as well as an understanding of living in a calm state of being which is not numbness. It is living as a pure aware being not influenced by a life of emotional conditioning. It is resting in the God of your being.

16. As you allow thoughts to rise and fall without dialoguing or responding to emotions, there is no personalizing, no suffering. Giving up the attachments to emotions (not the emotions) gives you the freedom of unconditional loving.

17. To realize in consciousness the personal from the impersonal, requires an alert practice of hearing the personal terms and silently knowing, I am an impersonal being. It is a spiritual principle to be realized and lived out from. Letting go of the attached personal sense of "I," means to identify yourself in the impersonal aware God Being — Oneness.

18. When you know your true identity, you know on this plane it is God-seeing, God-hearing, God-touching, God-smelling, God-tasting. You know the differences you attach to rising thoughts that may be held or withheld. Of course, it is necessary to use the personal terms to communicate in this relative world; however, knowing the truth is what makes you free.

19. When you keep yourself in neutral, thoughts or emotions cannot pull you to the left or right. You remain in a calm, peaceful center. "Thou wilt keep *him* in perfect peace, whose mind *is* stayed *on thee:* because he trusteth in thee" (Isaiah 26: 3).

20. Isaiah's use of the key instruction "stayed," means actively living your life with an aware consciousness of the Divine — your reality. With time, effort, and determined purpose, you may keep your mind fixed on the Lord and hear the teaching of the Holy Spirit in the name of Jesus Christ. "We are of God: he that knoweth God heareth us; he that is not of God heareth not us. Hereby know we the spirit of truth, and the spirit of error" (1 John 4: 6). Do not be distracted by the attractions of this world.

+ +

LESSON: 8 — ATTRACTION

ATTRACTION IS AN inherent occurrence within the vibrating energy states of individual expressions of consciousness.

1. Even before your birth on this plane, attraction is operational. Attraction is an inherent occurrence to be drawn toward, or to intentionally draw to you, an object or person of interest. To understand attraction, you must understand the spiritual supply source from which it draws the manifestations of vibrating energy (Lesson: 168).

2. It is said, "Opposites attract." Of course they do. This is the plane of opposites and you will attract, and be attracted to, both the positive and the negative attractions that your spiritual supply source manifest.

3. The individual expression of your conscious mental/mind vibrating energy, by means of your spiritual supply source, becomes manifested attractions. These appear as forms, conditions, and events.

4. It is risky to intentionally employ the mental state to accomplish your desire/wants. You may attract your interest however, it may misguide/disappoint you. The danger would be a misuse of your spiritual supply source of vibrating energy. The mental state is never satisfied with what it attracts. It always wants more of what it has, or something else. "Little children, keep yourselves from idols. Amen" (I John 5: 21).

5. When exclusively coming from the mental/mind state, the tendency is to reach out and constantly want to grab and hold on to what you may believe is your need. It is as if you are reaching for a gold ring from a horse on a merry-go-round.

6. As a truth student, you need never to grab hold of what is rightfully yours. The purer, finer, vibrating energy draws, with a certainty, all of your needs uninterrupted. Your entire Being is comfortable with the forms that are naturally manifesting from your inherent source of spiritual supply.

7. The occurrences of attraction may also tempt the illusion of *attachment*. Attachment is the bogy man hiding within desires and temptations. To become attached to what you are attracting will cause dissatisfaction and suffering.

8. Creation is within Consciousness. The conscious mind may identify with and become attached to that which is created. Once the mind identifies and is attached to a relative attraction, its actions/reactions are geared toward attaining the many desirable appearances associated with the attraction. "Why do the heathen rage, and the people imagine a vain thing?" (Psalms 2: 1).

9. As you continue to falsely identify with the many forms of attractions, so shall you continue to suffer. Desires are insatiable. You can only temporarily fulfill a desire. There is always another one awaiting your attention. "For what is a man profited, if he shall gain the whole world, and lose his own soul? Or what shall a man give in exchange for his soul?" (Matthew 16: 26).

10. Consciousness, mind/thoughts, and the senses, all rise in awareness and vibrate at different frequencies. Therefore, all may influence the appearances of the forms of attractions and the illusion of attachment.

11. As you progress on your spiritual journey, your vibrating energy frequency changes. This is one of the reasons many relationships do not last. Partners may become attracted to others, and others may be attracted to them. As your frequency of vibrating energy changes, your interest changes. As your interest changes, what and to whom you are attracted to changes. Your vibrating energy tends to attract and to be attracted to a like frequency. You are always more comfortable with those of your own vibrating energy frequency.

12. There is an important difference between attracting what you believe you want and what is necessary for your spiritual progress. The difference occurs in the intention of your individual expression

of vibrating energy. You may not always attract, or be attracted to what is necessary for your spiritual progress.

13. Attraction presents itself as a large grocery store with many items on its shelves. It is your selection that you are attracted to that will make the difference in your life. The junk food of this world may be more appealing, however, it is not the nourishment you need. It will not sustain you. "I will set no wicked thing before mine eyes: I hate the work of them that turn aside; *it* shall not cleave to me" (Psalm 101: 3).

14. Often, you are not aware of the many possible selections because you are so mentally focused on what it is you believe you want. This will hold you in the vibrating energy frequency that may bring forth your intended desire, but not your need. A natural power of attraction and spiritual supply exist within conscious awareness and if misused for selfish purposes, you build your life's progress on quick sand. "EXCEPT the Lord build the house, they labour in vain that build it: except the Lord keep the city, the watchman waketh *but* in vain" (Psalm 127: 1).

15. You are accountable for your actions (good or bad). "For the Son of man shall come in the glory of his Father with his angels; and then he shall reward every man according to his works" (Matthew 16: 27).

16. Mental practices to attract your desires may be a temporarily satisfying substitute for what is actually the inner hunger for the God - awareness of your Being. These types of practices will not manifest a lasting joy and peace. "And the peace of God, which passeth all understanding, shall keep your hearts and minds through Christ Jesus" (Philippians 4: 7).

17. As a truth seeker, trust that your permanent home is in the reality of your Being. The reality of your Being will effortlessly attract from your spiritual source of supply all that you will ever need for your spiritual progress on this plane. "*It* is better to trust in the LORD than to put confidence in man" (Psalm 118: 8).

18. There is never a time when you need to intentionally manipulate, force, or misuse the conscious vibrating energy for what is necessary on your spiritual journey. Remember, attraction is drawing from your God, spiritual, supply source and all that is necessary to meet your needs already exist. "Be not ye therefore like unto them: for your Father knoweth what things ye have need of before ye ask him" (Matthew 6: 8).

19. The peace, joy, and comfort you seek exist within an aware consciousness. You intuitively know the difference. The mental/mind state requires constant effort; the conscious aware state, is effortless. The mental state is limited and excludes. Aware consciousness is limitless, spacious, and all inclusive. All that is ever necessary on your spiritual journey is available for your short or long term use.

20. God knows your needs before you do. "Therefore take no thought, saying, What shall we eat? or, What shall we drink? or Wherewithal shall we be clothed? (For after all these things do the Gentiles seek:) for your heavenly Father knoweth that ye have need of all these things" (Matthew 6: 31 - 32).

21. God meets your need, not greed, in the appropriate time and manner. "And it shall come to pass, that before they call, I will answer; and while they are yet speaking, I will hear" (Isaiah 65: 24).

22. You are cautioned to recognize the difference between misusing truth or allowing the truth to guide you. The Holy Spirit in the name of Jesus Christ may free you of all unnecessary attractions. "And ye shall know the truth, and the truth shall make you free" (John 8: 32). Keep your attention on the realized goal — truth.

+ +

LESSON: 9 — ATTENTION

ATTENTION IS INTEREST "instantly" alerted by the rising of thoughts, senses, or sense impressions (acting as stimuli) within your conscious mind. Attention is instantly being aware of any thought, sense, or sense impression. It is an aware, conscious attraction - interest vibrating energy.

1. During a prayer practice, your attention is immediately attracted to whatever appears within your conscious mind.

2. You could simply say, attention is interest actively responding to any rising thought, sensation, or sense impression in the conscious mind or body. When attention is held by an object of interest, it is attentive concentration.

3. The senses; hear, see, touch, taste, smell, receive impressions through the physical body parts — eyes, nose, ears, etcetera and may draw your immediate attention.

4. The mind's contents, feelings, emotions, thoughts, and the sense impressions may often be conditioned. It is the mind's contents that may more often attract attention.

5. At an early age you may have been, positively or negatively, conditioned to believe what others say about you is true. You may have the tendency to accept the mind's conditioned content as real. Thus, you invest your God-given power in the conditioned content. Suffering and pain may easily attract your attention. Self-aggrandizement and elation may also easily attract your attention

6. As you practice the silent Christ Centered Prayer, you are instructed to become aware of your Spiritual Heart Center and rest in awareness. During your practice you may be attracted to any thought, sense, or sense impression as it rises. Instantly becoming consciously aware of any thought, feeling, emotion, or any particular sense, as it rises, *is* paying attention.

7. Your conscious attention of the different thoughts, senses, and the variety of sense impressions creates a sensory experience of moving toward or away (energy vibrating). It is the rising thoughts, senses, and impressions that cause an immediate change of the attention position from one moment to the next.

8. During a silent prayer practice, a thought or sense impression rises and you are immediately attracted. You do not ignore or pretend that the thought or the sense impression has not risen. Your attention is already there. You may, by choice, again become aware of your Spiritual Heart Center and rest in awareness.

9. During a silent prayer practice, thoughts or sense impressions of interest may constantly attract your attention. You may switch your attention intentionally (choice) from one content to another or again become aware of your Spiritual Heart Center and rest in awareness.

10. Example I: the sense seeing rises and the eyes are impressed with a vision of a tree. The tree interests you and has your attention. If you choose to continue to stay your attention on the tree, you may become consciously aware of every detail of its shape, color, leaves, branches, trunk, and size.

11. Example II: You are reading a book. Your focused attention is absorbed in your consciousness of the book. Someone enters the room and addresses you by name. You are so attentively interested in the reading of the book that you are not aware consciously of any sound. When your name is repeated, you may become aware consciously of the sense of hearing rising through the impression on the ear, and identify (conditioning) with the name. You may change your interested attention from reading the book to the sense impression of the presence of the individual vying for your attention through the rising sense of hearing.

12. Keep in mind, your attention may constantly be changing from one thought or sense impression to another as each rises and falls. At times, the changes are so subtle that you just do it without the conscious awareness of doing it. You are a conscious being but not always fully aware. With a silent prayer

practice, you become more aware within your practice and in your practical everyday life activities. Consequently, you are more aware of the rising of thoughts, or sense impressions as they occur. Your choices increase. The choice is yours.

13. If an individual appears (sense of sight) and is a bore while speaking (sense of hearing), you have the choice of tuning out. You may change your attention from one attraction to another, or easily become attached to one attraction or another.

14. If during a silent prayer practice, you enter into dialogue or emotionally respond to thoughts or sense impressions as they rise, your attention may be held captive/attached.

15. You may subject yourself to pain, suffering, or pleasure by attending and/or attaching to the sense impressions or the rising thought. It is your attracted interest that holds your attention. The greater the attraction the greater the attention. As your attention is attracted, it may seem to have a will of its own.

16. You are not the body. You are not the mind. You are not the senses. You are an aware conscious spiritual Being using and experiencing a mind, body, and senses. You have the ability of instantly paying attention to thought, or any of the sense impressions that attract your interest or not.

17. Thoughts and sense impressions are like a magnet. As they rise, they tend to draw attention to themselves. Thoughts and sense impressions serve a purpose on this plane. They allow a conscious flexible exploration of rising thoughts/sensations that may contribute to creativity or offer pleasure.

18. As you continue a silent prayer practice, the frequency and intensity of thoughts or sense impressions that attract may gradually decrease. You may gradually rest more and more as an aware Being. You have a greater awareness of your spiritual nature.

STUDENT'S STORY:

For some reason, I have received many "lessons" in airports. As a Gold Medallion frequent flyer, you know I do spend a lot of time traveling. One particular trip gave me four important realizations in one fateful and fretful day. Focus, attention, awareness, and detachment! Sometimes insights or realizations work that way. They come in bundles.

I was waiting for a flight to be called. I was sitting in the boarding area and since I was ticketed in section "1" the rest of the plane had to board first. That was fine with me, as I hate all the baggage slinging that goes on in the boarding period. So I decided to open my Lessons' book and read a bit while I waited for my section to be called. The more I re-read a lesson paper, the better it gets. I was sitting right smack in front of the registration desk with folks all around and the sound system in full swing.

I became so totally one-pointed with my Lesson on "Attention" that I was not at all "aware" that my name was being called, the plane was about to depart, and my ticket was being issued to a stand-by passenger in my place! While attentively focused and absorbed in the Lesson and enjoying every bit of the learning experience, I suddenly looked up, for some unknown reason, and realized that not only had I missed the boarding call, but also the door was shut and the plane was leaving! I had totally lost track of time and I was left behind!

I went up to the ticket agent and pleaded, "Wait, I'm supposed to be on that plane. Please open the door and let me in." She answered, "Who are you?" I gave her my name and boarding pass and she looked at me in utter disbelief. "Well," she said, "We have been calling your name for ten minutes and we gave your seat to someone else and the door is locked, the count is in, and you are not going anywhere right now." I pleaded for her to reconsider, however, airports have rules and I had better learn to obey. Fortunately, she had mercy on me. She couldn't believe I had not heard my name, and she was able to book me on the next flight. I did not suffer too great a delay on my journey, but did suffer a good dose of deserved embarrassment. It was clear I made the choice to move my focused-attention on the lesson paper to the exclusion of all else. However, I was grateful for the focused-attention-awareness realization, even though it came at a price of disrupting my travel plans. And, as if that were not enough, that same trip led to another spiritual realization (Lesson: 50).

+ +

LESSON: 10 — FORGIVENESS

THE PREFIX "FOR" translates away, apart, off. One of the definitions for "give" is to inflict punishment. Forgiveness isn't easy to comprehend or to put into action. It has been said, "I will forgive but never forget." Jesus asks you to forgive — to do away with, not to inflict punishment, seventy-seven times. "Jesus saith unto him, I say not unto thee, Until seven times: but, Until seventy times seven" (Matthew 18: 22).

1. Forgiveness is generic. It covers yourself and everyone who may come to mind. It is the gift of your nature that may be given freely and cause no harm. No caution labels are necessary.

2. You cannot talk about the forgiving part without talking about the "not" forgetting part. Jesus gives you a choice of retaining or not retaining. He leaves it up to you to decide. The admonition Jesus gave just before the given choice was, "Then said Jesus to them again, Peace *be* unto you: *as* my Father hath sent me, so send I you" (John 20: 21).

3. Jesus' life embodied forgiveness. Right up to, and through the crucifixion, Jesus was the personification of forgiveness. He asked the Lord to forgive those who did not know what they were doing. Although He gives you a choice, He also gives you the example for making that choice.

4. In the following of Jesus' example, your choice is forgiveness. The power lies in forgiving, *and* in the forgetting (the hurt/pain inflicted). In the Lord's Prayer, you ask for forgiveness but it is conditioned on your forgiving others. "And forgive us our debts, as we forgive our debtors" (Matthew 6: 12). And, "But if ye forgive not men, their trespasses, neither will your Father forgive your trespasses" (Matthew 6: 15).

5. If you believe you have forgiven and not forgetting (the hurt), you have recreated the hurt all over again. "Brethren, I count not myself to have apprehended: but *this* one thing *I do*, forgetting those things which are behind, and reaching forth unto those things which are before, I press toward the mark for the prize of the high calling of God in Christ Jesus" (Philippians 3: 13-14).

6. To forget does not mean you will no longer remember. Your memory stays in tact but when the memory rises the hurt will not rise and there will no longer be a negative emotional response. The emotional attachment to the event will have dissolved in the wash of Divine forgiveness and purification — your nature.

7. True forgiving is forgetting (letting go). Emotional wounds you inflicted or received are healed. The memory of the event is simply that, a memory. It is the discomfort, not the event, you are able to forget in the forgiveness and love of the Holy Spirit in the name of Jesus Christ.

8. Forgiveness always begins with you. Holding yourself at fault, being ashamed, accepting blame, and neurotic guilt feelings all must come to a space of forgiveness. This space is often provided for in a silent prayer practice. When the thoughts of your hurts and sufferings rise and you gently return to your Spiritual Heart Center, there is a "Holy Instant" — forgiveness occurs.

9. A present hurt (or past one) occurred once. With memory, you manage to repeat and repeat, duplicate and duplicate, multiply and multiply the original hurt many times over. This intensifies the pain and suffering. This is the reason the same thought (hurt) may rise many times during a silent prayer practice.

10. Each time this occurs, it is not the old original hurt but one of the many you have recreated. Dur-

ing a silent prayer practice, forgiveness and purification take place in the "Holy Instant" between each rising thought or emotion. The Holy Instant (Lesson: 84), may do away with the entire history of hurts during one silent prayer practice. It depends on the immediate lack of response to the rising memory or sense impression.

11. The most important work with forgiveness is not to take back (recreate) that which has been forgiven by responding through dialogue. Absolution *is* absolute. Once you have forgiven yourself, or others, the painful attached emotion no longer exists. Forgiveness is the necessary ingredient in the purification process.

12. Prepare to completely, totally give up all that you have held onto, have been attached to, and accept the forgiveness that has occurred during the silent prayer practice. Accept forgiveness and allow the grace of forgiveness to manifest in your life.

13. Forgiveness gives you the power to release others and it releases you from your own hurts through memory. It frees you to move on; it's a choice of loving or not. Forgiveness and loving are one. How can you have one without the other? Jesus was giving you an obvious choice, and as usual, He expects you to make the necessary one for your own salvation and sanity.

14. It is all about choice. You are the one who ultimately benefits. You are the one who receives the blessing. You are the one who is set free. You are the one whose trespasses are forgiven by the choice of forgiveness. In the process you also set others free. What is true for you is true for the one you forgive.

15. The power of forgiveness is given to you, the same power Jesus had when He walked the earth. The power God gave Him, He has given you. Realizing this, how could you not choose forgiveness?

16. Forgiveness is like a soft blanket that covers everything and gives you a warm, joyful spirit. It brings a most beautiful calm peace, a pliable peace that penetrates your entire being in all that you are and do.

17. Forgiveness, like love, is your nature, your true nature, it is not separate and apart from who and what you are.

18. Forgiveness is a natural, limitless gift of your spiritual Divine nature. Yes, to forgive is divine and purifies negative vibrating energy. The Oneness of God, is the source of your divinity.

BENEFITS OF FORGIVENESS:

A. Forgiveness may soften your spiritual walk through the straight gate and the narrow way.

B. Forgiveness may quicken your purification progress.

C. Forgiveness frees up the necessary energy for a more productive, practical life.

D. Forgiveness may give you a sense of freedom from past memory attachments and it may heal old hurts in all directions.

E. Forgiveness may give you the experience of a greater measure of joy.

F. Forgiveness may allow the rising of love to surface to meet your needs.

G. Forgiveness is the index finger of God touching your soul.

+ +

LESSON: 11 — PURIFICATION PROCESS

THE PURIFICATION PROCESS is a period in your life when you begin to turn toward an inner calling of a spiritual house cleaning — in other words, clean up your act! "Blessed *are* the pure in heart: for they shall see God" (Matthew 5: 8).

1. The purification process is a gradual cleansing of the misuse, distortion, and abuse of your pure

vibrating energy. Purification is necessary because you are the one who is responsible. You have caused the impurities and allowed them to have penetrated your heart and mind. You are the one responsible for submitting and opening to the purification process.

2. During your life, you may have caused pure energy to become polluted. Misguided (ignorant) words, thoughts, and deeds result. When self awakening begins, there is a slow, steady purification process that begins.

3. As you turn inward to the Spiritual Heart Center, rest in awareness and maintain silent prayer practice, the purification process intensifies. The process allows energy to be restored to its purity and words, thoughts, and deeds are no longer misguided/distorted

4. A silent prayer practice may speed up the purification process, however, purification is continually occurring when you are committed to the straight gate and narrow way. As you live more freely from the Christ of your being, attachments dissolve.

5. It is your intention of turning within that allows the purification process to begin. Good works, kindness, and charity are the natural outcome from the purification process. They are their own reward.

6. To harbor an expectation for something in return is commercialism not purification. Often "do gooders" of the world have caused more problems than the many who would withhold good works. Unconditional intention free from expectation of outcome, allows the purification process to unfold naturally and effectively.

7. In the purification process, a silent prayer practice is a valuable tool but not the only one. A silent prayer practice in combination with other traditional practices of purification (giving alms, fasting, and/or service) enhance the ongoing purification process. Practice your disciplines with a determined purpose.

8. Seek to realize your reality, and intensify the purification process in and out of a silent prayer practice. When you do this, many instances of purification take place continually under the direct inspiration of the Holy Spirit in the name of Jesus Christ.

9. As you come into compliance with your inner Christ nature, spiritual practices support a steady movement of the purification process. You may experience an unexpected release of tears or joy. You may find you seek silence, tend to speak less, and listen more.

10. Purification occurs during the silent Christ Centered Prayer practice in the "Holy Instant." It is the instant of not having dialogued or emotionally responded to the rising of a thought or emotional hurt.

11. Purification is a subtle activity within the Spiritual Heart Center in the Christ Consciousness of awareness. Its fruit is realized when no emotional upset or response accompanies the rising thought. The memory remains, however, it no longer threatens. It is no longer an irritating energy vibration. You are no longer hooked or attached emotionally. You are free.

12. Once purified, always purified. When similar events, fears, doubts, and desires rise they must also be purified. When rising thoughts again occur in the silent prayer practice, simply become aware again of the Spiritual Heart Center, without any dialogue, or response. Without any response to rising thoughts, they cease to multiply.

PURIFIERS:

A. Unconditional love (the most powerful) "He that loveth not knoweth not God; for God is love" (I John 4: 8)

B. Unconditional forgiveness, unconditional giving, unconditional receiving with openness, and unconditional acts of charity

C. Unconditional sharing what you receive, what you have, and unconditional laying down one's life for another, or others

D. Unconditional allowing, accepting, and respecting others to be wherever they are in their individual expression of consciousness

E. Being humble with a joyous spirit and acts of faith

F. Being deeply touched or transformed to a purer state of consciousness through an insight or realization

G. Expressing sincere gratitude

H. Realizing your true self and knowing others as yourself

I. Allowing yourself to be in the presence of an individual who has realized the Christ Consciousness may expose you to the purification process

J. Keeping an open heart to the teachings of the Holy Spirit in the name of Jesus Christ

+ +

LESSON: 12 — DETERMINED PURPOSE

IN A SILENT prayer practice, your determined purpose is the willingness to expend the necessary effort and time to accomplish or complete a goal.

1. When you consciously practice the silent Christ Centered Prayer, with a determined purpose, you may softly realize that blessed place within.

2. In the beginning of a silent Christ Centered Prayer practice, your determined purpose may only be to learn and to practice the method.

3. Your determined purpose will carry you as far in your silent prayer practice as you will allow. You will walk slowly or fast on your spiritual walk, according to your determined purpose.

4. As you acquire the necessary silent Christ Centered Prayer practice skills and maintain your silent prayer practice, the determined purpose may broaden to include the many steps on a spiritual walk.

5. It is when you have a determined purpose, you invest the time and energy in a spiritual silent prayer practice. The greatest value of having a determined purpose is not what you do for it but rather, what it may do for you.

6. To be determined in purpose may allow the silent Christ Centered Prayer practice to take you on an inner way graced with the things of God. You may realize, in the silent place in the Spiritual Heart Center, forgiveness, love, and the joy of being who or what you are.

DETERMINED PURPOSE EXPANSIONS:

A. Learn and maintain a silent prayer practice

B. Become aware and open the Spiritual Heart Center

C. Turn within and enter the silence

D. Understand and practice forgiveness and purification

E. Heal in forgiveness and purification

F. Realize the Christ within and the Oneness of being

+ +

LESSON: 13 — THE CHRIST CENTERED PRAYER

THE SILENT CHRIST Centered Prayer is a revelation from our Lord Jesus Christ. The Christ Centered Prayer practice guides you directly to the straight gate and narrow way. It acknowledges and builds upon all previous teaching, tradition, and biblical reference. It is a practice that drops the traditional aids and articulates a simplification of the ancient tradition. According to His revelation, the Christ Centered Prayer is a method "this generation is ready" to receive.

CHRIST CENTERED PRAYER METHOD:

A. Sit comfortably upright, feet on floor, head, neck, and spine aligned. If you prefer, sit on a cushion on the floor.

B. Close the eyes, rest hands gently in lap.

C. Slowly inhale deeply and slowly exhale relaxing the entire body. Continue to breath normally.

D. Consciously become aware of your Spiritual Heart Center (center of chest, between the breast) and rest in awareness.

E. If thoughts or sensations rise, do not dialogue, converse, engage, nor respond to their rising (your attention is already there). Allow them to rise and again just gently become aware of your Spiritual Heart Center.

F. Continue the practice in this manner. No matter how often thoughts, emotions, or any of the senses rise, gently again become aware of your Spiritual Heart Center.

G. At the end of your silent prayer period, take a few moments to become consciously aware of the mental and physical senses before returning to normal activity.

1. The silent Christ Centered Prayer practice is for you, who have an interest in the present "now" to respond to God "without mental or verbal words," in solitude, simplicity, and silence. "Blessed *are* the pure in heart: for they shall see God" (Matthew 5: 8).

2. A sacred word, verbally or mentally, is not necessary because *you are* the sacred "Word," the Word that existed in the beginning. "In the beginning was the Word, and the Word was with God, and the Word was God. The same was in the beginning with God. All things were made by him; and without him was not anything made that was made" (John I: 1-3).

3. *You are* the sacred Word, the Word that was made flesh. "And the Word was made flesh, and dwelt among us, (and we beheld his glory, the glory as of the only begotten of the Father) full of grace and truth" (John I: 14).

4. What is true of Jesus is true of you. "And the glory which thou gavest me I have given them; that they may be one, even as we are one" (John 17: 22).

5. You cannot separate yourself from that which was in the beginning and was made flesh. With the Christ Centered Prayer practice, through the Holy Spirit in the name of Jesus Christ, you may come to know the oneness of your reality. "At that day ye shall know that I *am* in my Father, and ye in me, and I in you" (John 14: 20).

6. After the initial long deep inhalation and exhalation, breathing should always be normal and with the diaphragm. Breathing should be smooth, no pauses. This allows the lungs to completely fill during inhalation and completely empty during exhalation. Diaphragmatically breathing, may contribute to your silent prayer practice and may improve your health.

7. Do *not* label any of the rising thoughts, emotions or senses. For example, a bird singing. All that is occurring is the sense of hearing is rising. The identity "bird" is a conditioning label, don't use it.

8. Be sure to remove eye glasses, loosen anything that is tight around the waist. When sitting on a chair, you may wish to sit on a chair with arms for support. The use of a prayer shawl is optional however, it may be an effective tool. It may help turn you inward.

9. Practice the Christ Centered Prayer at any time before a meal, at least two hours after a meal, and about an hour after liquid juices. Water is fine. Start your silent prayer practice with a few minutes allowing the prayer practice time to extend naturally. Be consistent. If possible, practice at least twice a day. If,

for any reason, you find it difficult to become aware of the Spiritual Heart Center area, place your hand upon the Spiritual Heart Center area for the first few prayer practices.

10. Do not separate your silent inner prayer practice from your outer practical living. All are spiritual activities. Washing dishes and scrubbing floors are spiritual activities, when you do them with conscious awareness.

11. The Holy Spirit in the name of Jesus Christ is guiding you in and out of a silent prayer practice. The guidance is seamless. Be as mindful of the Holy Spirit in the name of Jesus Christ in your practical living, as you are during a silent prayer practice, and the Holy Spirit in the name of Jesus Christ may become more obvious in your practical daily living.

12. The silent Christ Centered Prayer is easy to learn and its teaching direction is to the straight gate and narrow way within the Spiritual Heart Center. There is no extraneous dialogue, no stringent guidelines. There are no hindrances of any kind between you and Jesus Christ, the Holy Spirit, the awareness of your being, and beyond.

13. The silent Christ Centered Prayer practice, may gently take you directly into the Spiritual Heart Center and the awareness of your Being. "Because strait *is* the gate, and narrow is the way, which leadeth unto life, and few there be that find it" (Matthew 7: 14).

14. As a Christian, when you begin an inner, silent prayer practice, you are beginning a spiritual walk on a spiritual journey home to the Christ and you are accepting the guidance of Jesus Christ through a "straight gate and narrow way" to the awareness of your being. "Jesus saith unto him, I am the way, the truth, and the life: no man cometh unto the Father, but by me" (John 14: 6).

15. When you learn the silent Christ Centered Prayer method and maintain it with a determined purpose, the Holy Spirit in the name of Jesus Christ may grant the necessary progress. You are not unlike the prodigal child returning home to the Father's house. It is in silent prayer that you may open your heart to His healing presence and power as you ask, "Create in me a clean heart, O God; and renew a right spirit within me" (Psalm 51: 10).

16. The Christ Centered Prayer practice may awaken you to the entrance door of your inner life with Jesus Christ. "I am the door: by me if any man enter in, he shall be saved, and shall go in and out, and find pasture" (John 10: 9).

17. The Christ Centered Prayer practice may bring you into the realization of the present. A life lived in the present may hear His voice and open the door. "Behold, I stand at the door, knock: if any man hear my voice, and open the door, I will come in to him, and will sup with him, and he with me" (Revelation 3: 20).

18. The Christ Centered Prayer practice may support, strengthen, and deepen an ongoing relationship with Jesus Christ through the Power of the Holy Spirit "For through him we both have access by one Spirit unto the Father" (Ephesians 2: 18).

19. The hurts, sufferings, and emotional pain of this world may be purified and healed, when you can be present, answer as Samuel did, and are receptive to the grace of forgiveness of the Lord. "That the LORD called Samuel: and he answered, Here *am* I" (1 Samuel 3: 4).

20. The silent Christ Centered Prayer practice is a time set aside to witness the inner rising of the mind's content. An experience when the pure vibrating energy of the Christ Consciousness' Holy Instant may quicken the forgiveness and purification process, "And put no difference between us and them, purifying their hearts by faith" (Acts 15: 9).

21. The silent Christ Centered Prayer is a practice of inner silent awareness of God, the still small voice, Who is known by faith and dwells within you always. "Be still, and know that I *am* God: I will be exalted among the heathen, I will be exalted in the earth" (Psalm 46: 10).

22. As you faithfully practice, the Holy Spirit in the name of Jesus Christ, may slowly, carefully, and lovingly restore the remembrance of all the Son - God is, and you are. "For this *is* the covenant that I will

make with the house of Israel after those days, saith the Lord; I will put my laws into their mind, and write them in their hearts: and I will be to them a God, and they shall be to me a people" (Hebrews 8: 10).

....

STUDENT'S STORY:

This has not been a quick journey and I am still en route. There have been great moments of elation and huge valleys of despair. The one thread that has held me together has been fidelity to a practice of contemplative Christ Centered Prayer. The discipline in good times and bad has been non-negotiable. Just showing up and sitting down and returning to the awareness of my Spiritual Heart Center where I knew in faith the Lord dwelt, and the patient (and I mean patient) presence, and listening ear of my trusted teacher have sustained me.

During my thirty years of uninterrupted silent prayer practice, I have found that my inner practice has moved in the direction of less and less effort and to more and more awareness. The delightful and relative ease of the Christ Centered Prayer practice, compared to other prayer practices, holds sway in my life.

It is possible to teach Christian contemplative silent prayer bypassing the more traditional aids that suggest the use of sacred words, phrases, images, breath, etcetera. One may easily and effortlessly intend, consent and open directly to the awareness of the Divine presence within the Spiritual Heart Center. This awareness itself is the home to which all traditional practices point and ultimately lead. I realize this may be a novel idea. However, I have found in working with folks interested in a silent contemplative, Christ Centered practice, that it is possible to simply teach a person how to comfortably rest in awareness of the Spiritual Heart Center with a minimum of elaborate instruction.

Through direct invitation and guidance of the Holy Spirit, whom we know supercedes all methods, we are gently led to an awareness of the risen Christ who dwells in our inmost Spiritual Heart Center. Access to the Divine Indwelling is not only possible, but practical. Inspired and encouraged by this, I find the silent Christ Centered Prayer practice may assist us in the realization of the Divine Indwelling. It is to this Divine Indwelling awareness that the Christ Centered Prayer intends.

+ +

LESSON: 14 — POWER PRAYER

THE "POWER PRAYER," practice I and II, is a method that may allow you to address a particularly difficult issue that comes up repeatedly at various times. It is its own unique prayer practice and is to be used *only* when necessary. Its sole purpose is to remove invested power in a specific tormenting issue. It does not replace your twice daily silent Christ Centered Prayer practice. And, the prayer practices are never to be mixed during either prayer practice.

POWER PRAYER METHOD - PRACTICE I:

A. When you are plagued, tormented by a specific conditioned impression, sit in a comfortable position, close your eyes.

B. When the specific conditioned impression rises, silently, softly pronounce, "NO POWER, GOD IS" then immediately, gently become aware of your Spiritual Heart Center.

C. During your entire sitting Power Prayer practice, you continue to allow the rising of the specific conditioned impression and immediately repeat the sequence, "NO POWER, GOD IS," gently become aware of your Spiritual Heart Center, and rest there in awareness until the internal conditioned impression rises again.

POWER PRAYER METHOD - PRACTICE II:

A. As you go about your practical daily activities, you may internally practice the Power Prayer with one exception — you do NOT intentionally become aware of the Spiritual Heart Center. You internally repeat the words, "NO POWER, GOD IS" during your daily outer activities (when there is not a safety issue) as often as is necessary and refocus your attention immediately to the outer activity.

B. You never practice the Power Prayer while driving or operating any kind of mechanical equipment. Whenever your safety is at issue, you *do not* practice the Power Prayer. In fact, no silent prayer, of any kind, should be practiced during these times.

C. When you are plagued by an internal conditioned sense impression during your outer activities, that would not interfere with your safety, you may immediately silently, softly pronounce, "NO POWER, GOD IS" and go about whatever it is you are involved in.

1. When you are plagued by a particularly difficult internal conditioned sense impression, one that may contribute to disturbances, distractions, torments, and a low self esteem, the above practices may help.

2. The internal sense conditioned impression may be experienced as a solid steel form — non-penetrable. It may be the most difficult vibrating energy to purify. Because you have given it power by previously accepting a false belief in it; it may be a constant struggle just attempting to make the least dent.

3. As a young child or young adult, you were more receptive to the internal conditioning sense impression of those who would mold you in an image in which they may have been more comfortable. As a spiritual impersonal being created in the image of God, you may identify the internal conditioned sense impression and realize it has no sustaining power of its own.

4. The power is directly given to you from within and you are the one who invests or withholds the power. An internal conditioned sense impression, of itself, lacks the ability to attach. You attach, detach, give it life, give it death, and you may shed the false image with all of its internal conditioning.

5. You learn to forgive yourself and those who know not what they do. "I will give unto thee the keys of the kingdom of heaven: and whatsoever thou shalt bind on earth shall be bound in heaven: and whatsoever thou shalt loose on earth shall be loosed in heaven" (Matthew 16: 19).

6. It matters not whether you created the internal conditioned impression or others have created it for you. What matters is you have accepted it, have given it a home, a life of its own, and you continue to empower it to support its internal existence to distract and torment you. Therefore, you must accept the responsibility for withdrawing your God-given power from it.

7. The "Power Prayer" practice may bring you into a neutral zone of non- responding, restore your inner peace, and activate the forgiveness and purification process which is an integral part of the practice.

8. There are two ways to practice the Power Prayer. There is a quiet sitting time (not to be mixed with your regular Christ Centered Prayer practice time) and the times during your practical daily life activities.

9. How often and the length of the sitting Power Prayer practice is your individual choice. The method may be practiced periodically until you are no longer responding or affected by the specific conditioned impression.

10. The Power Prayer practice may effectively remove your belief in a personal attachment to the specific, internal conditioned impression that repeatedly plagues your time and attention.

11. This is not a "no" dialogue practice, like the Christ Centered prayer is. When you pronounce, the words, "NO POWER, GOD IS," you are doing a specific targeted dialogue practice. There is to be no mixing of the Power Prayer with the Christ Centered Prayer practice.

12. The major difference in a *no* dialogue practice (Christ Centered Prayer) and a specific, targeted dialogue practice (Power Prayer) is one of short term use. The Power Prayer practice is used in attaining the result of taking back your God-given invested power from a specific conditioned impression that would not respond during the ordinary schematic of events.

13. The Power Prayer, Practice I and Practice II, may eventually restore the vibrating energy to its original state, causing the necessary purification and healing, and allow continued progress on your spiritual walk. It is important that both Part I and II be practiced for a quickening of the retraction of the power and the purification process to occur.

14. That which appeared strong as steel, may bend to your will, and melt in the furnace of the realization a conditioned sense impression has, "NO POWER, GOD IS." All may be accomplished in the Spiritual Heart Center by the Holy Spirit in the name of Jesus Christ.

STUDENT'S STORY:

At the age of fifty-nine I have lived almost two-thirds of my life away from my family and far away from the familiar family homestead in New York. The negative influence and power of early child conditioning must be acknowledged and not trivialized. Although neither of my parents would ever describe themselves as "perfectionists," early on I intuited the message that there was, indeed, an unspoken standard of perfection and most often, and most certainly, I did not measure up.

My parents would often downplay or act embarrassed at my efforts to achieve. They didn't want me to become prideful and all I wanted was to be affirmed and acknowledged. This created a great dilemma for me. My self assessment on such occasions was a judgment that I was either too much or not enough. I decided I just had to work harder which, by the way never worked. I rarely felt "just right."

As an adult, these powerful childhood emotions had a way of re-surfacing. Often they would rise at family gatherings around holidays when my parents, children, and brothers would gather for a few days. Nothing like a few days of revisiting the homestead system to bring up unresolved childhood issues! Even after years of contemplative prayer, the power and influence of negative conditioning was impossible for me to ignore. The familiar feelings of anxiety, inadequacy, and failure would linger long after the holiday festivities were over.

I continued to be ill at ease with my own accomplishments and tended to trivialize, doubt, or apologize for successes and failures alike. It never occurred to me until fairly recently that the recurring cycle could be broken. I knew the source of my absolute true esteem lay not in parental upbringing or conditioning, but in an intimacy and realization of God's unconditional love and acceptance. Intellectual assent, however, was not sufficient to release me from the attachment nor did it heal the emotional wounds. I needed a powerful "intervention."

The Power Prayer practice came after a particularly difficult Thanksgiving season. Fully aware of the issues mentioned above, I needed a way to neutralize the negative thoughts and emotions rising in consciousness before they had a chance to seduce me into an emotional drama and I found myself at their mercy. Thus, the Lesson - Power Prayer, came into existence through my teacher.

The simple practice of "No Power, God Is" has been an enormous help in neutralizing these emotions before they get the best of me. The trick has been to initiate the practice as the thoughts rise before they get emotionally charged and certainly before any response or action is taken. Vigilant practice has paid off. The internal chatter seems overwhelming at times, but in not dialoguing with the rising thoughts, they fail to snare my imagination and hold me emotionally captive. This has been a great help in both growing in awareness and healing of childhood memories.

The Power Prayer is a practice I use almost daily in various situations. Developing a sensitivity, in consciousness, to the rising thought energy and noticing it, and choosing NOT to empower it with attention has made a big difference in my emotional life. I realize it has no power unless I empower it and that I do have a choice.

I think the clearest thing about the Power Prayer practice is the immediacy to respond, "No Power, God is." It cuts the attention off at the quick and getting in quick is key. With the help of the Power Prayer, I have been able to gradually stop blaming others for my emotional problems and begin to take personal responsibility for healing in cooperation with the Holy Spirit in the Name of Jesus Christ.

++++++++++++++++++++++++++

LESSON: 15 — HAND-TO-HEART PRAYER

THE SILENT HAND-TO-HEART Prayer method is to be practiced in a time of spiritual energy crisis or needed guidance.

HAND-TO-HEART PRAYER METHOD:

A. When you are besieged by inner vibrating energy turmoil or seek guidance, rest your hand over the Spiritual Heart Center (center of chest between the breast).

B. Take a deep long breath, exhale slowly, relaxing mind and body.

C. Rest your attention on your hand in the silence of awareness.

D. If necessary repeat several times.

1. Conscious awareness transforms. As you practice the silent Christ Centered Prayer, many inner changes may begin to occur.

2. An expansive consciousness may create times of highs and lows. At times your energy vibrates at such a rapid speed, you may feel as if you are on a roller coaster.

3. Whenever you have a silent prayer practice, purification may bring change and when there is a resistance to change, an inner struggle may occur.

4. There may be a variety of inner experiences that are inexplicable at the time. The conscious mind state may be struggling to understand the changes that are taking place. Changes that are beyond its comprehension.

5. You may need not necessarily understand what is happening and if immediate help is not available, the silent Hand-to-Heart Prayer practice may be a short term solution. This prayer method may be practiced anywhere, in any position, and during any activity.

6. The silent Hand-to-Heart prayer practice may help bring an immediate calm, and may restore the vibrating energy's balance.

7. This prayer practice may be used, as needed, during any spiritual vibrating energy crisis or when spiritual guidance is sought.

8. Do not be fooled by the simplicity of this prayer practice. Many times Jesus raised/used His hand to heal, to bless, or to still the waters. The Hand-to-Heart Prayer is empowered with the Holy Spirit in the name of Jesus Christ.

CHART I — THE CHRISTIAN SPIRITUAL JOURNEY: as applied to the Contemplative Invitation Teaching.

Christians have the Sacraments to participate in and receive, scriptures to read and contemplate, silent and verbal prayers to pray. These actions guide a Christian to the inner chamber of their Being — the Spiritual Heart Center.

As one rest within awareness, the arrows are reversed and a Christian's life is lived from the center of the Spiritual Heart Center enhancing the Scriptures, Prayers, Sacraments, and Service.

PART II

LESSONS: 16 – 207

LESSON: 16 — ACCEPT - ALLOW - RESPECT

To accept, allow, and respect expresses a reverence for all human beings.

1. On your spiritual walk, you meet individual expressions of consciousness on the same walk, on different walks, as well as those who are just sleep walking through life.
2. There is always the temptation to judge where you are on a spiritual walk, and where others may be. This is a trap easily stepped into. Therefore to accept, to allow, and to respect yourself and others gives you the freedom of movement among the many.
3. To accept, allow, and respect, may bring to your silent prayer practice an atmosphere of peace and quiet.
4. As you walk the straight gate and narrow way, it is not your responsibility to convert anyone.
5. You are always working on yourself. Your responsibility, as a truth seeker is, to accept, allow, and respect the One appearing as the many.
6. There are benefits received and given when you are able to accept, allow, and respect the differences presented in individual expressions of consciousness.

ACCEPT:
A. Acceptance frees you from judging.
B. When you accept others, you are accepting yourself, and in acceptance of yourself, is the expression of self-love.
C. To accept what is, at any given moment, reveals the present.

ALLOW:
A. When you allow others to be where they are on the path, expectations, stress, and struggle are greatly reduced,
B. You will lose less friends and family members if you allow and are patient with those who are not ready to seek truth. Don't try to drag others along with you.
C. Giving up criticizing of those who may have a different prayer practice, may deepen your own prayer practice

RESPECT:
A. Honoring others with the same respect you believe you deserve, contributes to a positive state of mind.
B. Respect for yourself and others may bring the recognition of the Christ light in others.
C. When you respect all faiths and religious beliefs, you suffer less from emotional turmoil.

++++++++++++++++++++++++

LESSON: 17 — ACCEPTANCE

Acceptance is the acknowledgment that Jesus Christ has welcomed you into the Kingdom of God.

1. You may find, after having realized the Christ Consciousness, you have a resistance to receiving the acceptance of the Christ of your being.
2. For a while, it may be difficult to accept the realization. Therefore, you may hesitate to acknowledge your acceptance of the Christ Consciousness and continue to ask for acceptance. "Let the words of

my mouth, and the meditation of my heart, be acceptable in thy sight, O LORD, my strength, and my redeemer" (Psalms 19: 14).

3. When you have realized the highest, purest expression of consciousness, it is not a matter of accepting it. You do not accept realization, you live it.

4. Because the mind cannot even begin to fathom the Christ, much less accept its acceptance, the mind struggles to believe the Christ's reality. "To the praise of the glory of his grace, wherein he hath made us accepted in the beloved" (Ephesians 1: 6).

5. Truth annoys the heck out of your analytical mind that wants to figure out and basically control everything.

6. The mind will never accept truth, but will gradually work with and for the Christ of your being.

7. Be patient, in time, you will come to rest in the Christ, not analyze it. "For the kingdom of God is not meat and drink; but righteousness, and peace, and joy in the Holy Ghost. For he that in these things serveth Christ *is* acceptable to God, and approved of men" (Romans 14: 17 - 18).

8. Because the mind has a difficulty in accepting the Christ realization, you move slowly from confusion, to conversion, to commitment, to communion, to celebration, and finally to total acceptance of being accepted through the Holy Spirit in the name of Jesus Christ.

+ +

LESSON: 18 — ADVERSITY

ADVERSITY IS A troubled, disastrous, or unfortunate state. On a spiritual walk, it may occur when desires or temptations and unwanted appearances rise to impose feelings of wretchedness.

1. An adversity may appear as a person, thing, or event, any of which may cause an adverse effect on your emotional consciousness' expressions.

2. There are times in life when everything around you may seem as a disaster and calamities abound. When you begin a silent prayer practice, you may often become more sensitive to the adversities in and around your life.

3. You can only be at the mercy of this world, its persons, and events when you are acknowledging this world is the greater power. To give this world, a relative world, such power is to deny the Jesus Christ divinity, the one power — the God of your Being.

4. Adversities are part of this plane of opposites and to rise above them is to overcome this world. "These things I have spoken unto you, that in me ye might have peace. In the world ye shall have tribulation: but be of good cheer; I have overcome the world" (John 16: 33).

5. It is during these times you may feel at the mercy of this world. There is the need to learn how to overcome sinking into the depths of emotional pain and suffering. "For whatsoever is born of God overcometh the world: and this is the victory that overcometh the world, *even* our faith. Who is he that overcometh the world, but he that believeth that Jesus is the Son of God?" (I John 5: 4 - 5).

6. The Christ Centered Prayer practice teaches you to allow all appearances to rise without reacting. It is this same attitude that needs to be applied to your daily life as you encounter adversities. "Him that overcometh will I make a pillar in the temple of my God, and he shall go no more out: and I will write upon him the name of my God, and the name of the city of my God, *which is* new Jerusalem, which cometh down out of heaven from my God: and *I will write upon him* my name" (Revelation 3: 12).

7. Stay alert and recognize the God-essence of the reality of your Being is always right where the adversity exits. It is vibrating energy creating whatever appears, whether distorted or not. "Remember therefore

how thou hast received and heard, and hold fast, and repent. If therefore thou shalt not watch, I will come on thee as a thief, and thou shalt not know what hour I will come upon thee" (Revelation 3: 3).

8. All expressions of consciousness are continuously rising and falling, coming and going. Know therefore, within the appearance of an adversity is the opposite waiting its turn to appear.

9. The appearance of an adversity is no different than an appearance of a joyful event. Both will rise, both will fall. It is your response that makes the difference. It is your work to remain calm and peaceful in that place between the rise and fall of either occurrence of joyfulness or sadness.

10. You make the choice of moving along with adversities or moving through them. Understanding the lack of power adversities possess, allows you to move through them with the Holy Spirit in the name of Jesus Christ. "For thou wilt light my candle: the LORD my God will enlighten my darkness" (Psalm 18: 28).

+ +

LESSON: 19 — ALONENESS

ALONENESS IS THE realization of your al-one-ness. It is the resting in the reality of your Being.

1. In aloneness, you may be alone but you are no longer lonely. You are aware of the impersonal Christ and the oneness of your divinity in relationship with Jesus Christ.

2. The emptiness and space is filled and a normalcy, of a kind, is established with those who would choose to come and go in your life.

3. The realization in consciousness, in awareness, from the loneliness experience to one of aloneness is subtle.

4. The practice of patience and trust is essential as you progress from one stage to the other. This process cannot be hurried nor forced. It must be lived/prayed through according to your individual disposition.

5. What loneliness and aloneness have in common is that they both carry the outer message of the inner revelation of "O-N-E." L-one-liness seeks the One and al-one-ness rests in the One.

6. As the Holy Spirit, in the name of Jesus Christ, awakens you in awareness to the Christ, there is a natural realization from loneliness to aloneness — and, you are contented.

+ +

LESSON: 20 — ANALYZING

ANALYZING IS THE intellectual bisecting of every morsel of revealed truth.

1. Truth is beyond the mind's intellect. Therefore, the mind/intellect finds it difficult to accept truth.

2. The mind's learned knowledge is usually in direct contradiction to revealed truth. "And to know the love of Christ, which passeth knowledge, that ye might be filled with all the fulness of God" (Ephesians 3: 19).

3. It is in mind's nature to bisect, scrutinize, and analyze what it cannot understand. "Trust in the LORD with all thine heart; and lean not unto thine own understanding" (Proverbs 3: 5).

4. Truth is not realized in its parts, because it has none. Truth is whole, perfect, and complete. "And ye are complete in him, which is the head of all principality and power:" (Colossians 2: 10).

5. You may waste life's journey examining truth with the mind's intellect and get caught up in a mire of darkness. "I thank God through Jesus Christ our Lord. So then with the mind I myself serve the law of God; but with the flesh the law of sin" (Romans 7: 25).

6. The mind's intellect is a wonderful instrument in the service of truth, but it becomes an emotional wreck when using its energy to analyze. "There *is* therefore now no condemnation to them which are in Christ Jesus, who walk not after the flesh, but after the Spirit. For the law of the Spirit of life in Christ Jesus hath made me free from the law of sin and death. (Romans 8: 1 - 2).

7. Mind becomes quickly tired and overburdened when it struggles with what is not in its domain. It is more beneficial to use the mind to gently ponder truth then to attempt to parcel it. Better still, become aware of your Spiritual Heart Center, and come to Jesus. "Come unto me, all *ye* that labour and are heavy laden, and I will give you rest" (Matthew 11: 29).

8. Contemplate the truth realized without making comparisons. Mind gets lost in comparisons. The truth of awareness has no comparisons, no equal. "Let this mind be in you which was also in Christ Jesus" (Philippians 2: 5).

+ +

LESSON: 21 — ANGER

ANGER IS AN emotion experienced as hostile feelings. Anger isn't a bad or good emotion. It just is, just an emotion and, at times, it may be a useful one. The anger emotion will rise whenever there is a need for it but it doesn't have to cause a heartburn, figuratively or literally.

1. Anger may be dissipated in the light of forgiveness. Once released, you may use the anger energy in a productive means.

2. You never want to repress anger. Allow yourself to experience it. Just admit, "I'm angry about such and such or so and so. I'm so angry I could scream," and if you are where you can scream, do it. If not, take a couple of long deep breaths. Then you may be able, if you choose, to express forgiveness and decide what action you need to take.

3. Anger is dissipated by forgiveness. When you can, not by force nor because you should, but from a truly forgiving heart, do not respond to the anger (including yourself for getting angry). Then the fire of anger is put out, its ashes used in a constructive way.

4. You take whatever action is necessary to protect yourself from those who would do you harm. Whatever action you do take is done in the forgiveness light of the Christ. You can act from a forgiving heart no matter what action/s you take. Jesus never asks you to do what is not in your nature.

5. Forgiveness is the tree that does bear the most delectable fruit. You don't have to get forgiveness or attain it. It is your true nature, you are not separate and apart from it. You only need to realize and awaken to it, that is why the choice is always yours. Know that you are the tree that bears the fruit.

6. Understanding the anger emotion allows you not to become angry with the anger, which serves to compound it. The best part is as you dissipate anger in forgiveness, you also come into the forgiveness realization. It's a bonus — two for one. What keeps the peace when anger rises, is the forgiveness that automatically rises with it. The "two for one thing."

7. All emotions rise as needed and as you are awakened, you are aware of whatever the emotion is in the present moment. It is in the present moment you have the choice of forgiving or retaining as you take whatever action is necessary.

8. It is the necessary action and the intention within the action that matters. The action may appear negative, however, it may contain the seeds of forgiveness and that is what may allow you to dissipate

the anger and move on in a productive mode. Example: your teenager has wrecked the car. You prescribe punishment, however, within the prescribed punishment exists your complete forgiveness and you are thankful to God no one was hurt.

+ +

LESSON: 22 — ANOINTING

THE SACRAMENT OF Anointing the sick, with Holy Oil or laying on of hands, may bring forth a clearer reflection of the spiritual perfection that exists. Anointing may heal, whether given or received, with the invested power as a blessing in the purest, finest of vibrating energy.

1. It is the pure emanating energy that heals, although it appears in the outer form of Holy Oil. "To another faith by same Spirit; to another the gifts of healing by the same Spirit;" (I Corinthians 12: 9).

2. The anointing healing power may be invested by the giver or the receiver. It is always the individual's consciousness that invests the power. Neither is denied what they believe is truth. "He giveth power to the faint; and to *them that have* no might he increaseth strength" (Isaiah 40: 29).

3. A healing is a revealing. It is the revealing of the wholeness of your being in the awareness . "For I reckon that the sufferings of this present time *are* not worthy *to be compared* with the glory which shall be revealed in us" (Romans 8: 18).

4. Anointing and healing of the sick, may occur without any outer symbol or ritual. A healing may occur through prayer, purification, and at holy shrines. The inner realization of awareness of Christ Consciousness may also result in a healing.

5. In awareness, there is neither health nor sickness. Health or sickness only appears on the plane of opposites (Lesson: 117).

6. Why then, once healed, may you again be effected by illness or health? It is because while you are upon this plane of opposites, you continue to be subjected to the law of opposites.

+ +

LESSON: 23 — AVOIDANCE

AVOIDANCE IS EVADING your spiritual practices through the use of false reasoning.

1. Entering the spiritual straight gate and narrow way, while involved with the activities of the world, lends easily to the avoidance of your spiritual practices.

2. A position in this world of responsibility that consumes your time and attention, may be considered a reasonable source for avoidance. It is not. Being self-realized, is your only responsibility on this plane. All else are activities of choice.

3. There are many excuses and justifications for avoiding spiritual practices that consist of a silent prayer, studies, exercise, or contemplating truth. There is never any good reason to do so. "And they all with one *consent* began to make excuse. The first said unto him, I have bought a piece of ground, and I must needs go and see it: I pray thee have me excused" (Luke 14: 18). And the Lord said, "For I say unto you, That none of those men which were bidden shall taste my supper" (Luke 14: 24).

4. Your spiritual practices are your priority. Whatever position you choose to accept or perform, is secondary to your spiritual practices. If for *any* reason, you believe you do not have the time — you need the practices the most.

5. All or anything you choose to do on this plane should contribute to your waking up. If anything interferes, a change should be considered. It is your responsibility to establish a balance between your spiritual practices and whatever capacity you serve on this plane. Service is an honorable activity but it is not an excuse for the avoidance of what should be your priority — self-realization.

6. To believe your work upon this plane is more important than time out for your spiritual practices is for you to exists in a bloated ego. The Holy Spirit in the name of Jesus Christ is constantly knocking at the door of your inner being. Not finding the necessary time to answer the call, condemns yourself to an avoidance habit that may linger. "Behold, I stand at the door, and knock: if any man hear my voice, and open the door, I will come in to him, and will sup with him, and he with me" (Revelation 3: 20).

+ +

LESSON: 24 — BAPTISM

THE SACRAMENT OF Baptism is the Baptizing with water in the name of the Father, and of the Son, and of the Holy Spirit. It is a response to the historical biblical invitation. It re-presents and enacts the outer, inner spiritual purification.

1. The Sacrament of Baptism is an initiation into the passion, death and resurrection of Jesus Christ as well as into a Christian community. Jesus submitted to the Baptism of John at the Jordan River and prior to His ascension commended His disciples to Baptize in the name of the Father and of the Son, and of the Holy Spirit. "Go ye therefore, and teach all nations, baptizing them in the name of the Father, and of the Son, and of the Holy Ghost" (Matthew 28: 19).

2. Although, many are baptized at an early age, awareness is ageless thus, the individual's consciousness is blessed by the light of the Holy Spirit.

3. The Sacrament of Baptism allows the Christian communities' youngest members to grow with a sense of belonging, exposing them to the Christian teachings through the Holy Spirit in the name of Jesus Christ.

4. The Baptism by water is the outward sign of an inward grace. Baptism represents and makes present a spiritual awakening (born again). "I indeed baptize you with water unto repentance: but he that cometh after me is mightier than I, whose shoes I am not worthy to bear: he shall baptize you with the Holy Ghost, and *with* fire" (Matthew 3: 11).

5. Scripture is replete with references to the Spirit of God and the promise of the Holy Spirit. "Then Peter said to them, Repent, and be baptized every one of you in the name of Jesus Christ for the remission of sins, ye shall receive the gift of the Holy Ghost. For the promise is unto you, and to your children, and to all that are afar off, *even* as many as the Lord our God shall call" (Acts 2: 38-39).

6. As with the Eucharist, the grace of Baptism contains and conveys all that is to effect an inner stirring and deepening experience of God's abiding presence.

7. The actions, Baptism and Eucharist, make present powerful purification seeds. Seeds, that may bear fruit through the activity of the Holy Spirit in the name of Jesus Christ.

8. And, as with all symbols or religious rituals, the Sacrament of Baptism may be invested with the power by the giver or the receiver.

9. The power of God's love and purity, imparted and received in faith, provides all that is necessary for an individual's consciousness future awakening. The seed is sown that is yet to be realized.

10. The power invested in Baptism, through the Holy Spirit, may have a strong positive influence in the lives of all those who are brought in faith come to the blessed waters.

++++++++++++++++++++++++

LESSON: 25 — BELOVED

BELOVED IS THE one within the many. The most dearly loved by the Power that is because It *is* the Power that is. "I and *my* Father are one" (John 10: 30).

1. You are the Beloved of God called into being. You are the "Word" spoken into life from all eternity. There is no other one like you. What greater testimony to God's infinite love for you is there? That you are here, and not someone else. "All things were made by him; and without him was not anything made that was made" (John I: 3).

2. You have your own vibration, your own tone of voice, your own thumb print. In the entire cosmos there is no other like you. "I will praise thee; for I am fearfully *and* wonderfully made: marvelous *are* thy works; and *that* my soul knoweth right well" (Psalm 139: 14).

3. God recognizes you as God's own. The Lord knows you in all your most finite ways. "O LORD thou hast searched me, and known *me*. Thou Knowest my down sitting and mine uprising, thou understandest my thought afar off. Thou compassest my path and my lying down, and art acquainted *with* all my ways. For *there is* not a word in my tongue, *but*, lo, O LORD thou knowest it altogether" (Psalm 139: 1 - 4).

4. To be so intimately known by God, so beloved by God, is to realize the dignity of being a human being. It is to realize who and what you are within the one reality of being. The Christ Spiritual Heart Center responds joyfully to the voice of its Beloved. "But now thus saith the LORD that created thee, O Jacob, and he formed thee, O Israel, Fear not: for I have redeemed thee, I have called *thee* by thy name; thou *art* mine" (Isaiah 43: 1).

5. Beloved, Beloved child of God, what more could you ever want or strive for on earth or in heaven? To be known as the Beloved of the Father within the heart of awareness, is your ascension in the Christ.

6. There is no time that you are not the Beloved of the Lord God of your being. "*And* of Benjamin he said, The beloved of the LORD shall dwell in safety by him; *and the LORD* shall dwell in safety by him; *and the LORD* shall cover him all the day long, and he shall dwell between his shoulders" (Deuteronomy 33: 12).

7. The Beloved cannot be separate and apart from its God's essence. "Beloved, now are we the sons of God, and it doth not yet appear what we shall be: but we know that, when he shall appear, we shall be like him; for we shall see him as he is" (I John 3: 2).

8. Through the forgiveness and purification process, you may identify as the Beloved of your God nature. And, as the Beloved, you have the responsibility to love as God loves. "Beloved, if God so loved us, we ought also to love one another" (I John 4: 11).

9. The Beloved serves at the Lord's pleasure, no matter the worldly consequences. "Then said the lord of the vineyard, What shall I do? I will send my beloved son: it may be they will reverence *him* when they see him" (Luke 20: 13).

10. As you awakened to your reality of being, your oneness is as the one Beloved, there is none other. "To the praise of the glory of his grace, wherein he hath made us accepted in the beloved" (Ephesians I: 6).

++++++++++++++++++++++++

LESSON: 26 — BIRTH - DEATH

BIRTH - DEATH are the coming and going upon the plane of opposites.

1. In the illusionary sense upon this plane, birth - death are the same event.

2. In general, and the simplest of terms, if you believe you are born and die, you are born and die. Investigate, study, and practice a silent prayer method to know God in spirit and in truth. "God *is* a Spirit: and they that worship him must worship *him* in spirit and in truth" (John 4: 24).

3. The ignorance of being attached to a false concept of an imaginary self with all its desires, creates an imaginary birth - death. "But put ye on the Lord Jesus Christ, and make not provision for the flesh, to *fulfill* the lusts *thereof*" (Romans 13: 14).

4. Birth - death are activities of a conscious mind gone amuck. "And God saw that the wickedness of man *was* great in the earth, and *that* every imagination of the thoughts of his heart *was* only evil continually" (Genesis 6: 5).

5. When you have awakened to the false sense of birth - death, you become aware of your real identity in the Christ of your Being. "Wherefore he saith, Awake thou that sleepest, and arise from the dead, and Christ shall give thee light" (Ephesians 5: 14).

6. The best part of being a follower of Jesus Christ and accepting the teaching of Jesus Christ, is that it is not necessary for you to believe in the illusions of birth - death to overcome this world. The most important life is always "now." "Come now, and let us reason together, saith the LORD: though your sins be as scarlet, they shall be as white as snow; though they be red like crimson, they shall be as wool" (Isaiah 1: 18).

7. Jesus taught of a baptism of water and spirit. One is of this world the other of the glory before the imaginary world of birth and death existed. "And now, O Father, glorify thou me in with thine own self with the glory which I had with thee before the world was" (John17: 5).

8. Jesus led the way, is the way, to the Christ Consciousness and pure awareness of being. He revealed an eternal spiritual life in a kingdom that was not this world. "Neither shall they say, Lo here! or, lo there! for, behold, the kingdom of God is within you" (Luke 17: 21).

9. All that Jesus was willing to suffer was to wake you up to the reality of your permanent spiritual being. Jesus is the way to the kingdom of your God source. "Fear not, little flock; for it is your Father's good pleasure to give you the kingdom" (Luke 12: 32).

10. For followers of Jesus Christ, the overcoming begins in the moment of accepting and waking up in the Holy Spirit in the name of Jesus Christ. The illusions are not necessary. Now, today you may be in paradise with Jesus Christ. When one of the thieves who had been crucified with Jesus, asked that he only be remembered by Jesus, Jesus replied, ". . . Verily I say unto thee, To day shalt thou be with me in paradise" (Luke 23: 43).

11. In pure awareness, birth and death do not exist. Remember, if there is a sense of birth, there must be a sense of death. Birth - death occur on the plane of opposites. They are not permanent occurrences.

12. Birth - death are not the reality of your being. All may be overcome on your spiritual journey home within awareness. "Him that overcometh will I make a pillar in the temple of my God, and he shall go no more out: . . ."(Revelation 3: 12).

+ +

LESSON: 27 — BODY

THE BODY IS a divine God source, vibrating energy created form. "All things were made by him; and without him was not anything made that was made. In him was life; and the life was the light of men" (John 1: 3- 4).

1. A spiritual healing of your body cannot be forced. You should never hesitate to consult with a

medical doctor for any physical condition. The body is not to be worshiped however, it is your divine image upon this earthly plane. Do not attack its appearance (God's image) on this plane. "And God said, Let us make man in our image, after our likeness: . . ." (Genesis 1: 26).

2. In spiritual terms: Void - Awareness - Consciousness - Mind - Body - Senses constitute a spiritual journey from the God-source into an imaginary world and back. It is a round trip fully paid for by many lessons learned. A trip that comes to a complete stop when you are fully aware the round trip was an illusion in time and space and ends in its beginning. "I am Alpha and Omega, the beginning and the ending, saith the Lord, which is, and which was, and which is to come, the Almighty" (Revelation I: 8).

3. When you falsely enter an imaginary world, false beliefs, attachments, experiences, and lessons determine what the human conditions will be.

4. The body is created by the divine God source and experiences the human condition. It's your method of transportation upon the plane of opposites. The transportation that allows you to walk a spiritual path, and travel a spiritual journey within the full awareness of your divine source.

5. The body is in your God control and guidance. "Know ye not that ye are the temple of God, and *that* the Spirit of God dwelleth in you?" (1 Corinthians 3: 16).

6. The body-sense appearance is not immortal, eternal. It does eventually become useless and decays (dies) but its spiritual flesh, its source, your life, is immortal, eternal. "And *though* after my skin *worms* destroy this *body*, yet in my flesh shall I see God" (Job 19: 26).

7. It is your divine God source that creates a body for *Its* use. "And the Word was made flesh, and dwelt among us, (and we beheld his glory, the glory as of the only begotten of the Father,) full of grace and truth" (John 1: 14).

8. Your life is the divine source, immortal, eternal. It's in the flesh (body) upon this plane you may glorify your divine source, God. So, be careful not to put God down. For God, through the Holy Spirit in the name of Jesus, is always lifting you up. "And I, if I be lifted up from the earth, will draw all *men* unto me" (John 12: 32).

9. It is the false belief of a personal separate identification and attachment with the body, that clouds your knowledge of the body's divine source. Forgetting your divine source, does not in any way dissipate it. "Judge not according to the appearances, but judge righteous judgement" (John 7: 24).

10. In the service of the Lord the body glorifies its God source. Therefore, as a vehicle in the service of the Lord, the body is not to be abused in thought, word, nor deed. Being the creation of the divine source, the body is to be cared for and lovingly accepted in all its necessary changes. All bodies are to be respected for their inherent dignity as "temples" of the Holy Spirit.

11. Too much social or cultural attention is focused on the cosmetic appearance of the body, making it the most socially conscious object. There is no justification for comparing the body you are using to others who may be obsessive with the concerns of the body. All too often, the criticism from others on behalf of your body is accepted. To do so, is to slap around a body that is carrying "you around" in the most loving, caring manner possible. "And the King shall answer and say unto them, Verily I say unto you, Inasmuch as ye have done *it* to the least of these my brethren, ye have done *it* unto me" (Matthew 25: 40).

12. The body you have been graced with isn't a form that is subject to the judgments or the condemnations of others. You cannot lay blame on the judgment or condemnations of others, when you emotionally accept a false sense-impression conditioning. To accept the judgments or condemnations of others is to do harm to the body, and is an insult to your divine God-source. Honor the dignity of yours and of all individuals.

13. It is your responsibility as the God source of the body, on this earthly plane, to guard it within your God Consciousness against those who would (intentionally or un-intentionally) do it harm in

thoughts or actions. The power of protection is not attachment to the body but lies in the realization of the truth about the body's source.

14. The body, as a manifested appearance sense-form in time and space, is subjected to change. Provide for the body's needs and take no further thought. The body's needs may include your consulting with a physician — whenever necessary. "Which of you by taking thought can add one cubit unto his stature?" (Matthew 6: 27).

15. Whenever you believe the body is separate from your divine source, you have created a false image. "Thou shalt not make unto thee any graven image, or any likeness *of any thing* that *is* in heaven above, or that *is* in the water under the earth:" (Exodus 20: 4).

16. The "likeness" of God does not change. It is only the personal sense image upon this plane that appears to change. The "likeness" of God is within pure awareness and *is* your life eternal. To damn the body you are using, desire a body other than the one you have been graced with, or desire that others may approve is to create a false god. "Thou shalt have no other gods before me" (Exodus 20: 3).

....

STUDENT'S STORY:

Months after receiving a Christmas present in the form of a (yet to be acted upon) membership to a local exercise gym, I found millions of reasons why I couldn't possibly get there. Maybe you have had such inner conversations about a well-needed outer change. I reasoned it was either too early, too late, I was too tired, too busy, had more important things to do. The list went on and on. Yet in spite of the protest and excuses, I still had an intuitive knowing that my body wanted some sort of physical aerobic, cardiovascular, weight bearing — you name it experience. My body kept sending me gut messages. However, my mind well exercised and armed with innumerable excuses held sway and for months the body didn't get to the gym! Overcoming inertia (entropy) is not easy however necessary for a healthy vibrant life. It is not surprising that it is known as one of the "seven capital sins!"

I do a lot of praying, reading, studying, etcetera. I needed to bring my "Mary" into balance with the nagging reality of my "Martha," which had been sadly neglected. How to move is not easy especially when it has been a long time. The status quo, lethargy, inertia, laziness — you name it, is a powerful motivator to stay put. The parabolic reality (guilt) that I may see my Christmas benefactor and have to confess I had not yet made it to the gym became a great motivator.

Finally, I moved into action. I decided it was time. I went, very tentatively and with great caution, into the arena called the gym that I knew little about. There is nothing like a little "beginners mind" to shake things up. I made an appointment with a trainer to show me how not to kill myself and I was treated with care and respect. I didn't find a lot of spandex or i-pod action in the gym as I had feared, and realized everyone seemed to be at this place for the same reason — careful attention to the physical body. It is, after all, the temple of the Holy Spirit and I decided it was high time to honor that fact appropriately and get my body moving. So, as a stranger in a strange land, I went from one room of the gym to another and at the end of an hour felt as if I had crossed an unknown sea and felt better for it. I had survived.

I write about this, not to suggest anyone else needs to go to a gym, but to acknowledge that we do have a responsibility of caring for the body, and for the silent, subtle power of inertia over it. Paradoxically, it can also serve as a grace or gift when recognized and acknowledged because it ultimately moves us, as in my case, to the gym not to the grave.

+ +

LESSON: 28 — BREATH

BREATH, IN THE simplest of terms, is the air you take into your lungs and then let out — inhalation, exhalation.

1. Breathing should always be done diaphragmatically and without pauses. This allows the lungs to completely fill during inhalation and completely empty during exhalation.

2. You may become aware that breathing diaphragmatically helps to calm the mind and body. When a stressful situation occurs, slowly taking a long deep diaphragmatic breath may allow the mind to function less emotionally and the body to become less agitated.

3. In scriptural terms, breath is God's life force infused into all living Beings. "And the LORD God formed man *of* the dust of the ground, and breathed into his nostrils the breath of life; and man became a living soul" (Genesis 2: 7).

4. Scripture relates the importance of the breath with your life in your God source. "And I will lay sinews upon you, and will bring up flesh upon you, and cover you with skin, and put breath in you, and ye shall live; and ye shall know that I *am* the LORD" (Ezekiel 37: 6).

5. Jesus demonstrated the power of the breath when He said, "Then said Jesus to them again, Peace *be* unto you: as *my* Father hath sent me, even so send I you. And when he had said this, he breathed on *them,* and saith unto them, Receive ye the Holy Ghost" (John 20: 21-22).

6. When you no longer are breathing, your life upon this plane has expired. "Thou hidest thy face, they are troubled: thou takest away their breath, they die, and return to their dust" (Psalm 104: 29).

7. A silent prayer practice is the silent praise of the Lord. "Let every thing that has breath praise the LORD, Praise ye the LORD" (Psalm 150: 6).

8. Through the Spiritual Heart Center, and Holy Spirit in the name of Jesus Christ, you may breathe and dwell in the secret place of the most High. "He that dwelleth in the secret place of the most High shall abide under the shadow of the Almighty" (Psalm 91: 1).

+ +

LESSON: 29 — CAN'T

CAN'T IS A defeatist word used by an individual who seeks not to begin or finish a task.

1. Can't is the most heard word uttered by new students on a spiritual walk. Can't is a good excuse but never a good reason.

2. I can't practice silent prayer sitting twice a day, I can't find the time, I can't sit still, I can't because I have company, I can't because I have so many things to do, I can't, I can't, I can't.

3. When you come to a silent prayer practice being sure you "can't" do it, you can't do it. You predispose yourself to defeating your purpose, if you ever had one.

4. Can't closes the door in your face and locks you out. You hold the key, drop the "t" and you are in.

5. On a spiritual walk, all things are possible with God. As Jesus said, ". . . With men this is impossible; but with God all things are possible" (Matthew 19: 26).

6. Trust you "can," and you can. It matters not if it requires mis-steps, stumbling, and repeating. Staying with it, not giving up, and continuing to walk towards the straight gate and the narrow way is the, "I can do it."

7. It is your constant, persistent effort that is the "can do." There are no failure moments on the spiritual walk only moments of "can do."

8. If you step up to do that which you are drawn to do on your spiritual walk, you can do it. All the Saints, Angels, and those who have walked the path before you will come to your aide through the Holy Spirit in the name of Jesus Christ.

++++++++++++++++++++++++++

LESSON: 30 — CELIBACY

Celibacy on the spiritual journey is the abstention practice from using sexual energy for sexual activity.

1. Celibacy, for the serious truth student, usually evolves over time of intense purification with a devotional single mindedness to a complete life service, in the oneness of a realized awareness of the Christ Consciousness.

2. The practice of celibacy cannot be a forced or voluntary decision. You do not get up one morning and say, "I'm a celibate." It won't work. It will cause an inner and outer struggle. "For I would that all men were even as I myself. But every man hath his proper gift of God, one after this manner, and another after that. I say therefore to the unmarried and widows, It is good for them if they abide even as I. But if they cannot contain, let them marry: for it is better to marry than to burn" (1 Corinthians 7: 7- 9).

3. Celibacy may or may not become a natural course taken in the life of one whose sexual energy has risen and is sustained within the Spiritual Heart Center. As one rises to the realized Christ Consciousness and maintains the state, the desires or titillating sensations for sexual activity may no longer rise.

4. Consequently, nothing is taken away, nothing is given up, nothing is forced. It is a falling away through your natural ascendence in the Christ Consciousness through the Holy Spirit in the name of Jesus Christ.

5. You are never asked to give up anything before its time has arrived. For those who would find a celibate life not possible — it is not possible nor is it necessary. "But he said to them, All *men* cannot receive this saying, save *they* to whom it is given" (Matthew 19: 11).

6. On the spiritual path there is all of eternity. You are in an individual expression of consciousness according to your disposition. There are stages along the spiritual path for you to evolve according to the lessons learned and lessons you seek to learn.

7. Jesus Christ is a gentle, loving guide and always patiently awaits your arrival in your own good time. At no time, does the Holy Spirit in the name of Jesus Christ push, shove, or take you where you are not prepared and ready to be.

8. The preparedness and readiness may always bring you to the realized consciousness where you belong. It becomes your free will to accept and maintain that for which you have been prepared and readied through the teaching of the Holy Spirit in the name of Jesus Christ.

STUDENT'S STORY:

In my growing up years, human sexuality rarely, if ever, was the topic of conversation. In elementary school our gender-segregated sixth grade health classes dealt with issues of puberty using a medical model. Classes were informative, scientific, academic, awkward, and brief. By sixth grade, the cultural taboo around such discussions was thoroughly in place and most of us had neither desire nor the language to carry on any kind of a meaningful conversation.

I realize much has changed today, but this was my experience growing up in the 50's. The only other mention of sex (outside of school) unfortunately came in religious instruction classes where it was very apparent that anything whatsoever to do with sex was either immoral, illegal, or intrinsically evil.

What I knew about my human sexuality in terms of its purpose, intent, content, meaning, and potential was distorted, limited, and in most cases inaccurate physiologically, psychologically, and spiritually. This was certainly not good preparation for negotiating the seas I encountered later in adulthood with one of the most important and powerful energies in human life.

By high school I knew more about balancing a check book than I did about balancing my hormones. I dealt with the issue by simply not dealing with it. This was certainly not the gift of celibacy but simply the better of two evils. What I did not know, feel, try, experience, talk about, touch, read, see, hear, etcetera could not hurt me and most importantly, could not land me in hell for all eternity. Playing it safe meant sex was not an issue because sex was just not an issue. End of story. Ha!

Obviously, at 59 with two grown children to testify to my human sexuality and its procreative capacities I have learned a lot and I have also had to unlearn even more. As I have grown in awareness and corresponding balance, every aspect of my human experience has been subject to reformation and transformation. I have come to acknowledge sexual energy as personal, occasionally problematic, procreative, playful, powerful, and purposeful. My primarily negative cultural and religious conditioning, around sexual issues, has often thwarted rather than facilitated my natural evolution towards self understanding and acceptance.

Fortunately, God took care of this deficit and began remedial work with me in the silence of my long standing contemplative prayer practice and discipline. Without even knowing it (and by the grace of God) I gradually became aware of my body self as whole, holy, sexual, creative, productive, positive, capable of love, joy, service, and compassion.

My aversion or attraction to expressions of sexual energy were gradually healed and normalized. I became capable of appropriate expressions according to my state in life. At this point I have come to recognize it was never sexual energy (itself, it is simply a fact, an energy) that was a problem but the right, proper understanding, use, and expression of sexual energy that was challenging. The importance of timing cannot be underestimated. Everything in due season. We must not deny, rush, shortcut, repress, or assume the presence or absence of our sexual nature. Celibacy (abstinence from the genital expression of sexual energy) is certainly within the parameters of legitimate human life and its capacity. In my attempts to grapple with this expression within the married and single state, one thing I know for sure is, it cannot be forced, willed, nor vowed. Quite the contrary.

The state of celibacy is arrived at and received as naturally and as appropriately as has each preceding stage. To pretend, assume, power over, battle or manipulate the mind or body prematurely into claiming a celibate lifestyle would not only be presumptuous and unnecessary, but ill-advised physically, psychologically, emotionally, and spiritually.

Likewise, for any who have not sailed that particular sea, it is equally unnecessary to claim it doesn't exist or that it is pathology. Like any gift of the Spirit, by the fruits you shall know. Transformed sexual energy, moved from the genital expression to the heart, manifests itself as universal compassion and unconditional love for all.

+ +

LESSON: 31 — CHARITY

CHARITY ENCOMPASSES THE love for yourself and all others. "Thou shalt not avenge, nor bear any grudge against the children of thy people, but thou shalt love thy neighbour as thyself: I *am* the LORD" (Leviticus 19: 18).

1. It is not just the charity of giving wealth, but also the charity of generously giving of yourself that scripture teaches. "And though I bestow all my goods to feed *the poor*, and though I give my body to be burned, and not charity, it profiteth me nothing" (I Corinthians 13: 3).

2. In this world of material appearances, you may accumulate many of the outward signs of success in business and your spiritual milieu. However, without charity you are an empty suit, dress. "And though I have the *gift of* prophecy, and understand all mysteries, and all knowledge; and though I have all faith, so that I could remove mountains, and have not charity, I am nothing" (I Corinthians 13: 2).

3. Charity is the spacious, all inclusive act of caring love. "And Jesus answered him, The first of all the commandments *is*, Hear, O Israel; The Lord our God is one Lord: And thou shalt love the Lord thy God with all thy heart, and with all thy soul, and with all thy mind, and with all thy strength: this *is* the first commandment. And the second *is* like, *namely* this, Thou shalt love thy neighbour as thyself. There is none other commandment greater than these" (Mark 12: 29 - 31).

4. The charitable love you have one to another, marks you as a disciple of Jesus Christ. "By this shall all *men* know that ye are my disciples, if ye have love one to another" (John 13: 35).

5. Charity brings you near the perfect image of the Divine. "And above all these things *put on* charity, which is the bond of perfectness. (Colossians 3: 14).

6. To limit your caring love to a few, is to believe charity has *its* limit. To realize the Divine's nature, you begin with yourself and all the other selves appearing in this world. "And above all things have fervent charity among yourselves: for charity shall cover the multitude of sins" (I Peter 4: 8).

7. Although it would seem the nature of charity asks much of you, its returns are generous. "Charity suffereth long, *and* is kind; charity envieth not; charity vaunteth not, is not puffed up, Doth not behave itself unseemly, seeketh not her own, is not easily provoked, thinketh no evil; Rejoiceth not in iniquity, but rejoiceth in the truth; Beareth all things, believeth all things, hopeth all things, endureth all things" (I Corinthians 13: 4-7).

8. Realize for yourself, though you possess faith and hope, on your spiritual walk, it is charity that may open wide your Spiritual Heart Center through the Holy Spirit in the name of Jesus Christ. "And now abideth faith, hope, charity, these three; but the greatest of these *is* charity" (I Corinthians 13: 13).

+ +

LESSON: 32 — CHANGE - CONVERSION

CHANGE - CONVERSION reveals itself within and out of your life as you progress on a spiritual walk. It is a sense of physical and/or emotional difference in appearance upon the plane of opposites.

1. When you are drawn to seek truth, your inner listening, hearing and silence deepen. You can be sure a sense of change - conversion has begun. It can be intentional or unintentional. "Who hath ears to hear, let him hear" (Matthew 13: 9).

2. Whenever you appear or "feel" differently, there is the tendency to refer to the difference as a "change." In reality there is no person to change or convert. There is no change - conversion because an illusion cannot be changed - converted.

3. In an illusionary world, you have been replacing one illusion with another and calling it change - conversion. You cannot change - convert what does not exist.

4. As an illusion, the One, God, appears as the many. In reality, there *is* only the One. What you are recognizing as change - conversion is your gradual awareness of the impersonal. As your inner world unfolds, your interest in the outer world may gradually lessen. And as you progress from a sense of the personal to an awareness of the impersonal, you may believe a "change - conversion" is occurring.

5. Emotions may seem to be gradually lessening and you are living in an arid, barren land. As the sense of the personal lessens, you may experience a sense of loss. The personal sense becomes less as you become more aware of the impersonal. "And the glory which thou gavest me I have given them; that they may be one, even as we are one: I in them, and thou in me, that they may be made perfect in one; and that the world may know that thou hast sent me, and hast loved them, as thou hast loved me" (John 17: 22-23).

6. Change - conversion may be difficult to handle and cause emotional turmoil when relating to others. As you attempt to adjust to a new way of being, family and old friends may become distant. It is difficult to describe the change because the change - conversion is impersonal, without words, or thoughts.

7. The impersonal is just be-ing without description, without definition — nothing more, nothing less. "And God said unto Moses, 'I AM THAT I AM: and he said, Thus shalt thou say unto the children of Israel, I AM hath sent me unto you. And God said moreover unto Moses, Thus shalt thou say unto the children of Israel, the LORD God of your fathers, the God of Abraham, the God of Isaac, and the God of Jacob, hath sent me unto you: this *is* my name for ever, and this *is* my memorial unto all generations" (Exodus 3: 14 - 15).

8. The old "self," with whom you were comfortable, may be slowly, and at times, not so slowly, dying. The less you resist the inner and outer change - conversion, manifesting, the quicker the change may occur. Allow the old "self" to go quietly in the night.

9. Now, there may be this new "self" whom you really do not yet know. The mind resists and fears what it does not understand. There may be a longing to return to the old self, the old ways. This temptation usually may occur during the alone times of despair, loneliness, or aridness.

10. For a time, change - conversion may cause an inner and outer struggle. You may be desperately trying to hold on to the old, while the new is being born. You may struggle with the temptation of the God awful feeling of having been forsaken, as did Jesus, "And about the ninth hour Jesus cried with a loud voice, saying, . . . That is to say, My God, my God, why hast thou forsaken me?" (Matthew 27: 46).

11. In daily activities, your life may have a certain dullness, uninteresting sense to it. It is when you are actively in the awareness of the Holy Spirit in the name of Jesus Christ, serving as the Holy Spirit, that you are beyond the emotions of emptiness, dryness, and a personal sense of being. "Thou wilt shew me the path of life: in thy presence *is* fullness of joy; at thy right hand *there are* pleasures for evermore" (Psalm 16: 11).

12. The sense of change - conversion on this earth is inevitable. In truth, you are and always have been a spiritual being. Waking up to reality makes all things new. "And he that sat upon the throne said, Behold, I make all things new. And he said unto me, Write: for these words are true and faithful" (Revelation 21: 5).

+ +

LESSON: 33 — CHOICES AND DECISIONS

THE CHOICES AND decisions, including the choice of the Christ Centered Prayer method and the decision to practice it, influence your spiritual walk's direction. There is no greater assistance on your spiritual walk than the choices selected and decisions made.

1. There is a very fine line between choices and decisions. You select a choice; you make a decision based on the selected choice.

2. Choices are two or more inner or outer appearances rising in consciousness from which you select a preference. When you have selected a preference, it is a choice. What to do with, or about the choice you have selected, is your decision.

3. For example, a simple choice would be: you are asked after dinner, "Would you prefer ice cream or pie for dessert?" You may think for a moment, but you don't have to concentrate intensely to select a choice. A simple choice doesn't require concentrated energy effort. Eating the entire dessert or part of it, is the decision you will make from the choice you have selected.

4. A simple or difficult choice is the initial selection you must choose from, and the choice you have selected, determines the decision and the amount of energy (will-concentrated energy) that is required to accomplish it.

5. The simple or difficult choices and decisions are differentiated by the intensity of the rising energy invested and the drawn interested attraction. In turn, each may attract your attention and the intensity of rising energy invested may increase, or decrease, depending on many variable conditioning factors.

6. During the Christ Centered Prayer practice, your choice is between staying with the mind, the rising sense impressions, or with a determined purpose, becoming aware of the Spiritual Heart Center. Once a choice is selected, the decision to do it kicks in.

7. In a silent prayer practice, every time you exercise the choice and decide to turn away from the mind or rising senses, you are giving up the conscious effort (will) to concentrate on the rising impressions. You are surrendering to the will of the Father. "And he went a little further, and fell on his face, and prayed, saying, O my Father, if it be possible, let this cup pass from me: nevertheless not as I will, but as thou *wilt*" (Matthew 26: 39).

8. You are constantly selecting from choices and making decisions along a bumpy, but straight gate and the narrow way. The rule of thumb is to select the choices that lead to the necessary decisions. It is the necessary decisions you make that helps guide your spiritual progress.

9. On a spiritual walk there are no right or wrong decisions. There is only what is necessary. You make your decisions based on what is needed at the moment or what is necessary for your spiritual progress, and in consideration of the need of others.

10. When a difficult decision must be made, the question to ask yourself is not, "Is this right or wrong" but, "Is this necessary?" The right or wrong of any decision making can only cause confusion, and may cause problems. It is impossible to judge the right or wrong of any given situation in the moment.

11. On the spiritual path, each momentary decision made is a momentary commitment and when each is a necessary decision, it becomes a steady resolved commitment to the reality of your being.

12. It is the committed decisions that may bring you into the awareness of the Christ Consciousness' presence. With every choice you select and every decision you make, you are constantly being asked, "And if it seem evil unto you to serve the LORD, choose you this day whom ye will serve; . . ." (Joshua 24: 15).

13. Choices and decisions should be considered possibilities or opportunities allowing you to prog-

ress more swiftly toward the awareness of the Christ Consciousness. You should consider carefully and wisely from the choices presented. A wise choice may allow you to make the necessary decision.

14. Choices and decisions are the sign posts that point the way, a map that shows the necessary way to take you there. Each choice and decision takes you near or far from your intended aware place.

15. In your life's journey upon this plane, choices and decisions are constant occurrences. By their very nature on the plane of opposites, choices and decisions rise.

16. As you continue your silent Christ Centered Prayer practice, becoming aware of your Spiritual Heart Center becomes less of a deliberate choice/decision and more a devotional love for the Holy Spirit in the name of Jesus Christ.

....

STUDENT'S STORY:

Choices and decisions have tremendous consequences upon our spiritual journey. The choices and decisions we make may allow us to sleep walk through life or awaken us in awareness to the Holy Spirit in the name of Jesus Christ.

I was not reared in the church and had no formal or informal religious training at home. However, at the age of eight I made a conscious decision to become a member of the Catholic Church. With my parent's consent, I was given religious instructions.

I grew up in New Rochelle, New York and most of my friends were Jewish. With one such friend, I would have long passionate theological conversations. We both decided for ourselves that what some of us were being taught could not possibly be true. He knew I was not going to hell and I knew he was not going to hell either. So with third grade mentalities, we dissented from official teachings and remained faithful to what we knew was true — that the God we knew loved and cared for all people and that all people would be together in heaven because that was the fair and just thing to do with good people no matter where or whether they went to church or synagogue.

My decision to leave the Roman church followed the more or less rebellious and exploratory stages of late adolescence. I was in college, Vatican II had hit, and the changes in Catholic and Protestant churches were all around. Everyone was listening to the Beatles, practicing Transcendental Meditation, visiting gurus in India, smoking pot, throwing away underwear, and going vegetarian.

There were so many choices, so many decisions. Viet Nam was on; students were taking over and being taken over by ideologies and causes. Bob Dylan was singing "How Many Roads Must a Man Walk Down." Peter Paul and Mary sang, "Puff the Magic Dragon." Holy Days of Obligation, fasting on Fridays, Easter duties, and such no longer held sway in my imagination, nor met my desperate needs for meaning and belonging.

My religious, Baltimore Catechism and public school education could not sustain or contain me. I had been forced to stretch my attitudes and opinions in every conceivable way and the elasticity of my religious indoctrination simply didn't have enough give. It snapped.

There were other choices and decisions to be made and I made them. I took college courses in comparative religion, philosophy, psychology and sociology. I visited the Congregational Churches and participated in the Campus Ministry programs. I met other Christians and together we struggled with the issues of racism, sexism, feminism, consciousness raising, war, peace, welfare, abortion, capital punishment, and of course, all of this under the constant shadow of an impending nuclear holocaust! I suppose it was a good time to either lose religion or, for heaven's sake, find religion. I did a little of both.

Later, I would be led by the Holy Spirit to make a choice of becoming a member of the Episcopal Church. By the time this choice was presented, my deep, devotional longing from childhood to be an ordained priest made the choice for me. It became a committed decision and surely, was the necessary one for me.

By the love of God, this choice and committed decision to follow through, once again put my feet firmly and consciously on a straight and narrow way. As a child, Jesus had pulled me into Himself and He never let go.

The world has not changed very much and we are all being confronted with pretty much the same choices and decisions. At one time, I based my choices and decisions on what I conceived to be right or wrong. However, as this lesson paper informs, there is another way—doing what is necessary.

+ +

LESSON: 34 — COMMITMENT

COMMITMENT IS THAT which gives you permission to agree with yourself to adhere to a silent prayer practice.

1. For some, beginning a silent prayer practice may seem easy. However, it is so easy, it may be difficult, and may even be boring. A sincere commitment may facilitate the sought after benefits.

2. When desires or temptations rise to pull you in other directions, a commitment may help keep you going towards the straight gate and the narrow way.

3. As a first time silent prayer student, curiosity may bring you to a silent prayer practice but a sincere commitment will bring you back. When you are committed to a silent prayer practice for even a short time, four - six weeks, chances are, you will want to continue.

4. It is your commitment that may strengthen your resolve and encourage the necessary discipline. To say, "I'll try," only builds in failure. To be committed may assure the possibility of success.

5. As a truth student, you never say, "I'll try it." You say, "I will do it." Success is your commitment in doing, not trying. Trying gives you a way out, doing gives you a way in — into all that you seek as a truth seeker.

6. Commitment may give you the freedom to open your heart and mind to inner realizations.

7. Commitment may keep you faithful to your silent prayer practice until your silent prayer practice is as necessary as breathing.

8. The stronger the commitment, the stronger and steadier your footsteps may become on your spiritual walk.

9. And, when there may be dark nights of the soul, commitment may help you to see the light at the end of the tunnel.

10. Whether the spiritual journey is a short one, or a long tedious one, a steadfast commitment may reap its rewards in the awakening activity of the Holy Spirit in the name of Jesus Christ.

+ +

LESSON: 35 — COMPANY

COMPANY MAY INCLUDE those with whom you may relate well or those with whom you may not relate well.

1. The company you keep and share your life with on your spiritual walk may help or hinder your spiritual progress.

2. There may be individuals who would demand much of your time away from your spiritual practices.

3. Culture and family imprinted conditioning may have instilled within you a sense of having to meet the demands of others.

4. There may always be those who would expect you to cater to their perceived needs. Your ultimate responsibility is to your self-realization.

5. Whatever leisure time you may have, should not be wasted constantly in the company of sleep walkers.

6. It is wise on your spiritual walk to keep company with like minded individuals: individuals who seek the things of a Godly nature.

7. As a serious truth student, the individuals who are necessary to share your spiritual journey may move in and out of your life according to your need.

8. In time, you may realize it is easier to be alone than in the company of those who would engage in idle verbiage. "But I say unto you, That every idle word that men shall speak, they shall give account thereof in the day of Judgment. For by thy words thou shalt be justified, and by thy words thou shalt be condemned" (Matthew 12: 36-37).

9. It is a blessing to have the opportunity to share the company of an enlightened being. However, no one may take you to the other side of the river. Under the guidance of the Holy Spirit in the name of Jesus Christ, you must row the boat to get there and you must be the one to experience what is there.

10. The company you keep is always your choice and decision. The best company you may ever keep is the Holy Spirit in the name of Jesus Christ.

+ +

LESSON: 36 — COMPARING

COMPARING IS THE evaluating of yourself in relationship to others in a negative or positive light.

1. Comparing yourself to the accomplishments or credentials of others gives you a false sense of separation.

2. As you rise to the awareness of your being, there are no others. There is always the one. The one, expressing in infinite variety. Not a lesser or better one but rather individual expressions of the same one. "And Jesus answered him, The first of all the commandments *is*, Hear O Israel; The Lord our God is one Lord:" (Mark 12: 29).

3. In the world of appearances there is the tendency to compare your self-worth by paper credentials. It may steep you in the habit of falsely judging yourself and others. "To whom will ye liken me, and make *me* equal, and compare me, that we may be like?" (Isaiah 46: 5)

4. Jesus' disciples were chosen from a variety of positions — from a fisherman, tax collector, etcetera.

5. Jesus taught His disciples truth and sent them forth to teach truth. Imagine a fisherman having to teach truth among scholars and well credentialed individuals.

6. Self-worth may never be found in a paper degree of any kind. Truth is not predicated on the amount of paper credentials this world has to offer.

7. No matter how many degrees you have earned in this world, you must go beyond them to realize truth. "I thank God through Jesus Christ our Lord. So then with the mind I myself serve the law of God; but with the flesh the law of sin" (Romans 7: 25).

8. You can only teach or share about Truth from your realization of it, not from what you may have learned from an attained degree. "They are of the world: therefore speak they of the world, and the world

heareth them. We are of God: he that knoweth God heareth us; he that is not of God heareth not us. Hereby know we the spirit of truth, and the spirit of error" (I John 4: 5-6).

9. Your self-worth, self-esteem is grounded in the conscious awareness of your being. All universal knowledge and Truth exist within conscious awareness and whatever is necessary for your use will manifest.

10. Who or what you are in reality has no degree of any kind. The awareness of your Christ Consciousness is the ultimate "degree." None other can compare to it or come even close to it. To want more of the Christ awareness realization is to want less of the approval of this world, not more of it.

+ +

LESSON: 37 — COMPASSION

COMPASSION IS GOD'S impersonal, unconditional love in a temporary moment's need during your spiritual walk on the plane of relative opposites.

1. Compassion knows the need and meets it at the level of appearance and as a child of God on this plane, you are the vessel through which the eyes, ears, hands, and intellect of God are actively engaged.

2. You are the administrator and the recipient of God's compassion through the Holy Spirit in the name of Jesus Christ.

3. Compassion is impersonal in the present moment-to-moment heartfelt response. It is in a moment of truth when you must either withhold or release to meet whatever the need may be at the moment.

4. As you develop your personal and impersonal relationship with Jesus Christ, the compassionate differentiation of either withholding or releasing comes from the inner prompting of the Holy Spirit in the name of Jesus Christ.

5. In your compassionate state you are constantly saying, "Yes Lord, I will serve; yes, Lord I am a child of God; and yes Lord, so are all who are in need. I am here Lord, send me." "Also I heard the voice of the Lord, saying, Whom shall I send, and who will go for us? Then said I, Here *am* I; send me" (Isaiah 6: 8).

6. Compassion moves on and does not remain in space or time. Compassion's impersonal, providing disposition is an expression of unconditional Love. Because compassion meets the need in any given moment, it frees you from the attachment to the rising need and to the needy.

7. Compassion blesses you with the gift of acceptance, allowance, and respect of those who choose to indulge in the desires and temptations steeped in greed.

8. It is your responsibility to discern the difference between need and greed.

NEED:

A. Need always meets or rises at the place in a moment of necessity.
B. Need is a temporary moment of comfort, and satisfies as a drink of water would satisfy a thirst.
C. Need takes precedent over desires and temptations at the moment of its expression or appearance.

GREED:

A. Greed extends beyond place and moment, and is insatiable.
B. Greed moves toward desires and temptations.
C. Greed drives you beyond your need and seeks to trample on the needs of others.

LESSON: 38 — COMPLACENCY

COMPLACENCY IS BECOMING satisfied at any given moment with the distance you have traveled on the spiritual journey.

1. The problem with complacency is that it may cause an unintentional drift. A drift that may hold you in a place that slows your spiritual progress.
2. Complacency's gifts of smugness, self-satisfaction, and a false release from your responsibility to awaken to the truth of your being are seductive, "As for me, I will behold thy face in righteousness: I shall be satisfied, when I awake, with thy likeness (Psalm 17: 15).
3. Complacency may occur for many reasons: emotional stress, mental exhaustion, and/or physical illness. No matter the reasons, you need to be alert to its nature and its potential to take you on a delayed or curved path.
4. You have worked hard, studied, and practiced a silent prayer. Many of the things you worked to realize have come to fruition. It is easy to want to enjoy the fruits of your labor — complacency may creep in.
5. Service to others, work responsibilities, social obligations have a way of distracting you from realizing all you ever have is the present moment. "But God said unto him, *thou* fool, this night thy soul shall be required of thee: then whose shall those things be, which thou hast provided?" (Luke 12: 20).
6. As a serious truth seeker, stay in an aware consciousness that allows you to avoid the complacency trap.
7. Through all of life's ups and downs, be consistent with the spiritual practices that are yours to nourish and bring you to a realized Christ Consciousness.
8. Through the Holy Spirit in the name of Jesus Christ, stand guard at the inner straight gate of the Kingdom of God and do not allow anything to approach that is not of a Godly nature.
9. Becoming too comfortable with your progress, is an invitation to complacency. Do not confuse resting in the spirit with resting from realizing truth.
10. It is at any of the following times that you are most vulnerable to be lured into complacency.

COMPLACENCY WARNING SIGNS:

A. Your progress is obvious and pleasing to you.
B. Everything seems to fall into place. Consequently, there may be a smug satisfaction with things the way they are.
C. You have attained many insights, realizations, and all is going well in your life experiences.
D. Your inner studies (includes: daily silent prayer practice and working with spiritual principles) are moved closer to a back burner, as your attention is placed more on outer activities.
E. You can justify to yourself and others why you do not have the time nor the energy to pursue your daily spiritual studies.

LESSON: 39 — CONCENTRATION

CONCENTRATION IS BRINGING the mind's vibrating energy to a one pointedness.

1. Placing your attention repeatedly on a thought, image, or sound may help concentrate the mind.

2. Concentration of the mind's vibrating energy requires continuous effort. Concentration is required to attract and manifest desires. The action/s to bring about the desired results are also necessary.

3. Example: to concentrate on becoming a doctor will not manifest the necessary schooling to become a doctor. Staying focused on your goal while *you* take the necessary steps to fulfill the requirements for medical school may assists you to accomplish your desire.

4. It is in the giving that you receive all that is necessary — not in the concentration of thought/s. "Which of you by taking thought can add one cubit unto his stature?" (Matthew 6: 27).

5. It is a mistake to solely use concentration of the mind to get something. Yours is a giving nature not a getting one. There is a spiritual principle of supply: all that you will ever need already exist. "Therefore I say unto you, Take no thought for your life, what ye shall eat, or what ye shall drink; nor yet for your body, what ye shall put on. Is not the life more than meat, and the body than raiment?" (Matthew 6: 25).

6. Entertaining positive thoughts may assist you in all that you do. As a truth seeker, the most direct practice for you to complete your spiritual journey is beyond the thinking mind — it is a silent prayer practice. "But seek ye first the kingdom of God, and his righteousness; and all these things shall be added unto you" (Matthew 6: 33).

7. There are many methods of deception to entice you to get caught up in the mental/mind state of consciousness. Bringing forth life's many desires through the concentration of the mind does not guarantee they will bring joy or peace. "Let us therefore follow after the things which make for peace, and things wherewith one may edify another" (Romans 14: 19).

8. Attracting what you desire, may bring forth more then you bargain for. So, be careful what you desire. You may very well get it. The mind alone is deceptive and easily seduced. It is better you put your trust in the Lord. "I will say of the LORD, *He is* my refuge and my fortress: my God; in him will I trust" (Psalm 91: 2).

9. The problem with using concentration to attract what you believe you want is its exclusivity. While you may get what you wish for, you may miss out on other options and possibilities that may support your spiritual progress.

10. There is a difference in what you may desire for yourself and what God may desire for you. There was a man who prayed day and night, "God please give me a new Ford automobile for Christmas." Sure enough, when he opened his front door Christmas morning, a shiny new Ford automobile awaited his use. The man was ecstatic and immediately fell to his knees, praised, and thanked God.

"Are you happy now," asked God.

"Oh yes," responded the man.

"Well I am glad," said God, "because I had a Cadillac planned for you."

11. A silent prayer practice is all inclusive. The spiritual principle of attraction rises within your inner awareness of Being — effortlessly. Your God-self is all inclusive and Its vibrating energy is always manifesting exactly what you need. "Be not ye therefore like unto them: for your Father knoweth what things ye have need of, before ye ask him" (Matthew 6: 8).

12. Yes, the mind can create a world. It is a world of false concepts. It is also of impermanence. Remember, what the thinking mind would create, must deteriorate.

13. The mind works with attraction *and* attachment. The attraction is: you to some one, some thing, desire, or temptation. What attracts attaches like flies to flypaper. The results are pain and suffering. The loss of freedom.

14. You need never create, through concentration, misleading attractions because your world with all of your needs already exists. The Kingdom of God exists now and throughout all eternity and it exists

within you. "Neither shall they say, Lo here! Or, lo there! For, behold the kingdom of God is within you" (Luke 17: 21).

15. The secret to fulfilling your life's needs (not desires) is to turn within. Rest in the silence of your Being beyond words and thoughts. Whatever you ask for, whatever you seek is available from within and will manifest as needed. "Ask, and it shall be given you; seek, and ye shall find; knock, and it shall be opened unto you" (Matthew 7: 7).

16. It is possible to become aware of the Kingdom of God while still in this world but not of it. "Thy kingdom come. Thy will be done in earth, as *it is* in heaven" (Matthew 6: 10).

17. "Thy will be done in earth, as *it is* in heaven." The thinking mind, full of desires and temptations, knows nothing of doing the will of God. Realizing the will of God is beyond the mind.

18. It is from the Spiritual Heart Center, the heart of God, that the will of God is revealed. The mind is a magnificent servant but a very poor master. When you live out from the heart of God, the heart and mind are one and the mind serves the will of God.

19. Go kindly and gently upon your spiritual walk and seek to know who/what you are before you seek the things of this world to bring fulfillment.

20. Attracting the things of this world to fulfill your desires is only a temporary fix. Turn within and you may become aware of a permanent fix through the Holy Spirit in the name of Jesus Christ.

+ +

LESSON: 40 — CONFIDENCE

CONFIDENCE IS THE stepping out in total trust and reliance on the Christ of your being.

1. Confidence in the Christ is knowing your divine heritage and claiming it. "For in him we live, and move, and have our being; as certain also of your own poets have said, For we are also his offspring" (Acts 17: 28).

2. Once you realize the truth, be confident and accept the responsibility for living it. Look no longer to others to fulfill that which is given you to do. "*It is* better to trust in the LORD than to put confidence in man" (Psalm 118: 8).

3. In confidence and with a determined purpose, you may holdfast to the truth you have realized. Do not live in fear nor separate your inner God-light from the world. "The LORD *is* my light and my salvation; whom shall I fear? The LORD *is* the strength of my life; of whom shall I be afraid?" (Psalm 27: 1).

4. In confidence, remain firm and grounded in the radiant light that shines within you and shines on all that you do. "Let your light so shine before men, that they may see your good works, and glorify your Father which is in heaven" (Matthew 5: 16).

5. With confidence in the Lord, you may live a quiet, contemplative life in a world of strife and turmoil. "Though an host should encamp against me, my heart shall not fear: though war should rise against me, in this *will* I *be* confident" (Psalm 27: 3).

6. With confidence, have the conviction, courage, and perseverance to walk towards the straight gate and narrow way. "For we are made partakers of Christ, if we hold the beginning of our confidence stedfast unto the end; while it is said, Today if ye will hear his voice, harden not your hearts, as in the provocation" (Hebrews 3: 14 - 15).

7. The confidence in your God-self, and the Holy Spirit in the name of Jesus Christ prevents you from turning back or looking forward. Take each step in place, in the present, on your spiritual walk.

8. Have confidence in all that you are in the oneness of the Divine-Christ Consciousness. Confi-

dently put on the armor of the Christ in the light of your God-awareness. "The night is far spent, the day is at hand: let us therefore cast off the works of darkness, and let us put on the armor of light" (Romans 13: 12).

+ +

LESSON: 41 — CONSCIENCE

CONSCIENCE IS THAT rising energy in consciousness which is effected by the exposure to "moral" conditioning. Conditioning dictates what is conceived of as right or wrong.

1. Conscience is similar to a sponge. Like a sponge, it absorbs the moral conditioning it is exposed to through the body sense impressions by the teachings of parents, peers, religions, and other institutions.

2. Moral conditioning may be what this world considers to be right or wrong, good or bad at any given time.

3. Right or wrong, good or bad, will vary according to the society and culture in which morals are established.

4. Conditioning reinforced over time instills a sense of the rightness or wrongness of any given choice, decision, or situation.

5. Once a moral conditioning is established in conscience, you are prone to respond actively or passively.

6. Your choices and decisions, therefore, are influenced by the accepted established moral conditioning, be they good or bad. It is wise for a society to choose carefully the moral conditioning it exposes to young consciences.

7. As a fully aware being, your conscious choices and decisions are made out of necessity. Your conscience is sensitive to the least leaning away from center.

8. When you are awakened to the Christ awareness of your being, there is never a question of doing the necessary in any given situation. You simply respond appropriately. As you are removed from the judgmental conditioned realm, your conscience is free to do what is necessary. "Judge not, that ye be not judged" (Matthew 7: 1).

+ +

LESSON: 42 — CONSCIOUSNESS - RECOGNITION

WHEN YOU HAVE realized, within awareness, expansive consciousness, the individual expressions of consciousness are recognizable. It is as if you were standing on a roof top looking down, viewing, and hearing everything around you. You come to know, recognize, and respect the individual expressions of consciousness.

1. Consciousness moves from the purest, fastest (expansiveness) to the slowest (less expansiveness) vibrations. A part of true mastering is to realize and recognize the individual expressions of consciousness.

2. All expressions of consciousness are flowing and vibrating within awareness and the differences you experience are sense differences. As when thinking arises, you sense a mind, as the physical sense rises, you sense a body. It is one even flow from the highest, fastest to the lower - slower expressions of consciousness' vibrating energy.

3. If you entered a room, closed your eyes, and listened to the individuals in that room, you would recognize each individual consciousness being expressed. Do it. It's a great practice in recognition.

4. It is your seeing the appearances (persons) that distract your listening - knowing gift or ability. Seeing interferes with hearing. It is your listening to what is being said and to what is not being said, in other words, the silent seconds between the words allow you to know.

5. That knowing individual expression of consciousness is similar to reading scripture for greater understanding. Once you understand there is more there than the written words, you begin to read between the words, between the letters, and you receive a new, greater meaning.

6. As you come to serve the Christ, you come to know or recognize and respect the various individual expressions of the Christ Consciousness. As you experience one expression of consciousness to another, whether asleep, mental, or physical, be aware of the smoothness — there is no space or time separation.

7. It is by realizing or recognizing the individual expressions of consciousness, you are aware of where an individual is at any given moment and may meet the necessary needs of others.

8. By realizing or recognizing the individual expressions, you know when not to disturb, or hurt other individuals. You know where they are coming from and where they may want to go.

9. You may know exactly what may help wake them up to the Christ Consciousness, or leave them where they are. And, leaving them where they are may well be a blessing at the moment. You can see the critical importance of recognizing individual expressions of consciousness.

10. By recognizing the individual expression of consciousness, you are aware if an individual readiness and preparedness is there to receive spiritual guidance.

11. If for the love of Jesus Christ you are to feed the lambs and the sheep, then you need to be aware of what it is you are to feed them. "He saith to him again the second time, 'Simon, *son* of Jonas, lovest thou me?' He saith unto him, Yea, Lord; thou knowest that I love thee. He saith unto him, Feed my lambs. He saith unto him the third time, Simon, *son* of Jonas, lovest thou me? Peter was grieved because he said unto him the third time, Lovest thou me? And he said unto him, Lord thou knowest all things; thou knowest that I love thee. Jesus saith unto him, Feed my sheep." (John 21: 16-17).

12. You can learn this by recognizing the individual expressions of consciousness. You have the ability to realize the expansive consciousness. Master It.

+ +

LESSON: 43 — CONSENT

CONSENT IS THE wisdom of agreement beyond the mind's understanding. It is with consent, trust, and love you do the Father's will. "Not every one that saith unto me, Lord, Lord, shall enter into the kingdom of heaven; but he that doeth the will of my Father which is in heaven" (Matthew 7: 21).

1. It was Jesus' consent to the will of the Father that allowed Jesus to suffer through persecution and the crucifixion. ". . . O my Father, if it be possible, let this cup pass from me: nevertheless not as I will but as thou *wilt*"(Matthew 26: 39).

2. Consent may bring you through the most difficult times with the saving grace that lifts you to the heights of pure awareness.

3. Consenting is not a giving up; it is a giving in and a willingness to do — to act in the name of Jesus Christ. It is a commitment to action, not retreat.

4. It is your consent that opens your Spiritual Heart Center. Consent vibrates unqualified love throughout your entire Being.

5. By the power of love within your consent you are a disciple of Jesus Christ. "By this shall all *men* know you that ye are my disciples, if ye have love one to another" (John 13: 35).

6. When you consent to do your prayer practice or to serve others, you are saying in the name of love, "I am, that I am." "And the world passeth away, and the lust thereof: but he that doeth the will of God abideth for ever" (I John 2: 17).

7. When Mother Mary gave her consent, in the finest of vibrating energy (pure love) Jesus was conceived. "And Mary said, Behold the handmaid of the Lord; be it unto me according to thy word. And the angel departed from her" (Luke 1: 38).

8. Consent may carry you over troubled waters of a life of corruption to the depth of a peaceful, calm spiritual baptism. "For he that soweth to his flesh shall of the flesh reap corruption; but he that soweth to the Spirit reap life everlasting" (Galatians 6: 8).

9. On your spiritual journey, you are constantly consenting as you walk gently and carefully through the maze of opposites on this plane through the Holy Spirit in the name of Jesus.

10. Consent, consent, consent and realize there is a joy at the center of whatever you are asked to do. "I delight to do thy will, O my God: yea, thy law *is* within my heart" (Psalm 40: 8).

+ +

LESSON: 44 — CONTEMPLATIVE

THE CONTEMPLATIVE IS one who accepts the invitation to receive the teachings of the Holy Spirit in the name of Jesus Christ.

1. It is a blessed thing to present yourself to the Holy Spirit in the name of Jesus Christ and walk the spiritual path in Its presence. You have heard His silent voice and have answered His call to come home to the Father's Kingdom. "And I appoint unto you a kingdom, as my Father hath appointed unto me" (Luke 22: 29).

2. The Contemplative, with dedication and devotion, turns inward to the Spiritual Heart Center's radiant warmth of the light of Jesus Christ. "With my whole heart have I sought thee: O let me not wander from thy commandment" (Psalm 119: 10).

3. While in service to humankind, the Contemplative practices a silent prayer method, studies, and ponders truth teaching. The Contemplative's intent is to realize and awaken to the teaching of the Holy Spirit in the name of Jesus Christ. "But the Comforter, *which is* the Holy Ghost, whom the Father will send in my name, he shall teach you all things, and bring all things to your remembrance, whatsoever I have said unto you" (John 14: 26).

4. The Contemplative lives in this world of knowledge that knows everything, but seeks the wisdom that is beyond this world. While immersed in truth, surrender, and obedience to the Christ, the Contemplative strives to maintain a balance in a worldly life. It's a constant reminder of being in this world but not of it. "They are not of the world, even as I am not of the world" (John 17: 16).

5. A Contemplative in this world, may struggle with desires and temptations. The Contemplative walks in His footsteps who leads by example. "Jesus saith unto him, I am the way, the truth, and the life: no man cometh unto the Father, but by me'" (John 14: 6).

6. The ever presence of the Holy Spirit in the name of Jesus Christ, gently and quietly, moves the Contemplative toward the realization of the Christ Consciousness within awareness.

7. A Contemplative's life is one in the wholeness of the Holy Spirit of Jesus Christ. "And this is eternal life, that they may know thee, the only true God, and Jesus Christ, whom thou hast sent" (John 17: 3).

8. Before the altar of all that is Holy, the Contemplative kneels before Jesus Christ and is welcomed

home. "And lo a voice from heaven saying, This is my beloved son, in whom I am well pleased" (Matthew 3: 17).

+ +

LESSON: 45 — CONTRADICTIONS

CONTRADICTIONS OCCUR ON a spiritual walk when the outer appears to conflict with the inner.

1. Truth seems full of contradictions. The worldly knowledge and insights, realizations, and truth do not usually mix well.
2. The moment you start a spiritual walk there are subtle contradictions between what knowledge you have learned and the truth that is revealed.
3. Truth, in and of itself, is simple. The contradictions rise in the outer interpretations and old habits.
4. You have been conditioned to think a certain way and organize your outer life accordingly. Now, the inner begins to surface to compete with your outer life.
5. Whereas, before you were able to devote 24 - 7 to an outer life of service, things and persons, now there is an urgency for change.
6. The mistake may be in believing you must give up one for the other. In reality, you are being forced to create a balance that more reflects the inner.
7. All of the service in this world is still of an illusionary nature. It is the reality of your being that insists you recognize any illusion for what it is and not allow it to overrun your contemplative life.
8. Service is a charge you have while upon this plane. However noble or honorable it may be, it is an activity upon this plane.
9. It is your intentioned response to the service that makes the difference. If you allow yourself to get caught up in the service *itself*, the ego will produce the most profound contradictions.
10. If you are to live a sane, seamless, inner - outer life upon this plane of opposites, a balance is necessary, and the balance must begin from the inner to the outer.
11. To attempt to balance the outer with the inner is to create confusion and contradictions. How can you balance an illusion with reality? You would be starting with an impossible premise. Weigh what it is you actually want from the Holy Spirit in the name of Jesus Christ on your spiritual walk, and conform the outer to realize it.
12. When you look into a mirror (the source) you may only be aware of the reflection (the outer). To become attached to the reflection is to lose the awareness of the mirror, your reality.
13. As you progress on the spiritual walk, the world comes from all directions to vie for your attention or service.
14. To attempt to fulfill the expectations of the masses at the cost of neglecting your contemplative life is folly. "For ye have the poor always with you; but me ye have not always" (Matthew 26: 11).
15. When you give more weight to what you are given to do than what the source of your being allows you to do, contradictions abound. True, you are not living in a cave. Few do. However, that does not mean a cave does not exists.
16. The Spiritual Heart Center is the cave of your inner being and the Holy Spirit in the name of Jesus Christ dissolves contradictions in the recognition of reality.

+ +

LESSON: 46 — COURAGE

YOU MIGHT THINK courage (being brave) may not be necessary in a silent prayer practice. However, it may often take courage for you to begin a silent prayer practice, and courage to maintain one.

1. The beginning of a spiritual walk, an inner journey, is one traveled by the courageous. Many times you may be challenged.

2. There is always the force of others and situations to distract you from your Christ intent. "... choose you this day whom ye will serve..." (Joshua 24: 15).

3. You are courageous, when you are willing to surrender with un-wincing faith to the inner guidance by the Holy Spirit in the name of Jesus Christ.

4. It takes courage to journey from the relative known to the reality of the unknown. It could require courage for you to accept the unconditional love and forgiveness in which your beloved Lord holds you.

5. There may be many times, during a silent prayer practice, you must rely on faith to continue. Standing firm in your faith during a difficult purification process may require all the courage you can muster.

6. As you come to realize truth, in awareness, your life tends to change and those around you aren't always receptive to the change. It may take courage to accept what others cannot.

7. You are returning to the Kingdom of God. When you know the reality of your being, it may require courage to continue to walk the straight gate and narrow way and to do the works of the Divine.

8. Your prayer practice may threaten relationships, you may be threatened with having to give up something, or someone; therefore, there may be pressure for you to give up your prayer practice. Courage may hold you steady on the path.

9. All around you there may be the temptation to please others, to take an easier path, a more familiar one. Stepping out in your Christhood and holding fast to the teaching of the Holy Spirit in the name of Jesus Christ, may require courage of the highest order.

10. To accept all you are given, and live out from truth takes a courage never before known. To do otherwise, is to insult your spiritual integrity — to deny the Christ of your being.

11. Peter denied Jesus three times. As a sleep walker, you have done so many times. Once you are awakened you are held accountable.

12. It took courage for Jesus to say, "Yes," to the Father and it takes courage for you to say, "Yes," to Jesus. The gate is straight and the way is narrow, but it is the only one to your Father's house. Have courage, come home, and stray no more.

+ +

LESSON: 47 — CREATION

CREATION IS ALL that may appear in consciousness within the light of awareness.

1. The universe, world, galaxy, and planets are all God's creation, vibrating energy, in consciousness within awareness.

2. All created appearances are by an omnipotent, divinely omniscient vibrating energy.

3. In the beginning is the Void (Lesson: 190). This Almighty God-Void that is not void-less, allowed there to be light and within awareness, Divine consciousness created all that was created. "And the earth was without form, and void; and darkness was upon the face of the deep. And the Spirit of

God moved upon the face of the waters. And God said, Let there be light: and there was light" (Genesis 1: 2 - 3).

4. To experience God's creations, came the creation of humankind. "So God created man in his *own* image, in the image of God created he him; male and female created he them" (Genesis 1: 27).

5. From the One came the many. "And God blessed them, saying, Be fruitful and multiply, and fill the waters in the seas, and let fowl multiply in the earth" (Genesis 1: 22).

6. Within awareness, consciousness rises and within consciousness, many individual expressions of consciousness vibrate.

7. It is the nature of God-Spirit to multiply. In infinite variety, your God source is constantly multiplying.

8. There is not anything that does not already exist. Humankind may have yet to discover all that exists but it does exist.

9. There is nothing new under the sun. It only appears new, as you become aware of it. "The thing that hath been, it *is that* which shall be; and that which is done *is that* which shall be done: and *there is* no new *thing* under the sun" (Ecclesiastes I: 9).

10. In infinite variety and with the utmost detail, the One God-Void, One Awareness, One Consciousness, One mind of God-Spirit created all that was created. "All things were made by him; and without him was not any thing made that was made. In him was life; and the life was the light of men" (John 1: 3 - 4).

+ +

LESSON: 48 — CRISIS - SPIRITUAL

A SPIRITUAL CRISIS is a crucial moment during a spiritual walk when you come to a crossroad of believing you are sufficiently realized and can handle a decisive dark moment. Such a moment may take you in the opposite direction of the path you had chosen to travel.

1. Into every serious truth student's life comes a spiritual crisis. After having realized the Christ Consciousness, a decisive moment of confusion may set in.

2. It is a time when you may be teetering between the Christ Consciousness and a previous individual expression of consciousness with all of its attached rising attractions. A time when you even distrust the teacher with whom you are working.

3. A spiritual crisis may be experienced as a spiritual drought and be painfully lonely. You may want to withdraw, cut yourself off from the very manna that is necessary for your continued progress. You may turn from your practice, your teacher, and contemplate less truth.

4. You may deceive yourself into believing you're a fully realized Being who is at the place where you can overcome temptations. You want what you want and that is as far as you can see at the moment.

5. Because you are not fully grounded in the greater consciousness and you lack the awareness of the greater purpose of being, you may want to stop your silent prayer practice.

6. Other individual expressions of consciousness are desperately competing for your attention and are attracting you as a magnet, toward a place of darkness. It is a spiritual crisis, and your steps on the path may not be as decisive.

7. If you hold steady for better or worse, you may be able to gain a glimmer of the original fall — how and why it could possibly have happened in the first place.

8. You may have asked your teacher many times, "How would, how could anyone want to stray from the Christ Consciousness, after having realized it?" If you are alert, you may have your answer.

9. It is during this juncture your choices and decisions are wrought with the idea you can handle it alone if you withdraw and be with yourself.

10. Your choices and decisions will not affect your teacher one way or the other. You are always working on yourself. You are always examining your own conscious mind.

11. If you are a fully awakened being, as Jesus was on the mountain, you would have the necessary clarity. Unfortunately, what you may not understand is the vicarious, fragile place you may be in and how easy it is to return to follow the imaginary path of this relative world.

12. After overcoming a spiritual crisis, you know the strong pull and overwhelming strength the attractions of this relative world presents. Taking a fall in consciousness is easy. Maintaining your realized Christ Consciousness is not. Stay alert!

+++++++++++++++++++++++

LESSON: 49 — DESIRES AND TEMPTATIONS

A DESIRE IS what you want. A temptation wants you. Desire is some thing, or some one you may want. A temptation wants your realized reality. In either case, they may become a detour from the straight gate and narrow way.

1. Desires and temptations hold hands with doubts. For all practical purposes, the goal is the same — attract you to things, and individuals of this world and to distract you from the straight gate and narrow way.

2. All desires must be fulfilled, or detached. All temptations must be overcome. Know as Jesus did, when He was tempted,"Jesus said unto him. It is written again, Thou shalt not tempt the Lord thy God" (Matthew 4. 7).

3. Desires and temptations require your time, attention, interest, and feed on the responses to the conscious mind's rising vibrating energy.

4. New silent prayer practitioners are prime targets. Desires and temptations will be as attractive as possible and make all the noise necessary to grab attention. No one on this plane is immune to temptations of this world. Don't fool yourself into believing you are beyond temptations.

5. Jesus was subjected to temptations. "And Jesus answered and said unto him, Get thee behind me, Satan: for it is written, Thou shalt worship the Lord thy God, and him only shalt thou serve"(Luke 4: 8). The temptation certainly wanted what Jesus had — His God realization.

6. Desires and temptations require your choice and decision for you to move in their direction. Once you have done so, they attach you to whatever the desire or temptation is at the moment.

7. A desire or temptation could be called "super glue." when either is fed by a response to the rising energy, it tends to stick until it's purposely released or overcome.

8. Desires and temptations are what this world offers and are believed by many to be required for a happy, successful life. They are all the things that aren't necessary for the Christ fulfilled being.

9. Desires and temptations are smooth talkers and polite. They often give you a choice between desire and desire, and between temptation and temptation. Be aware, they do not play fair.

10. Desires and temptations are always offering something, some place, or some one. You know the rightness in the offerings by the direction they would take you. Theirs is the wide gate and broad way. "Enter ye in at the strait gate: for wide *is* the gate, and broad *is* the way, that leadeth to destruction, and many there be which go in thereat" (Matthew 7: 13).

11. If given the power, desires and temptations will cause you to repeat lesson after lesson. You are the one to decide to give or withhold the necessary power to fulfill or detach from desires and overcome

temptations. "And I will give unto thee the keys of the kingdom of heaven: and whatsoever thou shalt bind on earth shall be bound in heaven: and whatsoever thou shalt loose on earth shall be loosed in heaven" (Matthew 16: 19).

12. Be ever vigilant of the distraction from your Christ Centeredness into a time and space of rising desires and temptations.

....

STUDENT'S STORY:

Parallel to my professed, one-pointed commitment to and longing for God, have run deep competing desires for children, financial security, job satisfaction, new houses, horses; travel, tennis rankings, jewelry, Laura Ashley clothes, Dooney and Burke purses, advanced academic degrees, Rolex watches, and public recognition just to mention a few!

As if these were not enough, temptations to drop or doubt whatever degree of spiritual awareness and awakening I may have managed to realize became prevalent. The temptation to return to the "important" things of life like becoming president of the United States and ending world hunger, never ceased to intrude into my sensitive consciousness!

The careful packaging of these desires and temptations was tailored to demand my attention with relative ease. And they did! Certainly Shakespeare's wisdom saying, "I think she doth protest too much," immediately comes to mind. Well, never mind.

Despite all the detours, time outs, dramatic righteous critiques, complaints, and back sliding, "by the grace of God," my spiritual journey has managed to continue. No mortal, (save my teacher, who is stuck with me) would ever put up with such continual nonsense for so long a time. Only God would or could. For such patience I can only say, "Thank you, Lord!"

All the scriptural passages in which Jesus recommends, "losing one's life, laying down one's life, letting go, giving away, being last, least, lost, poor, weak, silent, and ultimately dead," on first read suggests and inspires the generous and noble path of humility. I thought, "Oh, I'll just be humble." Easier said than done! Problems arose when I started to realize just what those cryptic statements actually meant in my most suburban, upper-middle class American life. They were not casual platitudes for discussion but blueprints mapping a total reorientation of my entire way of perceiving the world and what constituted success or failure.

The Beatitudes referenced in the gospel of Matthew (5:1-11), denote every possibility of this culture or kingdom paradox. Inevitably, every time I would feel I had "arrived" at some realization of the Kingdom of God in my own life, and felt I was actually living a particular Beatitude, some delicious worldly temptation or unfulfilled desire would raise its head in challenge.

The "war between the worlds" was no longer a science fiction story written on paper, but a battle being waged every moment of my life. Echoes of "Choose ye!" life or death, "God or mammon!" took on an entirely different meaning. I was confronted with the choice between total one pointed pursuit of intimacy with God and obedience to His will and my own whimsical desires for what I perceived was happiness based on my cultural-historical and familial conditioning.

More times than I would like to admit the world held sway. The candies of the world I pursued and thought would bring happiness began as sugar in my mouth only to turn to vinegar when fully digested. The short lived thrills left me with experiences of betrayal, anxiety, anger, frustration, envy, pride, grief, and discouragement. Needless to say, these fruits were not representative of a life lived obedient to the First Cause.

The purpose of these experiences was to alert me to the desperate shape I was in and the depth of self deception that desires and temptation present. In that case all things "work for good" for those who love God no matter how imperfectly at any given time. Thank God, God can work with that!

++++++++++++++++++++++++++

LESSON: 50 — DETACHMENT

DETACHMENT IS THE realization in conscious awareness when the witness falls away and all that is happening is the rising and falling of vibrating energy. There is no "self," no "I," no "witness" present.

1. This type of realization or enlightenment may come from an instant transcendental (supernatural) experience or the participating in an intensive silent prayer practice over a period of time. Becoming detached is the overcoming of the suffering of this world.

2. It is the realization there is no "you" to attach to any relatively temporary appearance. It does not matter how desirous, tempting, or impressive the momentary appearance is. There is the aware realizing, all is rising and falling, coming and going. It is not possible to hold on to any thing or any one. The freedom is now, "to take it or to leave it."

3. At first, the detachment realization may bring about a sense of loss of a personal "person." The person you believed you were, you are not, and never really were. It is the ultimate loss — dying to the false self, the illusionary sense of a separate personal life. It feels strange for a while, because there is nothing to cling to, no person or thing in which to identify. There is just pure being in awareness and this may take a little, or a lot, of getting used to. "He that findeth his life shall lose it: and he that loseth his life for my sake shall find it" (Matthew 10: 39).

4. You never have been a person or a body and this never has been your permanent home. Finding that out can be both devastating and radiantly uplifting at the same time. Truth seems full of contradictions because your life has been spent believing in a false sense of being.

5. When the sense of an, "I," a witness, personal self, falls away and there is the aware realizing only of the rising and falling energy of the senses, there is no attachment. Without the conscious witness, (I, me, my, mine) there is no one to attach any rising sense. There is just the rising and falling of the vibrating energy as thoughts, sensations, etcetera. That is all that is going on. This is the enlightenment of detachment.

6. Immediately after the detachment realization occurs, the realization may cause a disorientation for a time. It may be difficult for a personal sense of self to rise again. Thinking "I, Me, My, Mine" may not be possible for a time. This usually will not last too long; however, it is best to stay quiet and muse with it for a while.

7. Actually, realizing all that is going on *is* the rising and falling can at first be devastating. Being totally detached may take a little getting accustomed to. If possible, no immediate physical activity should be assumed. Time to readjust to your environment may be needed. Do not be in a hurry. Sharing with your teacher should be helpful.

8. For some, the detachment realization may be traumatic, an inner earthquake. The false mind sense has been the master. Now, the conscious awareness of your being is the master of the mind and the mind doesn't like giving up its control or habit. It means as a pure aware being, the heart and mind become one. You are of one mind, the mind that was in Jesus, the mind of God. "Let this mind be in you, which was also in Christ Jesus" (Philippians 2: 5).

9. Be patient, your world will never be the same. It may require a period of adjustment. This is a major realization or enlightenment and must be handled gently by you and a teacher if you have one.

10. The conscious mind is a wonderful instrument and servant when used to translate what is received from the Spiritual Heart Center. You live out from your realized Christ oneness as a pure aware being, not a separate person. There isn't any, and never has been any person to separate you from your true being.

11. Detachment does not mean that you do not continue to use what you need. Yes, you may use the things of this world. There isn't any ownership. Your house is *a* house, your car is *a* car. All will be left behind for the use of those who follow. All is created for your use. So, it is not the use of things you are giving up but the attachment to them. It is this false belief of possessive ownership that has created the illusion of separation from God. The things of this world have become "god." You are constantly being asked to make the choice between the impermanent and the permanent.

12. Detachment frees you from the suffering of being devastated whenever there is a loss of person or thing. It is the freedom in realizing who and what you are and living out from the realization. When you realize all of your needs are met before you ask and are constantly being met in the moment, you need not cling to anything.

13. Detachment is the freedom from the bondage of heavy burdens. It is to take the easier yoke and find rest. For the things of this world are weighty, and you may grow weary in the pursuit of them. "Come unto me, all ye that labour and are heavy laden, and I will give you rest" (Matthew 11: 28). "For my yoke *is* easy, and my burden is light" (Matthew 11: 30).

14. To be attached is to deprive yourself of the abundance that exists for your use. You cannot accept more when you are holding on to less.

15. The detachment realization helps awaken you to the illusions of this world. However it occurs, it must be realized for the truth seeker to come into a willing compliance with the demands of the spiritual life in devotion to Jesus Christ.

16. As a follower of Jesus Christ, the detachment realization may bring you to the understanding of the will of God through the Holy Spirit in the name of Jesus Christ. In a loving trust and obedience, it asks that you leave (detach from) all that you have in this world, and all that you believe you desire for the love of God. "But seek ye first for the kingdom of God, and his righteousness; and all these things shall be added unto you" (Matthew 6: 33).

....

STUDENT'S STORY: This is the continuation of my story from Lesson: 9 — Attention.

Due to my focused-attention on a Lesson, I had not heard my name called for boarding my airplane and consequently, missed my plane. However, I was strangely accepting of having missed my plane. I didn't think it would "fly" to try and explain to the stewardess that I was deep in focused-attention on a spiritual lesson paper concerning attention when I failed to be attentive to the boarding call, so I sat quietly down to await the next plane an hour away. I decided since I was tired now from all the excitement, I would CAREFULLY pray for a while. This time, mindful of security, I sat comfortably on my purse, placed my feet on my luggage, and with my alarm clock by my side, set to signal after a 30-minute prayer period, it would be just fine. I was backed up this time.

As I began to come out of my prayer period there was the very clear experience of the sense of hearing rising in awareness. The experience of hearing immediately rose. Just hearing sounds, that's all, one sound after another. For a few moments there was no conditioning associated with the immediacy of the sense of hearing. Just hearing was going on. Moving out of pure awareness, the experience of mind rising within consciousness was crystal clear. Then closely behind hearing, rose mind's interpretation of the sounds and language that suddenly was on the horizon. Then after the interpretation of hearing and language registered, the "I" translated the sounds based on my conditioning and "I" understood what was being said all around "me." Thank God, this time I did NOT miss my plane.

For those few moments before the "I" rose within conscious awareness, "I" *was* not. Detachment moved to attachment. First, the sense of hearing was rising in awareness. Then my conscious mind rose with intellect to interpret. Then Sandy was not missing her plane! I was really excited because although I had similar experiences of detachment a little less flashy, this one was crystal clear. Had "Sandy" not risen with "her sense of her-self," I am sure that the fact of hearing, seeing, touching, tasting, smelling etcetera would simply continue on unencumbered and unhampered by expectations, reason, intellect, discrimination, identity, or cultural conditioning. Lord knows what would be the state of airports after that! So my laugh was full. Who "was hearing" really "was" not! "Sandy" rose in conscious awareness in the field of awareness but prior to "her" appearance on the scene she didn't exist at all in reality. There was a split second of full realization about detachment, reality - impersonalization, awareness taking place in the noisy hub of the Houston Airport. Big deal? Well it was a big deal for me and a bit disconcerting.

I knew experientially exactly what was meant by senses rising and falling in mind, mind rising in consciousness, consciousness rising in awareness, and a separate false sense of self rising. I knew that the real-ity of "Sandy" is not something that rises and falls in awareness but is awareness *itself*. I also knew how important it is for me not to mistake the false self for the true self. To mistake the conditioned separate sense of self called "Sandy" for the one eternally aware impersonal reality that neither rises nor falls but exists always would be a totally understandable and acceptable (after all don't we all do it!) mistake but also a huge mistake. Who "Sandy" really is, is "Who She Is." "There is no other."

+ +

LESSON: 51 — DIALOGUE - INTERNAL

INTERNAL DIALOGUE IS a conditioned response to the rising conditioned thoughts, and/or sense impressions.

1. Internal dialogue is the busy work of the mind, mental. It may interfere with and stall a silent prayer practice. Internal dialoguing has no productive benefits. There is an attraction to inner dialoguing few of you can resist. It is a habit that will turn the attention away from the things of God.

2. Internal dialoguing attaches you to the past of hurtful memories, sufferings, and increases the painful emotional intensity. It may distract and weaken your determined purpose.

3. Internal dialoguing mainly deals with past (memories) and future expectations (planning). It successfully may hold you in the past or help focus your attention on future plans, neither of which exist in the present. In either case, during a silent prayer practice, dialoguing may cause the present moment of the silence and spiritual realizations of your God given nature to slip beneath the radar of your determined purpose of turning within.

4. There is an attraction to dialoguing you may find difficult to resist. When the vibrating energies rise in anger, resentment, or memories, dialoguing allows you to step into an emotional cesspool to indulge in imaginary vindictiveness. This causes the rising energies to be awash in impurities. It is best your spirit within earnestly seeks the Lord. "With my soul have I desired you in the night; yea with my spirit within me will I seek thee early . . ." (Isaiah 26: 9).

5. During a silent prayer practice, internal dialoguing serves no useful purpose. It may be given up without any repercussions. And, in fact, not dialoguing is beneficial.

6. The "not" dialoguing is the most important tool in the forgiveness and purification process.

7. Learning to listen more and speak less on the outer, will help your silent prayer practice. "For thus saith the Lord GOD, the Holy One of Israel; In returning and rest shall ye be saved; in quietness and in confidence shall be your strength: and ye would not" (Isaiah 30:15).

8. The practice of no dialoguing with the rising attractions of this world, in or out of a prayer practice, contributes to a smooth realization within pure awareness. "Be still, and know that I *am* God: . . ." (Psalm 46: 10).

BENEFITS OF <u>NOT</u> DIALOGUING:

A. The greatest benefit is the forgiveness and purification of the rising energies that occur.

B. Not dialoguing speeds up the entire process, moves it along, and allows the necessary space and silence for the forgiveness and purification in the "Holy Instant" of awareness to occur during a silent prayer practice.

C. During a Christ Centered Prayer practice, not dialoguing allows you to more easily become aware of the Spiritual Heart Center.

D. By not dialoguing, there is less of an emotional turmoil created. The energy rises and falls more quickly and you are not driven off course of your intended path.

E. Not dialoguing creates a more calm, peaceful, and less restless inner environment for a silent prayer practice.

F. Not dialoguing may allow you to realize detachment in pure awareness.

++++++++++++++++++++++++

LESSON: 52 — DISCERNMENT

DISCERNMENT IS AN inner clarity of heightened perception.

1. Discerning requires the understanding of the differences in the situation, or circumstance as they are appearing. Therefore, wisdom plays a significant role in the clarity of discernment.

2. Discernment is a subtle, quiet, knowing the necessary choice or decision that should be made in the moment. Discernment brings a quick resolution, solution, or conclusion to a present moment's need.

3. The awareness of discernment unfolds gradually as you progress on your spiritual walk. Inner realizations and insights create an environment where discernment may thrive.

4. As you become more balanced and centered on your spiritual walk, discernment may rise before the necessary choice or decision must be reached.

5. With discernment, your expansive consciousness absorbs the entire field of preferences presented. Like a sponge, discernment takes it all in and does not judge nor condemn, but rather, knows the thought, word, or deed that is the appropriate response.

6. When you have pure determined purpose, intention, and a devotional love of God, through the Holy Spirit in the name of Jesus Christ, you may be gifted with the highest discernment that pierces the illusion of what is considered good or evil. "To another the working of miracles; to another prophecy; to another discerning of spirits; to another *divers* kinds of tongues; to another the interpretation of tongues" (I Corinthians 12: 10).

++++++++++++++++++++++++

LESSON: 53 — DISCIPLESHIP

DISCIPLESHIP IS THE acceptance of the spiritual hand of Jesus upon your being. "The Spirit of the Lord *is* upon me, because he hath anointed me to preach the gospel to the poor; he hath sent me to heal the brokenhearted, to preach deliverance to the captives, and recovering of sight to the blind, to set at liberty them that are bruised, To preach the acceptable year of the Lord" (Luke 4:18-19).

1. In the awareness of the Christ Consciousness through the Holy Spirit, Jesus anoints, guides and directs your footsteps along the way to the Father's house. There is no greater anointing, no greater discipleship. "Herein is my Father glorified, that ye bear much fruit; so shall ye be my disciples" (John 15:8).

2. You are all that is necessary. You have the necessary where-with-all to accomplish whatever the Holy Spirit requires of you in the name of Jesus Christ. "Let your light so shine before men, that they may see your good works, and glorify your Father which is in heaven" (Matthew 5: 16).

3. Whenever you step up to the plate, in the name of Jesus Christ, the Holy Spirit may reveal your true nature. Trusting the Oneness of your being and surrendering may become as natural as breathing.

4. The confidence in your ability, on the spiritual walk, is placed in the Christ Consciousness. When you allow it, the unreal may recede and the truth, the real, may be revealed. Jesus is the way, you need only to follow. "And thine ears shall hear a word behind thee, saying This *is* the way, walk ye in it, when ye turn to the right hand, and when ye turn to the left" (Isaiah 30: 21).

5. You are here to wake up. The Divine will not let you down. The Lord hears your silent prayer and the Lord hears you among others. "And I knew that thou hearest me always: but because of the people which stand by I said *it*, that they may believe that thou hast sent me " (John 11: 42).

6. It is natural for the conscious mind, for a time, to shake at the changed wonders that it must behold. Accept your discipleship in the humility it expresses in its own way. Rejoice in realizing your being is formed in the reality of pure awareness.

7. Surrendering to your God-given discipleship will require you to control the conscious mind's impulses to believe it is not possible. "For with God nothing shall be impossible" (Luke 1: 37).

8. As a disciple of Jesus Christ, you're tested. The appearances of this world do not give up. Temptations come at you in a hundred different ways. Remember, temptation wants you and will appear in any fashion necessary to get what you have. "For all that is in the world, the lust of the flesh, and the lust of the eyes, and the pride of life, is not of the Father, but is of the world" (I John 2:16).

9. A disciple of Jesus Christ is humble, firm, grounded in uninterrupted truth, and loyal to the First Cause. Knowing always, "Ye are of God, little children, and have overcome them: because greater is he that is in you, than he that is in the world" (I John 4: 4).

10. A disciple of Jesus Christ is a servant who is rewarded in secret. Proceed with caution. The rewards, praise, or blame of this world are the same. "That thine alms may be in secret: and thy Father which seeth in secret himself shall reward thee openly" (Matthew 6: 4).

11. It is the reality of your being that makes all things possible. When others praise you, all you can do out here is to say, "Thank you" and move on to silently knowing, "Believest thou not that I am in the Father, and the Father in me? The words that I speak unto you I speak not of myself: but the Father that dwelleth in me, he doeth the works" (John 14: 10).

12. A disciple of Jesus Christ possesses the strength of the Christ in Jesus Christ and the Will of the Divine through the Holy Spirit. The Holy Trinity in action.

STUDENT'S STORY:

The genesis of formalizing these Lessons into a teaching and a manual is an interesting story. As with any "birthing," it had its accompanying labor pains and fears. I hesitate to say spontaneously, but as childbirth once set in motion, the inevitable occurs. Cooperating with the process certainly can help lessen the pain and perhaps shorten the delivery!

For about eleven years I was a retreat director and had been teaching Christian Contemplative Prayer under the auspices of an internationally respected, well known, and credentialed organization. There were "side benefits" that came along with this relationship. As an obedient and well schooled representative, I was able to "fly under the wings" of well known, respected, and published authors on the spiritual journey. By virtue of the organizations respectability I was rendered "respectable." The work was mutually enriching for the individuals I taught and I have only gratitude for the guidance and support I have received.

There is a lot to be said about such a relationship that is noble and appropriate. Unfortunately, it also has its limitation. Understandably, I was to present faithfully the teachings as I had been taught. This I did. However, there were times towards the end of my tenure with this organization when I deeply felt a desire to speak out of my own experience or add to a previously-revealed teaching. The latitude for such speech did not lay within the established boundaries of the organization.

The commitment I made to faithfully present this teaching and the challenge to that which was coming from my internal integrity created quite a crisis of loyalty. I tried my hardest not to leave and had numerous heated conversations with my teacher about "why I needed to stay for reputation, respectability, and access." After all, "Who was I to speak?" "Who was I to presume I could speak with authority" "Who would want to listen to Sandy!" It just seemed ridiculous to even entertain such a step. I recall lamenting and arguing these issues and said to my teacher, "How can I write a lesson or teach these spiritual principles based on my experience? And what about footnotes? Who would I footnote? Myself?" My teacher's response would always be a soft, "Yes."

The irony of my questions and her response was totally lost on me. It was inconceivable to me that a 57 year old Episcopal woman priest, trying to make ends meet in the woods of Wyoming would have something to add to the deposit of knowledge catalogued by the Spanish Mystics and great theologians of our day. It was beyond my wildest imagination. The thought of speaking in my own voice as a disciple of Jesus Christ was both compelling and terrifying. Nevertheless in spite of my protestations this was, in fact, laid before me. The directive was clear, "Choose."

Immediately the temptations rose. My initial impulse was to refuse, retreat and forget that I ever entertained the possibility. After a week of emails, between myself and my teacher, protesting such a move appealing to institutional loyalty, commitment, and obligations, etcetera — I had to face square on the real question, "Whom would I serve?" "To whom would I be faithful?" Would I be willing to trust and serve the Christ of my Being whose credentials were written in my heart and not on parchment? If I said, "Yes" to that Master then I knew my life would never be the same again because it would no longer be "my" life.

In utter terror, with few notable credentials, no reservoir of celebrities, and absolutely no footnotes, I decided to follow the inner prompting of the Holy Spirit and step out in faith and trust. I had no idea that the plethora of material and teaching found in these volumes would come forth as a result of that momentous decision. I thought I would have no books, no teaching, no method, no invitations to teach, no nothing. In fact, I have received everything and then some! As the woman giving birth with no previous knowledge of the gifts lavished by God on her child, I stand in awe of what is being brought forth into this world. And for that I can only give glory to God.

++++++++++++++++++++++++++

LESSON: 54 — DOUBTS

Doubts are inner rising mental vibrating energies which cause you to question your spiritual walk in all its phases.

THREE MAJOR POINTS ABOUT RISING DOUBTS:

FIRST: do not dialogue with the rising doubts that would tempt, challenge, and hold you hostage to the thoughts of a conditioned sense of a false personal self.

SECOND: the mental level cannot comprehend an experience that is beyond sense, word, and thought. Try as it will, it can't make good or bad sense of what goes beyond it and therefore, doubts must rise.

THIRD: realize the secret is in the judgment of good and bad. When you rest in pure awareness, you are beyond good and bad. Therefore, you are beyond the plane of opposites. Why expect a mind that is rising, falling, and is operating in the plane of opposites to be able to accept what is beyond it? It is natural that it would question this new Being who goes beyond opposites. You are not your mind!

1. There are no greater obstacles or hindrances to spiritual progress than the ever present, haunting doubts. They come from every direction at the most unexpected times.

2. Doubts trigger a chain reaction. Doubts - disbelief - wavering - distrusting - hesitation - lack of creativity that may slow your forward progress. At times, doubts may freeze your ability to move to the inner awareness. For all these reasons, doubts are taken seriously.

3. Doubts have no integrity and no respect for the serious truth seeker. They attack your self esteem, threaten your sanity, and will do anything to distract you away from the Christ Consciousness.

4. Doubts will take you down faster than a blow on the head. Doubts creep in before, during, or after a silent prayer practice. You may have doubts whether to stop, stay, or go forward on your spiritual walk.

5. Doubts will often rise to question if you are imagining your inner experiences. There may be doubts you are not practicing your silent prayer method enough and then, there may be doubts you are practicing too often. Doubts don't have a sense of proportion.

6. When insights and realizations come, doubts may rise to question if the ego or if pride has taken over. They may insist the ego has taken over and chide you for having the audacity to be so prideful.

7. There are doubts when there doesn't appear to be any spiritual progress and there are doubts, when there does appear to be progress. With doubts, it is always a no win — no win situation. Doubts will linger as long as possible. Be comforted in the knowledge that all truth seekers are plagued by doubts.

8. The rising mind contents are creatures of habit. Habits are not broken. You must transform or replace one habit with another. In the case of the mind habit of doubting, you replace it with the habit of reassuring the mind you do know what you are doing and you express sincere gratitude for its service. You are at all times kind, caring, and gentle with the rising energy that performs in the service of the Lord. This is true self-compassion.

9. Awareness is reality without opposites. As you realize awareness and rise again to the sense of a conscious mind, you experience the pure finer vibrating energy from the grosser vibrating energy.

10. To expect the mind to accept what it could not witness within pure awareness, is as if you were asking a first grader to converse with a college graduate student and to understand every word and knowledge the graduate student possesses.

11. Do doubts ever stop? Yes, they do, but only after you have been solidly grounded in the realized awareness of your reality. There comes a time, if you are faithful, trusting, and steadfast that a space is no longer available for rising doubts.

12. A fully awakened being has no reason for doubts to rise. Constantly, faithfully living out from the aware reality of your being guides you and leaves no room for a doubting mind to exist.

13. When you are grounded in the truth of reality, the mind or thought energies will come to serve your wishes to please the Christ. Obedience and discipline masters a wayward, unraveling mind of doubts.

14. When you are living as an aware Christ being, in all the Christ ways, serving your God, and knowing it's the Divine who does the work, you are beyond doubts and in a place where the eyes of God

are upon you. "For he performeth the thing that is appointed for me; and many such things are with him" (Job 23:14).

++++++++++++++++++++++++++

LESSON: 55 — DRAMA

DRAMA IS THE extreme hyper-response or reaction to inner insights and realizations that may require outer changes to occur.

1. You may be pulled into high drama as insights or realizations of truth are revealed.

2. As a serious truth seeker, your inner realizations may require outer changes you are not immediately prepared to make.

3. At times, truth feels like you have been struck with a bolt of lightning and you are left twisting and turning in a storm.

4. Enter the mind player. Mind creates high drama with every possible conflicting thought, impression, or argument it can make or reject the real for the world stage.

5. You may find yourself wanting to strike out at anyone and everyone. If there is a teacher, s/he will get the brunt of the acting out. If there is not a teacher, "Watch and pray that ye enter not into temptation; the spirit indeed is willing, but the flesh is weak" (Matthew 26: 41).

6. As the inner realizations begin to dissolve the outer veil of illusions, you are adjusting to inevitable life changes and, "EXCEPT the LORD build the house, they labour in vain that build it.: except the LORD keep the city, the watchman waketh *but* in vain" (Psalm 127: 1).

7. The remnants of attachment may be slow to fade, leaving you in these fits of temper, anger, and confusion. ". . . in quietness and in trust shall be your strength: . . ." (Isaiah 30: 15).

8. Patience with yourself and kindness with others are required while the adjustment to all things new are occurring. "Therefore if any man *be* in Christ, *he is* a new creature: old things are passed away; behold, all things are become new" (2 Corinthians 5: 17).

9. High drama is a natural result of a mind that cannot comprehend what is going on with you. It doesn't want to lose the old you and is fighting hard to hold on to the dream.

10. The best tool you can use during these moments is a good sense of humor. As with all outer struggles, this too will pass. Trust your teacher and the Christ of your being who, through the Holy Spirit in the name of Jesus Christ, will bring you through to the other side of the dream.

STUDENT'S STORY:

I can tell you that I have had my share of dramas on my spiritual journey. All my dramas, on the journey, have had amazingly similar structure, and they have differed in intensity and frequency depending on the length of recovery necessary for a lesson to present itself again. The all too common denominator for dramas in my life has been a defensive, negative conditioned response to the invitation for surrender and obedience to the Christ.

My inability and/or refusal to listen to the inner signals resulted in the drama eruptions with a vengeance. Instead of having a restructuring of life to address the necessary change to balance the outer life with the inner realizations in a patient rational manner, my more primitive instincts took over and I would blow up. I would become enraged, belligerent, and usually isolated from friends, family, and even God. This was not a very pleasant place to be and I have had a lot of experience with the landscape.

An intense purification or approaching realization could easily set a drama in motion. The stage directors, called reason and common sense, were braced and ready for the characters to arrive. They emerged out of the emotional storage rooms in the basement. The actors known as grief, loss, misunderstanding, indignation, and entitlement usually would come to center stage. They formed a chorus and each one reinforced the other until there was a cacophony of dialoguing vying for attention. Everyone was speaking and no one was listening. By this time, my silent prayer practice, no responding, return to awareness, had gone right out the window followed very closely by common sense.

Then, on center stage appeared a phone or computer! As an extrovert, I have traditionally searched for someone with whom I could process my upsets. In more recent years, it has been my teacher. These conversations were usually one sided. I would talk and she would listen. After speaking my piece and decrying the difficulty of being obedient to the Christ's demands and how the entire spiritual journey was overbearing, I would calm down. Then a certain feeling of relief kicked in which was very brief followed by embarrassment and remorse for having lost it yet one more time.

A variation of the drama theme was when I would get on the computer and email a similar tirade in the form of long lists with anywhere from 10-50 statements. They were terse, short, unedited, and raw. I would doubt everything and everyone, including my teacher. For some reason, sending this allowed me to get it off my chest and outside of myself. I would usually print out the soliloquy and wait for the return response. Remarkably, my teacher always pleasantly and promptly answered every single discomfort and complaint in minute detail concerning my struggle with resistance to surrender, obedience, change, and why.

In my attempt to conform my "outer" life to the inner realizations, I have had dramas of tragedy, comedy, documentary, debate, melodrama, and un-requited love stories galore. The emotional toll and strain on the body cannot be underestimated. There is a tremendous amount of energy that gets used up in dramas that might be better used if the drama had not taken place. These dramas erupted fairly frequently, when I was going through an intensive forgiveness, purification process, or struggling with adjusting to an insight or realization. Some dramas lasted a few hours. Some lasted a few days. Some lasted longer than I would care to admit. So at times I kept my teacher pretty busy.

I now have gotten to the point where I can pretty much anticipate a drama rising and even pinpoint the area of required change in my life. This is a fairly recent development. It certainly saves wear and tear on the system. What I have come to realize through my spiritual practices is that the best way to get hold of a drama is to catch it at its very root, when it begins its rising ascent. When this happens, the cycle can be broken. I have come to realize I can choose to prevent the dramas.

So far, so good, at the writing of this lesson reflection! I hesitate to say I will not conjure up another production, but I notice less and less interest in the theater and the actors seemed to have moved out of the basement and taken up residence elsewhere far away. Inner awareness has been the key to this change of behavior. In the past, I felt at the mercy of the drama. Now I know I have more of a clear choice. Given that choice, who in the world would want to go round and round the drama-go-round? Not I.

It isn't that I have overcome this propensity for high drama by might, force, or power of will, or even self-control. It has been the simple, quiet, subtle increase of inner insightful, awareness that has given me the interior freedom to choose to play the game or not. I have simply chosen not to play the game. And that has made all the difference.

++++++++++++++++++++++++++

LESSON: 56 — DREAMS

DREAMS ARE THE occurrences of images, thoughts, and deeds that may appear during sleep.

1. In general, for the truth seeker, dreams may be informative, instructional, and enlightening.
2. In sleep, you have given up control of your mind's contents. This allows the vibrating energy and

its contents to roam at will. Consequently, mixed up and totally unfamiliar images and events may appear.

3. In your dreams, you may not always recognize individuals or events that may occur. In your wakening world of illusions, you do not always recognize everyone who may appear.

4. There is usually a lesson that may be learned from a dream that is coherent. A vivid, coherent dream is your unconsciousness responding to a present need. A resolution may be revealed in your dream to a particular problem that you may have wrestled with during the day.

5. Your dream is your unconscious answering your conscious mind. All that rises in consciousness, whether awake or asleep contains its opposite. If you can conceive of a problem, the solution already exists.

6. It is the struggle with a problem that interferes with the rising of its natural solution. Therefore, the dream state allows for the free uninhibited flow of vibrating energy that may contain the necessary information or solution.

7. The best way to understand a dream is immediately upon awakening. Ask yourself, "How did I feel about what was happening? How was I responding?" Your answers may give you a clue to what the dream means as it applies to your life.

8. Dreams are easily affected by what has occurred during the day, what you may have eaten, or what someone may have said causing an impact/ impression on your unconscious and conscious mind.

9. Dreams may be considered positive by you and a horror by someone else. So, your dreams are individual and apply to you for your benefit.

10. If you are steeped into a silent prayer practice, scripture, and, in general, keeping your focus on the things of a Godly nature, your dreams may reveal remnants of truth.

11. You may have vivid dreams where Holy images appear. Many times, it is during a dream state that you may rise to the Christ Consciousness where Jesus may appear, teach you, and welcome you into His Holy Embrace.

12. Before entering sleep, be aware of the Christ Consciousness and receptive to the teachings of the Holy Spirit in the name of Jesus Christ.

+ +

LESSON: 57 — DRIFTING

DRIFTING IS A frequency change of your vibrating energy to a previous expression of consciousness.

1. You are walking a spiritual path between the opposites (Lesson: 117) on this plane. Allowing yourself to be pulled to an extreme toward either of the opposites, is drifting. To maintain the finer expression of consciousness and, at the same time indulge in a grosser expression is folly, an insult to your spiritual integrity.

2. If you are attracted to a previous expression of consciousness and attempt to express from it, an internal or outer struggle will occur. If help is available during these times, you should seek it.

3. When you are drawn to outer appearances, attracted to that which the spiritual principle of supply manifests, you may find yourself unintentionally drifting from your Christ center. A chain of internal disturbing emotions may rise.

4. Focusing on the many manifestations is to lose sight of the individuals who you may be called to serve. For example: regarding wealthy individuals you may be taken in by the opulence of others — and lost in the material manifestations. What you need remain aware of is the expression of consciousness that creates wealth.

5. It is always the individual's expression of consciousness that creates the outer appearances. To get caught up in the outer supply of manifestations is to drift from the Christ Consciousness into other individual expressions of consciousness as they are rising. You may find you too are drifting, reacting, and expressing from a previous individual expression of consciousness.

6. The more intense your prayer practice becomes the more it is likely that the temptation to drift may rise. There are many times, on a spiritual walk, when you may be tempted to drift from your Christ center. Doubts in minute detail may rise and a self-persecution follows. There is no place to go, no place to hide. Wherever you twist or turn the Christ is there. "If I ascend into heaven, thou *art* there: if I make my bed in hell, behold, thou *art there*" (Psalm 139: 8).

7. It is like the King who had a beautiful daughter and there were many young suitors who wanted to marry her. The King wanted the wisest of them for his daughter. The King invited the young suitors to come, and he told each one to take a live chicken and said, "Go where no one will see, and kill the chicken. The one who is able to do this will marry my daughter."

8. When they returned, one young suitor had not killed the chicken. The King asked, "Why have you not killed the chicken?"

"Sir, everywhere I went there was one who would see me kill it."

"And, who is that? asked, the astonished King.

"The chicken, sir. The chicken would see."

So amazed and impressed, the King said, "You are the wisest, you shall marry my daughter."

9. There is nowhere the Light of Awareness does not shine upon you. Nowhere the love of God does not know you. Temptation to drift, however, is so deceptive it may easily catch you unaware. Although, it isn't a death defying experience, at the time, it may feel as if it is. Drifting creeps up on you when it is least expected and wants to hang on for dear life — *its* conditional, temporary, relative life.

10. If you are to know and understand where anyone is and may be coming from at any given moment, you live out from an aware Christ Consciousness —no drifting allowed.

11. To remain in an aware state requires alertness. There are countless attractions and distractions to pull or grab you into any one of the many previous individual expressions of consciousness.

12. The grabbing of your attention is an illusionary tempting force to drift and move you away from the Christ Consciousness. In reality, there is no drift, no movement. All is a conditioned illusion in an illusionary plane of opposites.

13. The one becomes the many, therefore, when any one of the many returns to the one (its oneness) it is only natural for it to be drawn back toward the familiar. It is your responsibility to remain aware and to live out from the awareness of being.

14. You must be ever vigilant to the appearances that have drawn you initially into the arena of time and space, and possess the same energy force to lull you back to become once again a conditioned sleep walker.

15. Don't play the crazy head games of constantly dialoguing, "Am I good enough? Am I pleasing God? Am I pleasing others? Am I realized? Will I make it?"

16. The imaginings of a conditioned mind will play with charged emotions and cause you to drift into a dark night of the soul.

17. When drifting occurs, stop the dialoguing, become a witness, steep yourself in spiritual principles, scripture, remain disciplined with your silent prayer practice, and seek immediate help, if available. Do not linger in the darkness. You are living between two worlds and if you are not to drift, a balance is necessary for you to function as a practical being in a world of opposites.

18. There is no un-manifested consciousness. All of the repressed, suppressed, and conditioning impression craziness will rise at any moment of vulnerability. A drift may occur at your most vulnerable moment. It's an ideal time for you to work with the purification process.

19. A drift may be an opportunity for cleaning additional rooms in the mind's house. Take advantage of it. You work with it — not against yourself. The anger or attack mood that rises against yourself and others is the mind's way of defending itself against what it does not, nor ever can, understand.

20. You are the keeper of your realized Christ Consciousness. You are the guard at the entrance of the Kingdom. To guard wisely you stay awake and aware. To stay awake you are aware of the individual expressions of consciousness as they come and go, accepting, allowing, and respecting each and every one of them.

21. Although it is necessary to communicate with individual expressions as they pass by the gate of the Kingdom, the absolute necessity is not to (drift) leave your post, Christ Consciousness. For to do so, the gate to the Kingdom, for a time, may once again appear closed.

22. You have realized in awareness the Kingdom of God, the pearl of great price, the Holy Grail. It is an accomplishment of a lifetime — yours.

....

STUDENT STORY:

The sudden feelings of nausea and tightness in the gut of my stomach rose as I looked around and wondered what have I eaten?" "How did this happen?" "Oh, no, won't I ever learn?" "Not again!"

These were the feelings and thoughts that ran through my mind the afternoon I found myself enabling a needy, demanding, and quintessential drama member of my former congregation. This individual, feigned utter confusion and helplessness tossing out the, "Won't you join me in this misery?" Query.

The temptation to seduce me into leaving my post of genuine allowance, acceptance, and respect for the chosen state of an individual consciousness expressing itself. I bit the bait! I drifted into my previous expressed and all too familiar "messiah/savior" mode, as if Jesus needed help! When, in fact, the individual who most needed help was Sandy, not the parishioner.

Now we have two miserable co-dependents scrambling to fix it. I found myself picking this individual up, packing luggage, driving to the hospital, staying while the procedure was administered, and ultimately giving the invitation to stay at my house. I thought, "It would be better for me to care for this individual." The saying, "misery needs company" could not be clearer nor could the fact of my drifting from one state of consciousness to another be more apparent.

I was unable to maintain my Christ-centered awareness and appropriately lend the type of encouragement and support that might have helped the deteriorating situation. I found myself participating in the suffering and making it more complicated and ultimately worse. As the week went on the drift/enmeshment escalated to a pitch that forced me to see what had happened and to end the chaos.

Once I got that realization, the return to a proper expression of relationship between priest and parish member occurred quickly and without much fanfare. The individual decided the best thing was to go home to be with family. I couldn't get me to the car keys fast enough! After unloading the luggage, saying good-by and wishing the family well, I said my "act of contrition." I drove home, had a cup of tea, re-read my lesson on "drifting," went to the gym, meditated, had dinner, and went to bed! A lesson well learned, an invitation to be more alert.

The next time a temptation to drift into a previously traveled state of consciousness rises on my horizon I pray that I have the awareness to notice its stripes and consciously choose not to enter in. The blind lead the blind into a pit. In no way do I diminish or trivialize the suffering/fear of my friend. To have been of genuine/appropriate assistance under these dire circumstances, would have meant maintaining an awareness of the Christ of my/our being and not mistaking the appearances for the reality. Had I done that perhaps a "lifting up" would have occurred in a way that would have eased the suffering.

++++++++++++++++++++++++++

LESSON: 58 — EGO

EGO IS A false sense of importance. It is a bloated feeling of false humility run amok.

1. Stay alert and recognize the ego rising signs. Alertness and recognition will allow you to make the necessary correction. You are the one with the power to put the ego to rest and not be taken in by ego's many deceptive ways of engagement.

2. Keep a close watch on the rising thoughts of self-grandiosity and the ego will die a natural death.

3. On a spiritual walk, ego continuously struggles with humility. Its goal is to eliminate any resemblance of humility. Your goal is to be alert to the struggle and the opportunity to make a preferable choice.

4. Ego constantly casts a bright light on its self-interest, always wanting to take credit for the works of the Lord. "The getting of treasures by a lying tongue *is* a vanity tossed to and fro of them that seek death" (Proverbs 21: 6).

5. Ego is constantly vying for attention, praising itself, and always completely centered on the "person" it believes itself to be. "Let another man praise thee, and not thine own mouth; a stranger, and not thine own lips" (Proverbs 27: 2).

6. Ego sacrifices nothing, gives up nothing, shares nothing, and will take whatever it can get, whether or not it has a rightful claim.

7. Ego always works for "what's in it for me, what can I get out of it, and how will it benefit me?" It is always me, me, me, I, I, I. "Go from the presence of a foolish man, when thou perceivest not *in him* the lips of knowledge" (Proverbs 14: 7).

8. Ego will eventually smother itself in its own praise and take down the "person" it pretends to care for. "For sin, taking occasion by the commandment, deceived me, and by it slew *me*" (Romans 7: 11).

++++++++++++++++++++++++++

LESSON: 59 — ENLIGHTENMENT

ENLIGHTENMENT IS THE after-effect of truth realized.

1. Enlightenment is the result of the realization of the truth. Not always timed according to plan, enlightenment may occur when you least expect.

2. Do not be quick to think that one enlightenment is the total overcoming. There are many degrees of enlightenment within the totality of being a fully awaken, enlightened being.

3. There is not one grand enlightenment. In reality, there may be as many enlightenments as there are realizations.

4. With each spiritual realization, enlightenment penetrates the ignorance perpetuated by the illusionary world of your imagination.

5. Enlightenment requires a time to bathe in the pool of wisdom. As a fully awakened enlightened being, you live as an aware being in the world but not of it.

6. Through the Holy Spirit in the name of Jesus Christ, enlightenment casts a light of understanding within the realization of the reality of your being.

STUDENT'S STORY:

Consciousness is certainly an interesting phenomenon. At the start of my spiritual journey, like many folks, I thought of human existence in terms of being conscious or unconscious, alive or dead! I certainly had a notion of the waking state, dreaming state, and deep sleep states of consciousness, but that was about it. Concepts like transcendence, eternal life, resurrection, after life, and life after life held a certain curiosity, appeal, and fascination but hardly registered with any certainty of experience on my inner screen. I am now happy to report like Shakespeare that there really is, "More than meets the eye." Or Paul, "But as it is written, Eye hath not seen, nor ear heard neither have entered into the hart of man, the things which God hath prepared for them that love him" (I Corinthians 2: 9).

In looking back, I remember one trip over the Teton Pass in Wyoming on a beautiful sunny winter day. The trees were shining and the light was beautiful. As I approached the 10% grade, I had the very clear realization experience of a silent inner witness to the beauty in the midst of attending to the winding road, double white passing lines, and guard rails. The thought rose, "Is that It?" Is that "Enlightenment?" Is that the "whisper passing by the cave?" "That?" I remember laughing out loud. I had expected something a lot more spectacular for sure.

The silent abiding sense of being awake inside in the midst of all other activities certainly came with no bells or cymbals announcing, "You have arrived!" This was all quite effortless, normal, quiet, and natural. Isn't that what all the famous masters say, "Oh it is really nothing and you don't have to do anything . . ." Of course, that is after they have spent decades fasting, meditating, studying, serving, and waiting patiently preparing for such a natural unfolding!

In looking closely I have come to see that, "Enlightenment" is not simply an awareness of the witness state in the midst of activity any more than it is simply the unmistakable rising of spiritual energy through the spine. Over the years I have come to realize that what we typically call, "Enlightenment" is really a cumulative series of little awakening experiences of the truth of our being, over a long period of time.

+ +

LESSON: 60 — ENOUGH IS ENOUGH!

ENOUGH IS ENOUGH! The exclamation occurs when you are ready to give into a realization that is constantly tapping at your inner window for attention.

1. There are times when the same lesson rises repeatedly for your attention. This usually occurs when it is time for you to progress beyond the lesson through the forgiveness and purification process.

2. You are the one who attracts the necessary lesson to overcome, at any given time, on your spiritual walk.

3. You are the one who must accept the responsibility for the lesson and the spiritual practices that may give you peace and assist your overcoming, in the name of Jesus Christ. "These things I have spoken unto you, that in me ye might have peace. In the world ye shall have tribulation: but be of good cheer; I have overcome the world" (John 16: 33).

4. The rising of the same lesson over-and-over, may occur continuously or intermittently in similar or unfamiliar appearances. However it occurs, it will plague you until you are ready to realize the truth.

5. The realization in truth, is begging to spring forth but must await your weariness of repeating the lesson. You may continue to feel under attack on all sides and cry out for the relief you believe you deserve. "Mine enemies would daily swallow *me* up: for *they be* many that fight against me, O thou most High" (Psalm 56: 2).

6. Although you remain steadfast in your determination to overcome the tormenting illusion, in pain and suffering, you may come to question, "Will the Lord cast off forever? and will he be favorable no more? Is his mercy clean gone forever? doth *his* promise fail for evermore?" (Psalm 77: 7-8)

7. The intellectual understanding of the reoccurrence of the lesson does not lessen your continued struggle with the repeated rising of the lesson.

8. You may foolishly believe because you are ready and willing to give up part of the lesson, you can overcome the illusion it presents. Not so. "The way of a fool *is* right in his own eyes: but he that hearkeneth unto counsel *is* wise" (Proverbs 12: 15).

9. Truth cannot be parceled-out. Therefore, it awaits your readiness and willingness to detach from the illusion in its entirety.

10. Be assured, when you are hammered sufficiently with the same old, same old life's destructive, bruising lesson in this world of illusion and can claim, "Enough is enough!," you may be ready to leave the old behind and to embrace the new through the Holy Spirit in the name of Jesus Christ.

....

STUDENT'S STORY:

The time comes when "enough is enough." This was my experience around the root mistake of thinking my well-being and self esteem was to be found in the recognition of others and not in the Christ of my being through the power and grace of the Holy Spirit. The conditioning of the world and messages I received in order to feel "good" and be "well thought of by others," was that I must conform to their standards. These standards were not always clearly stated nor were they necessarily accurate.

Unfortunately, due to my lack of awareness of my true source of power and worth I was easily seduced and continually frustrated. Trying to please others as a means of insuring self-esteem and worth became a dead end street. Left unchecked, this situation creates a recipe for depression and self-deprecation. I was a living example of the suffering endured from "looking for real self-esteem, love, affection" etcetera—in all the wrong places.

My determination to be free and faithful is sincere and my spiritual practices are in place and, consequently, I have received numerable opportunities for purification. When I have failed to take notice, I have experienced an intensification of suffering as a result of my stubbornness. I have often said I am a slow learner.

Until a repeated, recycled all too familiar drama continued to rise and caused significant suffering, I would blithely disregard the profiles. The stickiness of my attachments along with the Spirit's desire to bring to my full awareness the real source of suffering is a dance that can play out during an entire lifetime. At the ripe old age of 59, I finally realized this teaching in its entire splendor and I might add humor!

The more I refused to see an issue as representing itself over and over with various lengths of reprieve between, the more the issue escalated in frequency and intensity. The Spirit's insistence that I "take notice" and "wake up" to the insanity of my drama remained constant until from the deepest center of my being, I agreed, "Enough is enough" and submitted to forgiveness, purification, and healing.

To be free, anything that enslaves whether it be an emotion, event, memory, habit, or whatever had to be brought to my awareness, accepted for what it is, and let go of in cooperation with grace. Forgiveness, purification, and healing does not happen in a vacuum, but within actual lived experience of mind, body, emotions, and spirit. That is a lot of territory to address and the spiritual journey takes it all seriously and no stone is ever left unturned. I am either free or not free. Anything in between is simply a way station.

+ +

LESSON: 61 — EUCHARIST

THE SACRAMENT OF Holy Eucharist is the ultimate gift of remembrance and new covenant. "And he took bread, and gave thanks, and brake *it* and gave it unto them, saying, This is my body which is given for you: this do in remembrance of me. Likewise also the cup after supper, saying, This cup *is* the new testament in my blood, which is shed for you" (Luke 22: 19-20).

1. The Holy Eucharist is Jesus' willingness to lay down His life for the love of humanity — for you and for me. There is no greater sacrifice. "Greater love hath no man than this, that a man lay down his life for his friends" (John 15: 13).

2. Jesus proved there is an end to the human personal separate sense of being and there is an immortal, eternal life in the awareness of your being within your God's Kingdom. Jesus was willing to sacrifice His physical personal sense form to prove this world is not God's Kingdom.

3. When Jesus spoke (John 6: 53 - 63) about having to eat of His body and drink of His blood, He made it clear He was speaking of beyond the physical sense of body and blood to that which is the Spirit *of* His body and blood. "It is the spirit that quickeneth; the flesh profiteth nothing: the words that I speak unto you, *they* are spirit, and *they* are life" (John 6: 63).

4. The strength of the bread and the wine taken, blessed, broken, and shared remain indelibly stamped in consciousness throughout generations. For as long as man walks on this plane of existence and breaks bread "do this in remembrance of me" and establishes the "new covenant in my blood," the possibility of waking up to the Christ Consciousness for those who would follow Jesus is enhanced.

5. To prove the physical sense body and blood were not your life eternal, Jesus was willing to lay His body and blood down. Jesus left the sacrament of remembrance that establishes a new covenant through His Holy Spirit. "But the Comforter, *which is* the Holy Ghost, whom the Father will send in my name, he shall teach you all things, and bring all things to your remembrance, whatsoever I have said unto you" (John14: 26).

6. The recipients of the Holy Eucharist, who would come with a sincere, deep, loving belief in the remembrance of the new covenant, are blessed in the communion of oneness in the Holy Spirit of Jesus Christ.

7. The Eucharist does not stop its spiritual activity at the altar. It has a continuous spiritual power in consciousness to awaken you to the spiritual teachings through the Holy Spirit in the name of Jesus Christ.

8. There is no greater remembrance and covenant that is given to you by Jesus Christ that would bring you into the presence of Jesus Christ. You are constantly being asked to remember the sacrifice, invited to the table to part take of the Holy Eucharist, and to accept the invitation to follow Jesus Christ. "And he said unto another, Follow me . . ." (Luke 9: 59).

STUDENT'S STORY:

During my eleven years of ministry as the director of a retreat center, I had the privilege of celebrating the sacraments of the church with folks from all over the country and from various Christian denominations. These celebrations were always "optional" and most retreat participants found them a powerful complement to their hours of sitting in silent prayer practice.

The most frequently celebrated action was Holy Eucharist. As its efficacy could not be mistaken nor underestimated, what I found particularly interesting were the powerful comments from people who had relatively little experience with sacramental action within their faith tradition, and their reports of profound experience of conversion, healing, and personal encounter with Christ. For many, joining with others around the altar to intentionally share the body and blood of Jesus Christ in simple gifts of bread and wine was life changing.

The words of institution proclaimed a clear intent, and when the outer word joined with the inner Word and disposition of consent to receive Christ, none were denied and all were satisfied. For those who had previously considered this ritual action to be either "restricted to only certain people," or not "the real presence of Jesus" a new spacious level of understanding and experience became evident. The presence of Christ in the prayers, offerings, scriptures, bread and wine was tangible, powerful.

Christ's real presence in and through and to persons of faith cannot be limited or restricted. Similarly, Christ's presence, although undoubtedly available to any, cannot be "forced upon" one who is not receptive. In Christ there is only patience, unconditional love, and acceptance. Jesus is neither a competing, compelling, nor a withholding Lord. Jesus is a present Lord and all we freely need do is be "present" to His Presence.

+ +

LESSON: 62 — EVIL

EVIL IS WHAT may cause harm to self or others.

1. Evil (like sin) is born of ignorance. Evil is ignorance of who or what you are in the reality of your being. Evil however, may go beyond sin in depth and breadth of doing harm to yourself or others.

2. Evil is self-inflicted through thought, word, or deed. You cannot think, speak, or do evil without inflicting it upon yourself.

3. Intentionally or unintentionally, evil is brought upon yourself or others by the choices and decisions you make and the behavior you engage in.

4. It would not be possible to do evil to yourself or others if you were fully aware of what you are doing. "Then Jesus said, Father, forgive them; for they know not what they do. And they parted his raiment, and cast lots" (Luke 23: 34).

5. If you are not aware of your reality, the appearances of evil in this world may easily disturb you. As you progress on a spiritual walk, it becomes difficult for you to invest your energy or power in doing evil.

6. The conscious awareness of who or what you are identifies others as yourself. You are less likely to harm others when you realize you are harming yourself and forgiveness for those who would do evil is your natural response.

7. When you are seriously going for the straight gate and narrow way, the understanding of the second commandment Jesus gave becomes clear. "And the second *is* like unto it. Thou shalt love thy neighbour as thyself" (Matthew 22: 39).

8. Evil need only to be reversed to l-i-v-e. Your spiritual walk, during a spiritual journey, awakens you from a sleep of ignorance to the Holy Spirit in the name of Jesus Christ.

+ +

LESSON: 63 — EXPANSIVE CONSCIOUSNESS

THE EXPANSIVE CONSCIOUSNESS may reveal experiences of different levels.

1. There may not be any particular experience you must have, and none should be expected. Whatever experiences necessary for your progress on a spiritual walk will manifest.

2. Expressions of consciousness are individual and different. What may unfold for one, may not be necessary for another.

3. Without a sense of your physical body, Jesus may escort you from the Spiritual Heart Center within the awareness of expansive consciousness. "And he carried me away in the spirit to a great and high mountain, and shewed me that great city, the holy Jerusalem, descending out of heaven from God," (Revelation 21: 10).

4. This may occur when the Holy Spirit in the name of Jesus Christ chooses to teach a lesson within the expansive consciousness. "After this I looked, and, behold, a door *was* opened in heaven: and the first voice which I heard *was* as it were of a trumpet talking with me; which said, Come up hither, and I will shew thee things which must be hereafter. And immediately I was in the spirit: and, behold, a throne was set in heaven, and *one* sat on the throne" (Revelation 4: 1-2).

5. You may be given the realization of no space. Eyes closed or opened, vibrating energy fills every inch of what you may be referring to as space. There is none. The Christ of your being will enable you to follow where Jesus leads, and learn the lesson presented.

6. The most minute expansive consciousness realization may awaken or stir an interest in a spiritual walk. At the core of your being is always the nagging sense of the knowledge, "There is more."

7. Initially, the realization of an expansive consciousness may raise doubts of your sanity. You may struggle with the experience of the expansiveness beyond the physical sense. There may be the temptation to convince yourself, "I must have been dreaming." However, the clarity and certainty of the experience validates its possibility.

8. There may be no verbal language spoken during an expansive consciousness experience. There is a transference of thought. There is conversation going on without uttering one word aloud. No interference, no mistranslation, nor misinterpretation can occur. The transference is direct, quick, and clear. The Holy Spirit in the name of Jesus Christ, speaks in silence and you hear every word.

STUDENT STORY:

It was the 4th Sunday of Pentecost. I was kneeling for the Confession of Sin after the Creed behind the high altar where the light is dim and the Rector and I are mostly hidden. I had my eyes closed, as is my custom. Peering inside of my eyelids, my common everyday awareness of the array of light and motion offered no distraction to my prayer. What did grab my attention in a most powerful yet subtle way was a realization that the inner landscape participated in the outer landscape without change or distinction.

I had not previously been aware of that until this strange morning. I thought it must be the lighting. After numerous "tests" of my perception, I became convinced that I actually perceived something about consciousness that I had not been consciously aware of before — energy in motion.

I am not suggesting the energy was "now in manifested flesh appearing" as if it just suddenly appeared on the scene, but rather that I was, now for the first time, able to see it eyes opened, eyes closed, and realize it as un-manifested vibrating energy.

I tested this over and over by ever so slowly having a sense of the light and its exact substance (sort of like light dancing particles). I carefully opened my eyes to behold eyes open what I had, in fact, been viewing interiorly when my eye lids were shut tight. It seemed as if I were seeing "through my eyes closed and I knew it.

I realized in an instant that there was no "empty space. There existed between the Rector and me, kneeling on either side of the altar, a pregnant field of lively vibrating energy that filled the entire altar area. If I had a sharp enough knife, it could be cut. Then I realized that the only thing at all that was really in that church was a massive energy field of vibrating consciousness at various speeds. Some wood, some metal, some bread, some wine, some song, some bodies, and yet, all one gigantic living breathing pulsating dancing Light.

I knew experientially the meaning behind Jesus' statement, "I am the Light," in a new and most delightful way. I also knew that in some mysterious, and not so mysterious way, we all dance in that Light and, in fact, are that Light. Amen.

+ +

LESSON: 64 — EXPECTATIONS

EXPECTATIONS ON A spiritual walk are conditioned anticipations of something you look for within yourself, others, or something you believe others may demand of you.

1. Whether self, superimposed, or believed imposed by others, the devastation expectations can cause in your spiritual life may be all consuming. The seriousness of this emotional state of mind easily may cause you moments of depressed creative energy.

2. In any case scenario, expectations usually set up a failure response or an unreasonable outcome. To have expectations of oneself or others is to anticipate what cannot exist in any moment in time and space.

3. You cannot sensibly meet the unwarranted expectations and demands placed on yourself or by others, nor should you.

4. You live on the plane of opposites where there is constant change by right of its temporary, relative existence. How can you at any given moment, hold anyone, including yourself, in graded expectations?

5. To hold yourself in a realm of expectations, whether imaginary or not, is to set yourself up for constant impossibilities, disappointments, and internal struggles.

6. You are not here to meet the expectations of others nor to artificially create them for yourself. You cannot do what is expected. You can only do who or what you are and that which you are does all things necessary. "EXCEPT the LORD build the house, they labour in vain that build it:. . . ." (Psalm 127: 1).

7. The fear you will not meet the expectations of others will cripple your spiritual progress and the misguided habitual focus on what is expected would interfere with your natural creativity.

8. As with all conditioning, allow the stressful emotional expectation energy to rise and fall without a justifying response.

9. Expectations are multiple emotional conditions that have been placed at your emotional door step. Expectations are deposited at an early age by parents, peers, teachers, etcetera, and reinforced by a culture you have come to rely on for your self-esteem. Expectations divert and often waste energy.

10. The Christ Centered Prayer practice may allow you to realize the reality of your being. It does not judge, condemn, nor hold you in expectations.

11. A silent prayer practice does not produce results on demand, nor does it compete with a relative plane of existence. To have expectations, judge, or anticipate any one of your prayer practice sessions or any of your life's actions, is to hold yourself in a conditioned state of being.

12. You possess the power to delete expectations from your emotional energy menu. Thus, as you should in your daily practical life, when you begin a silent prayer practice, push the delete key for expectations.

13. How can there ever be any more expected of who or what you already are? The Christ of your being, the Holy Spirit of your nature is whole and complete in awareness. There is never anything you

or others can expect of It. It is always being exactly what it is—no more and never less. "God said unto Moses, I AM THAT I AM . . ." (Exodus 3:14).

14. You, as a contemplative truth seeker, need only to accept and realize who or what you are as an impersonal spiritual Being and all imaginary expectations are seen for what they are — relative fantasies in an unreal world temporarily positioned to nag you into a fully awakened awareness.

15. If you allow, expectations may become the bars on a cell of fear. They will hold you prisoner to a dialogue of gigantic proportions. Shed the false belief that expectations have any validity or substance. The freedom in the Christ is the freedom without expectations. It is the realizing all that I am already is beyond expectations.

16. This world of expectations is naught compared to the wonder, the magnificence of God's Kingdom. "But, as it is written, Eye hath not seen, nor ear heard, neither have entered into the heart of man, the things which God hath prepared for them" (1 Corinthians 2: 9).

17. God in its infinite mercy has no expectations of that which It creates in Its image. All of the theatrical drama, candies, toys, and noise of this world serve but one purpose, "Be still, and know that I *am* God: . . ." (Psalm 46: 10).

18. When you give up the activity of self or superimposed expectations, you live the outer and inner life of openness and receptivity to the Holy Spirit in the name of Jesus Christ. You live in the moment. The eternal "now" effortlessly, appropriately, and spontaneously. This is a joyful life free of regret and expectations.

....

STUDENT'S STORY:

I have always had more difficulty receiving criticism than praise and only recently begun to have realized them as two sides of the same equation. On the one hand, there is nothing more grace-filled and humbling than to be the deliverer of God's Word in a faithful manner to a receptive congregation, and nothing more humiliating to have that same message misquoted, distorted, rejected, or criticized by the hearers.

I had come to rely on the prompting of the Holy Spirit and listening deeply to the movement of the Spirit when delivering my sermons. Part of that reliance was a practice of preparation which did not include a written text in the pulpit. I had discovered having a piece of parchment between me and God's people pinched my ability to be present to the Word of God as well as to His people to whom the Word was being addressed.

For several Sundays there was a parishioner who took exception to my preaching and decided to complain. The critiques were explicit, well thought out, sarcastic, and signed. Reading the note, raised tremendous fear in me and left me dumbfounded in light of the many positive comments I received about the same sermons. Thus, I was well schooled with the expectation of positive comments.

Unfortunately, my critic did not appreciate my style and had other expectations. The demand rendered was that I conform to preconceived established norms, published commentaries, orthodox theologies, oratory precision, etcetera, or this person would find another place to worship! Well that is a sweet message to get after a long hard week of study, prayer and preparation. Obviously, the sermon resonated deeply and powerfully within this person and resulted in an expressed attack towards me.

The human tendency to "get the hell out of Dodge" crossed my mind. The thought of never wanting to preach again crossed my mind. What did not cross my mind was the subtle signature of Expectation and Temptation. As defined in the Lesson Papers, "The freedom in the Christ is the freedom without expectation." And, "The fear you will not meet the expectations of others will cripple your spiritual progress and the misguided habitual focus on what is expected would interfere with your natural creativity."

My critic I am quite sure is unaware of the spiritual gift the criticism has given me. It took four days, and working intensely with my teacher for me to grasp, and realize, what really was going on. It was the expectation of not having my sermons criticized and the temptation to desist from trusting God in my preaching that caused my strong aversion and emotional upset. The temptation took the form of wanting to take away something very precious and hard fought for that I had; namely my trust in God to speak His Word to me in my inner most being and my willingness to give it voice when preaching.

The realization illumined me instantly to Jesus' caution against the gaining of the whole world and losing one's soul. Giving up expectations, turns the temptation into an opportunity to purify and strengthen a continued commitment and trust in the Holy Spirit in the name of Jesus Christ. To do otherwise would be to turn my back and run back to the dark woods from which Jesus has been calling me.

+ +

LESSON: 65 — EXPERIENCES - SPIRITUAL

ALL EXPERIENCES ARE spiritual. However, when you are serious on a spiritual walk during a spiritual journey, there may be specific experiences in the inner and/or outer world that may manifest.

POSSIBLE INNER EXPERIENCES:

A. Visions of Holy images may appear.
B. There may be hearing sounds or smelling odor of flowers.
C. Beyond physical body sense or heavenly singing may occur.
D. There may be the rising of stored energy (Lazarus rising) through spiritual centers.

POSSIBLE OUTER EXPERIENCES:

A. All needs for your spiritual progress are met.
B. The necessary reading materials or individual will appear.
C. When the Lazarus rising begins, there may be various physical manifestations.
D. Guidance and direction will become available as required. When you are ready, the "teacher" will appear.

1. As a silent prayer practice deepens, there may be experiences in the deeper, wider dimensions of consciousness. It is important you not get taken with what may appear. What is taking place is hearing, seeing, smelling, etcetera, and the purification process.
2. Inner experiences may differ individually. Experiences should not be compared, shared, or talked about except with a teacher.
3. Too much emphasis should not be placed on inner or outer experiences. Treat them as sacred and secret but do not become attached to them.
4. The true fruit of spiritual experience, inner and outer, is always realized in daily life with an increased willingness and ability to love, serve, and express sincere gratitude to God in the name of Jesus Christ through the power of the Holy Spirit.
5. Keep your heart opened without expectations and trust the Holy Spirit in the name of Jesus Christ is guiding you in all ways.

+ +

LESSON: 66 — FAITH

FAITH IS THE belief in the existence of the Kingdom of God. "Now faith is the substance of things hoped for, the evidence of things not seen" (Hebrews 11: 1).

1. A material minded world lends to judging yourself and others by material possessions. Faith in the outer appearances of the things of this world creates a stumbling stone on your spiritual walk. "Wherefore? Because *they sought it* not by faith, but as it were by the works of the law. For they stumbled at that stumbling stone;" (Romans 9: 32).

2. When Jesus multiplied the loaves and fishes, (John 6: 10-12) He was demonstrating the source not the effects. Jesus had faith His Divine God would feed five thousand, and have left-overs.

3. If you have faith, Jesus demonstrated God will meet your need in the moment (compassion). "Then touched he their eyes, saying, According to your faith be it unto you" (Matthew 9: 29).

4. The masses were so impressed they wanted to make Jesus their king. Jesus would be useful. They had not grasped the teaching. Jesus immediately removed Himself. "When Jesus therefore perceived that they would come and take him by force, to make him a king, he departed again into a mountain himself alone" (John 6: 15).

5. Jesus was teaching "faith." Faith, not in a king but in a Kingdom, the Kingdom of God — an unseen Kingdom. "If God so clothe the grass, which is to day in the field, and tomorrow is cast into the oven; how much *more will he* clothe you, O ye of little faith?" (Luke 12: 28). "But rather seek ye the kingdom of God; and all these things shall be added unto you" (Luke 12: 31).

6. The loaves and fishes were the means to demonstrate how faith meets all needs. Jesus was teaching to have faith in the source, the unseen Kingdom of God. He was teaching to live your daily life by faith. "Behold, his soul *which* is lifted up is not upright in him: but the just shall live by his faith" (Habakkuk 2: 4).

7. As a truth seeker, you come to a silent prayer practice with the full faith in the belief the Kingdom of God is not of this world, and you seek it within. "For therein is the righteousness of God revealed from faith to faith: as it is written, The just shall live by faith" (Romans 1: 17).

8. In this world faith has become one of usefulness. God is useful for the things sought after in daily life. There's more interest in the demonstrations than the source of them. The masses' faith was in what they could see and eat. The masses did not get the teaching. Do you? "Through faith we understand that the worlds were framed by the word of God, so that things which are seen were not made of things which do appear" (Hebrews 11: 3).

+ +

LESSON: 67 — FAITHFULNESS

FAITHFULNESS FOR THE realized individual expression of consciousness, is standing firm in the known Christ. "Trust in the LORD with all thine heart; and lean not unto thine own understanding. In all thy ways acknowledge him, and he shall direct thy paths" (Proverbs 3: 5-6).

1. Faithfulness is similar to obedience in that it brings you into the necessary discipline required on a spiritual journey. To do otherwise would be to stray from the straight gate and the narrow path, and only you can make the decision to stay or stray.

2. At times, being faithful to revealed truth may be difficult in a world that is constantly tempting

you to follow its created dogmas, rules, and insisting on loyalty to a cause or institution. The non-realized voices are a noisy background in a world of illusions.

3. Jesus is the best example of faithfulness grounded in truth. He stood firm against all odds of self-destruction. He was aware of His God-Christ being and could not be tempted by the principalities of this world. Jesus had a choice to make and He chose the one that would cost Him a King's ransom on this earth, for the Kingdom of God. A difficult decision for the non-realized but for the realized — a possible one, the only one.

4. At times remaining faithful to your Christ realization and revealed truth, may require a diplomatic disposition and a trust in an outcome not yet seen. Doubts with the acceptance of the reality of your being in all its glory is a common struggle for the realized in a world where doubts and confusion reign.

5. Faithfulness in what you know and others not know may cause confusion, conflicts, or breaking up of relationships. It is for this reason you, who are awakened, have the greater responsibility. "But the he that knew not, and did commit things worthy of stripes, shall be beaten with few *stripes*. For unto whomsoever much is given, of him shall be much required: and to whom men have committed much, of him they will ask the more" (Luke 12:48).

6. The responsibility involves a gentle, patient, kindness with those who have eyes but do not yet see, have ears but do not yet hear. Ultimately your faithfulness is to the Christ not to those who would thwart your direction with false claims of possessiveness.

7. A faithful servant of the Lord is one who follows the example of Jesus Christ and, at all times, willingly accepts for its known oneness in the Christ, the consequence of this world. "Love not the world, neither the things *that are* in the world, If any man love the world, the love of the Father is not in him" (1 John 2: 15).

8. The only flexibility within faithfulness to the Christ Consciousness and the awareness of your being is the one that love would allow. This occurs when others' resistance to your faithfulness is lessened or dissipates.

9. Faithfulness in all your ways to the Christ ways brings a continuous inward connection to the Christ and grounds you in uninterrupted truth. "For I the Lord thy God will hold thy right hand, saying unto thee, Fear not; I will help thee" (Isaiah 41: 13).

10. Faithfulness causes the Spiritual Heart Center to burst with the love of God and may allow continuous resting in the awareness of the Christ of your being. "I am crucified with Christ: nevertheless I live; yet not I, but Christ liveth in me: and the life which I now live in the flesh I live by the faith of the Son of God, who loved me, and gave himself for me" (Galatians 2: 20).

....

STUDENT'S STORY:

Every day (except Sunday), I continue to faithfully fall out of bed, meditate, slip on my sneakers, shorts and sweat shirt. I go downstairs for my cup of tea, piece of toast, and feed the cats. I watch 10 minutes of morning news and then set out on the one-minute walk around the corner to the gym. It is a habit now and I like it. My routine at the gym takes about 40 minutes from start to finish. It is a comprehensive work out. I meet with a trainer to insure I am safe and don't hurt myself or over do things.

You may say at this point, "So what?" Funny, I ask myself the same question. Well, let me see if I can answer that legitimate question. For one, without changing any of my eating habits I have lost over ten pounds. My clothes fit more comfortably, my balance is better, and I have more wrinkles! Not a bad trade off. My knee socks fall down and I have worn out two pair of sneakers for the first time in years! I feel better but not in a prideful way, rather a grateful way. Faithfully, patiently, and cautiously I have revisited my physical body and gotten to know it again. All the parts work and seem to enjoy being remembered on a regular basis. I realize that head and heart need the good support of leg and limb. I didn't have to "believe" going to the gym would make a positive difference in my life I just had to "belong" to the gym and faithfully present myself each day without demand or expectation. Having done so for a year, I can honestly report that I have, indeed, come to "believe." It has made a difference and it is a good one. I realize the physical disciplines are similar to spiritual disciplines.

Unrealistic expectations in either arena can be counter productive not to mention self inflating. If my expectations are too high disappointment is sure to follow. Too low, no progress/growth is made at all. Dropping expectations, demands, judgments, evaluations and just being "faithful" to the necessary discipline produces its own fruit in its own time.

This is what I have learned at the gym. "Doing" what is necessary to nourish, strengthen, and acknowledge each serves the common good. Matters of the heart, soul, mind, and body want to be attended to realistically. Faithfulness is its own reward.

+ +

LESSON: 68 — FALL - GRAND FALL

A FALL IS an individual choice of descent from a finer to a slower vibratory expression of consciousness within awareness. A Grand Fall is an individual choice to succumb to a temptation that would cause a steep decent from your greater heights of spiritual progress.

SIGNS OF A POSSIBLE FALL:

A. Drifting into more of this world (positions, service, things) and an increased attachment instead of a decreased one for the things of this world. "Christ is become of no effect unto you, whosoever of you are justified by the law; ye are fallen from grace" (Galatians 5: 4).

B. The connection with your silent prayer practice may gradually fade.

C. Avoiding a teacher (if you have one) and constantly finding a reason not to connect with a teacher.

D. Ferociously attacking your teacher with doubts, accusations, and distrust.

E. Attracted to previous individual expressions of consciousness.

F. Your spiritual, inner life is less and less of a priority. therefore, you make less and less time for your spiritual studies and silent prayer practice.

G. You justify why there isn't enough time to devote to your spiritual studies and silent prayer practice.

H. Your demeanor changes to one of discontent, restlessness, and striking out at anyone on the path. Darkness pierces your eyes and the light of Christ is dulled.

I. You feel abandoned by Jesus. Although it is a false sense, not a reality, it is heart wrenching.

GRAND FALL:

A. For a purified celibate, the temptation to use the purer, finer energy at a slower, denser rate would cause a starting over at the beginning of a spiritual walk.

B. If you are a celibate (not by persuasion, nor by choice, but through the purification process), you are constantly exposed to the possibility of a Grand fall. A celibate through purification is one who has raised the vibrating energy and is maintaining it within the Spiritual Heart Center.

C. The temptation to return the purified energy to the use of sexual activity is always just a heart beat away. Remember, temptations want something you have and temptations must be overcome one at a time, as often as they may rise.

D. The tormented memory of having once reached the awakened spiritual heights within awareness, only to reenter the dream, would make life most difficult. You may be once again caught up in the mind's mastery of emotional drama. A drama that would take you into the bowels of hell.

E. Even if you should lack the memory of all previous realizations, there would always be an incomprehensible insistent nagging throughout your lifetime.

F. Unfortunately, the grand fall has no degrees. It takes you down and may keep you on your knees throughout your lifetime.

HOW TO AVOID A FALL:

A. Be alert to the above signs. Don't convince yourself you can handle it alone.

B. Seek immediate help from your teacher or from another source, if available. A teacher or guide knows what you are experiencing and may help you to prevent a fall.

C. If you are on your own, stay connected with your silent prayer practice, no matter how insignificant it may seem at the time.

D. Sit and write a letter to Jesus and tell Him exactly how you are feeling. Don't be shy, sock it to Him. Jesus can handle it, and it may get you back on your feet toward the straight gate and narrow way.

E. Indulge less in the world's manifestations. Be kind, gentle, and patient with yourself and study more, not less, until the sense of darkness dissolves.

1. A fall may occur when you have attained a finer and faster rate of your energy vibration and intentionally, or unintentionally, succumb to temptation. This will cause your energy again to vibrate at a slower rate.

2. When you are attracted to and express your consciousness as a previous slower rate of vibratory energy, it is a fall from the straight gate and narrow way. There are, of course, degrees of falls. How serious a fall is would depend on how quickly you could get back on your feet.

3. Realizing what is happening and immediately doing something about it will lessen the degree of a fall.

4. The forgiveness and purification process lightens energy vibrations allowing it to vibrate at a faster rate. It is your responsibility to maintain that which you have realized.

5. A fall may cause struggle, distress, negative behavior, and a withdrawal from spiritual practices.

6. Any fall from the spiritual straight gate and narrow way, can take you into the shadow of darkness and may return you to a previous expression of consciousness. How long? That would depend on the intensity of the fall.

7. Because any fall is devastating, you want to prevent it from ever happening. Keep up your spiritual practices. "Wherefore the rather, brethren, give diligence to make your calling and election sure: for if ye do these things, ye shall never fall: For so an entrance shall be ministered unto you abundantly into the everlasting kingdom of our Lord and Saviour Jesus Christ" (II Peter 1: 10-11).

8. This world has a strong attraction. It is the reason you are here. However, you have the inner strength to prevent a fall and to stay with the straight gate and narrow way. The Holy Spirit in the name of Jesus Christ is the stronger attraction.

+ +

LESSON: 69 — FEAR

FEAR IS AN emotional stumbling block that you set before the entrance of the straight gate and narrow way. It is a paralyzing emotion that may delay the forgiveness and purification process and retard your spiritual progress. It is a restrictive force limiting your ability to act from an aware consciousness.

1. When you approach a silent prayer practice with trepidation, it may take you on an emotional roller coaster ride through the house of horror, walled by distorted mirrors. Your reality is so distorted there is a fear of realizing the truth that holds you prisoner to a personal separate false sense of being.

2. Fear on the spiritual walk may be so debilitating that it may override previous insights to the point of re-entrance into a belief of a personal separate false sense of being.

3. It is fear that holds your attention in the belief you are a personal, separate being. Fear of being hurt, physically or emotionally; fear of losing what you have; fear of what you conceal; fear of loneliness; fear of inadequacy; fear of lacking potential; fear of not being accepted; fear of illness; fear of death; and the ultimate fear — fear of God. The fear of knowing God; the fear of not knowing God.

4. The list of fears are incalculable. You are the creator of your fears, therefore, you have the power to attach fear to an endless emotional or physical false sense. "Fear thou not; for I *am* with thee; be not dismayed; for I *am* thy God: I will strengthen thee; yea, I will help thee; yea I will uphold thee with the right hand of my righteousness" (Isaiah 41: 10).

5. You walk into a wall of fear the moment you want anything or anyone, more than the reality of awareness and the Christ of your being. As you consciously progress with the straight gate and narrow way, concerns may transform into fears. There are fear moments of caution, moments of, "Can I do this?" "I can't do this." "How will it affect or change me?"

6. You may have a fear of having to give up that for which you have spent most of your lifetime protecting — losing or having to give up friends, position, and wealth.

7. Once you realize the Christ cannot be lost or ever be taken away, you know all else is replaceable. You could never be asked to leave, give up, or walk away from an awakened awareness of being. "And he said unto him, Son thou art ever with me, and all that I have is thine" (Luke 15: 31).

8. Everything of this world is for your use, position, cars, homes, all for your use. No thing is permanent. All is relative to this plane. All rises and all falls in relative time and space.

9. Fear is attached to that which does not permanently exist. It is the *attachment* to the personal separate false sense of being and to the transient things of this world you are constantly being asked to give up, not the *use* of them. Giving up the attachment is more difficult than giving up any thing.

10. As you rise in consciousness and your freedom from the attachment to things and individuals is realized, you are able to put all you receive to better use. Truth guides, teaches, and directs your intentional service.

11. When you hold fast to the purity of your commitment and walk the straight and narrow way, rather than losing or giving up anything, much is added. "But seek ye first the kingdom of God, and his righteousness; and all these things shall be added unto you" (Matthew 6: 33).

12. The Holy Spirit in the name of Jesus Christ only adds and multiplies — never subtracts. Whatever is given up at any given moment falls away willingly, and of your own accord.

13. Persons or things may come and go and what takes their place is of a higher order in the service and honor of the Christ of your being.

14. When a moment of choice rises and you are asked, "Choose ye who ye will serve?" It is your choice to make in fear or freedom. "No one can serve two masters: for either he will hate the one, and love the other; or else he will hold to the one, and despise the other. Ye cannot serve God and mammon" (Matthew 6: 24).

15. There is an incredible freedom whenever the choice is an immediate yes, Lord. Yes, Thy will be done. "Saying, Father, if thou be willing, remove this cup from me: nevertheless not my will, but thine, be done" (Luke 22: 42).

16. You move out of the limited fear box you have created into perfect love. Freedom in the Christ knows no fear. It is here that love casts out fear. "There is no fear in love; but perfect love casteth out fear: because fear hath torment. He that feareth is not made perfect in love" (1 John 4: 18).

+ +

LESSON: 70 — FLEXIBILITY

FLEXIBILITY GIVES YOU the freedom to adjust, correct, reconsider, and change.

1. When you begin a new silent prayer practice, you may find being flexible is difficult. You are taught to be consistent with your prayer time and place.

2. Once your time and place is established, making even a temporary change may be met with resistence. An active life style may require flexibility at anytime. Be prepared to adjust to new surroundings and accept the changes as they may occur.

3. There are times when you must adjust to a new routine. Being flexible will give you the ability to adapt your practice whenever and wherever necessary. Do not sacrifice your prayer practice in the fires of temptation.

4. If you are not flexible, traveling for a time to a strange environment could cause an interruption of your prayer practice. Do not trouble yourself with the outer appearances of change in your life. ". . . *the LORD seeth* not as man seeth; for man looketh on the outward appearance, but the LORD looketh on the heart" (I Samuel 16: 7).

5. All too often, you may become attached to a particular time, place, or sitting cushion. You want everything to be exactly the same — nothing out of order. In most situations, that would be ideal. As a dedicated truth student, you must be flexible enough to adjust to a moment of change as it presents itself.

6. Time, place, books, cushions, and shawls are useful tools but all you ever need to practice your silent prayer is "you." "But when thou prayest, enter into thy closet, and when thou hast shut thy door, pray to thy Father which is in secret; and thy Father which seeth in secret shall reward thee openly" (Matthew 6: 6).

7. As you may have to be flexible with your silent prayer time and place, flexibility also allows you to reconsider or correct decision making.

8. Necessary choices or decisions are not set in concrete. Flexibility gives you the greater vision for changing choices and decisions according to circumstances.

9. The Christ Centered spiritual walk is a direct one to the straight gate and narrow way. However, you are never locked into a rigid position on the walk.

10. Spiritual growth causes changes and requires flexibility for you to adjust and accept the changes, as they occur. "Behold, I shew you a mystery; We shall not all sleep, but we shall all be changed" (I Corinthians 15: 51).

+ +

LESSON: 71 — FOCUS

FOCUSING IS THE ability to remain single minded on the task at hand.

1. Attention gets you there. Staying attentive and focused (gentle concentrated energy) keeps you there.
2. Focusing may allow you to key in and penetrate exactly what it is you have placed your attention on.
3. Once your attention has been attracted, staying gently focused may give a clearer image on whatever it is you may wish to conceive or realize.
4. You may have heard the expression, "Pay attention" and "Focus on what you are doing." On your spiritual walk, there are many distractions. Staying gently focused, not a hard concentrated one, may be helpful.
5. There is always the temptation to drift away from the center of your being. Paying attention and staying focused are useful abilities.
6. Focusing on the choices and decisions you are making on the your spiritual walk is a natural ability of your rising vibrating energy.
7. When you are contemplating truth or a realization, staying gently focused may act like cleansing solution. It cleans away the mind's extraneous cobwebs.
8. The ability to focus is a neglected one by many truth students. One of great value, yet seldom used. Through the Holy Spirit in the name of Jesus Christ, you may easily perfect a gentle attentive focus with your spiritual practices.

+ +

LESSON: 72 — FOOD

ON A SPIRITUAL walk, food becomes a curious by product. Its selection, intake, and frequency are questions often asked. As a child you may have been wisely taught, "If you are true to your teeth, they will never be false to you." If you take proper care of the body, it will care for you.

1. Food is medicine for the body. Do not overdose.
2. Food is the body's friend. There is no need for fearing it. Too much, or too little is in your control. The control is within the mind, you are the master of the mind, and the mind the master of the body.
3. Mastering the mind is your natural responsibility. Once you realize the mind and body are not who you are, you accept the responsibility with a firm, but gentle, aware consciousness.
4. Over a lifetime of conditioning, food has been taken for comfort during times of stress, crisis, or depression. Seeking comfort by indulging in food unnecessarily is a conditioned impression attachment to an idea that is not born in reality.
5. During times of stress, crisis, or depression, it is the desire and *attachment* to the conditioned impression that causes the fear you cannot control, when it actually *is* in your power to control.
6. You may have invested your God given power in the attachment of the false belief that food will give you comfort. In truth, your comfort is in the reality of who you are. "And Jesus said unto them, I am the bread of life: he that cometh to me shall never be hungry; and he that believeth on me shall never thirst" (John 6: 35).
7. Ultimately, you are in charge. Don't spend a lifetime obsessing over food. ". . . Man shall not live by bread alone, but by every word of God" (Luke 4: 4). Give your attention to your silent prayer prac-

tice and you will have less time for food concerns. "Thou wilt keep him in perfect peace, whose mind is stayed on thee" (Isaiah 26: 3).

8. As your silent Christ Centered Prayer practice progresses, the selection of foods may change — to the lighter selections. Eating meat is not a hindrance in starting and maintaining a silent prayer practice.

9. As the energy is purified, the vibrating energy may become finer, lighter causing the digestion process to be more difficult to handle the heavy foods (meats). The mind and body will let you know when a change in any of the categories of food is necessary. You may need to adjust the selection accordingly. Do not force a change before its time.

10. Caffeine and refined sugar in food or drink products of any kind may be given up as soon as possible, but do it gradually. Don't try to jump a ten foot inner fence until your inner strength is strong enough to make the leap.

11. The body is your vehicle on this plane. You are probably taking loving care of your car. You expect it to operate properly at all times. It is the care you give it that will allow it to run well and last for the necessary time. Well, do the same for the body. Lovingly care for it, but don't over indulge it.

12. Realize the body, like a car, has a specific purpose on this plane — to serve you. The mind, senses, and body are all here to do a job for you. They are necessary on this plane. If you are to wake up, respect their position while they are here, use them wisely, but do not abuse them. "Know ye not that ye are the temple of God, and *that* the Spirit of God dwelleth in you?" (1 Corinthians 3: 16).

13. All food and drink should be done in moderation. Your spiritual progress will guide your needs. The awareness of your being takes care of every detail of your rising consciousness - mind - body. Pay attention, and be aware consciously of what the body may need, not the greed.

14. On your spiritual walk, the lust or over-interest in food, may be the most difficult to overcome. The conditioned fear and attitude of fighting with food choices, serves to increase the hold of the vibrating energies attention on food.

15. Food is not the enemy. Fear, depression, vanity, and pride may contribute to the obsession. Serve the Christ of your being in all your ways and food becomes a form of service.

16. The mind and body are rising in conscious awareness. Both mind and body, should be kept in the best of condition with a wise and balanced nutritious diet and proper exercise for the reception of the teaching of the Holy Spirit in the name of Jesus Christ.

SUGGESTIONS:

A. Approach food and drink knowing you have the sacred trust to properly care for the body.

B. Look directly at your hands as you reach for any food and food portions.

C. Decide as you reach for the food, if it is proper or necessary for the body's use. Do you glorify God in your choice? "What? know ye not that your body is the temple of the Holy Ghost *which is* in you, which ye have of God and ye are not your own? For ye are bought with a price: therefore glorify God in your Body, and in your spirit, which are God's" (1 Corinthians 6: 19-20).

D. Don't justify a desire to go against what you know to be the truth. "Be not deceived; God is not mocked: for whatsoever a man soweth, that shall he also reap" (Galatians 6: 7).

E. If you do give into an eye's choice or taste bud's salivation, don't spend time and energy condemning yourself. Start anew with a stronger conviction.

+ +

LESSON: 73 — FREE - TOTALLY

BEING TOTALLY FREE is what you are, "and ye shall know the truth, and the truth shall make you free" (John 8: 32). Truth is revealed by the Holy Spirit in the name of Jesus Christ and you are totally free in the revealed truth of the Holy Spirit.

1. A Christ Centered, fully awakened, is a totally free being. Totally free means being totally free beyond mind and body, beyond individual expressions of consciousness, and beyond consciousness' contents. It is realizing your supreme nature of awareness, a Holy Spirit. In truth, your spirit, as Jesus' is a pure Holy Spirit, the essence of a God which is truth and spirit. "But if the Spirit of him that raised up Jesus from the dead dwell in you, he that raised up Christ from the dead shall also quicken your mortal bodies by his Spirit that dwelleth in you" (Romans 8: 11).

2. Your total freedom is in the Holy Spirit of truth. "But when the Comforter is come, whom I will send unto you from the Father, even the Spirit of truth, which proceedeth from the Father, he shall testify of me" (John 15: 26).

3. An awakened, totally free being cannot be bound by a world that is constantly changing, rising - falling, coming - going. Being totally free may be a difficult adjustment. It may, at times, feel as if, "Totally free is killing me." It kills a false self who would believe itself limited, chained, and separated from God.

4. It is when you are within the Holy Trinity, waking up through the Son - Christ Consciousness - the Holy Spirit - God, and Be-ing pure awareness that you are a totally free Be-ing as the Truth.

5. You are a spiritual being and of course, as a Holy Spiritual Being you are not attached to this relative world — you are free, totally. This world knows nothing of the Holy Trinity of your Being. It cannot begin to comprehend the things of God revealed by your Triune nature. It can only marvel in wonderment of a Divinity it knows not.

6. The Holy Trinity of Spiritual Oneness is the essence of your Being. What of this world could ever touch it, ever imprison it, ever claim it? This world has no hands to hold it, no eyes to see it, no ears to hear it. It is as your aware spiritual nature, you are totally free, an unreachable spiritual being. "Furthermore we have had fathers of our flesh which corrected *us*, and we gave *them* reverence: shall we not much rather be in subjection unto the Father of spirits, and live?" (Hebrews 12: 9).

7. It is the realization that the light of awareness - Holy Spirit may testify to all the things of the Son, Jesus Christ, which reveals your reality as pure awareness. It is your aware spiritual nature of the Divine that is and always has been totally free.

8. As a seriously committed truth student, you seek to be totally free of the things of this world, to overcome, to be detached, and as the Master said, "These things I have spoken unto you, that in me ye might have peace. In the world ye shall have tribulation: but be of good cheer; I have overcome the world" (John 16: 33).

9. It is the awakening to the true reality of your being that allows the dropping away of the imaginary chains forged in the false concept of a rising mind that seeks to be attached.

10. You are not the mind nor a slave to it. You are always the master. You are the master and the rising mind is the servant. The self-identification with the mind and attachment to its contents are the chains that bind. If you don't identify with a personal mind-self that would cause a personal sense of a separate "you" from your God, then the chains that bind will break. This is waking up

11. When you claim your God-inherent freedom, the rising mind is a wonderful, obedient servant. Take charge of the rising mind in a loving, caring, master - servant relationship.

12. You are not attaining a totally free state of Being. You are waking up to the reality that you are, and always have been a totally free being within your God nature of pure awareness. You cannot be

bound by the things of this world. "Ye are of God, little children, and have overcome them: because greater is he that is in you, than he that is in the world" (1 John 4: 4).

+ +

LESSON: 74 — FREEDOM

FREEDOM — NOT the freedom that would chain you to a world of relative conditions, but a freedom based in the reality of the Christ Consciousness, within pure awareness. A freedom that allows your soul to soar to new and greater heights, to think new thoughts, releases creativity, and knows no fear. This is the freedom of being that is discussed here. Dare you live it? Dare you *be* it?

1. A fully awakened being is in the totality of the Christ Consciousness and awareness - reality. It is a reality of freedom which is experienced in its totality when you know who or what you are.

2. As an aware being, the attachment to this world no longer exists. Your allegiance is no longer to people or things. Freedom charges you with the faithfulness to the Christ truth. This world will always challenge and tempt your faithfulness to the freedom in the Christ revealed truth.

3. This world fears what it does not understand, or cannot destroy. This world thought that it could destroy (put to death) the freedom teachings of Jesus Christ. It could not. It did not.

4. The Spiritual Heart Center and a purified mind energy become one. It is from here you think and act from a deeper, purer place of being in freedom.

5. In the Christ reality of your aware freedom, you are aware of a freedom from the false beliefs, concepts, and conditions. You are detached from the desires that would bind you to this plane.

6. It is when you are accountable to the Christ of your Being you may realize the greatest freedom. When freedom exists with no restrictions, no boundaries for the rising and falling energy in the freedom of pure awareness, there is no - thing to possess and no - thing to possess you. This is true freedom.

7. During a silent Christ Centered Prayer practice, in the light of the Christ Consciousness, the power of forgiveness purifies the rising energy in consciousness. This process may free your consciousness to rise to ever greater heights of expansion in the Freedom of Being.

8. When there exists the freedom to forgive self and others, there is a trust in allowing all of life's energies to rise and be purified in the awareness of revealed truth in the Christ Consciousness.

9. In awareness of who you are is the freedom beyond words and thoughts. A freedom sought for, yearned for, and longed for, your entire lifetime.

10. Knowing you know, is the glory of the Freedom of Being. It existed before the world of illusion was, "And now, O Father, glorify thou me with thine own self with the glory which I had with thee before the world was" (John: 17: 5).

+ +

LESSON: 75 — FRUSTRATION

FRUSTRATION RISES AS an agitating emotional energy. Frustration usually rises when you are experiencing a spiritual drought.

1. When you are beginning a new silent prayer practice, a frustrating experience may occur. Doubts rise and your silent Christ Centered Prayer practice may seem in vain. It is usually more pronounced during an advanced prayer practice.

2. There will be times when you unintentionally move from the Spiritual Heart Center. The temporary relativity of this world becomes a distraction. It may become more difficult to maintain the necessary calm that would allow you to move more easily from the outer to the inner. Thus, the rising of frustration begins.

3. A yearning, aching heart for truth will move you in an inner direction. It is during these times you need to be more patient and persistent with your silent Christ Centered Prayer practice. The return to an inner calm is by way of trusting the Christ, "I am here Lord, I will wait for you." "TRULY my soul waiteth upon God: from him *cometh* my salvation" (Psalm 62: 1).

4. Because the waiting may become difficult, you tend to begin an examination and blame game on whatever you are doing and have done. In seeking to find reasons for the drift, you may cause more emotional frustrations and often anger will rise. Then you are caught in a vicious circle. Stop.

5. You may become frustrated because you no longer constantly feel emotions during a silent prayer practice, or you seek certain effects during your silent prayer practice. You have not come to realize, as your Christ awareness deepens, you are going beyond effects.

6. You tend to forget when you are being pure awareness, you are beyond the mind of feeling. So, of course, there are none of the mind feelings you have habitually experienced.

7. Emotions are all in tact and do rise as necessary. However, they have less of a feeling texture to them. In other words, you are less bound by them; therefore, you tend to think, "I am not feeling as before."

8. You have worked diligently and faithfully to become realized in the Christ Consciousness and the awareness of your being. The more you live out from awareness, the less you are attached within the world of mind feeling. It does not mean you will no longer feel but it does mean you will not be attached to those feelings, whether in or out of a silent prayer practice.

9. In the beginning when learning a silent prayer practice, you are taught not to judge your prayer practice. You are taught that there is never a good nor bad prayer practice. There isn't. When you judge a practice, you are setting up expectations. A prayer practice should not be judged. If you become attached to certain effects during a practice, you are creating barriers to moving to the deeper realized levels. Judging a prayer practice by how you feel, or do not feel, may hinder the simple return to the deepening of awareness.

10. All desires, wants, and expectations must be laid at the door of the Spiritual Heart Center. You enter without anything: desire, wants, or petitions. You come naked allowing the Christ to clothe you in His love, a love beyond understanding, beyond mind feeling.

11. During the most frustrating times, remember you can't lose what is your reality. So, with patience and kindness to yourself and those around you, you may gently become aware of that place of inner peace beyond understanding.

12. Your perseverance and earnestness may overcome any difficulty. On a spiritual walk, you are always beginning. In your reality there is no start, no finish; God is infinite. Express sincere gratitude for the dark nights as well as the bright days.

TO SOOTHE-PURIFY THE VIBRATING ENERGY:

A. First and foremost, keep a sense of humor.

B. Recommit, rededicate, and remind yourself that you are in it for the long haul. There are many temptations along the way.

C. Understand this is a phase all students encounter when in the midst of outer appearances. As your heart yearns to return to the Christ of your being, this phase will pass.

D. Do not dialogue with the frustrating disturbances during, nor after, a silent prayer practice. Be a witness but do not dialogue.

E. Read scripture either before or after a silent prayer practice. Read a word, sentence or verse, and ponder for a few minutes. Review Spiritual Principles (The Lessons), especially in the early morning hours.

F. If frustration is causing tears to flow, allow them — crying may be purifying. Be gentle and especially loving with yourself.

G. Energy rises to nag with frustrations and doubts of your spiritual progress and realizations. When this happens, rest in the realization that the mind knows not of which it speaks!

H. Continue to be faithful and persistent with your silent Christ Centered Prayer practice. Whenever there is a struggle between the inner and outer, the Christ is the stronger and it is an illusionary battle this world ultimately cannot win.

I. Accept, allow, and respect your silent Christ Centered Prayer practice wherever it is at any given moment. Be aware that from deep spiritual pain, struggle, or unknowing may come even deeper insights and a closer relationship with Jesus.

J. Don't give up, give in, and surrender to Jesus Christ, and renew your silent prayer practice with your original determined purpose.

++++++++++++++++++++++++

LESSON: 76 — GIFTS

GIFTS OF THE Holy Spirit in the name of Jesus Christ may be the necessary assistance you need to complete your spiritual journey home. Your God is a giving God. God gives eternally and in infinite variety.

1. The infinite gift of mercy, love, and forgiveness is the nature of God — thus, yours by birth right. What you may lack is the realized awareness of it.

2. Once awakened and realizing God's true nature, you too are able to share the infinite gifts of God's nature — your nature.

3. What is prodding you to want to wake up? Look at why the sinners followed Jesus. They wanted to be in His presence and to take a meal with Him. He offered them the gift of mercy yet, it was not enough.

4. They would always want more from Him. They had a need to know this man called Jesus. This man who fed the masses, who taught of caring for each other.

5. Jesus' need was to teach them to know the Father through Him and to follow Him to the God's Kingdom that was not of this world. He wanted them to wake up to the reality of the Father. "And I appoint unto you a kingdom, as my Father hath appointed unto me;" (Luke 22: 29).

6. Within a loving heart and wrapped in the nature of God, the following are a few of the gifts offered. Gifts are always available and awaiting your acceptance. They are free, no strings attached. It is your responsibility to unwrap and wake up to the spiritual gifts resting in the love of God. "And he said unto him, Son, thou art ever with me, and all that I have is thine" (Luke 15:31).

GIFTS TO AWAKEN YOU:

A. The greatest gift is the nature of God, eternal life. "For the wages of sin *is* death; but the gift of God *is* eternal life through Jesus Christ our Lord" (Romans 6: 23).

B. The awareness of God's love.

C. The gift of repentance, turning away from the laws of man to the love of God. "Cease ye from man, whose breath *is* in his nostrils: for wherein is he to be accounted of?" (Isaiah 2: 22).

D. The gift of a restful surrender to the inner guidance of Jesus Christ. "Come unto me, all ye that labour and are heavy laden, and I will give your rest" (Matthew 11: 28).

E. The gift of commitment to the God of your being. "And the LORD came, and stood, and called as at other times, Samuel, Samuel. Then Samuel answered, Speak; for thy servant heareth" (1Samuel 3: 10).

F. The gift of inner and outer guidance of teachers, angels, and saints drawing you near to your inner journey. "The eternal God *is thy* refuge, and underneath *are* the everlasting arms: and he shall thrust out the enemy from before thee; and shall say, Destroy *them*" (Deuteronomy 33: 27).

G. The gift of God awareness. Within it, are contained all of the necessary gifts. "Be still, and know that I *am* God: I will be exalted among the heathen, I will be exalted in the earth" (Psalm 46: 10).

+ +

LESSON: 77 — GRACE

GRACE IS GOD'S expressed eternal nature bestowed on its many manifestations. It is the light of awareness within which all images rise.

1. Grace is God's expression of favoring Its creation. And, as by the expressed Grace of God you are created in his image,

2. Grace is God favoring you with Its eternal nature — life. It is by the Grace of God you are sustained.

3. Grace is the "does" in "the Father does the works." "And he said unto me, My grace is sufficient for thee: for my strength is made perfect in weakness. Most gladly therefore will I rather glory in my infirmities, that the power of Christ may rest upon me" (2 Corinthians 12: 9).

4. Grace is the light that shines during your darkest moments. "Even when we were dead in sins, hath quickened us together with Christ, (by grace ye are saved)" (Ephesians 2: 5).

5. Grace is the guiding light that eventually attracts your attention and allows you to see the straight gate and narrow way. It is by the guiding light of Grace the prodigal child finds its way home to the Kingdom of God.

6. Grace is the spiritual favored embrace of God touching, holding, comforting, and protecting Its own. "And of his fulness have all we received, and grace for grace" (John 1: 16).

+ +

LESSON: 78 — GRATITUDE - EXPRESSED - SINCERE

EXPRESSED, SINCERE GRATITUDE is the appreciation of all you are. It is the glorifying joy of knowing the reality of your being. You are grateful for realizing who you are, not for whom you may have wanted to be, and for what you have, not for what you may have wanted. You know wherever you stand is holy ground. "And he said, Draw not nigh hither: put off thy shoes from off thy feet, for the place whereon thou standest *is* holy ground" (Exodus 3: 5).

1. Expressed, sincere gratitude is the one sign carefully watched for by a teacher, because it reveals a transparent spiritual progress. Its importance in your spiritual unfoldment can't be overrated.

2. Expressed, sincere gratitude is most important because the expressed sincerity in the "thank you"

is beyond the spoken words. It is assurance the necessary spiritual progress has occurred which allows for the greater enlightenment.

3. Whenever you express sincere gratitude, in the inner or outer world, there is a tender but firm new resolve. It's this new resolve that strengthens your commitment, deepens your inner connection, and allows you to become established in truth. "But he answered and said, It is written, Man shall not live by bread alone, but by every word that proceedeth out of the mouth of God"(Matthew 4: 4).

4. In expressed, sincere gratitude, you may realize, I am in my perfection and what I have is perfect. "Be ye therefore perfect, even as your Father which is in heaven is perfect" (Matthew 5: 48).

5. Expressed, sincere gratitude may give you the trust that your needs are now, and always will be met. You follow and acknowledge the guidance of Jesus Christ in all your ways. "My help *cometh* from the LORD, which made heaven and earth" (Psalm 121: 2).

6. Expressed, sincere gratitude may hold firm the conviction of all that cannot be seen, heard, or touched, in this world. It may move you to an inner closeness, which lets you know, "Yes, I can do it. I can enter the straight gate and walk the narrow way. I can go forth in the Holy Spirit, in the name of Jesus Christ, revealing Its truth, and keep my attention focused on the BELOVED Christ." "Now we have received, not the spirit of the world, but the Spirit which is of God; that we might know the things that are freely given to us of God" (1 Corinthians 2: 12).

7. Expressed, sincere gratitude may bring to the surface an inner awareness graced with a spiritual strength never before consciously experienced. It may help you to gain entrance into the straight gate and a sure footing on the narrow way.

8. Expressed, sincere gratitude may give you the awareness of replacing the old with the new, and may give you a steady footing as the new smooths the way between the old and the new — gently, and in its own time, the old falls away. "And he that sat upon the throne said, Behold, I make all things new. And he said unto me, Write: for these words are true and faithful" (Revelation 21: 5).

9. When expressed gratitude is sincere, there may be an awakening to the caring love that envelops you. You may experience a tremendous bountiful knowing of your spiritual worth. You may realize truth is for you, the one lost sheep, for which Jesus would leave the ninety-nine. It may cause the tears of gratitude to flow easily. "What man of you, having an hundred Sheep, if he lose one of them, doth not leave the ninety and nine in the wilderness, and go after that which is lost, until he find it? And when he hath found *it*, he layeth *it* on his shoulders, rejoicing" (Luke 15: 4-5).

10. Expressed, sincere gratitude may softly elicit a willingness to bring into compliance the necessary obedience that encourages a sweet surrender. It never insists, it just may take you to a place of wanting to please the Christ in all *Its* ways.

11. Expressed, sincere gratitude may define less of this world as more — and more of this world as not necessary. It may wash away greed and may bathe you in a total love commitment for your God. "Jesus said unto him, Thou shalt love the Lord thy God with all thy heart, and with all thy soul, and with all thy mind" (Matthew 22: 37).

12. Expressed, sincere gratitude may bring to mind those whom you may have offended, and those who may have offended you. It may allow you to enter a space of silence where forgiveness resides. A forgiveness that may cover a multitude of stored hurts and may release you from the pain and suffering of holding on. The releasing may create tears of purification.

13. Expressed, sincere gratitude may be a constant reminder of the power and love that resides within you. It may be yours freely to unconditionally share. It may permit you to receive truth in abundance, without limits, and you may share the abundance — without limits. "The thief cometh not, but for to steal, and to kill, and to destroy: I am come that they might have life, and that they might have *it* more abundantly" (John 10: 10).

14. Expressed, sincere gratitude warms the Spiritual Heart Center to an ever-greater expansion in the

light of the Holy Spirit in the name of Jesus Christ. "As long as I am in the world, I am the light of the world" (John 9: 5).

15. Expressed, sincere gratitude may take you to your knees in adulation of the Christ and may bring you to your feet in pure joyful humility. "This *is* the day which the LORD hath made; we will rejoice and be glad in it" (Psalm 118: 24).

16. Expressed, sincere gratitude is the expression of love without the commercialism. There are no shadows, no pretense, only the true self spreading its loving, gentle kindness. It may touch the heart of an indescribable God.

+ +

LESSON: 79 — GRIEF

GRIEF IS A gut wrenching, heartfelt emotional experience usually rising from a conceived loss.

1. Do not believe, once you are an awakened being, grief will no longer rise to penetrate your heart. It will — and it does.
2. Be not fooled, all your emotions remain intact on the spiritual walk and as joy exists, so must grief.
3. Grief is no respecter of individual expressions of consciousness. It may stalk all individual expressions of consciousness that enters the plane of opposites.
4. The plane of opposites exist in the illusion of birth and death. Accept, allow, and respect its relative comings and goings. Recognize the opposites and their timely occurrences. "A time to weep, and a time to laugh; a time to mourn, and a time to dance" (Ecclesiastes 3: 4).
5. On the spiritual walk, you are not taught to forcibly repress your grief/sorrow. You experience it. You are aware of its rising and its falling. You accept it for what it is — rising vibrating energy expressing as an emotion and let it go.
6. Grief rises as an emotion of excruciating, heartfelt, interior, deep sorrow born of the threatened loss of the false concept of self and/or the loss of a false appearance (death) of a dear one.
7. Grief may rise to fill a temporary vacuum created by the loss of a dear one. It is the attachment to grief that keeps you from moving beyond it. You are always alone inside with your grief. There isn't anything or anyone outside of your Being who can lessen the grief. It is yours to do with as you wish.
8. Grief may hold your emotions in an intense focus on the conceived loss and produce sporadic involuntary tearing and crying. And no one else, no matter how sympathetic, can enter your space of rising, sorrowful, emotional intensity.
9. Grief may not easily pass. It may cling for a time then subside and fade in the background only to rise at intervals. Memories, stained with the heartfelt sorrow you experienced, may rise again and again to trigger the emotional sorrow of your loss.
10. Since within any opposite exists its opposing force, the transformation of the memory from sorrowful grief to loving joy may occur when you are willing to express sincere gratitude for the time spent, love received, and life shared with the one you lost.
11. In gratitude, a loss may become a gain. You are the recipient of all the love expressed, an heir to all that has gone before. You may release your love one not to a grave but to the Holy Spirit in the name of Jesus Christ in the awareness of oneness.
12. A loving relationship is a spiritual gift that remains with the giver and receiver. It is an expression of your Christ being. You may convert your tears of sorrow to tears of joy by knowing that which touches your heart is your heart.

13. You may exercise your grief in the taking of pen and paper and express exactly what emotions are rising, the intensity, and the sorrow that overshadows your heart. Feel it, write it, and release it. Only the attachment to the rising grief can hold you prisoner to it.

14. The grief for the loss of a dear one is the result of having the privilege of sharing another unique individual expression upon this plane. Rejoice that you were chosen to share the love and companionship.

15. Celebrate the passing as you did the coming. Allow the dear one's love to rest in your heart with the same joy you welcomed the arrival of the dear one into your heart.

16. The consoling truth is in the realization — "And God shall wipe away all tears from their eyes; and there shall be no more death, neither sorrow, nor crying, neither shall there be any more pain: for the former things are passed away" (Revelation 21: 4).

STUDENT'S STORY:

Grief naturally rising is purifying and ultimately healing although, at the time, it may be most disconcerting. It may come and go in waves depending on the depth of loss. Grief may vary in flavor but basically it runs the same course until it has run its course. Repressing the rising of grief is not a good idea. Take it as it comes is a good motto to follow. Neither encourage it into a drama nor ignore it as if it were not rising.

Grieving appropriately at the loss of a loved one, or object of affection, is relative. To exaggerate grieving is neither therapeutic nor healing. I have learned this lesson recently with the impending loss of Calico my long time friend. While she is a feral kitty that adopted me many years ago, she has never hissed, scratched, or bitten me. I have witnessed her give birth and nurture kittens and she has never wavered from her duties.

The loss of friendship, love, and physical presence may be an occasion for grieving. The deeper the love, the deeper the capacity to grieve the apparent loss. I say apparent because I am fully aware the relationship that I have and I am certain that, although it will change in outer appearance, my friend will dwell in the bosom of my heart always.

Grief is a most peculiar phenomenon. Deep sadness, sobbing, tears, and at times, gut-wrenching contractions. It is not unlike giving birth, and in some mysterious way, also like "giving death" which is nonetheless another birthing. The awareness of this has been through the physical feelings I have had in my heart and gut while going through the grief process. There seems to be a correlation between the spiritual, physical, and mental, that cannot be denied.

+ +

LESSON: 80 — HABIT

A HABIT IS an act of interest often repeated. This lesson refers to replacing the habit of one spiritual silent prayer practice with another.

1. When you initially want to learn the silent, Christ Centered Prayer practice, you may already have formed the habit of practicing a different silent prayer method.

2. An established habit is not always easy to immediately discontinue, especially, if it is one of long standing.

3. If you are disturbed by a previous silent prayer practice, you need only to know that the easiest way to drop an old habit is by replacing it with a new one.

4. In the beginning of a silent Christ Centered Prayer practice, if the habit with a previous silent prayer practice rises to compete with the new practice you are attempting to form, do not get upset.

5. Struggling or forcing the new practice in the place of the old one will only perpetuate the old habit's strong hold on your attention with it.

6. With loving kindness, you allow the old established practice prayer method to rise and give it equal time with your new prayer practice method during the same sitting.

7. Gradually, lessen the time of the old silent prayer practice method and increase the time with the new silent prayer practice method.

8. As the new silent prayer practice method becomes stronger and deeper, the old silent prayer practice method will weaken until it no longer exists.

9. A change of a silent prayer practice need not be an arduous task, but a natural progression on the spiritual walk.

10. The Holy Spirit in the name of Jesus Christ has been waiting for you. It will gently and lovingly welcome the change.

+ +

LESSON: 81 — HEALING

HEALING IS A physical or emotional sense manifestation of change — "The blind receive their sight, and the lame walk, the lepers are cleansed, and the deaf hear, the dead are raised up, and the poor have the gospel preached to them" (Matthew 11: 5).

1. A healing is the revealing of your inner source of vibrating energy purifying from a denser vibration to a finer one.

2. Jesus demonstrated the manifestation of healing. "There came also a multitude *out* of the cities round about unto Jerusalem, bringing sick folks, and them which were vexed with unclean spirits: and they were healed every one" (Acts 5: 16).

3. Healing may occur with or without an outer source of intercession. The power you invest in the belief in your God-source may bring into manifestation a healing.

4. The major difference between the Christ Consciousness awareness and a mental/mind healing is that the physical or mental healing illness may reoccur.

5. There is the laying of hands upon self or other type of healing. This healing may occur either as a mental healing or an Christ Consciousness awareness healing. As a mental healing, it is with concentrated energy. As the Christ Consciousness awareness healing, it is the purification that cleanses the negative energy appearing as a negative condition.

6. A healing may be received even though you may be miles away from the individual healing practitioner you call upon. That is because there is no time nor space in reality. It is important to understand; healing is an innate power source of revealing the truth and may be accessed through the purification process, a silent prayer practice, acts of charity, faith, and surrender to the will of God.

7. When you come with an open heart to the Holy Spirit in the name of Jesus Christ, healing may be gifted — "To another faith by the same Spirit, to another gifts of healing by the same Spirit" (1 Corinthians 12:9).

8. There are many kinds of healing. They all come under one of the two types of healing. The mental healing or the Christ Consciousness awareness healing.

MENTAL/MIND HEALING:

A. The mental level of physical or emotional healing may occur when there is present a mental concentrated energy.

B. This kind of healing may be assisted by the intercession of an outer source. It requires the intercessor's mind to be well concentrated.

C. Whenever there is great effort to bring about a healing, it has occurred through the use of the mental concentrated energy.

D. There are specific mental practices that would concentrate the mind and allow it to develop a "healing practice." This type of practice commands a great deal of time and effort. It must also be maintained.

CHRIST CONSCIOUSNESS AWARENESS HEALING:

A. Christ Consciousness awareness healing is often referred to as a spiritual healing. However, all vibrating energy is spiritual. The difference is the speed of the vibrating energy.

B. Christ consciousness awareness healing of the physical or emotional sense may occur during instances of fervent prayer, silent prayer practice, or surrender. In truth there is no healing. What occurs is the more perfect revealing of your real nature. It is in the nature of awareness to reveal itself as whole — complete without good or bad health.

C. There have been many who have been healed when attending Holy shrines, and many who have not. Shrines and Holy places may possess a pure vibrating energy and for those who come in a surrender mode to this vibration, a healing may occur.

D. Many may be disappointed because they did believe and did not receive. However, it requires a belief beyond the mental level.

E. Often, the healing received may not be the one you are seeking. The Holy Spirit in the name of Jesus may touch that which it knows needs healing.

F. A Christ Consciousness awareness healing is a permanent one. Once healed, it remains whole because the vibrating energy has been purified. The mind is limited but awareness of being is limitless.

G. However, when vibrating energy is again misused physically or emotionally, a new negative condition may appear.

+ +

LESSON: 82 — HEALTH - SPIRITUAL

Spiritual health is an aware conscious state of wholeness.

1. In the physical sense of manifestation there exists the appearance of good or poor health.

2. In pure awareness, there are no opposites. You are always just being. There is neither good health, nor poor health.

3. As you practice the silent Christ Centered Prayer, you may be brought into an awareness of your true nature.

4. It is as your true God nature, you may be aware of being beyond good or poor health. There is a lightness of Being which is beyond the physical sense.

5. You don't realize the nature of God as good health or poor health because in God there is no need for either.

6. In God there is perfection in all things. "Be ye perfect therefore, even as your Father which is in heaven is perfect" (Matthew 5: 48).

+ +

LESSON: 83 — HOPE

HOPE IS TRUSTING in your spiritual progress through the straight gate and narrow way. For thou *art* my hope, O LORD GOD: *thou art* my trust from my youth" (Psalm 71: 5).

1. Hope freshens the internal well spring of eternal truth. It allows truth to be ever new, ever satisfying your thirst for truth.
2. Hope softens each step of your spiritual walk in the Christ of your being. "And every man that hath this hope in him purifieth himself, even as he is pure" (I John 3: 3).
3. Hope allows you to quietly wait on the Lord. *"It is* good that a man should both hope and quietly wait for salvation of the LORD" (Lamentations 3: 26).
4. Hope springs eternal. It picks you up after a fall on your walk and holds your hand as you continue with the straight gate and narrow way.
5. When your faith has temporarily withered, hope is what allows you to say, "yes" to all that the good Lord asks of you.
6. It is the Christ in you, the hope of glory that carries you through the mysteries and shadows of doubts and dark nights of the soul. "To whom God would make known what *is* the riches of the glory of this mystery among the Gentiles; which is Christ in you, the hope of glory:" (Colossians I: 27).

+ +

LESSON: 84 — HOLY INSTANT

A "HOLY INSTANT," is an instant of forgiveness and purification that occurs during a silent Christ Centered Prayer practice. It is a "Holy Instant" that may heal harmful memories and long held attachments.

1. When harmful memories rise during a silent Christ Centered Prayer practice and you immediately do not dialogue, respond, nor react, a "Holy Instant" of forgiveness and purification may occur.
2. A "Holy Instant" may occur at an instant of silence as you do not respond and again are about to become aware of the Spiritual Heart Center and rest in awareness. It cannot be measured in time nor space. It does not exists in time or space.
3. A "Holy Instant" cannot be felt nor emotionally experienced. Feeling is of the mind, and a "Holy Instant" is beyond the mind. What may be realized is the result. It is in the effect of the "Holy Instant" that you may be aware of its having occurred.
4. You may know forgiveness and purification has taken place, in a "Holy Instant," as a harmful memory rises again and you are no longer negatively affected. The memory remains intact but the suffering attached to the memory's event no longer exists.
5. Not dialoguing, not responding, nor reacting to whatever rises during a silent Christ Centered Prayer practice may allow the benefit of a "Holy Instant."
6. It is because the Christ Centered Prayer practice is a subtle, calming practice in the Christ Consciousness within awareness that a "Holy Instant" may occur. To forgive *is* divine and the "Holy Instant" is an instant of your divinity.

+ +

LESSON: 85 — HOLY SPIRIT

THE HOLY SPIRIT is the teaching member of the Holy Trinity. It is an active pure, vibrating energy force through the resurrection of Jesus Christ. "But *there is* a spirit in man: and the inspiration of the Almighty giveth them understanding" (Job 32: 8).

1. As long as Jesus walked the plane of opposites, the spirit of Jesus was an expression of consciousness individualized as a personal physical sense being.

2. The incarnation of Jesus was without sin. It was pure energy; therefore, the process of purification wasn't necessary. However, "For he hath made him *to be* sin for us, who knew no sin; that we might be made the righteousness of God in him" (2 Corinthians 5: 21).

3. Thus, Jesus identified with all things human. In doing so, He too had to overcome this world of ignorance. Jesus experienced desires as you do, He was tempted as you are, He had to care for the flesh, as you do, and He displayed emotions as you do.

4. Because Jesus had taken upon Himself a personal physical sense of being, the personal sense of the rising energies were subjected to the possibilities of impurities. Jesus progresses through the purification process by ever remaining awakened to his incarnated individual expression of realized consciousness.

5. It is as Jesus overcame this world and said yes to God's will to lay down His life for you that Jesus' vibrating energy rose through the purification process in the identity of His impersonal God Self, a "Holy Spirit."

6. It is when Jesus Christ resurrected and ascended to the Christ Consciousness of the Father the promise could be fulfilled: "But the Comforter, *which is* the Holy Ghost, whom the Father will send in my name, he shall teach you all things. And bring all things to your remembrance, whatsoever I have said unto you" (John 14: 26).

7. When Jesus The Christ ascended, the Holy Spirit in the name of Jesus Christ impersonally could descend, multiply, differentiate, and impart the teachings of the Divine as received by Jesus Christ while upon this plane. "And I, if I be lifted up from the earth, will draw all *men* unto me" (John 12: 32).

8. Thus, the Father in the child, the Spirit, Holy Spirit, of the child resides in you. "For there are three that bear record in heaven, the Father, the Word, and the Holy Ghost: and these three are one"(I John 5: 7).

9. It is because you are a descendant of the one Divine Father, you may become aware of your Holy Spirit through the ascending Holy Spirit of Jesus Christ. "And I will pray the Father, and he shall give you another Comforter, that he may abide with you for ever" (John 14: 16).

10. As you recognize, accept, and realize the Christ Consciousness you may awaken to your true awareness of being and seek to return to your Divine expression of the Christ Consciousness.

11. It is the Holy Spirit in the name of Jesus Christ that points the direction toward the straight gate and narrow way, once traveled by Jesus. It is also the Holy Spirit in the name of Jesus Christ that is guiding you in the way to the knowledge of all things Godly.

12. There is never a time when the Holy Spirit in the name of Jesus Christ, the Father Consciousness, and an individual expression of consciousness is separate or apart from that which has ascended. "Jesus saith unto her, Touch me not; for I am not yet ascended to my Father: but go to my brethren, and say unto them, I ascend unto my Father, and your Father; and *to* my God, and your God"(John 20: 17).

13. The Holy Spirit in the name of Jesus Christ is the light that shines through the darkness of the ignorance of your being separate from your God essence.

14. Who or what you truly are is a child of God. "And what agreement hath the temple of God with idols? For ye are the temple of the living God; as God hath said, I will dwell in them, and walk in *them*;

and I will be their God, and they shall be my people." (II Corinthians 6: 16). "And will be a Father unto you, and ye shall be my sons and daughters, saith the Lord Almighty" (II Corinthians 6: 18).

REVIEW:

A. The Christ Consciousness manifests as the individual expression of consciousness — the son, Jesus.

B. Jesus, in the consciousness awareness, rises as an individual expression of consciousness and a physical sense of body enters the plane of opposites which assumes the personal physical sense.

C. Jesus' determined purpose is to awaken other individual expressions of consciousness to the reality of being one in pure awareness.

D. Jesus, the personal physical sense of being, rises through the purification process from the personal physical sense of being (the overcoming) to Jesus Christ, the impersonal.

E. After the resurrection and ascension the pure Jesus Christ Spirit, the Holy Spirit, in the name of Jesus Christ descends to continue the Divine teaching and to show you the way to God's Kingdom of consciousness in awareness.

+ +

LESSON: 86 — HUGS

HUGS ARE THE gift of an acceptance greeting or parting embrace.

1. On a spiritual walk, gentle hugs usually abound among those who practice silent prayer.

2. You may tend to hug those with whom you feel comfortable, or whom you may believe have kind intentions toward you.

3. All of which is well and good in its limited purpose. Hugs are underappreciated in all they may accomplish among your brothers and sister on this earth plane of opposites. To restrict or limit hugs to a particular group of individuals, is to restrict or limit your infinite nature of giving.

4. Hugs should not be given as an after thought, or kind gesture. They should be thoughtful, caring, gentle, and given without a desire for compensation — (if you give a hug, you may be liked better).

5. A hug isn't just a feel good expression of warmth. It is a non verbal communication which allows vibrating energy of either or both recipients to express without words a heartfelt caring through the sense of touch.

6. Hugs allow you to share your calm vibrating energy, energy that may bring a calm where there is disruption, depression, or fear. "And after the uproar was ceased, Paul called unto *him* the disciples, and embraced *them* . . ." (Acts 20: 1).

7. The greatest benefit a gentle hug offers is you cannot give a hug without, at the same time, receiving one.

8. Hugs are the visible proof of the spiritual principle: in giving, you receive.

9. A gentle appropriate hug may allow you to express in a general, uncompromising way your God-loving nature. Hugs may give comfort, joy, and at times when most needed, a spiritual lift.

10. When you are presented with an opportunity to hug another whom you do not know well, and you do reach out in a non-threatening, gentle, and loving embrace, the blessings you may receive are many fold.

11. Hugs have a rescuing power. Within a gentle hug's endearing embrace, is the strongest power of the One — God's love.

12. Because of the inherent power of God's Love in every hug, healing of mind, emotions, or body may occur.

13. As a truth seeker you may be constantly seeking the experience of the embrace of God. Be aware God's embrace *is* yours.

14. The only way in which you may experience the embrace of God on this plane, is for you to embrace another. You are the heart, arms, and hands of God. You have the ability to gently hug the God of others, as the God of yourself.

+ +

LESSON: 87 — HUMILITY - A HUMBLE SPIRIT

WHEN JESUS SAID, "Yes," to the Father, "Thy will be done," He consented to suffer a torturous persecution and crucifixion. He allowed man to strip Him of His human dignity. He was the ultimate in humility. "Humble yourselves therefore under the mighty hand of God, that he may exalt you in due time" (1 Peter 5: 6).

1. Jesus was aware there was no personal sense of an "I" to defend. In this world of conditioning, you are always on the defensive. You are always in a ready mode to defend, protect, or justify your beliefs/actions.

2. Humility is within your God essence. It is waiting to surface from just beneath this world of false concepts and conditioning. With the least crack of your worldly armor (conditioning), humility may be revealed from within you. Usually, it will rise during a humiliation experience, when you know, absolutely, you are "right." Once realized, humility is ever ready to gently express itself.

3. Humility is not easily realized. You may be approaching your silent prayer practice and temptations as you do with many tasks in your daily life with, "I can do this." The misconception is there is a personal "I" who must or can do anything. "I am the vine, ye *are* the branches: He that abideth in me, and I in him, the same bringeth forth much fruit: for without me ye can do nothing" (John 15: 5).

4. The realization that may move you into a humble spirit is, "Of myself I do nothing." Therefore, there is no "self, I" to defend, protect. It is realizing "Of myself I do nothing" that may bring you to the doorstep of humility. It may give you the permission and freedom to reach within for whatever the need is at the moment — and that includes humility. "If ye abide in me, and my words abide in you, ye shall ask what ye will, and it shall be done unto you" (John 15: 7).

5. You may find humility difficult to realize and able to flow from every pore of your being until you, too, realize as Jesus did, "Believest thou not that I am in the Father, and the Father in me? The words that I speak unto you I speak not of myself: but the Father that dwelleth in me, he doeth the works" (John 14: 10).

6. It may be difficult for you, because humility is a quality of being that does not seek anything and gives up the intentional outer show when fame, honors, and platitudes are presented. "Whosoever therefore shall humble himself as this little child, the same is greatest in the kingdom of heaven" (Matthew 18: 4).

7. Pride may be a hindrance to the admission of being humble. "Pride *goeth* before destruction, and an haughty spirit before a fall. Better *it is to be* of an humble spirit with the lowly, than to divide the spoil with the proud" (Proverbs 16: 18-19).

8. Humility is not necessarily a soft spoken voice, an embarrassing smile when others praise you, nor a display of false modesty. You are asked to be humble, but firm, in all you may do through the Holy Spirit in the name of Jesus Christ.

9. The humble in spirit holds on to nothing, realizing there is never anything to hold on to because in the Kingdom of God all my needs are already met. You come as a child of God, open and trusting.

10. In humility, you know there is nothing out there that can be added to your already complete, perfect pure awareness of Being. You are aware that all is here for your use and, in reality, there is no ownership. You cannot own the temporary which is relative to the plane of opposites.

11. It may be possible for you to be a truth student of long standing and continue to struggle with the humility of your Christ Conscious realization. The lack of obedience and discipline may prevent the recognition of true humility.

12. As a humble spirit, you surrender to the Christ of your being without question and believe beyond a doubt in the path you have chosen. Then the inner and outer help that is necessary for the continued guidance for your progress on the spiritual walk is received.

13. Jesus struggled with the choice He was given. He struggled with its difficulty. "And he went a little further, and fell on his face, and prayed, saying, O my Father, if it be possible, let this cup pass from me: nevertheless not as I will, but as thou *wilt*" (Matthew 26: 39). However, Jesus never questioned His path's direction, the Father's motives, nor doubted what was asked of Him.

14. Jesus was humble in spirit and obedient. He trusted the Lord did know and understood His struggle, "Not as I will, but as thou *wilt.*"

15. When the willful pride of your stubbornness is awash in humility, you accept that which is asked of you. Throughout all your trials, temptations, struggles, on this walk, Jesus Christ gives you help and transmits it to you in ways you may not always understand.

16. Whatever the need is, there is some thing or some one who appears to assist. It is always you, who must accept the way Jesus may select to assist you. "Humble yourselves in the sight the Lord, and he shall lift you up" (James 4:10).

17. While you are still in this world and doing the service given you, it is with a humble spirit you shall overcome attachment to the rising appearances of this world.

18. Humility brings you before the Christ awareness of your being. It asks for all that you are. It allows you to remain in this world but not be of it. It is with discipline and obedience a humble spirit may fill your silent Christ Centered Prayer practice allowing you to grow in the teachings of the Holy Spirit in the name of Jesus Christ.

19. You may come to recognize that the extraordinary awareness of your Being allows you in a humble spirit to bow your head and bend your knees before the Divine of your Being. And, when you rise again, you are immersed in the realization of this "I am," that you are, and there is no higher, no lower only that which you are, always have been, and will be throughout all eternity. "And God said to Moses, I AM THAT I AM . . .'" (Exodus 3:14).

20. Humility gives you permission to drop haughtiness, pridefulness, and strips you of all pretenses. When you are humble in spirit, you walk in humility, speak in humility, see in humility, touch in humility, and love in humility. You are the Grace of God expressing *Its* existence in a humble spirit.

STUDENT'S STORY:

For years, I have prayed for the grace of humility. I knew genuine humility had something to do with "humiliation" and I have certainly had my share of humiliating experiences. It's just that they had not resulted in humility. Quite the contrary! More often than I would like to admit, the humiliating events resulted in a renewed effort to rationalize, defend, deny, or blame someone/thing else for my indignation, embarrassment, discomfort and stubbornness.

When my pride was pricked or fragile self-esteem challenged, the conditioned response was anything but humble. I discovered, quite by an opportunity, that genuine humility is at once naturally subtle and yet incredibly powerful. Its presence actually dissolves any sense of self-aggrandizement or self-consciousness. Let me tell you my story.

After a long week of preparation for a parish retreat Quiet Day, I was tired and had a million things to remember. I got up early on a Saturday morning rushing to get ready for Morning Prayer at 8:00 am sharp in the church. I was not the only one that had a lot on their mind that Saturday morning. Our Sexton had an equally full schedule. Sextons do much of the work on Saturday, when fewer people are around. In my case, we were on the calendar and scheduled for our Quiet Day. Just before starting the prayer service I had an occasion to encounter the Sexton coming down the hall.

The footsteps and body language alerted me. I intuitively knew something was a miss. Hurriedly, we spoke in the hall, and I quickly learned that a message confirming the Quiet Day had not reached the Sexton's desk until the night before! This is not good. This was a "sudden" inconvenience of great proportion! Of course, I had given proper notice, placed a note in the mail box with ample time, and followed instructions. I was in the "right." The bottom line, however, was one very unhappy staff member. My righteous, and less than compassionate streak, could be felt rising up my spine with a vengeance. Knowing enough not to have the, "Didn't you get it? I put the memo in your mailbox Wednesday" conversation at that moment, I went to my office to get my Prayer Book. I took a deep breath, gathered my thoughts, and decided to set the record straight at the next opportune time. I didn't have to wait long.

Noticing the Sexton pushing the coffee cart into our meeting room, I approached. Then a strange thing happened. I found myself oddly relaxing and out of my mouth came, "I just wanted to let you know how much I appreciate all you are doing to make this day a success." I spoke sincerely and kindly. As I left I couldn't believe my words! It was as if someone else had spoken those words.

Now, you may think this is crazy, but it was true. I did not unload with my righteous words that would have created more upset. I actually spoke the real truth, which was gratitude. The room was set, the coffee was made, and getting up on my "high horse" was totally irrelevant at this point. "What does this have to do with humility?" Well, everything! At that moment in the hallway it didn't matter a bit to be "right." The freedom I experienced as I reflected back on my passing comment, cannot be underestimated. I felt at peace, unencumbered, and light.

The fact that the Sexton would remain justified in her critique and irritation at my "neglect" did not occur to me. I did not feel the need to justify or to clarify my actions or exercise any authority. The truth was simple. I really was grateful. No one was more surprised than I was with what came out of my mouth. Call it whatever you want. Overshadowed by Holy Spirit, God . . . it really doesn't matter. All I know is that I realized the peace that passes understanding. It made no sense. I realized it nonetheless. I realized "freedom" and had no need or desire for "power," at the expense of someone else. The rest of the day went without a hitch. The split second of responding with kindness and gratitude for what was actually happening changed my experience from self-righteousness to grace-filled humility. This is not how I thought humility would be revealed. It was not acquired. Humility simply rose in me and remains an unforgettable reality of my being. For this I am grateful.

+ +

LESSON: 88 — HUMOR

HUMOR IS THE state of mind that allows you to appreciate the comical in times of stressful situations.

1. Humor on a spiritual journey is one of the best relaxers for the serious student.
2. As many students tend to do, you may begin to take yourself too seriously. It is important to maintain a sense of humor on your spiritual walk. "Then was our mouth filled with laughter, and our tongue

with singing: then said they among the heathen, The Lord hath done great things for them. The LORD hath done great things for us; *whereof* we are glad" (Psalm 126: 2-3).

3. Being a serious truth student is necessary. However, you must not lose your sense of humor. In times of sadness remember the great thing the Lord is constantly doing for you. Learn to laugh at the obvious foolishness of this world. It may keep you from getting caught up in its illusions.

4. The spiritual journey is difficult enough and without an appreciation for the comical, it is next to impossible.

5. Humor may lighten a serious situation. Many Masters will teach lessons by telling amusing stories.

6. A teacher was impressing upon his students not to be too quick to follow the crowd. He told a true story about a large, heavy set (really big) naked man who would stand on a street corner and spit upon anyone who came by. The locals referred to him as a big fool.

7. One day a taxi driver came by and was spit upon. Well, the driver had the best work day ever. So, he came by the following morning before starting his work day to be spit upon again. He had told other taxi drivers about why he believed he had been so lucky that day. Upon hearing this, many taxi drivers also came by early the next morning to be spit upon.

8. The lesson the Master was teaching was: the bigger the fool, the bigger the following. When you consider the foolish things you say and do, you can realize the Divine must have a great sense of humor.

+ +

LESSON: 89 — IMAGININGS

IMAGININGS ARE THE illusions that may occur during an intensive silent prayer practice. They are usually steeped in ego creations.

1. During intensive silent prayer practices, imaginings of self-importance may rise.

2. Imaginings of being a great teacher, holding a position of power, and doing great things in this world may grab your attention.

3. Your creativity may be heightened in the production of entire scenarios with great detail, playing out in your imaginings.

4. Imaginings are very attractive and may hold sway for a time during a silent prayer practice. Curiosity in wanting to know the outcome of imaginings prolong their multiplicity.

5. Because these imaginings are so thorough, they may be temporarily believable. Suddenly, you may believe what your destiny is and convince yourself of its truth.

6. Imaginings are temptation traps to step into. You can easily get snared by the imaginings of a mind momentarily side tracked.

7. Constantly giving attention to the self-aggrandizement during silent prayer practices slows down your steps on a spiritual walk.

8. Imaginings have no reality. As you withdraw interest in them, they will pass. Once you free yourself of indulging in imaginings, you may find the Holy Spirit in the name of Jesus Christ is there waiting to more quickly move you along.

+ +

LESSON: 90 — IMITATING

IMITATING IS TO assume for yourself another's spiritual journey.

1. You can never imitate the spiritual journey of another individual's expression of consciousness.
2. When you read or hear of how someone else may have traveled their spiritual journey, you may be tempted to imitate their spiritual walk.
3. You may seek the places he or she visited. You may seek the teacher with whom he or she studied.
4. You may attempt to imitate another's spiritual journey in great detail only to be disappointed that you did not attain the same results.
5. To read or hear about another's spiritual journey may encourage and inspire you on your spiritual walk. However, you can never imitate experiences, insights, realizations, or enlightenments of another individual's expression of consciousness.
6. Each individual expression of consciousness may share their spiritual journey with others, however, each individual expression of experiences may vary in some way.
7. True, realizations and enlightenments are the same for all; however, getting there may involve different twist and turns on the way.
8. Imitating good works is admirable and will certainly assist you with your purification process. Your intentions and response to good works may not be comparable to others. Consequently, it may affect the end result of your purification.
9. Experiences are shaded and presented differently in each spiritual journey. There is no imitating, no exact duplicating the steps on the way from here to here.
10. Be inspired, learn from others but do not get caught up in the false expectation of imitating others to gain some specific result.
11. Your spiritual journey is unique to you. Your lifetime events may take you where you need to be and to those you need to meet. Books, tapes, sermons, and teachers will appear as you are ready.
12. Jesus Christ would be the most worthy to imitate and yet, do you imitate Him? You may learn and accept His teachings through the Holy Spirit. You may follow, in some form, Jesus' footsteps experiencing all that He realized. Follow Jesus.

++++++++++++++++++++++++++

LESSON: 91 — IMPATIENCE

IMPATIENCE IS WHEN you press hard against the gates of heaven.

1. You may be progressing well on your spiritual walk then suddenly, you believe you are at a stand still. Restlessness and impatience may set in.
2. You may feel stalled, as behind a large truck that has suddenly stopped. You can't see around or up ahead so you are anxious. You blow the horn, yell obscenities, and just plain cannot understand what is happening, and why you must sit still so long.
3. You were making such good time, driving along well and now all of a sudden this complete stop. You turn the steering wheel sharply to the left, step on the accelerator, and pull full speed around and ahead of the truck.
4. You impatiently proceed only to find there has been a landslide. To the horror of the truck driver, you plunge off the washed-out road several hundred feet below. In other words, you crash.
5. Impatience may have similar effects on your spiritual practices. Because you cannot know what is

yet ahead, at times, you may move too quickly to seek negative practices that cause you to crash into the depths of darkness and despair.

6. You want to move on, you want what you want, and you want it now! These are times when you may be easily mislead by the outer world of attractive appearances of tricks and magic.

7. There is a difference in the guidance of this world and the guidance of the Spirit of God within you. "For as many as are led by the Spirit of God, they are the sons of God" (Romans 8: 14).

8. On your spiritual walk, something is always going on whether or not you are aware of it. Do not be quick to blindly force your way onward, when it may be a time for resting in the spirit. Resting in the spirit is also progress. "Come unto me, all *ye* that labor and are heavy laden, and I will give your rest" (Matthew 11:28).

9. When the tormenting times of impatience rises, "Rest in the LORD, and wait patiently for him: fret not thyself because of him who prospereth in his way, because of the man who bringeth wicked devices to pass" (Psalm 37: 7).

10. The spiritual journey is one that consists of pauses, time outs, and waiting. "I WAITED patiently for the LORD; and he inclined unto me, and heard my cry" (Psalm 40: 1).

++++++++++++++++++++++++

LESSON: 92 — IMPERSONAL

THE IMPERSONAL IS your immortal Divine source — that which you were in the beginning before the world was. "And now, O Father, glorify thou me with thine own self with the glory which I had with thee before the world was" (John 17: 5).

1. The impersonal is all that the personal is not. The impersonal cannot be identified with nor attached to persons, places, or things.

2. The conscious mind, body, senses are impermanent, not real. The impersonal is permanent, real.

3. The impersonal cannot be separated from its Divine source. Its immortal life is the source and the essence of the Divine.

4. On the spiritual walk, the spiritual activities, including a silent Christ Centered Prayer practice, contribute to the detachment and to the overcoming of the separate "personal" false sense concepts, allowing you to awaken to your impersonal eternal Divine life.

5. When Jesus spoke to His disciples of having overcome this world He was referring to the personal false sense concepts. "These things I have spoken unto you, that in me ye might have peace. In the world ye shall have tribulation: but be of good cheer; I have overcome the world" (John 16: 33)

6. Follow Jesus' example, heed His words, and overcome this world of personal, false concepts. "He that hath an ear, let him hear what the Spirit saith unto the churches; To him that overcometh will I give to eat of the tree of life, which is in the midst of the paradise of God" (Revelation 2: 7).

7. The entire spiritual journey is the conquering and overcoming attachments to the things of this world. "He that overcometh, the same shall be clothed in white raiment; and I will not blot out his name out of the book of life, but I will confess his name before my Father, and before his angels" (Revelation 3: 5).

8. As a fully awakened impersonal being, you return to the Kingdom of God and journey no more in a world of imaginary illusions. You have awakened to the Sabbath of your eternal life. "Him that overcometh will I make a pillar in the temple of my God, and he shall go no more out: and I will write upon him the name of my God, and the name of the city of my God, *which* is new Jerusalem, which cometh down of heaven from my God: and *I will write upon him* my new name" (Revelation 3: 12).

LESSON: 93 — INNER - OUTER

WHEN A SILENT Christ Centered Prayer practice is begun and you turn within, the "inner" is referred to as the inner world of realization of the reality of your being. The outer is the world of impermanency. The world you experience through the senses.

1. As you practice a silent prayer, you go within and, in awareness, thoughts of vibrating energy rise in consciousness creating a sense experience of moving from an inner to an outer expression of consciousness — an inner world to the consciousness of an outer world. To maintain a healthy balance in an outer world of appearance, the outer world must conform to the inner not the other way around.

2. An awakened Christian being, within the awareness of the Christ Consciousness, realizes truth through the Holy Spirit in the name of Jesus Christ and translates it in the language of this world. It is an experience of the inner and the outer as one.

3. When you are a fully awakened being, there isn't the Christ Consciousness and other separate expressions of consciousness. There is only the One expressing as the many. "I will not leave you comfortless: I will come to you" (John 14: 18).

4. The more alert and aware you are, the more you live out from the Christ Consciousness. As you consciously express at a slower speed of rising vibrating energy, thinking rises and you have a personal sense of being an "I, me, mine" in the outer, this world.

5. When you are realizing pure conscious awareness (the inner) and you are beyond the witness state, you are a detached Be-ing. There is no I talking; there is talking going on. There is no I eating; eating is going on, there is no I thinking; thinking is going on. All is rising within awareness, the inner. A detached world cannot know the inner. "O righteous Father, the world hath not known thee: but I have known thee, and these have known that thou hast sent me" (John 17: 25).

6. There is no "personal, person." There is just the rising and falling of the vibrating energy as thinking, feeling, and sensations constantly rising - falling, coming - going. It is the rising vibrating energy you have come to identify with as a person, the outer in this world of relativity. As Jesus could not separate from God the Father, nor can you. "I and *my* Father are one" (John 10: 30).

7. As you are aware of the Christ Consciousness, you are able to identify the different individual thoughts, sense expressions within consciousness.

8. It is the vibrating energy at the individual speeds that is referred to as the different individual expressions of consciousness. Living from the Christ Consciousness and yet aware of other states of individual expressions is what Jesus referred to as being in the world but not of it. "They are not of the world, even as I am not of the world" (John 17: 16).

9. Within pure awareness, you realize who or what you are — the nature of God being. There is no space for the rising of doubts or desires. You are completely detached and although you may experience being a stranger in this world, your identity in the Christ Consciousness is well established.

10. You are the rising breath of God. "Then the LORD God formed man *of* the dust of the ground, and breathed into his nostrils the breath of life; and man became a living soul" (Genesis 2: 7).

STUDENT'S STORY:

There is a strangeness about this type of life. It is not my own. It is God expressing Itself. It has been hard for me to meet the demands of the inner life and the outer temptations. For many years, I have tailored the inner life to fit into the time and mold of the outer life. I did make time for my prayer and meditation but the outer "unreal" world came first.

It is so interesting for me to realize that most of my life I have lived the outer life and taken the inner life as a "practice." I realize it is really the other way around and it is no wonder that establishing a balance between the two has been skewed. Reversing to conform the outer "unreal" to the inner real one is not something that happens overnight. It has taken a long time. The continual movement between the two worlds has slowly begun to reverse itself.

What I have come to "value," consistently, reliably, efficiently, and effectively meets my need. Over the years my contemplative prayer practice and daily discipline have consistently, reliably and effectively met my need to be in relationship with Jesus Christ and grow in intimacy with God through the power and presence of the Holy Spirit. Therefore, prayer is a serious value in my life. And it is time tested.

As my relationship with Jesus has changed over the years I have gradually become more aware of a spacious silent inner presence and reality that co-exists with the outer world and its ceaseless demands, noise, distractions, and challenges. Balancing these two realities (inner and outer) has not always been easy and more times than I would like to admit, I have fallen flat on my face.

The disregard (whether conscious or unconscious) of this balance between resting in God and engaging the marketplace has had dire consequences. Burn out, irritability, ineffectiveness in work and mistrust of myself, God and anyone else for that matter, to name but a few.

The healing of this situation required a reorientation of my value system gone awry. Instead of conforming my prayer inner spiritual life to the world's schedule, I had to turn it upside down and re-conform the world's schedule to honor and respect the demands of my spiritual life. Jesus' admonitions to "finding and losing" one's life and the teaching taught in this Lesson Paper resonated loudly once this realization dawned on me or should I say hit me over the head!

The "real" world to which I belong, where true happiness is realized, needs appropriately and ultimately met, is in Christ Jesus who dwells in the inner most Spiritual Heart Center of my being. This "Holy of Holies" is the pearl of great price, the treasure hidden before all ages, and the Kingdom worthy of seeking.

+ +

LESSON: 94 — INSIGHTS AND REALIZATIONS

SPIRITUAL INSIGHTS ARE moments of intellectual understanding and realizations are awareness of truth revealed.

1. There is a subtle but important difference between insights and realizations. Insights are of the mind; realizations are beyond the mind.

2. An insight you get. A realization you are. When you come to a spiritual walk with an open heart the mind, insights and realizations work hand in hand. "Let this mind be in you, which was also in Christ Jesus" (Philippians 2: 5).

3. An insight may hold your interest when you are tempted to wonder off a spiritual path, and may move you toward the direction you want to go where a realization may be waiting for you when you get there. "BEHOLD, what manner of love the Father hath bestowed upon us, that we should be called the sons of God: therefore the world knoweth us not, because it knew him not" (1 John 3: 1).

4. Through the Holy Spirit in the name of Jesus Christ, you may gain an insight giving you a better understanding of whatever truth teaching you are pondering. "Consider what I say; and the Lord give thee understanding in all things" (II Timothy 2: 7).

5. You could then work with the insightful understanding until you realize the truth the teaching is about. If neglected, not acted upon or worked with, an insight may fade over time. A realization if neglected may recede but does not go away. It will return to tug at your heart strings another time.

6. Insights are the intellectual store candies that keep you coming back for the awareness of the whole store. An insight is like a boat on the surface of a lake that allows you to touch the waters of life and if you dare to, dive deep into the depths of the waters of life (realizations).

7. Insights and realizations work together to fully awaken you to the awareness of being.

8. Practicing the silent Christ Centered Prayer, pondering truth, and reading Scripture in the recognition of the Holy Spirit in the name of Jesus Christ, may ignite an insight into a fire of realization.

+ + + + +,+ + + + + + + + + + + + + + + + + + + +

LESSON: 95 — INSPIRATION

INSPIRATION IS WHAT colors the black and white pictures of your life.

1. Inspiration rises from the spiritual essence of your Being. It is inherent in your God nature. "But *there is* a spirit in man: and the inspiration of the Almighty giveth them understanding" (Job 32: 8).

2. Whether inspiration appears to rise from within you or from other individuals, its spiritual essence is always the same one spiritual essence of your God nature.

3. Your inspirational ability exists 24 - 7. There is never any time that you lack the ability to be inspired.

4. You are always capable of reaching into the well of your existence and supply the water to quench the thirst of those who are in need of the greater vision.

5. Do not ever be fooled into believing there is a lack of inspiration because boredom sets in. Boredom is merely a momentary "timeout" from your inspirational attention on individuals and events.

6. All that is ever necessary during the times of dryness or boredom, is for you to quietly create the space for the inspirational creativity to rise from within your Being.

7. It is within your inspirational nature to express beyond any imaginable present appearances in the world of opposites.

8. Develop a reflective, contemplative mood. Allow yourself moments of day dreaming and give the thinking mind a rest.

9. You may trust that you possess the inspiration to solve any problem or find the solution necessary at any given moment. Hold fast to your belief in yourself and the Holy Spirit in the name of Jesus Christ. "Jesus said unto him, If thou canst believe, all things *are* possible to him that believeth" (Mark 9: 23).

10. Stay aware that inspirational spirit of God is within you. Therefore, inspiration begins from within you. You are self-inspiring, self-creative, and you also may drink from the well of your inspirational waters and be renewed.

+ +

LESSON: 96 — JESUS- PRE-EXISTENCE-PERSONAL-IMPERSONAL

JESUS AS THE manifestation of the Son of God, pre-existed, became the personal Jesus, son of Mary, and ascended as Jesus Christ the impersonal.

1. PR-EXISTENCE:

A. Jesus' pre-existence was in the awareness of God the Father before the world was. "And now, O Father, glorify thou me with thine own self with the glory which I had with thee before the world was" (John 17: 5). This is Jesus' pre-existence.

B. Taken to the mystical experience, the Oneness, the Word, the Son of God, the One of God, the only One of God always has been, and always will be. It is the One appearing as the many.

C. The prodigal son, each of you, returns home to your Father's house-consciousness - awareness - void before the world was. "For in him we live, and move, and have our being; as certain also of your own poets have said, For we are also his offspring" (Acts 17: 28).

D. Of course, like the many, there was never a time when Jesus did not exist. The essence of Jesus' pre-existence is the same as your pre-existence — pure God awareness. "In the beginning was the Word, and the Word was with God, and the Word was God. The same was in the beginning with God. All things were made by him; and without him was not any thing made that was made. In him was life; and the life was the light of men. And the light shineth in darkness; and the darkness comprehended it not" (John 1: 1-5).

E. Your belief that you are out here in this world, is a distortion of the truth. Truth is within. "And when he was demanded of the Pharisees, when the kingdom of God should come, he answered them and said, The kingdom of God cometh not with observation: Neither shall they say, Lo here! Or, lo there! For, behold, the kingdom of God is within you" (Luke 17: 20-21).

F. As you realize pure awareness, as Jesus did, you realize the pre-existence essence of Jesus and your pre-existence is the same, the One that becomes the many. All rises within awareness.

G. Pre, as pre-consciousness, pre-mind, pre-body, pre-world. "He stretcheth out the north over the empty place, *and* hangeth the earth upon nothing" (Job 26: 7).

2. PERSONAL:

A. The personal Jesus, son of Mary, existed and inhabited a human sense body that had all the biological needs.

B. Jesus of Nazareth the personal, was mother Mary's baby boy who was taught to crawl, talk, walk, and played as all little baby boys and girls do.

C. Jesus the personal, grew as all boys do through all physical phases of a young man.

D. Jesus of Nazareth, the son of Mary, experienced the mental and physical states of consciousness.

E. Jesus expressed human emotions, anger, love, and disappointment. He confronted desires and overcame temptations. Like you, Jesus could identify with the needs of the physical body and mind senses.

3. IMPERSONAL:

A. The impersonal Jesus Christ exists to manifest God the Father. "Neither pray I for these alone, but for them also which shall believe on me through their word; that they all may be one; as thou, Father, *art* in me, and I in thee, that they also may be one in us: that the world may believe that thou hast sent me" (John 17: 20-21).

B. The personal Jesus overcame the world, resurrected, and ascended as the impersonal Jesus, The Christ.

C. The impersonal Jesus Christ is one with the Father Christ Consciousness. "If ye had known me, ye should have known my Father also: and from henceforth ye know him, and have seen him" (John 14: 7).

D. It is within and from the Spiritual Heart Center that the Christ Consciousness vibrates the finest, purest energy. It is within the impersonal Christ that the forgiveness and purification process is quickened.

E. The impersonal Christ is a constant within your Spiritual Heart Center. "At that day ye shall know that I *am* in my Father, and ye in me, and I in you" (John 14: 20).

F. Jesus Christ, the impersonal, is one within the Father Christ Consciousness, like you are one with the Father, the Son, and the Holy Spirit. "I and *my* Father I are one" (John 10: 30).

....

STUDENT'S STORY:

As I was struggling with having to give a sermon about the personal Jesus, it occurred to me that Jesus' birth is sooooooooooo counter cultural and sooooooooooo bottom up. Jesus descends into the world to raise the world. The world thinking it is already risen, takes no notice of its need either to be forgiven or raised. So instead of repenting of the self righteousness, self aggrandizement, and egocentric idea that "we can take care of ourselves and earn our way by obeying the law, thank you," they set out to get rid of the messenger to "preserve' the temple and of course, the status quo.

Having a humble mother, Jesus comes into this world unpretentious, and yet a great saviour, Lord, Son of God born to lead the way back to our Father's Heart. The miracle of Jesus' birth is that He came as one of us, a baby, for all of us. Jesus' beginning is our beginning, His birth is our birth. He came as the Son of God, we also come (born) as a child of God. It is the miracle of our relationship — oneness that we are. That is the saving grace, the salvation born of a little baby saviour, Jesus. The greatest reason for a personal Jesus's birth is the connection we have with that birth. Although a virgin birth for some, it is a human birth for all.

The personal Jesus turns the entire way of operating upside down. Jesus challenged the value system of His day and ours today. Jesus reaches out across the sea of Galilee from Jew to gentile and back and forth, and back and forth. I love that Jesus completes my life and that He fills my moments with His presence. Can anything matter more than that? I think not.

+ +

LESSON: 97 — JOY

Joy is the inner contentment of Jesus Christ's presence.

1. There comes a certain contentment of joy as you are established in the presence of the Lord Jesus Christ. "Thou wilt shew me the path of life: in thy presence *is* fulness of joy; at thy right hand *there are* pleasures for evermore" (Psalm 16: 11).

2. It is a joy that comes from the realization that you are not alone. Jesus is a reality. One with whom you may have a relationship.

3. It is the reality of a promise Jesus made and this day, in you, may be fulfilled. It is a joy you do not want over shadowed for any reason nor can anyone take from you. "And ye now therefore have sorrow: but I will see you again and your heart shall rejoice, and your joy no man taketh from you" (John 16: 22).

4. Once you have experienced this inner joy of the Christ, it adds color to your outer world. To lose the inner joy would be to return to a black and white world. It is a joy that rests in a peace beyond understanding. "And the peace of God, which passeth all understanding, shall keep your hearts and minds through Christ Jesus" (Philippians 4: 7).

5. It is a soft, gentle joy of the Lord that sees you through the sadness of worldly events. "Then he

said unto them, Go your way, eat the fat, and drink the sweet, and send portions unto them for whom nothing is prepared: for *this* day *is* holy unto our Lord: neither be ye sorry; for the joy of the LORD is your strength" (Nehemiah 8: 10).

6. Joy is the gift that is never giddy, nor pretentious, but obviously flaunts its pleasure in the Christ. There is an abiding joy in being consciously aware of the Holy Spirit in the name of Jesus Christ.

+ +

LESSON: 98 — JUDGING

JUDGING ON THE spiritual walk is to bring into question your own silent prayer practice or the prayer practice of others.

1. Judging your own spiritual walk, silent prayer practice, or others can be a serious stumbling block. "Judge not, that ye be not judged" (Matthew 7: 1).
2. Judging places limitations and boundaries where there are none. Until you are fully awakened, it is impossible for you to know where you are on your spiritual walk, or where anyone else may be.
3. It is a mistake to get caught up in judging a silent prayer practice as good or bad. Judging spiritual practices is to stall your own spiritual walk. A silent prayer practice may go beyond the plane of opposites. Judging holds on to the plane of opposites.
4. The path is the straight gate and narrow the way. The obstacles encountered may vary according to individual expressions of consciousness.
5. There is no right or wrong silent prayer practice on a spiritual journey. There is only the necessary. You cannot judge by appearances. The outward fool may be an inward saint.
6. Individual expressions of consciousness may have similar or different experiences. It is not for you to know the hearts of others. "And God, which knoweth the hearts, bare them witness, giving them the Holy Ghost, even as *he did* unto us; And put no difference between us and them, purifying their hearts by faith" (Acts 15: 8 - 9).
7. Be compassionate and cautious with yourself and others. "And thinkest thou this, O man, that judgest them which do such things, and doest the same, that thou shalt escape the judgment of God?" (Romans 2: 3)
8. The Holy Spirit in the name of Jesus Christ knows exactly what each of you may need. Trust that all, including yourself, are receiving exactly what is necessary.

+ +

LESSON: 99 — KINGDOM

THE KINGDOM OF God is beyond the mind's comprehension. "And in the days of these kings shall the God of heaven set up a kingdom, which shall never be destroyed: and the kingdom shall not be left to other people, *but* it shall break in pieces and consume all these kingdoms, and it shall stand forever" (Daniel 2: 44).

1. When God's will is done, it is God's Kingdom, not the earthly one, that is brought into manifestation within your life, "If any man will do his will, he shall know of the doctrine, whether it be of God, or *whether* I speak of myself" (John 7: 17).
2. Spending your life building earthly kingdoms is like building sand castles on a beach. With the

first wave all is washed away. "Except the LORD build the house, they labour in vain that build it: except the LORD keep the city, the watchman waketh *but* in vain" (Psalm 127: 1).

3. Jesus taught the Kingdom of God was at hand if you would repent, turn toward God for the things of God. "And saying, Repent ye: for the kingdom of heaven is at hand" (Matthew 3: 2).

4. The Kingdom of God is eternal because it is within you, now and always. It is in the awakening to the realization that God's Kingdom does exist now.

5. God's Kingdom is your natural inheritance into all that is God's. "All things that the Father hath are mine: therefore said I, that he shall take of mine, and shall shew *it* unto you" (John 16: 15).

6. When God's will is done, God's Kingdom comes into a reality within you. "Nor will they say, 'Look, here it is!' or 'There it is!' For, in fact, the kingdom of God is within you" (Luke 17: 21).

+ +

LESSON: 100 — LANGUAGE

LANGUAGE IS A silent, spoken, and universal expressed form of communication. "Let the words of my mouth, and the meditation of my heart, be acceptable in thy sight, O LORD, my strength, and my redeemer" (Psalm 19: 14).

1. SILENCE:

A. Within the awareness of the Spiritual Heart Center, through the Holy Spirit, in the name of Jesus Christ, is a silent language translated by the intellect.

B. The heart and mind of God are one, and speak the language of silence. "Be still, and know that I *am* God . . ." (Psalm 46: 10).

C. On your spiritual journey, you may find you speak less and seek the language of silence more.

D. With a silent prayer practice, you may hear a silence that is deafening.

E. In the silent language of God, the Holy Spirit teaches you the truth in the name of Jesus.

F. In the silent language of your being, you may awaken to the reality of your God awareness.

2. SPOKEN WORD:

A. When the silent Word of God was spoken aloud, it became visible; it became flesh. "And the Word was made flesh, and dwelt among us, (and we beheld his glory, the glory as of the only begotten of the Father,) full of grace and truth" (John 1:14).

B. The spoken word possesses power. Feelings may be hurt, lies may be told, and wars may be started. All with the use, or misuse, of language. There are many spoken words within the many different languages. Language is subjected to culture conditioning. It evolves and expands through the thought process.

C. Language is conditioned through the use of culture. The nuances and attached specific word meanings evolve through the communication interactions among its people. The meanings and differences in words may challenge you to go beyond the spoken word.

D. Scripture tells the story of a prideful people who would build a city and a tower of Babel. "And they said, Go to, let us build us a city and a tower, whose top *may reach* unto heaven; and let us make us a name, lest we be scattered abroad upon the face of the whole earth" (Genesis 11: 4).

E. As mortals they could build a city, a tower, or whatever they wish, but they were not mortals. They were children of God. Therefore, they were scattered over the earth speaking in many different languages. "So the LORD scattered them abroad from thence upon the face of all the earth: and they left off to build the city" (Genesis 11: 8).

F. They would no longer be a one identifiable people unto themselves. They had become the many peoples of the earth, for God creates in infinite variety. Individual expressions of consciousness were not created to pridefully build cities and towers.

G. God expands and differentiates individual expressions of consciousness. The people of the earth were driven to go beyond the barrier of one language and of the false sense of being mortal.

H. The people of today continue to build cities and towers that reach the heavens, but they will not find God in them. As with the Babel story, more confusion is created. However, often within confusion, clarity is found.

3. UNIVERSAL LANGUAGE:

A. There is a universal language of the purest vibrating energy that all the peoples of the earth may share — Love/Caring. It is a language all understand and may respond to favorably.

B. Because love is your God nature, it does not have to be learned. It need only be gently expressed. "And we have known and believed the love that God hath to us. God is love; and he that dwelleth in love dwelleth in God, and God in him" (I John 4: 16).

C. Love is easily expressed with the silent, spoken language, or with the purest vibrating energy. It, therefore, is threefold in its ability to communicate.

D. The universal language of God's love, your nature, is unconditional. It requires no translation, has no nuances. It causes no harm and may bring comfort where needed. "Love worketh no ill to his neighbour: therefore love *is* the fulfilling of the law" (Romans 13: 10).

E. Love may be transmitted with a twinkle in the eyes, a gentle touch, a hug, kind words, acts of charity, or sharing moments. "And this commandment have we from him, That he who loveth God love his brother also" (I John 4: 21).

F. When you are not aware of the silence or lost for words, speak the universal language of love, and the cities and towers you are building will reach into the heart of God.

+ +

LESSON: 101 — LAYERS

THE THREE MAJOR layers are spiritual, psychological - mind, and physical, and within each major layer exist many levels. The mistake that may be easily made is for you to get hung up in one layer or the other.

PHYSICAL SENSE LAYER:

A. It is an attachment to a physical sense body that is a drag on a spiritual walk.

B. Being obsessed with the physical sense of a body, keeps you in the body consciousness until you progress beyond it. "Therefore I say unto you, Take no thought for your life, what ye shall eat, or what ye shall drink; nor yet for your body, what ye shall put on. Is not the life more than meat, and the body than raiment?" (Matthew 6: 25).

C. The body should be cared for and its needs met. It is a valuable instrument of transportation on a spiritual walk.

D. As with an automobile, keep the body in top condition and it will serve you well.

E. The physical sense of body is to be respected, but not worshiped. It is what is within you that is sacred. "Know ye not that ye are the temple of God, and *that* the Spirit of God dwelleth in you?" (Corinthians 3: 16).

PSYCHOLOGICAL - MIND LAYER:

A. The psychological layer is similar to the physical layer. However, this is a layer in which you may more easily get caught up in for a longer time.

B. This layer at the many different levels contains the possibilities of bliss, holy visions, fortune telling, and a manipulative mental power of the physical sense layer, all of which may be difficult to move beyond.

C. There may be prayer practices that are grounded in scientific or psychological models. It is not necessary for you to bog yourself down with scientific or psychological theories.

D. All of the psychological knowledge you learn on this plane is relative to this plane. You will be unlearning as you realize truth.

E. An illusion is an illusion, no matter in what layer or level it appears.

F. A silent prayer practice is to assists you to go beyond the physical sense of body, mind, science, and psychology. Worldly knowledge is useful as an occupation in a specifically related field. To apply these theories to a silent prayer practice is to prolong your spiritual walk.

G. It would be as if you had purchased an airplane ticket with many stops before you arrived at your final destination. The silent, Christ Centered Prayer practice is a direct, non-stop flight — the straight gate and narrow way into the Spiritual Heart Center, and the awareness of your being.

SPIRITUAL LAYER:

A. The spiritual layer is the purer, finer vibrating energy, and its many levels may not be any easier to go beyond than the two previous ones.

B. The spiritual layer is expansive, may be blissful, express the appearances of Jesus, Blessed Mother, saints, and loved ones. Therefore, it may hold your attention and interest longer than necessary.

C. You are not asked to give up the spiritual layer, nor any of the other two. You are passing through them to the reality of your being of pure awareness.

1. You are born on the earth plane through the spiritual vibrating energy layers, the psychological, and the physical sense. You return within the reality of your being through the same layers in a reverse order. There is no skipping any layer nor any necessary level within the layers.

2. How long you may remain in each layer - level, on your return journey, depends on the identity and attachments you form while in any of the layers and any of the many levels. Each level within any layer must be overcome. There is no progressing from a first level within a layer to the tenth level. All work within any level must be finished. "I have glorified thee on earth: I have finished the work which thou gavest me to do" (John 17: 4).

3. Because the three layers exist in consciousness, you may experience any and all of the three layers while in the world. However, you must be completely detached from each layer - level to realize fully the awareness of your being and your glory before the world was. "And now, O Father, glorify thou me with thine own self with the glory which I had with thee before the world was" (John 17: 5).

4. All three of the layers remain available for your use once you are fully realized. The difference being, you will have realized you are not in the expressed three layers, the three layers are within you. "I am the door: by me if any man enter in, he shall be saved, and shall go in and out, and find pasture" (John 10: 9).

5. You do not have to drag yourself through the three layers and their many levels any longer than is necessary. The reality of your being, in pure awareness, is beyond consciousness and the layers expressed in it. The spiritual journey through these layers, in consciousness, are necessary but are not your permanent reality.

6. The work of the Holy Spirit in the name of Jesus Christ, is to progress you as smoothly as possible

through each of the layers until you rest where you never left. "This *is* my rest for ever: here will I dwell; for I have desired it" (Psalm 132: 14).

+ +

LESSON: 102— LAZARUS RISING

THE LAZARUS RISING refers to the dormant energy stored at the base of the physical sense body's spine.

1. Many of the Bible events have a deep profound teaching. "And when he thus had spoken, he cried with a loud voice, Lazarus, come forth. And he that was dead came forth, bound hand and foot with graveclothes: and his face was bound about with a napkin. Jesus saith unto them, Loose him, and let him go" (John 11: 43-44).

2. For Christians, Jesus bringing forth Lazarus from the dead, at the metaphysical - mystical level, translates to the energy rising from the base of the physical body sense form. The Lazarus energy, that may activate and rise, has been dormant at the lower spinal level.

3. Calling, "Lazarus, come forth," represents the dormant energy and the, "loose him, and let him go," is the untying of the knots (purifying). As you purify your energies, the dormant energy may slowly rise through the spiritual centers to the crown of the head.

4. When you begin the forgiveness and purification process, the dormant energy may begin to rise automatically and awareness may expand.

5. The activation of this energy may also be forced by certain practices. But these types of practices may cause all kinds of negative behaviors to occur and should be avoided. When you are doing good works in thought, word, and deed, the purification process is a natural process. It should never be forced.

6. Always, when you close your eyes to practice the Christ Centered Prayer, be conscious that Jesus is your inner guide and if the Lazarus rising energy should become active, consciously allow Jesus to bring forth the Lazarus rising. Stay aware, but do not attempt to guide or direct the energy yourself.

7. As this occurs, it allows the energy to rise through the spiritual centers. For some, it may cause shaking of the body or other effects may occur. When it is ready to move to the top of the head, it will move smoothly and rapidly from the bottom up.

8. Your body may feel as though it is a foot, or more off the cushion. You may even feel you are going to leave (die) this plane. If it should overwhelm you or frighten you, repeat, "God *is*, God *is*," until you feel consciously in control again. Then consciously bring the energy back to the Spiritual Heart Center. It is here you may maintain it.

9. If you wish to have additional information, talk with a teacher. For now, what is most important is that you are aware of what may take place and be receptive.

10. The process has its benefits and gifts. You may be gifted with certain realizations and spiritual gifts. It is best to have an experienced teacher to work with you. However, you are not alone. Jesus is present with you on this inner journey and holds you close in the Christ Consciousness.

STUDENT'S STORY:

The following is an entry in my journal that was written on the fourth day of a 10 day silent prayer retreat. At the time, I was 40 years old.

June 15, 1988, this is what I learned today:

1. There is an energy in me that is more powerful than I would have ever imagined.
2. This energy is invulnerable.
3. This energy is *so* powerful
4. My body contains this life energy force and can be empowered by it
5. This energy expresses itself to me in great waves of power rising up my spine and circulating around and around like an orbit.
6. I am more than my body.
7. I AM connected to God and I AM held in God's palm.
8. I AM loved by the ONENESS of life

When this experience occurred, it was undeniable. I became aware of the intense energy when it spontaneously began in my lower gut area and rose with speed and intention and intensity that could not be modified. I simply rode the wave of pulsating energy for several minutes. While the energy circulated in a motion that rose up my spine to the top of my head circling back up through my feet to my head and around and around and around, I could see the trail of light completing the circuit. I experienced my finger tips and saw light emanating from them at a distance of about one foot. The energy beams of light were very clearly visible to my opened eyes and the energy extended out of each of my fingers. It was like a laser of white light and it was so powerful that I had little control.

I experienced an energy that came from deep within my own core that up until that moment I had no first hand experience, although I had read about such energy in spiritual books. Without my intending, expecting, or manipulating, the energy simply came, appeared, and ran its course. The muscles in my body had a difficult time containing the intensity of the energy while it was moving. There was a contraction and jerking of my muscles as they accommodated this phenomenon. It was not painful, it was remarkable and I just sat there in awe of what was taking place fully aware that in some mysterious way I was being shown something about my body self which I had never known before.

This was not a dream, not imaginary, nor esoteric. This was just Sandy having a peek into a reality she had up to that point never realized. When the experience subsided I found myself relaxing and had the sense of being energy without boundaries. Of course, I certainly was in my body and the boundaries were there at the same time as this unbounded spacious sense of an energy field in which I existed also.

The comments above are the reflections on this experience. The knowledge through this experience and the assimilation and integration of it has taken years. On the one hand, it seemed extraordinary and, on the other, it was just a matter of fact. I absolutely knew that I was certainly more than meets the eye.

Words are not great at explaining this experience, but suffice to say, it was as real as any other sensory learning I have had. Realizing my essential nature, body, mind, personality, was shot through with light and energy certainly re-orientated my understanding of the depth and breadth of the fact that we are truly more than we appear and at the same time, we appear as we are.

The paradox of form and energy and energy and form for me was no longer an intellectual curiosity, construct, or argument; it was simply a reality — a vibrant reality that continues to be active and is maintained in my spiritual heart center. I have since come to understand that if this energy is forced to ascend before the readiness exists, harm may occur to an individual's mind and/or body. Therefore it is a stage in our spiritual journey that must be respectfully allowed to unfold in its own time.

What difference it made in my life was simply in the area of insight, understanding, purification, and awareness. Another curtain had been pulled aside and I was privy to a dimension of reality. The interchangeability of matter and form and energy seemed to clarify. What may have seemed beyond my ability to comprehend or believe no longer was a mystery.

+ +

LESSON: 103 — LESSONS - MISTAKES - ERRORS

Lessons, mistakes, and errors are your playground of learning opportunities.

LESSONS:

1. Lessons are the manifested guidance necessary for you to overcome the attachment to this world. "I will instruct ye and teach ye in the way which thou shalt go: I will guide thee with mine eye" (Psalm 32: 8).

2. The first lesson may appear immediately upon your attachment to the rising false belief in a personal sense of "I." "Shew me thy ways, O LORD; teach me thy paths" (Psalm 25: 4).

3. Lessons come in many forms, shapes, sizes, and descriptions. They may cause a sense of pain and suffering. "Though he were a Son, yet learned he obedience by the things which he suffered" (Hebrews 5: 8).

4. You attract the necessary lesson/s created by your attachment to your false beliefs. It is your response to the lesson that will determine whether a lesson will be repeated. Lessons have a way of pricking at your illusionary dream state of this world. "And all thy children *shall be* taught of the LORD; and great *shall be* the peace of thy children" (Isaiah 54: 13).

5. Usually, lessons are not welcomed on your earthly sojourn. They are often unexpected and seldom understood. Lessons may aggravate, irritate, or stimulate you into beginning a spiritual walk toward a spiritual journey within.

6. A lesson may often come unannounced and hang around until it causes a spiritual itch within your consciousness. A lesson is thorough and may repeat many times and in various ways before you "get it."

7. A lesson may come in parts or sections. So, believing you have learned a lesson in its entirety may be deceptive. The same lesson may appear in different form, as often as is necessary. Just when you may believe you have learned the necessary lesson and are completely off guard, it may resurface in another form.

8. Lessons always teach you where you are not on the spiritual walk. "For when for the time ye ought to be teachers, ye have need that one teach you again which *be* the first principles of the Oracles of God; and are become such as have need of mild, and not strong meat" (Hebrews 5: 12).

9. Lessons continue their appearances until the detachment enlightenment occurs, a personal sense of "I" no longer exists in your consciousness, and you are fully awakened. "For we know in part, and we prophesy in part. But when that which is perfect is come, then that which is in part shall be done away" (I Corinthians 13: 9 - 10).

MISTAKES — ERRORS:

1. Mistakes and errors are lessons waiting to happen. They may take you in an unintended direction. "When I was a child, I spake as a child, I understood as a child, I thought as a child: but when I became a man, I put away childish things. For now we see through a glass, darkly; but then face to face: now I know in part; but then shall I know even as also I am known" (I Corinthians 13: 11 - 12).

2. Mistakes and errors present opportunities for learning experiences. "Wherefore he saith, Awake thou that sleepest, and arise from the dead, and Christ shall give thee light" (Ephesians 5: 14).

3. Mistakes and errors give you the opportunity to begin again and again and they teach you humility while they tug at false pride.

4. Mistakes and errors may be warning signs to slow you down and keep you in the present. Learn from them and then drop them. Reviewing and regretting mistakes is a waste of time and energy and may give cause for repeating them.

5. You may have the misconception that making a mistake or error, while on a spiritual walk, is a

lack of progress on your spiritual walk. The opposite is true, if you are alert to the lesson you may realize from a mistake or error.

6. You are always perfect. Your perfection has and always will exist. Perfection does not exclude mistakes and errors. Mistakes and errors are within perfection — learn from them. You have all of eternity to travel to where you are. Don't hurry through a task you are given. Savor each moment of any task, as though it were your last.

7. There are no such things as mistakes or errors on your spiritual walk. All mistakes and errors are teachings through the Holy Spirit in the name of Jesus Christ. Value the days of mistakes and errors as you would value the days without them.

STUDENT'S STORY:

Lessons do appear sequentially as I have been ready to receive them but they never stop once they make their way into my conscious awareness. If anything, they seem to recycle round and round supporting and fine tuning from every angle. I don't finish with the humility lesson and move on to detachment. Quite to the contrary! Once gained twice maintained would be my caution.

The recycling of lessons has helped etch them in my mind and heart. I find that I am quicker to recognize a particular lesson by its stripes and respond appropriately by either letting go or refusing to empower. I continue to have my share of mistakes and errors. However, each lesson realized, and overcome moves me in the direction of interior freedom and peace. A peace which most definitely passes understanding.

+++++++++++++++++++++++++

LESSON: 104 — LISTENING

LISTENING IS THE inner ability to hear the silent voice of God. It is in the silent stillness, within the Spiritual Heart Center, you may come to know God. "Be still, and know that I *am* God: . . ." (Psalms 46: 10).

1. As you rest in your Spiritual Heart Center within awareness, the silent voice of God may be heard. And, patiently listening allows you to wait on the Word of God. This is possible whether in or out of a silent prayer practice.

2. Over time, listening to the inner silence within your Spiritual Heart Center, you may find there is a silent, sacred language that speaks to you, one you may come to understand more easily than any language of this world. "The tongue of the wise useth knowledge aright: but the mouth of fools poureth out foolishness" (Proverbs15: 2).

3. As you practice the silent Christ Centered prayer, the ability to tune a listening ear into the stirring of the Holy Spirit and hear the word of God may increase. "Then said Jesus to those Jews which believed on him, 'If ye continue in my word, *then* are ye my disciples indeed; and ye shall know the truth and the truth shall make you free'" (John 8: 31-32).

4. The inner silence may become so deafening it is loud, clear, and listening with the attitude, "Speak LORD," opens the inner ear to the silence within. ". . . Speak, LORD; for thy servant heareth . . . (I Samuel 3: 9).

5. Listening to the inner silence, may assist you in the ways and direction your spiritual walk in the outer may take.

6. Listening to the silence within the awareness of your Spiritual Heart Center, may rest the mind

and calm the vibratory energy. Over time, you may find you listen more and speak less because whatever you hear from within translates to your outer action of doing.

7. If you form the habit of turning within to your Spiritual Heart Center, with a listening ear, you may acquire the necessary guidance in your every day practical living.

8. Because there is a reverence for the words the message carries, less words are more. The mind and heart of God are one.

9. When necessary, the mind may obediently translate that which rises from within your Spiritual Heart Center.

10. The more you rest in a listening mode within your Spiritual Heart Center, the more you may hear. The Holy Spirit in the name of Jesus Christ is always communicating with you. Listen and you may hear.

+ +

LESSON: 105 — LONELINESS

LONELINESS IS THAT God awful forsaken feeling deep inside.

1. The major difference between loneliness and aloneness is one of knowing your reality of being. Loneliness is seeking, aloneness is resting.

2. Pure awareness is the calm, peace, and love that you are. It is your oneness, all in the One. Realizing this, and then having to return to a world of the mind's imaginings, where you are not able to express or embrace all with the Christ's love, causes an all pervasive loneliness.

3. As you progress with a silent prayer practice, many emotions are experienced. Loneliness may be the most devastating and threatening emotion to your prayer practice. It may begin to rise early in your practice, however, loneliness usually rises as you are progressing more toward the pre-advanced or advanced stages of your practice.

4. You may feel totally cut off and disconnected from personal relationships (not to be confused with detachment), have a heart that aches for understanding the depth of your loneliness, and a strong desire for the company of others. When this occurs, there may be moments of loneliness that border on despair.

5. At times even God may seem to have forsaken you. The old life is dying and until the new is fully born, your heart may ache for human companionship, as your soul cries out for God. ". . . My God, my God, why hast thou forsaken me?" (Mark 15: 34).

6. During these difficult times, you may need to be reminded to eat, rest, and care for the form that serves you on this path. It may be wise during the extreme loneliness to engage in a relaxed activity — a movie, a swim, a walk, a fine restaurant. These activities may, for a time, remove your focus on the depth of the emotion.

7. The lonely experience desires the company of others, wants it. For a time, you may find you must go through a period when no thing nor anyone can fill the empty space inside. Your silent prayer practice is actually creating the emptiness and space which allows the loneliness to rise in preparation for knowing the truth of your being.

8. The loneliness you struggle with is the truth of seeking the recognition of your own reality. It is this for which you are longing, and it is this for which the emptiness and space has been created.

9. As you begin to wake up to your reality, it isn't easy to live in a world of the mind's creation. You cannot hold on to anything nor anyone. You are learning it is not possible to hold on to what is constantly rising and falling. All here must deteriorate.

10. No one seems able to fill the emptiness inside, not even a teacher. You just want someone, something and until you realize you are complete and whole, the empty lonely feelings may upset your inner calm.

11. The best you can do during these times is to know all is just going on. Talking is going on, walking is going on, work is going on. There is no one doing anything.

12. It is all happening. Whatever needs to get done will get done. You are a witness to it all. And yes, it can be a helpless and lonely feeling at times, but that too rises and falls.

13. Jesus understands the depth of your loneliness. He experienced it. "O Jerusalem, Jerusalem, *thou* that killest the prophets, and stonest them which are sent unto thee, how often would I have gathered thy children together, even as a hen gathereth her chickens under *her* wings, and ye would not!" (Matthew 23: 37).

14. All rises and falls within awareness and as you live out more from your reality, that which you are becomes more pronounced and this world less. As this world fades, you are where you never left and in the awareness of your being there is no loneliness.

++++++++++++++++++++++++++

LESSON: 106 — LONGING

LONGING IS THE inner yearning for that which you are. It is the longing within your heart to know the mystery of God.

1. Longing prompts you to seek, investigate, ponder, and walk a spiritual path.

2. It is an unidentified longing that may turn you in the direction of your inner reality with the help of the Christ Centered Prayer practice.

3. When you have strayed from the straight gate and narrow way, longing brings you back.

4. Longing instills a belief there *is* more during the dark days and darker nights on the walk.

5. Longing is an itch that can't be scratched. The deeper the itch, the greater the courage to enter the Spiritual Heart Center.

6. Longing never lets you forget there is something beyond the plane of opposites. It may cause a restless twisting and turning, until the turning is within.

7. The longing on a spiritual walk creates an inner longing for the Holy Spirit of truth in the name of Jesus Christ. "My soul breaketh for the longing *that it hath* unto thy judgments at all times" (Psalm 119: 20).

8. At the end of your spiritual walk, you may find that the inner longing is only contented in the resting within the awareness of your being through the Holy Spirit in the name of Jesus Christ.

STUDENT'S STORY:

Trinity Sunday falls each year on the first Sunday after Pentecost. Its challenge to preachers cannot be understated. Unlike Pentecost Sunday, full of vivid drama with descriptions of wind, tongues of fire, and newfound faith, Trinity Sunday asks preachers to articulate a doctrine articulated in 325AD at the Council of Nicea, and read it back into the scriptural texts provided. It is the only Sunday that celebrates the doctrine and in this instance that of God as One in Three Divine Persons: Father, Son, and Holy Spirit. The Trinity, as it is commonly referred to.

This is perhaps the quintessential mystery of Christian faith. As I approached this task, I had my usual array of scriptural commentaries, exegetical books, Bible dictionaries, concordances and the like all piled neatly under my coffee table. For some reason I found myself in a quandary unable to find any inspiration whatsoever for the sermon. As each day passed, I thought, "Surely tomorrow will bring some clever new insight or story." These never appeared.

It was Saturday night and still nothing for the sermon, not even an opening line let alone a closing statement. I began to feel a deep panic, if not despair, settling in as I went to bed Saturday night knowing full well that I would, in fact, appear at St. Francis the next morning whether I had a sermon or not and "Not" was an experience of which I had no previous knowledge at all! Even after my early morning traditional cup of tea and a piece of toast not to mention the shower (where very often I would find some last minute sermon insights), nothing rose in my imagination. I knew that perhaps the day would come when "I" would have to give way to "Jesus" in a way that preempted "My" organizational plans. My teacher had said many times, "All you ever need do is to totally trust Jesus." I just wasn't prepared for Trinity Sunday 2005 to be that Sunday of total trust. But it was.

As I prepared and reviewed the order of worship with the acolytes and organist, I appeared calm and collected, however, inside I was anything but! My internal dialogue went something like this, "What am I going to say?" "What am I going to do? "I have no sermon." If there were a way out I would have taken it. There was not. This day I knew the only way "out" was in fact, the way "in." All I had to hold on to at that point was the last line from the gospel of Matthew I was about to read, Jesus says, ". . . and, lo, I am with you always, *even* unto the end of the world. Amen." (Matthew 28: 20).

As the congregation sat down I stood perfectly still, feet firmly planted on the wooden floor for balance, and in utter silence. My mind was a total blank. I stood for what seemed to me like an eternity and then suddenly a thought rose. I began to speak. "Today we are supposed to reflect on the mystery of God. Our news is full of rhetoric on Intelligent Design, Darwinism, and Evolution of the Species. Everyone seems to have the answer to what is fundamentally a mystery. The mystery of creation and the origins of life. What I have come to believe is that dogmas, doctrines, platitudes, books and words do not save. When everything has been said and done, they each fall short of the mark. When trying to find the words, trying to articulate the mystery of God in creation, the mystery of God in Christ, the mystery of God in Spirit, and the mystery of God given in Baptism to each of us, I find I am absolutely lost for words." I paused and stood still.

At this time, I was unaware that tears were welling up in my eyes and starting to literally drip down on my alb. I continued to wait on the Lord, and again a thought came this time from deep, deep in my heart. I said slowly and through the tears, "All that I know is that in my life I have longed in the deepest part of my heart for that which I cannot understand, for that which I cannot find words because the longing comes not from my head but from the silence of my heart. I have spent my entire life in hot pursuit of that mystery. And what I can say to you today is only this; that mystery for which I have so deeply longed for has even more deeply longed for me."

Again I paused and at this point I was aware of the tears and tinge of embarrassment at what I might say next. I concluded, "My message to you is, long for that which you cannot know in your head, cannot write on a piece of paper, has no name, no form, but can only love. Then take that mystery which longs for you and for me, and embody it, enact it, and give it to every person, plant, and animal on the planet and in that way, you shall know God."

The sermon ended in the same silence in which it began. I turned around with tears of gratitude. Not only had I preached, but also more importantly I had received a message and a teaching. I knew for a certainty, that mystery I had so deeply longed for, longed even more deeply for me. My life, my heart, my head, and my preaching, for that matter, have since never been the same.

++++++++++++++++++++++

LESSON: 107 — LOVE (GOD'S)

LOVE (GOD'S) — poets write about it. Romance novels are full of it. You use and misuse it and yet seldom understand its true nature, purpose, or meaning. It is a word you often use with limits placed on it. "I'll love you, if you love me. I love you because you love me, or I love this one but not that one."

1. Although many have tried to imitate God's love with pen in poems, prose, and novels, its true essence is never quite captured through speech, nor by the written word. God's love is purest of the pure, without ingredients or mixture of any kind. It cannot be bisected, analyzed, or commercialized. It competes and compares only with Itself. "BEHOLD, what manner of love the Father hath bestowed upon us, that we should be called the sons of God: therefore the world knoweth us not, because it knew him not" (1 John 3: 1).

2. God's love is acknowledged presence of Its creation. It is God's acceptance of the responsibility for you who have been created in Its image.

3. In its simplest expression, it colors the grass, it paints the sky, it explodes a mustard seed, and allows the sun to rise and rain to fall indiscriminately. "The LORD hath appeared of old unto me, *saying,* Yea, I have loved thee with an everlasting love: therefore with loving kindness have I drawn thee" (Jeremiah 31: 3).

4. God's love gives all to all, and holds back nothing from those who would share in the constant multiplying of the loaves and fishes. God's love does not subtract. It can only multiply and add.

5. God's love empowers you with unimaginable courage, sacrifice, obedience, and a firm direction. It is the most caring of your nature. God's love feeds you when you are hungry, it holds you when you are lonely. God's love cares for you through the wilderness times of your life, and it walks with you through the valley of death. "Yea, though I walk through the valley of the shadow of death, I will fear no evil: for thou *art* with me; thy rod and thy staff they comfort me" (Psalm 23: 4).

6. God's love transcends the physical appearance, gender, mental thought, or the attachment to people and things. God's love radiates and may penetrate the most hardened of hearts and the most closed minds.

7. It is in God's love you may experience a heart that expands to include all individual beings, all of God's creation. It knows no limit, has no boundaries. Since it is beyond space and time, there is never a moment when it does not exist. God's love has a natural ability to spread its tentacles into every expression of consciousness.

8. God's love is Its own nature, and the splendor of Its Truth is in knowing It is a natural cause in your existence. Thus, when you rise to the heights of the Christ Consciousness, you possess the natural inclination to want to share God's love and it is in the sharing of God's love, you come into the awareness of your God-nature.

9. God's love is like the wind you cannot see, but which can be felt and known by all it touches. Because God's love is the purest of the pure, it may bind old wounds, mend broken hearts, and heal relationships.

10. When you are weary of the world's promises, it is God's love that fills the hole in your heart, the emptiness in your life, and sets a table of all your life's needs asking only that you love your God and others as yourself. "Jesus said unto him, Thou shalt love the Lord thy God with all thy heart, and with all thy soul, and with all thy mind. This is the first and great commandment. And the second *is* like unto it. Thou shalt love thy neighbour as thyself. On these two commandments hang all the law and the prophets" (Matthew 22: 37- 40).

11. Jesus is the Love of God personified. He is the example of God's compassion for all Its children, all Its creation. "That Christ may dwell in your hearts through faith; that ye, being rooted and grounded

in love. May be able to comprehend with all saints what *is* the breadth, and length, and depth, and height; And to know the love of Christ, which passeth knowledge, that ye might be filled with all the fulness of God" (Ephesians 3: 17-19).

12. God's Love has no beginning, no end. It is a gift constantly being delivered every moment of your life. God's love is never withdrawn, never withheld, and always available. It never requires proof of identity — It always knows *Its* own!

+ +

LESSON: 108 — LOVING - DIVINE

LOVING - DIVINE is God expressing *Its* nature, God in Action — the Heart Beat of an indescribable God. "As the Father hath loved me, so have I loved you: continue ye in my love" (John 15: 9).

1. You choose whom you are loving. You use loving to focus your affection on those closest to you. You give or you withhold your loving, as though it is a coin in your pocket to spend whenever you please or not. Coins are useless unless you are spending them. Loving is worthless unless you *are* loving.

2. On this plane of opposites, there is good-bad, up-down, love-hate. God's awareness be-ing has no opposites. There is no giving nor withholding. You say, "God is love" and leave it at that, but God's b-eing is much more than an unconditional inactive l-o-v-e. God loving is the loving Jesus Christ expressed when He was willing to lay down His life for you.

3. God is divine, unconditional, loving. Its nature is pure divine L-O-V-I-N-G. In Its truest sense, loving is the act of expressing itself. God loving is constantly expressing Itself in the caring for your need, not greed.

4. God's loving expresses Itself through all the supply that will ever be necessary. God's loving is available before a need is ever realized. Is not that what God is doing — Loving? "Be not ye therefore like unto them: for your Father knoweth what things ye have need of, before ye ask him" (Matthew 6: 8).

5. If you look around, you will know this earth produces all you shall ever need. It is not God that limits your supply or causes hunger. It is man's manipulation of Divine Supply.

6. Actually, you have never been put out of the Garden of Eden. All of God's loving supply is the Garden of Eden. God doesn't love one and not another. God is loving all, always.

7. All that comes forth, all you receive is God expressing, manifesting Its Divine Loving. Loving, God's Loving, isn't an abstract you cannot touch or see. It is in everything you are, and in all you do. You are the manifestation of God's Divine Loving.

8. Every individual, every creature, is God's loving expression of Itself. From the one who places the seed into the ground, the one who toils the soil, the one who gathers the goods; the one who packages it, ships it, stocks it, and buys it to prepare for your consumption; all is an expression of God loving.

9. You can't eat a meal without knowing that all upon the table, the least upon the table, is an expression of God loving.

10. The supply and consumption is for all. Man decides who will partake when it commercializes its availability. You aren't required to bargain for God's loving expression. God is constantly expressing Its unconditional loving. It is what God is, it is what God does.

11. God only knows how to express Its Divine unconditional loving. God gives, man withholds.

12. Yours is a loving, caring, and giving nature — God's. You are the loving expressive image of God. If you wish to see an expression of God loving, look into a mirror and the face smiling back at you is God loving Divinely.

++++++++++++++++++++++++

LESSON: 109 — MARRIAGE

THE SACRAMENT OF marriage, in a religious content, is defined according to time in the religious culture and history.

1. Marriage on the plane of opposites may be more fluid than many would want to consider.
2. Different cultures and societies may define marriage according to the mass consciousness of that culture and society. The laws governing marriage may tend to change in order to meet the needs of a culture and society.
3. In the old Biblical times, a man had many wives. Wives were taken and discarded at will. Jesus came along and instructed according to the then present needs of all concerned and He reminded them, "But from the beginning of the creation God made them male and female" (Mark 10: 6). Creation is a reflection. It is not the reality of what is beyond male and female. Man has moved out from the beginning into the attachment of a false physical separate sense of being.
4. It matters not upon this plane who are joined together by man. It is those who were joined together from the beginning that cannot be separated. "What therefore God hath joined together, let not man put asunder" (Mark 10: 9).
5. The struggle to change the laws of marriage in the present culture and society is an on- going festering wound. If as Jesus did, the present needs of culture and society are examined, there would be the ointment/answer to heal an ever growing infection.
6. On the plane of opposites, laws of marriage may be necessary. A physical sense union may be encouraged, promoted, and blessed. However, it is temporary, relative to this plane. It will not survive beyond it. Thus, the seed of truth in, "Till death do us part."
7. The sacrament of marriage as with all other symbolic rituals, may be blessed with the power invested in its belief by a realized individual officiating or the individuals accepting the blessing as sanctified.
8. It is a nice time honored tradition in or out of a religious sanction. However, it matters not how marriage is defined, practiced, or sanctified. In reality, it does not exist. You cannot protect that which does not exist in reality. "Jesus answered and said unto them, Ye do err, not knowing the scriptures, nor the power of God. For in the resurrection they neither marry, nor are given in marriage, but are as the angels of God in heaven" (Matthew 22: 29-30).
9. On the spiritual path there is no right nor wrong, good nor bad, only what is necessary and if a lawful state of marriage is believed necessary for yourself, then marry and be happy.
10. It is from a realized expression of the Christ Consciousness that marriage of opposites may no longer be desired. Marriage on this plane is but a reflective temporary attempt to recreate in the outer appearance, with the use of opposites, that which already exists as one.
11. In God's heavenly kingdom, before creation, there is no one married, nor taken in marriage. In the awareness of being, there is only the impersonal oneness of being. There are never opposites to unify in any form of marriage. "God *is* a Spirit: and they that worship *him* must worship in spirit and in truth" (John 4: 24).
12. As the God-consciousness manifest as the many individual expressions of consciousness, the false belief in separateness rises. Your desire to return to oneness and your natural state in awareness is falsely sought in an opposite physical form.
13. All individual expressions of consciousness eventually awaken to awareness as it is always being. What God has always held in oneness is never parted. Marriage is the symbolic ritual or representation of the oneness of God.

14. It is the false belief in a separate being that turns you outward toward the appearance of opposites and a belief through the joining of the personal physical sense act of sexual energy that you are again momentarily one — an illusion.

15. It is not in the sexual act nor in the abstaining from the sexual act that you are at one in awareness, but rather, it is by the rising in God-consciousness within that realized spiritual Oneness.

16. In the awareness awakening through the activity of the Holy Spirit in the name of Jesus Christ, an individual expression of consciousness will gravitate toward its own likeness — its own God-Self before creation occurred. "And now, O Father, glorify thou me with thine own self with the glory which I had with thee before the world was" (John 17: 5).

+ +

LESSON: 110 — MEMORY - RECALL

MEMORY - RECALL is selective attention on a "past" present thought, word, or deed.

1. What you wish to "remember" is a present thought, word, or deed that is considered the "past" but in reality, is always present in consciousness.

2. It is a present impression consciously stored and imprinted on your vibrating energy. Therefore, memory and recall are in the moment and present anytime you wish to place your attention on them.

3. Since all is in the present, the conscious mind and thoughts have the power to be present with what you consider to be a memory.

4. You are the master of the mind and thoughts rising in your consciousness. All are rising and vibrating in conscious awareness. You are a conscious aware being. As a conscious aware being, you have the conscious aware power to remember and recall that which has occurred actually in the present.

5. Nothing is ever lost. Sounds strange but the "past" actually has nowhere to go but in the present.

6. It is a matter of placing your aware consciousness of the present that contains the thought and action you are presently remembering — which is constantly vibrating as the present.

7. All you ever have to do is to direct the mind to the present to bring forth whatever it is you may want to remember at any particular present moment. It is not as much "remembering," as it is switching your selective attention to what is always presently available.

8. You don't need to be constantly clogging your attention with what is considered a "past" or "future" action. Once you have imprinted the need for the action, it is always presently available. It is all in the present. Past, future, and present thought, word, and deed are vibrating present energy.

9. When, in the present, a memory of an act or thought rises the memory *is* the present. Your attention may just not be on what you may consider to be a "past" action or thought.

10. Whatever you have imprinted in your conscious mind at any given present moment is available in any given present moment. Manifestations past, present, and to come, exist in a present moment of time — "now." "And the devil, taking him up into an high mountain, shewed unto him all the kingdoms of the world in a moment of time" (Luke 4: 5).

+ +

LESSON: 111 — MIND

MIND IS THAT which is referred to as thinking, memory, feelings, and emotions.

1. In reality, there is no such "thing" as *a* mind. What rise in consciousness are thoughts, memories, feelings, and emotions and they are called mind.

2. As vibrating energy rises as thoughts, memory, feelings, emotions, etcetera, within consciousness, you receive impressions through a physical sense body form (organs) and identify with the impressions.

3. As there is no mind in reality, there is no person. However, when the thought, "I, Me, My, Mine" rises you identify with the mind's contents as an individual separate person. This is how mind acquired its mastership. As the result of a false separate sense of self, you have accepted a master that is a false concept.

5. As the personal "I" dissolves, you may become aware and distinguish the unchanging in the changing, the inactive in the active. The false fades as it has no substance in reality leaving only what is true.

6. When concentrated, mind's rising vibrating energy may be a powerful force. However, the real power is beyond the rising vibrating energy of mind.

7. You may falsely believe, you of yourself, possess power through the use of a mind. "Jesus answered, Thou couldest have no power *at all* against me, except it were given thee from above: therefore he that delivered me unto thee hath the greater sin" (John 19: 11).

8. The rising thoughts - memories, feelings, and emotions are rising in consciousness. Consciousness is rising within awareness. Since all rises within awareness, all power emanates from within.

9. As you awaken to the reality of awareness, you will find the mind and its concentrated power is your dutiful servant.

10. The mind's rising contents is of great use in the service of the Lord, and therefore should be respected and guarded. The world's conditioning which you feed the mind affects its response and its response affects the physical sense body.

11. Exposing the mind's thoughts, feelings, and emotions to constant pictures of violence and degrading materials will result in a mind prone to respond in like manner.

12. As a fully awakened being, the heart and mind become one and the mind's contents serve the Holy Spirit in the name of Jesus Christ. "I thank God through Jesus Christ our Lord. So then with the mind I myself serve the law of God . . ." (Romans 7: 25).

++++++++++++++++++++++++++

LESSON: 112 — MOTHER MARY - SPIRIT OF MARY

THE SPIRIT OF Mary vibrates from the purest, highest Christ Consciousness. It supports you and those you serve through the Holy Spirit in the name of Her Son, Jesus Christ.

1. The spirit of Mary's Immaculate Heart is an open door to her Son's Sacred Heart. "And Mary said, My soul doth magnify the Lord, And my spirit hath rejoiced in God my Saviour" (Luke I: 6 - 47).

2. The Spirit of Mary encourages the praying of the rosary. The rosary prayer shares her life and her son's life experiences on *her* spiritual journey. As Mary walks with you on your spiritual walk, the spirit of Mary's primary activity is to patiently guide you to Her Son, Jesus Christ.

3. For those who are not ready to follow Mary's Son, Mary remains the intermediary who is ever ready with a mother's love and understanding. A devoted mother who stood by the cross till her Son drew His last breath. "Now there stood by the cross of Jesus his mother, and his mother's sister, Mary the *wife* of Cleophas, and Mary Magdalene" (John 19: 25).

4. The spirit of Mary is a tender, gentle force that allows you to bathe in an unconditional mother's love. It is like a warm hug that dulls the chill of life's crises.

5. It's the spirit of Mary that reaches out to comfort you when you lack a loving relationship with an

earthly Mother and, if you would allow this Blessed Being, she would teach you to forgive and to love your earthly mother, as you would love Mother Mary.

6. In the spirit of Mary, you may come into forgiveness for an earthly mother and/or father you believed has fallen short.

7. In the spirit of Mary, you may rest in a mother's expression of consciousness. When you feel unloved, unwanted, and not appreciated, it is Mary's spirit that dries your tears and tenderly holds you.

8. The spirit of Mary loves you in places you could never conceive — in the deepest crevices of your heart, in the most disparate moments of your life, and during your most unlovable moments.

9. When all else seems to fail, the spirit of Mary may be a living active presence. It is an ever present presence that needs only to be acknowledged.

10. The spirit of Mary is a Holy, healing spirit, so quiet, so silent you are often unaware of this dedicated Blessed Holy Being who wants only for her children to come follow her son, Jesus Christ.

+ +

LESSON: 113 — MOTIVATION

MOTIVATION IS STIRRED by an intense interest (positive or negative) with reason and intent, and may be influenced by desire or temptation.

1. On a spiritual walk, the purity of reason and intent of your motivation is determined by your relationship with the Holy Spirit in the name of Jesus Christ.

2. Jesus' life was an example of pure motivations because He sought to do the will of the God. ". . . not as I will, but as thou *wilt*" (Matthew 26: 39).

3. When you are motivated by doing the will of God, your actions/services cease to be grandiose. Seeking to do the will of God automatically removes self-interest or impure motives. It also frees you from evaluating the outcome of your service.

4. Motivation grounded in the desire for recognition and rewards is self-serving. "Take heed that ye do not your alms before me, to be seen of them: otherwise ye have no reward of your Father which is in heaven" (Matthew 6:1).

5. You know that your motivations are pure when you act/serve without the concern for a personal desired result.

6. When you act, not react, to objects, events, and/or persons you are acting from a purer state of mind and heart. "Blessed *are* the pure in heart: for they shall see God" (Matthew 5: 8).

7. Christ inspired motivation will always serve the greater good when you are not looking over your shoulder in the hopes that someone may be watching. "Therefore when thou doest *thine* alms, do not sound a trumpet before thee, as the hypocrites do in the synagogues and in the streets, that they may have glory of men., Verily I say unto you, They have their reward" (Matthew 6: 2).

8. When you are motivated to act/serve from your heart, your left hand will not know what your right hand is doing. "But when thou doest alms let not thy left hand know what thy right hand doeth" (Matthew 6: 3).

9. Although your motivation to act/serve may be seen in public, it is held secret when it comes from the sacred place of the heart. "That thine alms may be in secret: and thy Father which seeth in secret himself shall reward thee openly" (Matthew 6: 4).

10. As you progress on your spiritual journey, your motivations may rise to a purer, higher compassionate calling through the Holy Spirit in the name of Jesus.

+ +

LESSON: 114 — NEGATIVITY

NEGATIVITY IS THE destructive conditioned impression used with conscious vibrating energy in thought, word, or deed.

1. This world of opposites consists of the choice of using your vibrating energy source as a negative or positive expression of consciousness.

2. It is your choice. Which of the opposites do you accept in this relative world of opposites? Your choice of one or the other creates your mental and physical environment.

3. If you select to express the positive, an inner knowledge of truth rests in a sea of calmness allowing an inner peace. "Grace and peace be multiplied unto you through the knowledge of God, and of Jesus our Lord" (2 Peter 1: 2).

4. If you select to express the negative thoughts, words, or deeds, it attracts a restless, destructive (considered impurities) nature to the mind and body vibrating energy.

5. The vibrating energy you use for the purposes of negativity must be eventually purified to its original calm vibrating state. It is for this reason as you begin a silent prayer practice, the forgiveness and purification process occurs.

6. With the forgiveness and purification process of non-responding to the rising negative conditioned impressions, you are given the opportunity to return the vibrating energy to its natural vibrating expression of neutrality.

+ +

LESSON: 115 — "NO."

"NO," IS THE guard at the door of egotism. It may protect you from the lack of humility.

POLITELY SAYING, "NO.:"
  A. "I am not available."
  B. "Schedule is full at present."
  C. "Will be pleased to make an appointment with you."

PRESENCE REQUESTED:
  A. "Allow me to consider it and get back to you."
  B. "It does not fit into my schedule at the present time."
  C. "I appreciate your asking me; however, I cannot accept."
  D. "Thank you but I am not available."
  E. "I will need to check my schedule first."
  F. "Perhaps at another time."

1. As you move toward the direction of being a realized being, more of this world will want more of you. Darkness is always attracted to the light, and your light of awareness shines brighter as you become an aware being.

2. As a realized being you are vulnerable to the request and pull from others. One of your most difficult lessons may be simply learning when too much, *is* too much.

3. Constantly over-scheduling because you believe you must not say "No" or can't bring yourself to refuse whatever is asked of you, is to fall into an ego trap. The ego wants to feed you the false belief you are the only one who could possibly serve any particular request or situation.

4. You may find it difficult at times to just say "No" because it may be perceived as a negative. However, there are other words or terms available that will convey the same message.

5. Remember, even Jesus withdrew from the pull of the masses. He was well aware the outer world would always want some "thing" of Him. Jesus came to awaken individual expressions of consciousness to the inner reality of the Kingdom of God. Your journey is the same as an awakened Being,

6. If you do not pen your daily schedule carefully, you will be of little use to yourself or to others. Meeting the needs of others is noble but meeting the needs of yourself is necessary if you are to remain noble.

7. You are constantly given choices and decisions to make. Choose and decide wisely. Learn to pause and think before you respond. Responding from the top of your head, will keep your heart in an emotional turmoil.

8. In whatever activity you may be engaged, individual expressions of consciousness will seek you out. Serving others is what you are all about. You must also serve yourself. The Christ cares for all, including you.

9. A balance must be maintained in the outer world to maintain your realized inner world. A conflict exists when the outer becomes more and the inner less. Your inner world of reality within awareness is the bedrock of your being. The outer world and its demands are temporary and you may be constantly asked to place bandages on the hurts of this world.

10. Of course you do whatever you are able. Your service to Christ is ultimately to being a fully-awakened being who recognizes the inner reality of the many.

11. In order to maintain a constant inner awareness and connection to the Holy Spirit in the name of Jesus Christ, down time for your silent prayer practice, study, rest, and being with that which you are, must be a priority. Over indulgence in the activities, including service of this world, may bring you back to a previous expression of consciousness.

12. Ultimately, the greatest service to other individual expressions of consciousness is for you to remain an awakened being. "And I, if I be lifted up from the earth, will draw all *men* unto me" (John 12: 32).

+ +

LESSON: 116 — OBEDIENCE

OBEDIENCE IS THE adherence to the inner teachings by the Holy Spirit in the name of Jesus Christ.

1. Here's the problem — balance. In order to establish a balance, your inner life must take priority to perform the outer activities as a Christ servant.

2. When you are obedient to your inner life and silent Christ Centered Prayer practice, a balance exists. The constant moment-to-moment expression from the inner consciousness to the outer is quiet, smooth, and uninterrupted one. "Then Peter and the *other* apostles answered, and said, We ought obey God rather than men" (Acts 5: 29).

3. When you neglect your inner silent prayer practice in deference to the outer world, you are convincing yourself, "After all, "I am serving." You tend to place more importance on the outer than is necessary. The outer service becomes an ego trip and it is the glory of this world you seek. "For they loved the praise of men more than the praise of God" (John 12: 43).

4. The greatest importance of obedience to the teachings of the Holy Spirit in the name of Jesus Christ and a silent prayer practice is its service *to* you. There's a contradiction for you! But true obedience serves to help you awaken to pure awareness. "If ye abide in me, and my words abide in you, ye shall ask what ye will, and it shall be done unto you" (John 15: 7).

5. As you awaken to pure awareness the inner requires an obedient attention to maintain a steady balance. The inner is the real; the outer is the relative, temporary.

6. The real requires an obedient, attentive balance when you are experiencing outer relative, appearances. Make any sense? This is key to understanding obedience to your inner life. It *is* the real. It is your reality, your true identity, and your permanent home.

7. Establishing a balance between the inner world and the outer world is a bit tricky at first. Eventually you may realize there really is only one world. The difference between the inner world and the outer world is the constant change of the vibrating energy's speed of your expression of consciousness.

8. At first there is a disobedient resistance to having to constantly come from a pure rising of the Christ Consciousness into the many vibrating energy-sensed individual expressions of consciousness.

9. There may be times of struggle when you're not obedient to your inner guidance. You will not let go of the outer appearances nor surrender totally to that which you are.

10. It is perfectly natural in the beginning to lean toward the inner or outer world while struggling to maintain an obedient balance. When more of the outer is chosen, an imbalance occurs.

11. In time you may come into the realization of how demanding the inner life is. It does require time and attention and yet, at the same time, requires you to live among the other individual expressions of consciousness and to do it in a loving, caring way.

12. The spiritual path requires a steady, alert, obedience between inner and outer to remain balanced. Sometimes you may feel you are walking a tight rope and you do not dare look left, right, nor especially, down. It is your obedience to the Christ of your being that assists you to maintain the necessary balance.

13. Your balance at times may get a little wobbly and fear kicks in. The fear of not living out from the Christ Consciousness is more devastating then all the king's horses and all the kings men. In other words, all that this world could ever offer — you then straighten out fast.

14. It isn't blind obedience Christ requires, but total obedience. Total obedience establishes balance; moving from one expressed consciousness to another is effortless.

15. Without obedience Jesus' disciples would not have followed, not have listened, and not have realized all that Jesus taught them.

16. You are not alone when you obediently surrender to the God of your being. It is God's battle, not yours. Allow God to do Its work. ". . . for the battle *is* not yours, but God's" (II Chronicles 20: 15).

17. When you are obedient, truth unfolds without limits. The Christ is serving you. When you are obedient, you may reach into the silence of awareness and may hear, "And lo a voice from heaven saying, This is my beloved Son, in whom I am well pleased'" (Matthew 3: 17).

18. Obedience is joyous when every moment of your life is lived in obedience to the Word. "Thou wilt shew me the path of life: in thy presence *is* fulness of joy; at thy right hand *there are* pleasures for evermore" (Psalm 16: 11).

STUDENT'S STORY:

I realize the truth behind the statement in the obedience Lesson that the Christ ultimately is serving the one who is obedient and not the other way around. Yielding to the guidance of the Holy Spirit in the name of Jesus Christ at times seems like giving in and surrendering control. I suppose it is but the paradox is that in losing control and giving in, I received one hundred fold. To lose is to gain.

This is such a hard lesson and one that has taken and continues to take me by surprise. It is also a lesson that the more I resists, the more it presents itself. It is a lesson that I have strained with much of my life. I have usually insisted in doing things "my way" even when claiming I wanted to obey Jesus Christ. Often my "obedience" was convenience rather than fact! There is a huge difference between selective, convenient obedience and total radical obedience to Christ. Like a horse taking the bit, I would often take hold and go where I wanted rather than where I was being led. More than not I ended up bruised in a brier patch! Learning to yield to the bit, listen, and obey the guiding hands of the Master has not come naturally.

When my first test of obedience presented itself and I failed miserably, my teacher emailed, "Well, now that you have failed your first attempt at obedience, let's do this . . ." Thank God, for her sense of humor. I often argued, "How was I supposed to be autonomous, self sufficient, self reliant, pliable, and obedient at the same time? How was I supposed to understand obedience in a spiritual context when the world conditioned a cultural message of rugged individualism and demanded self-sufficiency?"

The world taught me I had to be strong. I had to rely on myself. I had to be sure that I took care of myself because I doubted anyone else's ability and even questioned God's. It is only recently I have come to see that true obedience to the spirit's legitimate authority in the name of Jesus Christ and consenting to being led, fed, and provided for that my struggles, instead of getting worse, actually got easier.

The paradox of radical obedience leading to radical freedom was something that has and continues to take me a long time to grasp and appreciate. Freedom in Christ is a challenge to everything that I grew up being taught and everything that was modeled for me. Consequently, I often mistook surrender in obedience through the Holy Spirit in the name of Jesus Christ to my teacher as a sign of weakness. To obey was to give in and to lose, and to lose was just not part of my growing up curriculum. The "My way or the highway" attitude, often left me not on the mountain top, but in the ditch! "Pride certainly cometh before the fall!"

Realizing that I was patiently and persistently being addressed by the Christ of my teacher's being through the power of the Holy Spirit manifesting in her has helped me respond more obediently to legitimate requests that were being made. I have begun to appreciate experientially that the straight and narrow spiritual path of total obedience to the Christ, affords not a straight jacket or limitation of freedom, but rather, is the door to spacious creativity and infinite possibilities without obstruction. The more obedient to the Christ — the more free. The more free — the more creative. The more creative, the more obedient. I have come to acknowledge this truth and this "truth has indeed set me free."

+ +

LESSON: 117 — OPPOSITES

OPPOSITES EXIST ON this earth plane. Birth - death, male - female, good - evil, up - down, in - out, wealth - poverty, etcetera.

1. Your very first appearance (birth) on this plane begins the process of opposites (death). Opposites come in every possible condition, situation and conceivable manifestation. In truth, in God awareness there are no opposites. "Hear O Israel: The LORD our God *is* one LORD:" (Deuteronomy 6: 4).

2. By your birth you are an opposite — female or male. And within your individual expression of consciousness (personality), opposites exist. There also exist opposites from other individual expressions of consciousness that you encounter on this plane.

3. Your entire sojourn on this plane involves dealing with, overcoming, and transcending opposites. It is why this plane is called the earth plane of opposites. When you are dealing with the pleasantness of

this world, you may tend to forget that what is pleasant one moment carries within it the seed of unpleasantness. "But of the tree of the knowledge of good and evil, thou shalt not eat of it: for in the day that thou eatest thereof thou shalt surely die" (Genesis 2: 17).

4. Within pure awareness, there are no opposites. Man is creating them. Look about you, praise and blame, joy and sadness, and peace and wars, are all man made. "O Timothy, keep that which is committed to thy trust, avoiding profane *and* vain babblings, and oppositions of science falsely so called:" (I Timothy 6: 20).

5. In reality, there are no opposites. It is the same vibrating energy being used to create a pleasant situation, as an unpleasant one. Therefore, there is no opposition to opposites.

6. This may become obvious when practicing the forgiveness and purification process during silent prayer practice. When a "negative" remembrance rises and you do not respond but gently become aware of your Spiritual Heart Center and rest in awareness, the rising energy of the appearance of a negative memory is forgiven and purified.

7. This is the same energy that may now be used for a "greater good." Can you not see within the bad is the good waiting to come forth — the same energy?

8. Opposites manifest as lessons to be learned. They may come in praise or blame. Either may teach you to go beyond and know the Christ of your being. The Christ of your being requires neither praise nor blame.

9. You attract the necessary individuals, situations, and lessons that come forth in your life. God does not deal in opposites. There are no opposites in truth. Right there where an opposite seems to appear, your God-source exists. It is the God-source, pure in its nature, that is being used or misused for the creation of opposites, not by God, but rather by you and other individual expressions of consciousness.

10. Go beyond the appearances of opposites to your God-source and realize the light of Jesus Christ shining forth and loving you always. The realization of the light of Jesus Christ may help bring an inner peace and joy in your life because it allows you to go beyond the appearances — good or bad — and rest in the awareness of your being.

+++++++++++++++++++++++++++

LESSON: 118— OVERCOMING

OVERCOMING IN THE grand scheme of your spiritual journey is the constant moving through the many illusions presented on this earth plane of opposites.

1. You may hear the term overcoming tossed about in many of the areas of your spiritual walk. The ordeals you are overcoming are the washing of your robe (expression of consciousness) in the blood of Jesus. "And one of the elders answered, saying unto me, What are these which are arrayed in white robes? And whence came they? And I said unto him, Sir, thou knowest, And he said to me, These are they which came out of great tribulation, and have washed their robes, and made them white in the blood of the Lamb" (Revelation 7: 13 - 14).

2. The overcoming is progressively occurring through the forgiveness - purification process. "How much more shall the blood of Christ, who through the eternal Spirit offered himself without spot to God, purge your conscience from dead works to serve the living God" (Hebrews 9: 14).

3. The more serious truth seeker you are, the more likely the overcoming pace increases. "Come now, and let us reason together, saith the LORD: though your sins be as scarlet, they shall be as white as snow; though they be red like crimson, they shall be as wool" (Isaiah 1: 18).

4. A lesson repeats itself until you are cleansed of its hold on your consciousness. "For whatsoever is

born of God overcometh the world: and this is the victory that overcometh the world, *even* our faith" (1 John 5: 4).

5. When you have finished with a lesson, you have overcome it. There must be a time when you wake up to the totality of lessons that make up an imaginary world. "He that hath an ear, let him hear what the Spirit saith unto the churches; To him that overcometh will I give to eat of the tree of life, which is in the midst of the paradise of God" (Revelation 2: 7).

6. You have the example and assurance of Jesus Christ that this world can be overcome. "These things I have spoken unto you, that in me ye might have peace. In the world ye shall have tribulation: but be of good cheer: I have overcome the world" (John 16: 33).

7. Through the Holy Spirit in the name of Jesus Christ, your daily overcoming of this world is gradually waking you up to your rightful inheritance as a child of God. "To him that overcometh will I grant to sit with me in my throne, even as I also overcame, and am set down with my Father in his throne" (Revelation 3: 21).

8. Overcoming is progress. To have overcome this world is life eternal. "He that overcometh, the same shall be clothed in white raiment: and I will not blot out his name out of the book of life, but I will confess his name before my Father, and before his angels" (Revelation 3: 5).

+ +

LESSON: 119 — PATIENCE

PATIENCE IS THE nature of God that allows you to stay in place. "My soul, wait thou only upon God; for my expectation *is* from him. He only *is* my rock and my salvation: *he is* my defence; I shall not be moved" (Psalm 62: 5-6).

1. God has infinite patience and all that the Lord has, you have. Therefore, patience isn't acquired. It is as available as love and as potent.
2. Patience is the kindness you share with yourself and others. "Now we exhort you, brethren, warn them that are unruly, comfort the feebleminded, support the weak, be patient toward all *men*" (1 Thessalonians 5: 14).
3. Patience allows you the necessary time to learn spiritual practices. "But if we hope for that we see not, *then* do we with patience wait for *it*" (Romans 8: 25).
4. With patience, you may work through and deepen realizations and insights.
5. Patience keeps anger, frustrations, and agitations at bay.
6. Patience sees flaws in yourself and others, in the light of forgiveness.
7. When a ground swell of chaos seeks to touch your life, patience reminds you, "This too, will pass."
8. Patience holds relationships together and establishes new ones.
9. Patience slows your response in the guidance of yourself and others giving you clarity in the present.
10. When there are those in your life who would try your patience, you may count on patience being infinite, without end. You may be as generous as you wish with patience, for it can never be depleted.
11. For many, patience may be slow to surface. However, all should try it. It has a natural ability to increase in stamina, "But let patience have *her* perfect work, that ye may be perfect and entire, wanting nothing" (James 1: 4).
12. Patience bears fruit, which is its own reward, "But that on the good ground are they, which in an honest and good heart, having heard the word, keep *it*, and bring forth fruit with patience" (Luke 8: 15).

13. Tapping into patience is to drink from a well spring of pure, cool water on the hottest of days.

14. Come to the eternal well spring of your soul's nature and with the hand of God, draw from within. "In your patience possess ye your souls" (Luke 21: 19).

+ +

LESSON: 120 — PENANCE

PENANCE IS THE gift that restores relationships. "But why dost thou judge thy brother? Or why dost thou set at nought thy brother? For we shall all stand before the judgment seat of Christ" (Romans 14: 10). "And this commandment have we from him, That he who loveth God love his brother also" (I John 4: 21).

1. On the spiritual path there is no self-punishment. There is self-forgiveness, purification, and the giving up of attachment to harmful actions to yourself or to others.

2. With most repentant individuals comes the desire to make amends and to cleanse the conscience.

3. Of course, in daily life whenever positive amends can be accomplished, by all means, do so.

4. A sincere apology to others, or yourself, is always a welcoming gesture of caring thoughtfulness.

5. Effective penance is consciously loving others as you would yourself in thought, word, or deed. "By this shall all *men* know that ye are my disciples, if ye have love one to another" (John 13: 35).

6. Genuine penance accepts the gift of restoration and intends not to ever repeat the same harmful behavior.

7. The sincerity of the renewed relationships in the love of God penetrates the forgiveness and purification process allowing you to move more easily within the Spiritual Heart Center and rest in awareness.

8. The penance of sincere restoration exposes one to the Spiritual Heart Center and the cleansing power of the Holy Spirit in the name of Jesus Christ.

+ +

LESSON: 121 — PENTECOST

PENTECOST IS A time in your life when the Holy Spirit is a reality.

1. Jesus instructed He would send His Father's promise. "And, behold, I send the promise of my Father upon you: but tarry ye in the city of Jerusalem, until ye be endued with power from on high" (Luke 24: 49).

2. On the seventh Sunday (Pentecost) after Easter, the Lord's promise was received by those who waited and believed. "And they were all filled with the Holy Ghost, and began to speak with other tongues, as the Spirit gave them utterance" (Acts 2: 4).

3. It did not stop then and there. The Biblical Pentecost event, although celebrated once a year, may be a daily event in your life. The glory and power of Jesus Christ through His Holy Spirit exists always. "Teaching them to observe all things whatsoever I have commanded you: and, lo, I am with you always, *even* unto the end of the world" (Matthew 28: 20).

4. If you believe in Jesus Christ, the Lord's "promise," the Holy Spirit in the name of Jesus Christ is available to teach you all things unto the end of the world.

5. The Pentecost of your life may occur when you believe in Jesus Christ and open your heart to Him. Jesus' Holy Spirit is available 24 - 7. Why separate yourself from Its possibilities?

6. The Holy Spirit in the name of Jesus Christ is a living teaching activity. Say, "Yes," to Jesus Christ and the Pentecost of your life is now.

+ +

LESSON: 122 — PERSECUTION AND CRUCIFIXION

THE PERSECUTION AND crucifixion are literal, metaphysical, and mystical initiations of enlightenments on the spiritual journey.

1. As you progress on the spiritual path, the Bible scriptures progress with you from the literal, to the metaphysical, to the mystical.

2. The symbols, signs, and teachings within the letter of the scriptures reveal metaphysically and mystically what the Holy Spirit in the name of Jesus Christ taught then and continues to teach now.

3. Jesus's promise is a continuous one. "But the Comforter, *which is* the Holy Ghost, whom the Father will send in my name, he shall teach you all things, and bring all things to your remembrance, whatsoever I have said unto you" (John 14: 26).

4. Jesus Christ is the way. Follow in His footprints and they are yours. "At that day ye shall know that I *am* in my Father, and ye in me, and I in you" (John 14: 20).

PERSECUTION:

A. From the moment you have a personal conscious sense that is separate and apart from the impersonal God, the persecution begins.

B. There came a time when Jesus Himself was asked to give up His personal sense for the realization of the impersonal Christ. "Greater love hath no man than this, that a man lay down his life for his friends" (John 15: 13).

C. Jesus struggled with the idea of giving up; the personal sense of being. "And he went a little further, and fell on his face, and prayed, saying, 'My Father, if it be possible, let this cup pass from me: nevertheless not as I will, but as thou *wilt*'" (Matthew 26: 39).

D. Ultimately, you, as Jesus did, may realize the will of God. ". . . O my Father, if this cup may not pass away from me, except I drink it, thy will be done" (Matthew 26: 42).

CRUCIFIXION:

A. Afer the persecution of a personal sense of a false self, you take up the cross, your personal being and follow Jesus Christ through the crucifixion.

B. Betrayal — the sense of a personal self.

C. Whipping — the pain of accepting a physical sense of being.

D. Crown of thorns — the adoration you seek in an imaginary world.

E. Cross — *You* are a living cross, the cross which you are instructed to take up and follow Jesus. "Then said Jesus unto his disciples, If any *man* will come after me, let him deny himself, and take up his cross, and follow me. For whosoever will save his life shall lose it: and whosoever will lose his life for my sake shall find it" (Matthew 16: 24 -25).

F. Nails — desires and temptations that hold you to the cross.

G. Piercing — the final giving up of the false sense of a physical life.

H. Death — a false concept of eternal life.

++++++++++++++++++++++++++

LESSON: 123 — PERSON

A PERSON IS that which appears to be who you are in this world. It is the illusion of your imagination born of a false sense of a mind and physical body. "What is born of the flesh is flesh, and what is born of the Spirit is spirit" (John 3: 6).

1. There is no person. Never was, never will be. "But ye are not in the flesh, but in the Spirit, if so be that the Spirit of God dwell in you. Now if any man have not the Spirit of Christ, he is none of his" (Romans 8: 9).

2. The mind self-identifies and attaches with itself and the objects it creates. Thus, there is a dream world of attachments to an imaginary person, personality, and events. The mistake is living out from the mind rather than the aware consciousness of having a mind rising within consciousness.

3. There is nowhere you could go or be, other than who or what you really are. What you call yourself by name is an image appearing on a conscious screen of awareness and when the light goes out the image disappears. "Where can I go from thy spirit? Or where can I flee from your presence?" (Psalm 139: 7).

4. It is the light of an aware consciousness that allows the person and its objects to be seen. They are reflective of a reality within. "My substance was not hid from thee, when I was made in secret, *and* curiously wrought in the lowest parts of the earth" (Psalm 139: 15).

5. That which you believe to be a person consists of vibrating energy rising as mind - thoughts, feelings, physical body sense, sense impressions, and perpetuated in memories and habits — all impermanent. A shadow of your spiritual reality. "Are ye so foolish? having begun in the Spirit, are ye now made perfect by the flesh?" (Galatians 3: 3).

6. The real is permanent, eternal. In all that appears real, a person cannot be found — not in yourself nor in an other individual expression of consciousness. There is noooooooooo person. "For he that soweth to his flesh shall of the flesh reap corruption; but he that soweth to the Spirit shall of the Spirit reap life everlasting" (Galatians 6: 8).

7. When you are identifying yourself as a person, you are also identifying other expressions of consciousness as persons separate and apart from yourself. This may cause the rising of stressful emotions attached to the approval or disapproval of yourself by others.

8. The spiritual walk and the spiritual journey within, awakens you to the impersonal reality you are and always have been. "Then shall the dust return to the earth as it was: and the spirit shall return unto God who gave it" (Ecclesiastes 12: 7).

++++++++++++++++++++++++++

LESSON: 124 — PERSONALITY

PERSONALITY IS THE appearance of your distinctive qualities you express as an individual expression of consciousness.

1. As consciousness rises in awareness and mind self-identifies with a personal "I." The belief that "I" am this or that creates the birth of a personality.

2. A personality is what displays unique characteristics that you have accepted as your own expression of consciousness.

3. Personality characteristics may be noticeable soon after your birth. Many personality traits may be learned or hereditary.

4. Your personality is constantly evolving from parental association, cultural conditioning, and spiritual awareness. "But all these worketh that one and the selfsame Spirit, dividing to every man severally as he will" (1 Corinthians 12: 11).

5. A personality may be influenced by the exposure to extreme events or change.

6. There is no such thing as a fixed personality. As one who has a silent Christ Centered Prayer practice, you may find your personality either instantly or gradually changing as you realize the mind of Christ Jesus in the Christ Consciousness. "Let this mind be in you, which was also in Christ Jesus" (Philippians 2: 5).

7. As you begin dying to the old self (false concepts), a new self with marked personality changes emerges. Often it may take a period of adjustment to become acquainted with the new self and its personality changes. Be patient. "That ye put off concerning the former conversation the old man, which is corrupt according to the deceitful lusts; And be renewed in the spirit of your mind; And that ye put on the new man, which after God is created in righteousness and true holiness" (Ephesians 4: 22-24).

8. For a time, you may be uncomfortable with the new personality but as you allow old ways and habits to fall away, you wear the new personality with less discomfort. However, you may find old friends also fall away. Others may find the new personality not to their liking.

9. Like the mind and body, a personality is a useful tool for change and growth. Like the mind and body, the personality serves a purpose and has no real existence in pure awareness or void. There must be an "I" to identify with a personality.

10. As you become more awakened to your reality, personality changes may be subtle or extreme. Your individual expression of consciousness begins to reveal the image that is in God's likeness — God's personality. A personality that is grounded in unconditional love and forgiveness.

+ +

LESSON: 125 — PIERCING

Piercing is the attempt by others to penetrate your Christ armor.

1. As you progress in the Christ with trust and confidence, there will always be those who will attempt to throw spears and arrows to pierce your confidence. "My soul *is* among lions: *and* I lie *even among* them that are set on fire, *even* the sons of men, whose teeth *are* spears and arrows, and their tongue a sharp sword" (Psalm 57: 4).

2. For many in this world, piercing with an un-controlled tongue is a favorite past time. If you take them seriously, you will constantly be plugging the holes in your confidence.

3. When you no longer want anything of anyone, the piercing of your confidence will not be possible.

4. Spears and arrows cannot pierce what you no longer fear and do not accept as your own. "The LORD *is* on my side: I will not fear; what can man do unto me?" (Psalms 118: 6).

5. Do not rely on the confidence of others. "*It is* better to trust in the LORD than to put confidence in man" (Psalm 118: 8).

6. Confidence and trust are in the Christ of your being. "And this is the confidence that we have in him, that, if we ask any thing according to his will he heareth us:" (II John 5: 14).

7. Jesus knew that even the piercing of His side could not penetrate the Christ of His oneness with the Father. "But one of the soldiers with a spear pierced his side, and forthwith came there out blood and water" (John 19: 34).

8. There is nothing out there that anyone can give you that you do not already possess. Criticism and doubts belong to those who would attempt to use them against you. They will ricochet and hold their sender prisoner in the fear they would create.

+++++++++++++++++++++++++++

LESSON: 126 — POSITION

POSITION IS A particular type of job responsibilities you may hold that allows you to perform specific work activities.

1. There are a variety of positions you may aspire to attain in this world. The garb, surroundings, and/or circumstance of a position may be an ego's best friend.

2. Whether seeking a position or maintaining one, the spiritual principle is the same. A position is not who you are. It is what you do. It is through a position you may serve yourself and other individual expressions of consciousness.

3. If you identify with a position, attachment is surely to follow, and the mistaken belief that you must protect the position at all cost.

4. There are positions that may be considered, more or less, of greater importance. As an individual expression of consciousness seeking self-realization, you may become aware a doctor, waitress, lawyer, janitor, or priest positions are of the same importance.

5. Because certain positions in this world may be given more importance than others, it may be easy to get caught up in the super-imposed importance of a position.

6. A position does not create the importance. The Creator creates the importance in the position. If you are not alert, you may very well find yourself serving the position rather than its intended purpose.

7. There may be a tendency to worship the service rather than the source within that makes the service possible. "Jesus answered them and said, Verily, verily, I say unto you, Ye seek me, not because ye saw the miracles, but because ye did eat of the loaves, and were filled" (John 6: 26).

8. A position does not adequately reflect your reality. It may give you the opportunity to express from your reality. Although Jesus spoke with great authority and wisdom the masses identified Him with the position He held. "Is not this the carpenter's son? Is not his mother called Mary? And his brethren, James, and Joses, and Simon, and Judas?" (Matthew 13: 55).

9. Individuals have not held great positions. Great (realized) individuals have held positions. There isn't any position that can demand respect from anyone.

10. The demand for respect is a sign of seeking reward in this world. "Blessed are ye, when *men* shall revile you, and persecute *you*, and shall say all manner of evil against you falsely, for my sake. Rejoice, and be exceeding glad: for great *is* your reward in heaven: for so persecuted they the prophets which were before you" (Matthew 5: 11-12).

11. As a truth seeker or self-realized individual expression of consciousness, there is never a need for respect or demand of any kind during your performance of service. "Doth he thank that servant because he did the things that were commanded him? I trow not. So likewise ye, when ye shall have done all those

things which are commanded you, say, We are unprofitable servants: we have done that which was our duty to do" (Luke 17: 9-10).

12. To expect all individuals to be politely receptive to the position you hold or service you render is to cling to the results of that service. Jesus knew His mission was not always as a peace giver. "Suppose ye that I am come to give peace on earth? I tell you, Nay; but rather division" (Luke 12: 51).

13. The power of importance within any service rendered is within your realized consciousness, not the appearance of the service.

14. You are not giving anyone anything at anytime. You are sharing your realized light with others. Do not cast dispersion upon those who cannot yet see nor yet hear the truth of their being. "Having eyes, see ye not? And having ears, hear ye not? And do ye not remember?" (Mark 8: 18).

15. Your very presence may cause a disturbance with an individual. Darkness always struggles with the light. "In him was life; and the life was the light of men. And the light shineth in darkness; and the darkness comprehended it not" (John 1: 4 - 5).

16. There will always be individuals who will not appreciate what you may have to share. Jesus certainly experienced that throughout His ministry. "And they were offended in him. But Jesus said unto them, A prophet is not without honour, save in his own country, and in his own house" (Matthew 13: 57).

17. A rejection of your service is not a rejection of who you really are. No one can reject what they do not recognize. They are only rejecting an appearance that may not please them due to their own individual conditioned impressions.

18. Jesus rose above the ultimate rejection. His example may be your realized moment. "Then said Jesus, 'Father, forgive them; for they know not what they do.' and they parted his raiment, and cast lots." (Luke 23: 34).

+ +

LESSON: 127 — POWER - ABUSIVE

POWER - ABUSIVE is the misuse of the trust a student may have in a spiritual teacher, guide, or leader.

1. A teacher, guide, leader - student relationship is a delicate one that requires a caring balance. One that is forged in trust and obedience.

2. Teachers, guides, leaders may come to have power over their students. Masters have been known to put students to a test by requesting total trust and obedience to specific instructions. Instructions students may, at times, find difficult.

3. Instructing students to trust and obey a teacher's teachings may be easily misunderstood.

4. Students may not always willingly follow blindly where a teacher would lead. There may exist a strong conditioning for independence and skepticism. Trust, surrender, and obedience may come slowly.

5. Bringing a student into compliance with the Holy Spirit in the name of Jesus Christ at times — can be a challenge for the Christ Centered teacher.

6. Christ Centered truth teachers should not abuse their power and cause harm to anyone in their charge. It is a sacred trust. You are cautioned not entirely to give up your skepticism.

7. Harm could be caused by misguided teachers, guides, or leaders (Christians and non-Christians) who would lead their followers on an outward journey. The guidance should always be one of directing you within your being. There is no grandiose pretense in this world that will enlighten you. If ever you have doubts, walk away.

8. Use common sense. You may know intuitively when a teacher, guide, or leader is abusively using his or her power. The Christ within your Spiritual Heart Center is your caution light. It may warn when there is impending danger. Stay tuned in.

9. As a follower of Jesus Christ, you are taught to wake up to the awareness of your being. You come to realize the self as a false concept of who you really are through the Holy Spirit in the name of Jesus Christ. At no time would this allow you to willfully destroy the sense of the mind or body in your care.

10. Christ-like teachers would not deplete your finances, cause harm to others, nor encourage or participate in mass suicide of their followers. The straight gate and narrow way may be a long one, but it does not end in destructive behavior.

+ +

LESSON: 128 — PRACTICAL LIVING

PRACTICAL LIVING IS day to day responsibilities, activities, and service performed.

1. A silent prayer practice is not stopped when you open your eyes and go about your outer activities. In your silent prayer practice there is the element of mindfulness. You are mindful of all that rises. This mindfulness should be carried into your world of outer practical living.

2. A silent prayer practice should be practical in your every day life. The thinking should not be this is spiritual, this is not. Judging what is spiritual and what is not is a slippery slope you do not want to step on.

3. Be consciously aware of all you do in thought, word, and deed. Stay alert and pay attention to your thoughts, spoken words, and deeds as they rise inviting participation on the plane of opposites.

4. If you are aware of what you say before you say it, you may prevent suffering for yourself and others. Acts or deeds will be more appropriate, if you weigh whether they are necessary.

5. Your silent prayer life should be practical in all that you do. What you learn during a silent prayer practice may be practical in your daily living. The no responding, the no dialoguing, and being gentle with yourself may help you when you are actively involved with others.

6. Do not separate your inner prayer practice from your outer practical living. When you are consciously aware of what you are doing, all are spiritual activities. Washing dishes and scrubbing floors are spiritual activities when you do them with conscious awareness.

7. The Holy Spirit in the name of Jesus Christ is guiding you in and out of a silent prayer practice. The guidance is seamless.

8. Be as mindful of the Holy Spirit in your practical living as you are during a silent prayer practice, and the Holy Spirit will become more obvious in your practical daily living.

+ +

LESSON: 129 — PRAISE AND BLAME

PRAISE AND BLAME are opposites that rise in the same vibrating energy source that may illicit an emotional response.

1. Praise and blame are the same. Both are directed at a false, personal sense of being. You may be praised one day and blamed the next. Both must be overcome.

2. To get emotionally caught-up in either praise or blame is to take them personally. You are not a person. You are a spiritual being.

3. Praise or blame cannot affect the impersonal Christ of your being.

4. It matters not if you are praised or blamed. It is the same vibrating energy being used or misused. Your work is to recognize either one for what they are; opposites that have no reality.

5. You cannot accept praise and then get upset when you are blamed - criticized. If you are to accept one, then the other must follow. Give them both up and you are free from the negative effect either may have upon you.

6. You may make the mistake of working very hard in overcoming your emotional response to blame but revel whenever praise is heaped upon you.

7. You should guard against a personal emotional high. It is much easier to be deceived by the praise of the world than the blame. Be alert. "For they loved the praise of men more than the praise of God" (John 12: 43).

8. For praise, a soft outer "Thank you" is enough, while knowing it is the Father who does the work. When others praise you, you should silently give praise to God. "While I live will I praise the LORD: I will sing praises unto my God while I have any being" (Psalm 146: 2).

9. Blame should be received with one major difference. Your response should be a soft *inner*, "Thank You." You can always learn from blame. Whether you believe it to be justified or not, it puts daggers into the heart of an ego and holds at bay false pride.

10. You cannot overcome one and not the other. Both must be neutralized in the forgiveness and purification process through the Holy Spirit in the name of Jesus Christ.

STUDENT'S STORY:

Unfortunately, it has taken me a long time to acknowledge the damage and distortion resulting from attachments to positive feedback and overt praise and adulation. Because praise registered on my emotional screen as "pleasant to the touch" I never suspected it as a distortion of the truth. These pleasant variations on the fundamental error never caused me much alarm. It never occurred to me that such inflations were as equally misleading as the desolations I experienced with the least little bit of blame flung my way.

Oh, yes, my teacher repeatedly reminded me, "praise and blame are the same" and "what goes up must come down," but rarely, until very recently, did I really "get" what would be necessary to become free of the see saw, roller coaster, and emotional ride I'd been on all my life. Now it seems so obvious, but trust me, it was not an easy lesson. It was with great suffering and sadness caused by repeated and intense blame/criticism of my preaching style, content, and delivery, that I realized that to get "rid" of the pain I must be ready and willing to get rid of the gain. It was the intense emotional pain that moved me to see that praise and blame were the same. I was willing to do *anything* to be rid of the negative lows that I experienced when criticized by others. To be rid of the lows would entail my willingness to be rid of the pleasurable highs that accompanied the praise and adulation. I was willing.

For the first time, I saw the entire equation. I opted to take responsibility for the choice to let go of both distortions of the truth. My choice was for freedom from attachment and for emotional equilibrium coupled with the freedom to respond appropriately to praise or blame and to know them for what they really were — energy rising.

The true source of my well being and self-esteem is the abiding surety of God's unconditional love and presence in the heart of my being. In that certitude I can now receive praise with a gracious "thank you" and blame/criticism with an equally gracious, "thank you" and having responded, get on with my day without any emotional drama, dialogue, or regret. "Truly my soul waiteth upon God: from him *cometh* my salvation. He only *is* my rock and my salvation; *he is* my defence; I shall not be greatly moved" (Psalm 62: 1 - 2).

+ +

LESSON: 130 — PRAYER METHOD - SILENT

A SILENT PRAYER method is a means you may use to become aware of truth.

1. Within the Christian tradition, a silent prayer method is referred to as contemplative prayer. In recent times, some refer to this prayer method as meditation. For the sake of clarity The Lessons use the term silent prayer method or silent prayer practice.

2. There are many types of silent prayer methods. You have a wide range of choices to choose from and the decision should be based on whatever is necessary for you. There is no right or wrong method. The choice of any one of the silent prayer methods should be one of comfort and relatedness to your spiritual integrity.

3. A silent prayer method may have many other benefits — stress reduction, calming, peacefulness, feeling of well being, and flexibility. These are some of the fruits realized in daily life as a result of the faithful practice of a silent prayer method.

4. The most important decision you can make is to choose a method and commit your time and effort to the practice. If you find the choice does not fit, you will be aware of it almost immediately. Indecision may be excruciatingly stressful and binds the energy you could be using to awaken to the Christ within.

5. It is a mistake to continuously bounce about from one method to another. There must be a moment when one of the methods is chosen and, with determined purpose, is practiced. The sooner you are able to surrender, trust, and become committed to a chosen silent prayer method, the sooner any and all of the help you may need on the spiritual path may appear.

6. A silent prayer practice may assists with the purification/forgiveness process. With a silent prayer practice, you may find all of the necessary assistance be they books, situations, travels, teachers, etcetera are attracted to you as the need arises.

7. As those who roamed in the desert for forty years, perhaps you may fear knowing the truth. Remember how the Israelites sent Moses to go up the mountain to meet and talk with God? Moses could then come back and tell them about what God may have wanted of them. In the meantime, they created a false idol. Isn't that what you may be doing? You go to church to hear about God, but resist turning within where you may know God for yourself.

8. A silent prayer method is a most useful tool. Begin your silent prayer practice today. The only equipment necessary to practice is "you." You have all of the necessary parts to get started. A silent prayer method may allow you to bring the busy mind to rest and to enter the chamber of sacred silence.

+ +

LESSON: 131 — PRAYING - PRAYERS

PRAYING PRAYERS IS a conscious aware act of petition, intercession, thanksgiving, praise, and/or a devotional intent. For followers of Jesus Christ, prayers may be an integral practice of faith.

1. Praying prayers and a silent prayer practice are different. When you are intentionally praying prayers, you are using the mind. In a silent prayer practice, you are allowing the mind to rest.

2. Praying prayers, whether aloud or in the silence, requires concentration, thinking, and memory.

3. Praying on a spiritual walk is encouraged. Praying prayers and/or pondering Scripture may prepare the mind for its rest before beginning a silent prayer practice.

4. Praying prayers at anytime, except during a silent prayer practice, may have its benefits. Praying prayers may deepen a faith, expand spiritual contemplation, and may help to steady your steps on a spiritual walk.

5. In prayers, scripture, and a silent prayer practice, you are always being invited into the Spiritual Heart Center to walk with Mary and Jesus through the power of the Holy Spirit.

6. Praying prayers and a silent prayer practice should not be mixed. Praying prayers may occur anytime before or after a silent prayer practice. Christians have many forms of prayers. The following are the three prayers many Christians often pray.

THE HAIL MARY:

A. In the Hail Mary, you recognize Mary's purity, "To a virgin espoused to a man whose name was Joseph, of the house of David; and the virgin's name *was* Mary. And the angel came in unto her, and said, Hail, *thou that art* highly favoured, the Lord *is* with thee: blessed *art* thou among women" (Luke 1: 27 - 28).

B. You acknowledge, blessed is the fruit of her womb that she had conceived, you praise her as the Mother of God, and ask her to pray for our sins. "And the angel answered and said unto her, The Holy Ghost shall come upon thee, and the power of the Highest shall overshadow thee: therefore also that holy thing which shall be born of thee shall be called the Son of God" (Luke 1: 35).

C. The Hail Mary honors a young woman who willingly gave Her consent to a virgin conception. "And Mary said, Behold the handmaid of the Lord; be it unto me according to thy word. And the angel departed from her" (Luke: 1: 38).

D. Praying the Hail Mary allows you to bring to mind a blessed Scriptural event.

E. Praying the Hail Mary with full awareness of recognition, praise, and blessedness may bring you to the experience of a closer relationship with the Blessed Mother.

THE LORDS PRAYER:

A. "After this manner therefore pray ye: Our Father which art in heaven, Hallowed be thy name. Thy Kingdom come. Thy will be done in earth, *as it* is in heaven. Give us this day our daily bread. And forgive us our debts, as we forgive our debtors. And lead us not into temptation, but deliver us from evil: For thine is the kingdom, and the power, and the glory, forever. Amen" (Matthew 6: 9-13).

B. This one short prayer contains the complete instructions to begin an interior prayer practice; maintain it, and journey home to the kingdom of God.

C. The Lord's Prayer begins with Jesus guiding your attention - conscious awareness directed toward Our Father, the God state which resides-vibrates within your heart. "And hope maketh not ashamed; because the love of God is shed abroad in our hearts by the Holy Ghost which is given unto us" (Romans 5: 5).

D. In the salutation, "Our Father in heaven," Jesus clearly establishes the God consciousness state as a place other than geography of this world. "So then after the Lord had spoken unto them, he was received up into heaven, and sat on the right hand of God" (Mark 16: 19). This is referring to heaven as a higher state — "up." "For I came down from heaven, not to do mine own will, but the will of him that sent me" (John 6: 38).

E. Jesus gives the most high, sacred praise, "Hallowed be your name." Scripture gives praise to this

Divine Spiritual God. "God *is* a Spirit: and they that worship him must worship *him* in spirit and in truth: (John 4: 24).

F. "Your kingdom come. Your will be done on earth as it is in heaven." It is this Holy Sacred Kingdom, and Will that Jesus instructs you to experience — the kingdom, God's "will" within you, while you are yet on the earth plane. The kingdom that is not of this world. "Jesus answered, My kingdom is not of this world: if my kingdom were of this world, then would my servants fight, that I should not be delivered to the Jews: but now is my kingdom not from hence" (John 18: 36). "For the kingdom of God is not meat and drink; but righteousness, and peace, and joy in the Holy Ghost" (Romans 14: 17).

G. "Give us this day our daily bread." It is not man made bread Jesus is instructing you to request. "And Jesus said unto them, I am the bread of life: he that cometh to me shall never hunger; and he that believeth on me shall never thirst" (John 6: 35).

H. "And forgive us our debts, as we forgive our debtors." One of the greatest Spiritual Principle for you to learn and realize is the forgiveness of yourself and others. "For if ye forgive men their trespasses, your heavenly Father will also forgive you" (Matthew 6: 14).

I. Forgiveness touches every phase of your life because it allows the purification process to cleanse your heart, purify your energy, rid yourself of judgment and bitterness, and it releases you of negative conditioning impressions. If you don't move beyond holding on to old hurts/impressions, you deny yourself the blessing of the purification process in lightness and freedom of being.

J. "And lead us not into temptation, but deliver us from evil." Jesus was not referring to God leading you into temptation but that you not enter into temptation as it rises. You are asking for the protection, as temptation rises, that God not allow you to be led into it. Simply put, when you are faced with a temptation that would lead you away from the kingdom, you are asking God to lead you not in that direction but rather away from it (evil). "Watch ye and pray, lest ye enter into temptation. The spirit truly *is* ready, but the flesh *is* weak" (Mark 14: 38).

K. Jesus teaches in a few words the direction of the kingdom of God. "Neither shall they say, Lo here! Or, lo there! for, behold, the kingdom of God is within you"(Luke 17: 21). "Ye are of God, little children, and have overcome them: because greater is he that is in you, than he that is in the world" (1 John 4: 4).

L. The Lord's Prayer constantly guides you to the silence of your being, the God within you. Through the Holy Spirit in the name of Jesus Christ, the Lord's Prayer begins from the letter of the word, rises to the metaphysical, and carries you to the mystical. "And this is life eternal, that they might know thee the only true God, and Jesus Christ, whom thou hast sent" (John 17: 3).

M. The Lord's Prayer, given to you by Jesus, teaches you the holiness of God, the coming of the Kingdom, and doing God's will on earth as it is in heaven. It is an informative and instructive prayer for any serious truth seeker on a spiritual walk.

THE ROSARY:

A. Ah! The Rosary. It contains all.

B. Praying, not just saying, but praying the Rosary with the help of rosary beads may take you on an experience of the spiritual journey as none other.

C. Slowly, mindfully, praying the Rosary, takes you from the beginning of the recorded scriptural events of Mother Mary and Her Son to the end of its promised beginning of an awakened life.

D. Praying the Rosary allows you to be with Mary when she is asked to conceive Jesus, be with Jesus as He grows into manhood, travel with Him as He teaches, is persecuted, crucified, and is resurrected.

E. You are there beneath the cross with His Mother, when He asked John to care for her.

F. You hear Jesus ask the Father to forgive them who crucified Him, and you witness the pain in a Mother's heart when her son dies upon a cross.

G. You are also there for the burial, resurrection, and ascension. All given to you by praying the Rosary.

H. Ah! The Rosary, the power and the glory of praying the Rosary. Prayed with respect and sincerity of heart, touches your heart, and may strengthen your resolve on a spiritual walk.

+ +

LESSON:132 — PREPAREDNESS-READINESS-WILLINGNESS

PREPAREDNESS - READINESS - willingness are the results of slow methodical learning. Through your lifetime you are being nudged by the activity of the Holy Spirit in the name of Jesus Christ to the moment of awakening within pure awareness.

1. From a lifetime of yearning for and seeking truth, intentionally or unintentionally, comes the necessary preparedness that brings you to a state of readiness and willingness for the moment of awakening to your reality.

2. As you consciously begin a silent Christ Centered Prayer practice and gradually become aware of awakening, questions often rise. "How did it happen? "Why now?" "Why not sooner?" You may find it difficult to accept that "now" is all you have and a lifetime of "now" has prepared and made you ready for this "now."

3. When you become a serious truth seeker, it is because a state of preparedness, readiness, and willingness exist. It is an indication that the necessary spiritual work and practices have been done enabling you to walk towards the straight gate and the narrow way, to turn within to deeper inner insights and realizations.

4. All that has gone before brings you to a time of prepared readiness. The unwanted events, uninvited struggles, pain, and suffering were the tonics for a needed cure — waking up.

5. The darkness of trials and tribulations presented the opportunities to move to the brighter light of the Christ Consciousness in awareness. "Lord, thou hast been our dwelling place in all generations" (Psalm 90: 1).

6. Although a rough and rocky road at times may yet be necessary, the curves in the road are becoming straighter and more narrow until there is only the straight gate and the narrow way. The light at the end of the path will let you know it was the Lord who prepared you, who made you ready and willing to accept the invitation to follow in His footsteps. "I will go before thee, and make the crooked places straight" (Isaiah 45: 2).

7. Nothing is ever wasted. All that you have experienced in the outer world of illusionary appearances serves to bring you to the "now," when knowing your reality takes predominance within an inner journey. "This *is* the day *which* the LORD hath made; we will rejoice and be glad in it" (Psalm118: 24).

8. When you have been well prepared, made ready, and are willing to receive the truth teaching through the activity of the Holy Spirit in the name of Jesus Christ, you consciously begin a spiritual walk to an awakening. Your "now" has come. "Arise, shine for thy light is come, and the glory of the LORD is risen upon thee"(Isaiah 60: 1).

STUDENT'S STORY:

There is a Time For Everything Under Heaven . . . .

My mother always told me, "Sandy, in life timing is everything." I have also come to realize that in addition to "timing" are preparedness, readiness, and willingness! When all three are present, change results and moments of conversion occur. Although cautious and tenacious by nature, there have been occasions in my life when I have chosen to step out of my comfort zone and "go for it." These moments necessitated letting go of the familiar and venturing out into the unknown. They occurred when my "need exceeded fear." On these occasions, I moved and my life changed as a sign of the times!

To consider letting go of some highly cherished practice, discipline, or idea on the spiritual journey is not always easy. However, it may be necessary! Doubts rise and loyalties are often challenged whether they are to a person, place, or practice. For close to twenty years I had practiced an Eastern method of meditation and found it to be helpful and thought it was not in competition with my prayer or sacramental life as a Christian. What I was not aware was the attachment I had developed to this daily practice. Perhaps some of this attachment was due to years of sitting not to mention the amount of money I had spent on publications and advanced courses! I was invested to say the least. It did not occur to me that I might be overly attached until one day it was suggested I drop the practice and devote time and attention exclusively to my Christian disciplines and prayer.

Initially, I became defensive and annoyed; a sure sign a nerve had been accurately touched. Mind you, NOT the practice, but my attachment to the practice had been uncovered and this triggered an immediate emotional response. The intensity of my resistance to defend the discipline alerted me to the degree of my attachment and lack of freedom. There is one thing I know about the Christ Centered journey — it is a journey that moves out of slavery into freedom. To be free in Christ Jesus through the power of the Holy Spirit asks us to be unencumbered and light of burden.

My Eastern practice was deemed as restrictive by the simple fact that I was unwilling to let it go. What Jesus did with that revelation was to graciously wait on me. In response to my initial hesitancy, a casual comment from my teacher, "Perhaps you are not ready," allowed me to examine the attachment for what it was. I suppose in some way that statement appealed to my competitive nature and my desire to please and excel. Who me not ready? No way! The time between the invitation from my teacher and my dropping of the mantra practice was about a week.

God even makes use of our hesitations to effect His greater purpose. Jesus desired my exclusive attention. The working of the Spirit in the name of Jesus Christ wanted Sandy on the "straight and narrow" path. It was time. I could no longer ride down the spiritual river with my feet in two boats. My moment of "now" had come, I had to move, and I was invited to choose. I did.

My Eastern practice, which had served me well, graciously gave leave in the Christ awareness and wished me well. I had been well prepared and was ready. The mantra dissolved in the light of Christ and I continued on my way with gladness and singleness of heart.

++++++++++++++++++++++++++

LESSON: 133 — PRESENCE

THE PRESENCE IS the realization of the Oneness Spirit of Jesus Christ.

1. The presence of the Spirit of Jesus Christ is a strong, knowable, and viable presence emanating within the awareness of the Christ Consciousness.

2. In His presence is a sweet joy like none other. There is the wholeness of being complete, perfect as

One. The Spirit of Jesus Christ's presence is an unconditional, non- judgmental, pure vibrating energy always within your reach.

3. Follow Jesus' two commandments and you will be in the presence of Jesus Christ. "Jesus said unto him, Thou shalt love the Lord thy God with all thy heart, and with all thy soul, and with all thy mind" (Matthew 22: 37). "And the second *is* like unto it, Thou shalt love thy neighbor as thyself'" (Matthew 22: 39).

4. The Christ Centered Prayer practice of the awareness of the Spiritual Heart Center may help guide you to the door of the Christ Conscious Spirit of Jesus' presence.

5. Jesus is the example and the way to follow, and as you live a life of loving kindness you begin to move in the direction of Jesus' presence.

6. Live every moment of your conscious life as though you were in the presence of Jesus Christ. Do as He would do, in thought, word, and deed, and the presence of the Spirit of Jesus Christ may penetrate every pore of your existence.

+ +

LESSON: 134 — PRESENT

THE PRESENT IS an instant "now" of awareness. It is always in the present "now." There is never a behind, nor beyond.

PRESENT "NOW:"

A. Sit in a comfortable position, close eyes, and rest hands on lap.
B. Become aware of your breathing, the rising and falling of the abdomen area.
C. Breathe normally, being aware of the inhalations and exhalations from beginning to end. Do this several times.

1. The above is an experience of the aware be-ing present "now:" If you were able to do the above practice, you were experiencing the present, "now" with every aware breath. The present "now" is not something you can feel. It is the experience of be-ing itself.

2. The past consists of memories. The future consists of anticipations and expectations. The present "now" is life lived at its fullest.

3. A past memory may only be considered in a present "now" as a rising thought.

4. A future anticipation or expectation may only exist at the time of its present "now."

5. Neither a past memory, a future anticipation, nor expectation can be in the present "now." You may think about a memory but don't waste the present "now" on it.

6. You may make future plans in the present but don't spend or waste the present "now" in the anticipation or expectations of the possible outcome.

7. All you ever have is the present "now." To live in its fullest fruition requires your conscious aware attention.

8. If you are using the mind to remember a memory, in anticipation or expectation of a planned future event, you are wasting vibrating energy of the present "now".

9. To be fully aware is to be in the present "now." It is in the present "now" that a realization, insight, or wisdom is received. As you learn to live in the present "now," your inner hearing deepens and you are in tune with the necessary inner and outer guidance.

10. Within awareness there is no time, no space. When you re-enter the mind thoughts-body sense, you are back into relative time and space.

+ +

LESSON: 135 — PRIDE

"Pride goeth before destruction, and an haughty spirit before a fall" (Proverbs 16: 18).

1. On a spiritual walk, pride is an expression of consciousness of a false sense of being independently separate from your God source.
2. To live out of a state of willful pride blinds you to the light of God's radiance, the warmth of God's love, and a relationship of the Holy Spirit in the name of Jesus.
3. Prideful claims to your works, service, and seeking worldly awards or recognition are signs of immaturity on the path.
4. A boastful pride works against you, a loving humble Christ nature works for you.
5. Prideful attachment to this world denies the reality of what is.
6. A stiff neck pride may slow down, hold back, or retard your progress on the spiritual path.
7. Opinionated pride attacks what it does not understand, narrows your vision — restricting the light of awareness.
8. The haughtiness of pride prevents you from hearing clearly the Word of God, reading the Word of God, and closes your mind and heart to the love of Jesus, stifling possibilities on the path.
9. The stubbornness of pride may cause drifting and prevent you from seeking help when you may need it most. A prideful sense of being stalls mental flexibility that would invite Jesus to light the dark crevices of your mind and heart.
10. The arrogance of pride prevents you from being fully exposed to the teachings of Jesus Christ and a possible close relationship.
11. Pride in the belief that you do the work, you of yourself are independent creates a false sense of a separation from your higher, pure source of awareness.
12. A prideful being steeped in its self importance attempts to hold to the illusionary things of this world believing its identity is confirmed by what it possesses.
13. With the attachment of pride you display and boast of material wealth while disregarding spiritual worth.
14. Self-pride collects that which goes from dust to ashes, destined to leave you in a state of perpetual dissatisfaction.
15. False pride creates a sense of separation from the source and a false belief that you must fend for yourself.
16. All that you may accumulate, all that you may accomplish in this world in the name of pride, cannot ever bring to your nature the joy of living in the name of Jesus Christ. "For what is a man profited, if he shall gain the whole world, and lose his own soul? Or what shall a man give in exchange for his soul?" (Matthew 16: 26).

OVERCOMING FALSE PRIDE:

A. A prideful disposition is dissipated in the recognition, "Believest thou not that I am in the Father, and the Father in me? The words that I speak unto you I speak not of myself: but the Father that dwelleth in me, he doeth the works" (John 14: 10).

B. It is a humble spirit that dispels the false pride of being. "Whosoever therefore shall humble himself as this little child, the same is greatest in the kingdom of heaven" (Matthew 18: 4).

C. We are God's nature expressing God's will. How then, are you to boast of your good works, your loving ways? It is in God's nature you prosper and share all good things manifested for your use.

D. The silent Christ Centered Prayer practice with determined purpose, Holy Scripture, and an ever deepening love for Jesus Christ may move you from under pride's shadow into the light of a loving God.

+ +

LESSON: 136 — PROGRESS

Progress is a constant, subtle, inner vibratory energy, frequency change.

1. Progress on a spiritual walk is not something that is easily detected.
2. You cannot judge your progress by outer appearances or on whether you believe your silent Christ Centered Prayer practice is good or bad.
3. You are more likely to know where you are *not* than where you may be on a spiritual walk and that, too, is progress.
4. Many times, you may believe you have learned a lesson only to have it reappear in another form of desire or temptation.
5. Ups and downs, repeated lessons all contribute to your progress. Inner and outer activities are opportunities for you to work with. Be mindful your progress does not stop when you leave your prayer cushion.
6. Your or others' progress should not be judged or discussed. When you invest time and attention to spiritual activities with determined purpose, in or out of a silent prayer practice, you are progressing.
7. Your least amount of devotion to your spiritual activities in or out of a silent prayer practice, lends itself to progress on your spiritual walk.
8. Trust that as long as you are a serious devoted truth seeker, progress is constantly occurring through the Holy Spirit in the name of Jesus Christ.

+ +

LESSON: 137 — QUESTIONS

Questions are what rise when there is a need for a greater clarification about a truth teaching. They may be prompted by doubts, curiosity, cynicism, and an earnest love of truth.

1. There are no foolish questions.
2. Questions may be valuable teaching tools. They may be the doorway to insights and realizations.
3. Questions may work for you. They may allow you to work through the illusionary world of opposites to the center of your being.
4. Never shy away from asking questions before a teacher or guide, whether you are alone or in a group setting.
5. Ask questions and question the answers. Ponder the questions and the answers.
6. Each question that rises may casts light on that which you seek to realize.
7. Questions may rise to help assist you to stay alert and delve into the truth.
8. Questions may cause you to progress on your spiritual walk through the Holy Spirit in the name of Jesus Christ.

LESSON: 138 — QUIET

QUIET IS THE peaceful rest you gently, lovingly, and purposely allow the mind.

1. There is never a forcing of the mind to be still. Never in your silent prayer practice do you intentionally stop thinking. It is always a gentle allowing the rising thoughts, emotions, and senses to rise and fall and again becoming aware of the Spiritual Heart Center and rest in awareness.
2. Patiently practicing your silent prayer method will softly allow and invite the mind to a quiet, restful, peaceful state. It isn't necessary to manipulate nor ignore any rising manifestations.
3. You are not practicing to rid yourself of the mind. You are practicing to allow the mind to quietly rest.
4. The mind, although a poor master, is a wonderful servant. Respect it, give it its quiet rest, and use it as necessary.
5. If you are faithful with the Christ Centered Prayer practice, the mind will become less and less active and more quiet.
6. No inner dialoguing creates a quiet restful space for the rising vibrating energy to quickly fall.
7. As you practice the Christ Centered Prayer as you were taught, you may reap the reward of the mind's effortless restful quietness.
8. The Christ Consciousness within awareness you seek is yours within the Spiritual Heart Center through the Holy Spirit in the name of Jesus Christ.

LESSON: 139 — QUITTING

QUITTING IS A time when you want to give up your spiritual journey.

1. There may be many times during your spiritual journey when you want to quit, walk away, give up, and return to your world of illusionary being.
2. The highs may keep you going but the lows may cause you to want to quit.
3. You may even attempt to stop all spiritual practices and block out the truth you have realized. It won't work! Usually, you will find yourself returning to begin again.
4. Perhaps you may believe you have had enough and want time off; however, even during a time off, the inner truth realized will tug at you for attention.
5. Quitting really is not an option. You may believe at the time it is, but whether now or later, your spiritual journey will be continued.
6. Quitting may slow your progress but it does not impede your eventual waking-up. Not possible!
7. The Christ and the awareness of your being does not go away — does not disappear. That which you are is always being you — awake or asleep.
8. When you seek to quit, run away, you are running in place. When you begin your spiritual practices again, you are exactly where you left off.
9. Your conscious spiritual journey begins at your center through the Holy Spirit in the name of Jesus Christ. Your quitting and your beginning again occur at your center through the Holy Spirit in the name of Jesus Christ.
10. The illusionary circle you travel in this world always ends where you began. Realize your center and go around no more.

LESSON: 140 — RECOGNITION - JESUS'S PRESENCE

RECOGNITION - JESUS' Presence is a conscious awareness of an inner sacred presence.

RECOGNITION OF THE CHRIST PRESENCE WITHIN YOU:

   A. An inner nagging of wanting peace and quiet in your life.
   B. The urge to reach out to others in need.
   C. An expression of love.
   D. Seeking truth.
   E. Turning within.
   F. Not being totally contented with the things of this world.
   G. Questioning the validity of your life.

1. The above and many other signs are easily overlooked when you are racing through your days and nights. Recognition may bring acceptance and acceptance gives salvation. There are times that you may miss the obvious due to the closeness of it.

2. Although the presence of Jesus is always present, you may not always recognize it because you are living a busy life. You may seldom pause to recognize there is more in your life than the things of this world.

3. You cannot access what you do not recognize. If you are very poor and a relative willed you a million dollars and it sat in the bank without your ever knowing it was there, you would still be very poor.

4. You cannot spend what you do not recognize as yours nor can you enjoy the presence of Jesus Christ without recognition of it.

5. You are either like the many who walked away from Jesus' presence or like Peter who recognized Jesus' Holy presence and stayed with Him. "And we believe and are sure that thou art that Christ, the Son of the living God" (John 6: 69).

6. Jesus' presence is a light within you. Recognize and accept Jesus' presence and It will penetrate the darkness in a world of illusion through the Holy Spirit in His name.

LESSON:141 — RECONCILIATION-ATONEMENT-SALVATION

"FOR IF, WHEN we were enemies, we were reconciled to God by the death of his Son, much more, being reconciled, we shall be saved by his life. And not only so, but we also joy in God through our Lord Jesus Christ, by whom we have now received the atonement" (Romans 5: 10-11).

1. Jesus Christ gave His life for the atonement of humankind. How then, may you experience the reconciliation, the at-one-ment, the salvation?

2. Your reconciliation - atonement - salvation are not in "getting" what already has been given but rather, in "accepting" that which already has been given.

3. The Christ Centered Prayer practice, with a determined purpose, may gently guide you to that place where you may begin to open your heart and mind to the gift of reconciliation - atonement - salvation.

4. During your prayer practice, you are turning away from an outer world of right or wrong to an inner spiritual path of reconciliation with Jesus Christ in the acceptance of atonement, salvation.

5. When you purposely turn within, to the Holy Spirit in the name of Jesus Christ, you are liberating yourself from the worn false conceptions of this world. Your redeeming salvation is in the turning away to the turning within.

6. Through the activity of the Holy Spirit in Jesus Christ, you may share in a deeper relationship with Jesus Christ. The experience of reconciliation is in the acceptance of reconciliation.

7. When you cease to dialogue with rising thoughts during your silent prayer practice, you allow the purification and forgiveness process to rest in the "Holy Instant" of pure silence. Here you may experience reconciliation and at - one - ment.

8. By redeeming the purity of the vibrating energy that has been, intentionally, or unintentionally misused, you share reconciliation - atonement - salvation. Purification and forgiveness occur in the Holy Instant. "And Jesus said unto him, Verily I say unto thee, To day shalt thou be with me in paradise" (Luke 23: 43).

9. In God's Kingdom, that which is past is past. All impurities are cleansed in the reconciling - at-one-ment of the Divine's presence by the Holy Spirit in the name of Jesus Christ. "Come now, and let us reason together, saith the LORD: though your sins be as scarlet, they shall be as white as snow; though they be red like crimson, they shall be as wool" (Isaiah 1: 18).

10. The Christ of your Being in reconciliation - atonement - salvation welcomes you to the inner sanctum of your Being. Jesus calls you to a place where silence reigns and peace is established. This is the Holy of Holies. "But the LORD *is* in his holy temple: let all the earth keep silence before him" (Habakkuk 2: 20).

STUDENT'S STORY:

The experience I am going to share happened many years ago. When it happened, it was seared indelibly in my consciousness. It is as true for me today as it was many years ago. What has changed, however, is my understanding of what happened. As I worked with this Lesson, forgiveness and wisdom grew, deepened, and matured.

At first I had no theological language to speak of this experience. I didn't tell it to anyone for many years. I eventually shared it with my teacher. When enough time had passed with some historic distance and glimmers of some wisdom around it, I did begin to speak of it in the context of retreats when discussing the celebration of the sacrament of reconciliation. In no way did I plan, expect, or intend to have this experience. It had me is more accurate. So here it is:

During my second year of seminary at The Oblate School of Theology, I took a class called: Sin, Reconciliation, and Pastoral Care. The course was taught by a learned priest and professor of moral theology. The purpose of the course was to prepare clergy to celebrate the sacrament of reconciliation of penitents.

I studied the scriptural precedents for reconciliation in the life, actions, and teachings of Jesus, as well as the historical and cultural traditions developed throughout church history. I also learned that conversion was at the heart of the human experience of reconciliation and with God's grace it signaled the readiness to reconcile and the possibility of restoring of broken relationships. It was also the experience celebrated in the sacrament of reconciliation. All this sounded so exciting that I decided to apply it to my own life.

Since the class took place during the Spring Semester and Lent fell during that time, I intended to take the six week period and devote myself to a thorough honest investigation of my life. I opened myself to the possibility of conversion, transformation, and reconciliation. I studied and reflected on scripture daily, maintained my usual prayer periods, examined my conscience, fasted, and gave alms. All are traditional lenten disciplines.

I had spent a lot of time reviewing my life as openly and honestly as I could. The scriptural definitions of sin as "missing the mark," rebellion, mistake, and putting something created in the place of the Creator, all helped me assess my situation to date. It was an interesting six weeks.

Maundy Thursday I went to sleep and had an experience of encounter with Jesus, my Risen Lord, that was vivid, lucid, audible, and etched in my consciousness. I do not know exactly how long this encounter lasted, but I do know that it took as long as was necessary for me to get the point of the visit. Jesus wanted me to know the essence of reconciliation, divine union. When I emerged from the experience, I wrote it verbatim. To this day, I have never changed a word of it. The following is the verbatim. I will later offer reflections.

> "Clothed in brilliant white, face unseen yet known.
> Tall in splendor knowing, He says to me,
> 'Come home.'
> From deep within His being, He gently beckons me,
> 'Let go of all your sorrows. Come in me and find your peace.'
> One moment, Lord. I close my eyes, I need to go within.
> A second to reflect, I thought, before I can begin.
> Time then stopped in stillness. How long I cannot say.
> Lost somewhere within His love my Lord in me did pray.
> What of our encounter, Lord?
> You know we never had our chat.
> 'Hush, my child. Be still. Can you see? It's over just like that.'
> But Lord, it was too easy, to forget myself in thee.
> I wanted to tell you all there was.
> But you only wanted me."

Jesus simply appeared to me in full radiance and filled my entire conscious awareness. The brightness of the light was indescribable. Jesus' invitation and gesture to come home was explicit.

When everything stopped and the only language I can use to describe this time is utter stillness, nothingness, void. This was a long "nothing" and only after returning to awareness and again conscious of Jesus' presence did I know I had been lost somewhere although I had no knowledge or memory of where I had been or how long. The fact was Jesus had pulled me into Himself and beyond any radiance of Himself into THAT place is something I had no earthly knowledge of nor ability to understand until fairly recently.

Whatever did go on in that gap prepared me for the culmination of our encounter. Initially failing to realize the full impact of the gap, I resumed the conversation trying to remind Jesus that I had not even mentioned my litany of sins. The conversation was personal, direct, and respectful.

To my astonishment as in the biblical story of the Prodigal Son, there was absolutely no interest on Jesus' part to hear any of my stories. Rising to the occasion, of course, I told him to wait a minute so I could get myself in order before I began my rehearsed litany of sins. Jesus was not about to entertain that litany nor was He interested in the past. I will never forget Jesus' look of amazement when He simply responded, "Hush, my child. Be Still. Don't you see, it's over just like that." The humor was lost on me at the moment and continues on to this day. It seems to be my nature not to be able to leave well enough alone. I continued, "No, no, no, Lord that is not the way it is intended to be. It's supposed to be hard, humiliating, and embarrassing."

I suppose I was going to give Jesus a lesson on how to hear a confession! It was at that moment of remonstration with Jesus that I finally understood. Ah! I get it. I wanted to tell Jesus all there was. However, Jesus was only interested in me and Jesus only wanted all of me! The split second that realization dawned in my consciousness, Jesus disappeared. Not one second sooner or later. The moment I had the realization of true forgiveness, to put away punishment and experienced reconciliation, at - one - ment, a complete sense of peace and light filled my entire being. My true nature was not separate from God but deeply one in God through Christ. Amen!

Now, years later, I realize the infinite patience and tolerance my Lord has had for my dramas. I also know that there comes a time when He draws the curtain! I know what is true for me is true for all. It is for this reason that I share this little story. It profoundly illumined my mind and healed my heart. Forgiveness truly means to do away with, or to put off punishment. Jesus was not interested in my mistakes but He was keenly interested in my well being and having all of me. In the same way Jesus saw health and wholeness beneath all appearances and apparent distortions of my human broken-ness. He saw Sandy as beloved, holy, and restored her to wholeness. Just like that!

To be invited, loved, acknowledged, and drawn into intimacy and union with Christ by the power of the Holy Spirit is a powerful experience of reconciliation. We simply have to be willing to go there and having been in that embrace give gratitude and thanksgiving to God who in Christ is reconciling us and the world and everyone in the world to Himself.

+++++++++++++++++++++++++

LESSON: 142 — REFERENCE

REFERENCE IS THE place in truth where you are able to discern what others may say or write about truth.

1. When you read or listen to lectures, sermons, and theories about truth do so with interest and pleasure, while guarding against an outer pull to drift into intellectual speculations.

2. As you listen or read others' interpretation of truth, you should constantly be checking it in reference to the truth as *you* have realized it.

3. There is the subtle temptation to get swayed by written or oral speech. The rising mind is always inviting you to seek truth in the outer appearances. "Behold, I come quickly: hold that fast which thou hast, that no man take thy crown" (Revelation 3: 11).

4. You may find yourself getting caught-up in the speech or writings of others. New ideas and scientific progress may easily excite and stimulate the mental vibrating energy.

5. There is much written and spoken about truth, You have an inner gauge, realized truth, by which you may be consciously aware of the most minute differences.

6. The mind's intellect falls in love and may easily be carried away when it can wrap itself around interesting words and thoughts. "My little children, let us not love in word neither in tongue; but in deed and in truth" (I John 3: 18).

7. Read and listen with a reference to what you know is truth from within not what others may write or say about it.

8. Be as balanced when you are listening or reading, as you are when you are practicing your silent prayer.

9. Read and listen to others in a calm, centered conscious awareness, allowing the thoughts and words of others to be gently, quietly, and throughly filtered through *your* realization of truth.

10. The truth you have realized is your reference point for holding fast. Outer intellectual interpretations of truth may continue to tempt, but you remain true to realized truth.

+ +

LESSON: 143 — REFLECTION

ALL THAT APPEARS upon this earth is but a reflection of the light of your impersonal true God source. "All things were made by him; and without him was not anything made that was made" (John 1: 3).

1. The only way to see a reflection of God on this earth plane is to look into a mirror or into the eyes of another you. That which created you is the essence reflected within you.
2. Jesus came as a son of man appearing as a personal reflected male image on earth.
3. Mother Mary is the personal reflection or image of the feminine on earth.
4. If you wish to see a feminine reflection of the image of God on earth, then all a woman or girl need do is to look to herself.
5. On the plane of opposites, the impersonal One God appears reflected as the many, male - female. In truth there are no opposites — no male, female. "There is neither Jew nor Greek, there is neither bond nor free, there is neither male nor female: for ye are all one in Christ Jesus" (Galatians 3: 28).
6. All creation is but a reflection of the greater God source within conscious awareness. "And the scribe said unto him, Well, Master, thou hast said the truth: for there is one God; and there is none other but he" (Mark 12: 32).
7. The One becomes the many in infinite reflected personal opposites as male - female upon this earth plane. The reflections are not the reality. In spirit there is neither male nor female. "Jesus answered and said unto them, 'Ye do err, not knowing the scriptures, nor the power of God. For in the resurrection they neither marry, nor are given in marriage, but are as the angels of God in heaven'" (Matthew 22: 29-30).
8. The Holy Spirit in the name of Jesus Christ guides the infinite personal opposites, back to their Oneness of eternal being. "I will overturn, overturn, overturn, it: and it shall be no *more*, until he come whose right it is; and I will give it *him*" (Ezekiel 21: 27).

+ +

LESSON: 144 — REGRESSION- SPIRITUAL

REGRESSION - SPIRITUAL is the review of the past experiences of your present life through the memory bank.

1. On your spiritual journey, the rising of thoughts, words, and deeds that you have buried in consciousness may rise for your attention
2. Many times on the spiritual path your most recent actions are brought to your attention. You may be given the opportunity to review your past experiences.
3. During a silent prayer practice many of your experiences in your life may rise. You are being allowed to purify, let go of any attachments to past persons, or events.
4. This is an important time in your life therefore, the regression into these experiences through memory may allow you to move on and progress more rapidly on your spiritual journey.

5. Regression of a few hours, days, or years of your present life may be a valuable teaching tool. The regression of the memories occurs in the present "now."

6. The present is "now," and it is always "now" when you may wake up.

+ +

LESSON: 145 — REJECTING REALITY

REJECTING REALITY IS the temptation to turn away from the spiritual journey.

1. There are times during your spiritual walk when you may find yourself deliberately rejecting reality.

2. There may come a moment, when you wish you could return to what you, and those around you, called "normal." "And Jesus said unto him, 'No man, having put his hand to the plough, and looking back, is fit for the kingdom of God" (Luke 9: 62).

3. It is interesting, because rejecting usually occurs when there is a quiet in your life. All is going well — there are no ups nor downs. And yet, these are the times you may want to return to the illusions of this world.

4. You may question your sanity. You may question whether the truth that you are, and come to have realized, *is* reality.

5. You may wonder, did I imagine the realizations? Which is the dream, this world or the Christ of my being?

6. You may even for a time be tempted to slip into the old skin of imaginings. "And he said unto them, Full well ye reject the commandment of God, that ye may keep your own tradition" (Mark 7: 9).

7. You may struggle with the idea of having to be an awakened Being while those around you are not yet awakened.

8. You may experience the feelings of being lost, not fitting in, and therefore wanting to reject the new for the old. The problem is, once awakened, there is no longer the "old."

9. You may play head games and attempt to convince yourself you can go back for a while. However, rejecting realized truth, leaves you with an itch that cannot be scratched.

10. Be comforted in the knowledge that rejecting the Christ at one time or another may come to any serious truth seeker. The temptation has always existed.

11. Remember Peter; he, too, rejected the Christ with a denial when he was asked if he knew Jesus. "But he denied before *them* all, saying, I know not what thou sayest" (Matthew 26: 70).

12. If such a moment tempts you on your journey, know that staying with the straight gate and the narrow way may be less difficult than meandering. Better to spend a time-out resting in the Holy Spirit in the name of Jesus Christ than to find yourself restlessly wondering.

+ +

LESSON: 146 — RELATIONSHIPS

RELATIONSHIPS ARE FAMILY and friends you know and the strangers you may meet on your spiritual walk.

1. When you begin a silent prayer practice, others in your life may not understand or be in agreement with the practice.

2. Family and friends may feel left out and think of the activity as odd.

3. There may be some attempt to discourage the continuance of a silent prayer practice.

4. It is your responsibility to hold fast to your determined purpose to walk a spiritual path.

5. You cannot bring along anyone who is not ready for an inner silent prayer practice.

6. In the beginning, this may be difficult for you to accept. When truth is revealed, it is natural to want to share it with those closest to you.

7. To attempt to force your way on others may do more harm than good. Your spiritual walk is specific to your spiritual need. In general, you may attempt to share and invite, but you cannot push or pull others in your direction.

8. The best rule for you to follow is to accept, allow, and respect where your

family, friends, and others may be at any given moment.

9. Patience and gentleness with family and friends may be required.

10. As you progress on the spiritual path, you may find family members become more receptive and less judgmental. Old friends may move out of your life and new ones may enter.

11. For a time, you may go through a transition where you are without old friends. Strangers, on your spiritual walk may become your new friends. You are comfortable with those of the same mind. There is an attraction towards those of like individual expressions of consciousness.

12. You may find, in time, your relationships change. The Holy Spirit in the name of Jesus Christ may attract a spiritual family and new friends from strangers. "For whosoever shall do the will of my Father which is in heaven, the same is my brother, and sister, and mother" (Matthew 12: 50).

+ +

LESSON: 147 — REMORSE

REMORSE IS A deep sorrow or regret from a particular thought, word, or deed committed against oneself or others.

1. Remorse is accepting the responsibility for your belief of having done harm to yourself or others. It is a deeply felt sorrow for your actions in thought, word, or deed.

2. Remorse may rise when there is the conscious knowing you may have insulted your own or another's spiritual integrity.

3. True remorse includes the recognition of a misconduct in thought, word, and/or deed. The torment and guilt from such conduct may in time turn to repentance. "The Lord is not slack concerning his promise, as some men count slackness; but is longsuffering to us-ward, not willing that any should perish, but that all should come to repentance" (II Peter 3: 9).

4. When you are consciously remorseful and turn away from misconduct in thought, word, and deed, you are making room for Jesus Christ in your life. "And who *is* he that will harm you, if ye be followers of that which is good?" (I Peter 3: 13).

5. Sorrowful remorse may allow the "Holy Instant" of forgiveness and purification to take place. Your life may be turned in a different direction. "In all thy ways acknowledge him, and he shall direct thy paths" (Proverbs 3: 6).

6. Do not wallow in remorseful quilt. Call upon the Lord, your God, and accept forgiveness through the Holy Spirit in the name of Jesus Christ. "Rejoice the soul of thy servant: for unto thee, O Lord, do I lift up my soul. For thou, Lord, *art* good, and ready to forgive; and plenteous in mercy unto all them that call upon thee" (Psalm 86: 4 - 5).

+ +

LESSON: 148 — RESURRECTION - ASCENSION:

JESUS OF NAZARETH rising from the dead in an enclosed tomb is the New Testament's account of Jesus rising from the dead. It is the rising from the grave of a false sense of birth and death. It is a resurrection of enlightenment through the Holy Spirit in the name of Jesus Christ.

1. Birth and death are relative to the plane of opposites. In the belief of a birth, there is death. What is born upon the plane of opposites must die.

2. The resurrection is beyond gender and the concept of birth or death, "But they which shall be accounted worthy to obtain that world, and the resurrection from the dead, neither marry, nor are given in marriage. Neither can they die any more: for they are equal unto the angels; and are the children of God, being the children of the resurrection" (Luke 20: 35-36).

3. The resurrection is the overcoming of the belief in the opposites. In the resurrection, you rise beyond the belief of birth or death.

4. The grave/death that you shall be resurrected from is your belief in an illusionary world where light and darkness exist, "And have hope toward God, which they themselves also allow, that here shall be a resurrection of the dead, both of the just and unjust" (Acts 24: 15).

5. For example, Martha questioned Jesus when he assured her, ". . . Thy brother shall rise again" (John 11: 23). Martha's understanding of the resurrection was of a future event. "Martha saith unto him, I know that he shall rise again in the resurrection at the last day" (John 11: 24).

6. In reassuring Martha, "Jesus said unto her, I am the resurrection, and the life: he that believeth in me, though he were dead, yet shall he live" (John 11: 25).

7. Jesus taught if you would believe in the teachings of His Father, then the resurrection and life that He is, you are. Jesus taught, before He was crucified, the importance of the resurrection - overcoming this world. "These things I have spoken unto you, that in me ye might have peace. In the world ye shall have tribulation: but be of good cheer; I have overcome the world" (John 16: 33).

8. To rise to the resurrection, all corrupted and dishonored vibrating energy must be purified and exist again in its original lightness of being. The false sense of body can, through the forgiveness and purification process, rise through the resurrection of your Christ Being to the awareness of life eternal. "So also *is* the resurrection of the dead. It is sown in corruption; it is raised in incorruption: It is sown in dishonour; it is raised in glory: it is sown in weakness; it is raised in power" (1 Corinthians 15: 42-43).

9. Jesus said, "I am the resurrection and the life." He added you must believe. "Now if Christ is preached that he rose from the dead, how say some among you that there is no resurrection of the dead? But if there be no resurrection of the dead, then is Christ not risen: And if Christ be not risen, then *is* our preaching vain, and your faith *is* also vain" (1 Corinthians 15: 12-14).

10. Jesus Christ's resurrection and overcoming this world is a living on, going on, now occurrence. It is truly good news! In and through Jesus Christ's resurrection the promise and reality of your own resurrection from a false sense of being is assured when you choose to obey, wake up, and follow in His foot steps. "And God hath both raised the Lord, and will also raise up us by his own power" (1 Corinthians 6: 14).

ASCENSION:

The ascension is the New Testament account of Jesus the Christ ascending to the Kingdom of God on the 40th day after Easter. It is an awakening within pure awareness. "And it came to pass while he blessed them, he was parted from them, and carried up into heaven" (Luke 24: 51).

1. This is a round trip spiritual event home to a finer vibratory energy. "And no man hath ascended up to heaven, but he that came down from heaven *even* the Son of man which is in heaven" (John 3: 13).

2. The spiritual journey on this plane of opposites is from the heavenly finest vibratory energy to the sense of a solid earthly one and back to the realization of the finest vibratory energy within awareness.

3. There is a sense of a progression descending to the earthly plane of opposites and a sense of regression ascending to the awareness of being. "(Now that he ascended, what is it but that he also descended first into the lower parts of the earth? He that descended is the same also that ascended up far above all heavens, that he might fill all things)" (Ephesians 4: 9-10).

4. The forgiveness and purification process resurrects a false separate sense of a personal physical body. When you are fully awakened, you may ascend to the finest vibratory energy within awareness.

5. When Jesus' disciples were astonished at His teaching "eating me to live," He quickly added, "*What* and if ye shall see the Son of man ascend up where he was before? It is the spirit that quickeneth; the flesh profiteth nothing: the words that I speak unto you, *they* are spirit, and *they* are life" (John 6: 62-63). Many turned away from Jesus on that day.

6. Jesus existed somewhere else before His birth on this plane and it was possible for Him to return. "In the beginning was the Word, and the Word was with God, and the Word was God" (John I: 1) "And the Word was made flesh, and dwelt among us, (and we beheld his glory, the glory as of the only begotten of the Father), full of grace and truth" (John I: 14).

7. As the son of man, Jesus' body-flesh was not His life, nor is it yours. "And now, O Father, glorify thou me with thine own self with the glory which I had with thee before the world was" (John17: 5).

8. You too, have descended from within the most high and you too, are spirit, not flesh. You too, will ascend to where you were before. Jesus was teaching the way, He is the way, the way to follow, and the way to ascend to your God reality of Being. You may have forgotten from where you descended but the return trip is as it was in the beginning. "In the beginning was the Word, and the Word was with God, and the Word was God" (John 1: 1).

9. As you descend this world, it exists for you. When you ascend fully awakened, in awareness, it will no longer exists. In reality, you are always where you began and never left.

10. Birth, persecution, crucifixion, death, resurrection, and ascension apply to you as they did for Jesus. Jesus' spiritual walk upon this earthly plane and His spiritual journey home is the same straight gate and narrow way you are traveling through the Holy Spirit in His name.

+ +

LESSON: 149 — RETREAT CENTER

A RETREAT CENTER is a place to visit where you may learn a silent prayer practice or visit for spiritual renewal.

1. In general, retreat centers usually provide for all your basic needs that allow you to reflect, contemplate, practice silent prayer, and pray undisturbed. The time you may spend in a retreat center is usually optional, according to the center's schedule and yours.

2. A silent retreat is not for everyone. It is wise to start a first silent prayer practice retreat for a weekend. It will allow you to discover if you are ready for the change from a busy worldly environment to silence. If you find it to your liking, you may later want to increase the time. As you become more disciplined with your silent prayer practice, you will become more comfortable with a retreat center setting.

3. A retreat center may be supportive and beneficial in helping you to rest. However, you need be prepared for the solitude and the possible purification, forgiveness, and healing that may occur as your silent prayer practice intensifies.

4. There are retreat centers that allow individual non-guided silent prayer programs. You probably would have to create a prayer schedule for yourself. A retreat schedule may consist of alternating your sitting silent prayer practice with other silent activities such as, eating, walking, reading scripture, napping, and taking care of personal needs.

5. Christian retreat centers may offer a variety of Christian activities. Be sure you select one that is conducive to your silent prayer practice, whichever method you practice.

6. There are many Christian retreat centers listed on the internet. Know what it is you want, then investigate exactly what they offer. Ask questions about cost, what you should bring, and if there would be a consultant or teacher there, should you need assistance. If for any reason, you are not satisfied with a retreat center, leave.

7. It is the noise of the world that keeps you asleep. It is the silence within that awakens you to the awareness reality. "But thou, when thou prayest, enter into thy closet, and when thou hast shut thy door, pray to thy Father which is in secret; and thy Father which seeth in secret shall reward thee openly" (Matthew 6: 6).

8. The purpose for a silent retreat is to deepen your silent prayer practice, immerse yourself in the teachings of the Holy Spirit in the name of Jesus Christ, and awaken you to the reality of awareness. "And he said unto them, Come ye yourselves apart into a desert place, and rest a while: for there were many coming and going, and they had no leisure so much as to eat" (Mark 6: 31).

+ +

LESSON: 150 — SACRED AND SECRET

SACRED AND SECRET is the protective environment you create for your spiritual walk.

1. You will find your spiritual practices, insights, and realizations deepen when you hold them in sacred and secret protection.

2. The less you talk about your inner experiences the more likely you will progress on your spiritual walk. Too much talk causes doubts and temptations to rise.

3. When first you realize the Christ of your being, It is as a baby Jesus whom you must protect from the Herods of this world. Hold your baby Jesus close within your Spiritual Heart.

4. As Mary and Joseph had to protect the baby Jesus from the Herod of their world, you must do likewise. ". . . Arise and take the young child and his mother, and flee into Egypt, and be thou there until I bring thee word: for Herod will seek the yong child to destroy him" (Matthew 2: 13).

5. Allow the inner experiences to grow to maturity in a sacred and secret place within the Spiritual Heart Center.

6. Do not be too quick to share or proselytize. Wisdom is slow to follow enlightenments and realizations. If you think yourself to be wise, you are not. Wisdom is not a thought. The mind dabbles in falsities.

7. To run your mouth off about what you do not yet fully understand in wisdom is folly. It may turn others away and give cause to question your sanity.

8. Waking up does not make you better than others. All that you are, others are also. You are waking up and they have yet to wake up. Therefore, be patient with what you have and are receiving. Even Paul waited a number of years before he began his ministry.

9. If you should have a truth teacher or guide then of course, share with him or her. It is necessary to establish a close working relationship with your teacher or guide.

10. If you do not have a teacher or guide, it is your responsibility to practice the discipline of sacred secretness. When your time has come, the Holy Spirit in the name of Jesus Christ will speak for you.

+ +

LESSON: 151 — SENSES

THE SENSES ARE your means for experiencing the plane of opposites through a physical sense of a mind and body.

1. The senses, hear, sight, touch, taste, and smell are constantly recording no matter what the learned conditioned is.

2. On the plane of opposites, the senses respond to learned conditioning.

3. The rising senses do not change in their intended function. The learned conditioning may change. Realizing hearing, seeing, touching, tasting, and smelling, is all the senses are constantly doing, is a realization within pure awareness.

4. You may become aware consciously of sight, touch, taste, or smell as they rise in conscious awareness. Examples: a vision of a rose appears. Actually, the only thing that is occurring with the sense of sight is seeing.

5. The learned-conditioned impression, concept received and interpreted is "a rose." Seeing is all that is going on. A car horn is heard. The only thing occurring is hearing. The learned, interpreted conditioned impression is "a car horn."

6. Seeing is the same sense when it sees a cat, dog, or person. It does not matter what the perceived conditioned impression is, the sense of seeing remains the same. This is true for all of the senses.

7. When you identify yourself with the senses or the body, you have created a false concept of self.

8. When receiving conditioned impressions remember, many of the conditioned impressions are created for you by your culture, family and friends. The importance of understanding the senses is in the realization you are not the senses — you, as an individual expression of consciousness use the senses.

+ +

LESSON: 152 — SENSITIVITY

SENSITIVITY IS TAKING personally the hurtful criticisms others may heap upon your outer works in the service of Jesus Christ.

1. As you progress on a spiritual walk, knowing the inner realizations of the Holy Spirit in the name of Jesus Christ creates outer changes. At times, you will be tempted to deny the changes. Peter did. "But he denied before *them* all, saying, I know not what thou sayest" (Matthew 26: 70). "And again he denied with an oath, 'I do not know the man'" (Matthew 26: 72).

2. Old habits may fall away. Your dislikes and likes may change. These outer changes may be seen or felt by some as a threat. What others don't understand about you may be threatening. As a result, there may be criticism of how you approach your outer activities or responsibilities. "And the light shineth in darkness; and the darkness comprehended not" (John 1: 5).

3. No matter what the position or responsibilities you have in this world, your allegiance is to the Christ of your being. Your kingdom is not of this world. "Jesus Answered, My Kingdom is not of this world . . ." (John 18: 36).

4. You are a new being and your thoughts are not the old thoughts of those around you. "For my thoughts are not your thoughts, neither *are* your ways my ways, saith the LORD" (Isaiah 55: 8). "Therefore if any man *be* in Christ, *he is* a new creature: old things are passed away; behold, all things are become new" (II Corinthians 5: 17).

5. You are being fed from within, not as those who would have you as one of them. This world can't comprehend the manna you share with Jesus Christ. "But he said unto them, I have meat to eat that ye know not of" (John 4: 32).

6. There are times when the critics will prick at your sensitivities and you must take on the armor of the Christ and shake off the dust of the critics. "And whosoever shall not receive you, nor hear your words, when ye depart out of that house or city, shake off the dust of your feet" (Matthew 10: 14).

7. Returning to old ways (theirs), is intentionally returning to a previous expression of consciousness. It carries serious consequences. It would be a denial of the Christ Consciousness. "But whosoever shall deny me before men, him will I also deny before my Father which is in heaven" (Matthew 10: 33).

8. As you grow in the Holy Spirit in the name of Jesus Christ, the straight gate and narrow way at times may be more difficult. It means, as Jesus did, you must also do. Jesus never denied the Divine, and you cannot ever deny Jesus. You *are* a new teaching. Your very Christ being exudes the teaching of Jesus Christ. "For he taught them as *one* having authority, and not as the scribes" (Matthew 7: 29).

9. There are subtle ways of denying Jesus. Many times it is a denial of omission. Quietly changing or hiding your light to allay the fears of others. "Ye are the light of the world. A city that is set on an hill cannot be hid" (Matthew 5: 14). You have a choice of denying Jesus or denying yourself. "Then said Jesus unto his disciples, If any *man* will come after me, let him deny himself, and take up his cross, and follow me" (Matthew 16: 24).

10. The masses will not welcome you with open arms. The masses crucified Jesus and if He walked the earth today, they would crucify Him again. Those who realize the Christ of their being through the Holy Spirit in the name of Jesus Christ are Jesus walking the earth today. Yes, in denying yourself, you do take up your cross and in your sensitivities you are crucified in the name of Jesus Christ.

11. That which pricks is the crown of thorns; bearing the Word of God is carrying the cross; tearing down your self-esteem is striping of the garments; hammering away at your (Jesus's) ways; the nails in the wrist; and trying to destroy or kill the Christ light, is the piercing of the sword in the side. In all things you do identify with Jesus Christ unto your salvation, resurrection, and ascension. "And I, if I be lifted up from the earth, will draw all *men* unto me"(John 12: 32).

12. The temptations (critics) of this world are infinite in number and appearances. Temptations (critics) aren't always immediately recognizable. They come in all sizes, shapes, and often may be disguised as friends. Your defense is the same one Jesus used. "Get thee behind me, Satan! . . ." (Luke 4:8).

13. Truth casts a bright light which may cause a disturbance among many. And, at times, it may cause your heart to ache for those you cannot reach, as it did Jesus. "O Jerusalem, Jerusalem, thou that killest the prophets, and stonest them which are sent unto thee, how often would I have gathered thy children together, even as a hen gathereth her chickens under *her* wings, and ye would not!" (Matthew 23: 37).

14. As Jesus is, you are with all things and persons: kind, loving, and patient. Praise or blame are the same. Jesus knew then, as He does now, whether they were singing His praises one day or crucifying Him the next, that the God of His being is perfect. He never used the mighty power of God to prove it. He

was aware all would bow before the Lord of hosts in a time prepared. ". . . Not by might, nor by power, but by my spirit, saith the LORD of hosts" (Zechariah 4: 6).

15. To allow the critics of this world to prick your sensitivities is to seek the praise and glory of men. "For they loved the praise of men more than the praise of God" (John 12: 43).

16. You suffer the stings (criticisms) of this world because of the attachment to a belief in the personal sense of a separate self, who you believe needs protecting. The light of the Lord cannot be put out, and it is yours. "The LORD *is* my light and my salvation; whom shall I fear? The LORD *is* the strength of my life; of whom shall I be afraid?" (Psalm 27: 1).

+ +

LESSON: 153 — SERIOUS

SERIOUS IS WHAT you are when your spiritual walk is your priority.

1. When you are a serious truth seeker, you are self-motivated.
2. As a serious truth seeker, your outer life conforms to your inner one.
3. You do maintain a sense of humor while staying on the straight gate and narrow way you have chosen to follow.
4. As a serious truth seeker, you are grateful for all that has been given to you. However, you do not rest on what you have until you are fully awakened.
5. Being serious allows you to concentrate on the teachings and studies to which you are exposed.
6. As a serious truth seeker you find the necessary time for your silent Christ Centered Prayer practice.
7. Being a serious truth seeker may assure you a steady progress on your spiritual walk.
8. When you are a serious truth seeker, all you will ever need is available through the Holy Spirit in the name of Jesus Christ.

+ +

LESSON: 154 — SERVANT I - THE CHRIST

FROM WITHIN THE Kingdom of God, with a grateful heart, you are a Christ servant of your God source. You are an acceptable, good and worthy servant when you are obedient, loyal, and do all things the Holy Spirit in the name of Jesus Christ asks of you. "Wherefore we receiving a kingdom which cannot be moved, let us have grace, whereby we may serve God acceptably with reverence and godly fear"(Hebrews 12: 28).

1. Your servant ear and sight are always on the Master. Your attention is not distracted by the things of this world. You may have and enjoy the things of this world but they are not your priority. As a Christ servant you are always on call. Your interest is to do the Master's bidding. ". . . Speak, LORD, for thy servant heareth . . . " (1 Samuel 3: 9).

2. You are a Christ servant who is humble unto God. Without humility you would seek recognition, titles, and honors from others and your head would be turned by the applause of this world. Your response is always consent to the demands of the Christ. "Also I heard the voice of the Lord, saying, 'Whom shall I send, and who will go for us?' Then said I, Here *am* I; send me" (Isaiah 6: 8).

3. Hear the "still small voice" that reveals truth. Follow in the steps of Jesus joyfully. Allow the separate personal sense to drop away, as you come to identify with your Lord and Master in the silence of your being. "Verily, verily, I say unto you, The servant is not greater than his lord; neither he that is sent greater than he that sent him. If ye know these things, happy are ye if ye do them" (John 13: 16-17).

4. The Christ servant knows his Master as himself. In knowing in reality that it is you, yourself, whom you serve, you cease to rely on or seek this world's recognition, titles, and honors. The service itself is your reward.

5. The Christ servant is at the mercy of his Master, a merciful God. Therefore, he shares in the nature of his Master — God. "For thy mercy *is* great unto the heavens, and thy truth unto the clouds" (Psalm 57: 10).

6. As a Christ servant, you never ask, "Whom shall I serve now God?" You are aware no matter how many or whom you serve, it is God you serve. To serve in the Christ army of One, is to lead a balanced life — not being pulled in different directions by the candies of this world.

7. Jesus asks you not to lose heart if your service is not appreciated. Those who do not welcome your service in a worthy manner are the unfortunate ones. "He that receiveth you receiveth me, and he that receiveth me receiveth him that sent me" (Matthew 10: 40).

8. You are the servant and the receiver of all acts of service. Be worthy of both expressions. The heartfelt joy experienced from pure, unconditional service is like none other. The Christ servant is always on the giving *and* receiving end. The Christ serves the Christ.

STUDENT'S STORY:

One of the clearest examples of this teaching occurred when I was seeking to change jobs. After several disappointing and humiliating rejections, and my incredibly strong negative reaction to them, I had to admit I was more interested in a "job" than in Jesus Christ as the source of my emotional, spiritual, and financial security! I claimed, "All I want is God," but my frustrated emotions reported more accurately, "No, what you really wanted was the damn job!"

Arriving at a state of contentment and peace with or without the job would indeed take a lot more purification, conversion, repentance and grace. Fortunately, God continued to give me opportunities to see the "forest from the trees." Opportunities, I might add, I neither wanted nor enjoyed, but were absolutely necessary.

Eventually I was offered a job. It was not the job I had expected. This happened only after I admitted to my deeply disguised self interest and began to see how powerfully it commanded and controlled my time, attention, and emotional life.

Once I became available to the grace of God who forgave that mistake, new avenues for intimacy opened and so did a new job! The most appropriate and necessary position for me would be as a genuine Christ servant. A position to serve as the Associate Rector in a large Episcopal parish came to my attention. Although it certainly had not been on my radar screen (the world would see that as a demotion), I was given the grace to see and understand this job as a promotion. I had not been ready, willing, or worthy of this Christ servant job until now. I was too busy pursuing the various versions of what "I" considered to be a Christ servant. Jesus' choice for this presumptuous child of God would be quite different.

The embodiment of humility and service vividly referenced in Jesus' washing of the disciples' feet is clear and straight forward. "Verily, verily, I say unto you, The servant is not greater than his lord; neither he that is sent greater than he that sent him. If ye know these things, happy are ye if ye do them" (John 13: 16 - 17). I finally "Understood this," and the jury is still out on whether or not I am humbly and happily able to "do it."

\+ +

LESSON: 155 — SERVANT II - INDIVIDUAL TYPES

As a servant of Jesus Christ, there are four types of individual expressions of consciousness you may serve: family and friends, the many various individuals, an individual, and the serious truth seeker. There are individual differences within the four types you serve. Of course, in reality, they are all the ONE.

FAMILY AND FRIENDS - TYPE I:

1. Family and friends require a special kind of service because of the long time relationship you may have with them and the open, personal, and up-close relatedness that may, at times, be difficult to manage.

2. If your family and friends are not aware of your commitment to a contemplative life, and they usually are not, maintaining an on-going relationship may be challenging. Family and friends have special needs and usually expect your immediate attention and time. With children, there remains a responsibility of nourishing and being available. With friends there is always the supportive attention and contact that has developed over the years.

3. As a Christ servant realizes detachment, family and friends may become the most difficult folks to relate to because of their expectations and demands. With these individuals there may be expected unspoken lifetime contracts, and unless they wish to dissolve them they will expect you to keep the terms. This may cause a falling away or releasing of a relationship.

4. Family and friends require loving kindness, attention, availability, tons of patience, and a compassionate ear and tongue. There will be times when the Christ servant begs Jesus for help to negotiate the relationship.

THE MANY VARIOUS INDIVIDUALS - TYPE II:

1. I am sure you are well familiar with this type. Not all individuals served will be cooperative. Some may be obstinate, especially in the beginning.

2. There will always be various individuals within the many type who will vie for special attention and apply unwanted pressure. Within the many various individuals, the Christ servant must gain trust and tolerance.

3. The many type requires loving kindness, flexibility, caring consideration of their needs, tons of patience, and compassion in all that the Christ servant is called upon to do. There will be times when the Christ servant begs Jesus for help to cope with the relationship.

THE INDIVIDUAL - TYPE III:

1. When the Christ servant is called upon to serve one particular individual in a close working relationship, it is a little different. This service requires loving kindness, tons of patience, and a good deal of flexibility.

2. The Christ servant must remember who makes the final decisions, and stepping back when the individual being served insists on doing it his/her way.

3. The Christ servant suggests rather than insists and tends to the small things as though they were the large ones. The Christ servant humbly walks and works in the shadow of the individual being served and is compassion at all times and under all circumstances.

4. Although the Christ servant's primary responsibility is to serve the individual, types one and two are not to be excluded. The Christ servant is constantly progressing and expanding his or her ability to serve. There will be times when the Christ servant begs Jesus for help to sustain the multitude of relationships.

THE SERIOUS TRUTH SEEKER - STUDENT - TYPE IV:

1. When serving a serious truth seeker, the commitment of service takes a totally different slant. It requires a Christ servant teacher who serves, teaches, and guides. This relationship requires total trust and obedience from the start, not that the Christ servant teacher always gets it.

2. First and most important, the Christ servant teacher must maintain his or her presence in the Christ Consciousness. S/he must serve, teach, and guide the serious truth seeker as directed by Jesus Christ. When the serious truth seeker is ready to receive truth, it must be shared clearly and often requires repetition!

3. The Christ servant teacher must maintain a balance between the "two worlds," and must assist in establishing the same balance for his/her charge.

4. As with type 3, tons of patience, loving kindness, flexibility, humbly working in the serious truth seeker's shadow are required. Stepping back when the serious truth seeker insists upon doing it his or her way is also required of the Christ servant.

5. The Christ servant teacher must be available and quick to respond to the serious truth seeker's needs. There may be times when the Christ servant teacher holds his or her breath, not knowing if the student has chosen to break the contact.

6. The Christ servant teacher must be able to discern the individual differences that exist among serious truth seekers.

7. The Christ servant teacher has the responsibility for the serious truth seeker's spiritual welfare (always aware that it is Jesus who has given the Christ servant teacher the charge).

8. The Christ servant teacher must tend to the serious truth seeker's mental and physical health because spiritual progress effects both.

9. The Christ servant teacher must know the signs and the conditions the serious truth seeker labors under. The Christ servant teacher must be sensitive to the disposition of the serious truth seeker.

10. Compassion must always exist in consideration for the serious truth seeker's needs. At times, compassionate discipline may be required and tons more patience may be necessary. As with the previous, the Christ servant teacher may often beg Jesus for help to get himself or herself through difficult situations.

SUMMATION OF THE FOUR TYPES:

1. The additional requirement for type four is more constant and closer contact between the serious truth seeker and Christ servant teacher.

2. The major difference with type four is that the Christ servant teacher is held accountable for his or her charge and never gives up as long as the serious truth seeker remains committed. With number 2 or 3, the Christ servant can change positions or jobs. The serious truth seeker also has a list of requirements that s/he must fulfill to maintain the relationship with the Christ servant teacher.

3. There are additional requirements that exist for the Christ servant teacher when the serious truth seeker is totally awakened.

4. Although the four different types appear individually and have individual differences, they do share the ONE most common thread — the Christ Consciousness. When you are serving the multitudes as individual expressions of consciousness, the Christ servant teacher has a responsibility to be aware of the reality of all s/he serves — the ONE

5. Most importantly, a Christ Servant teacher must attend to his or her own spiritual needs with the time and attention necessary to maintain his or her own inner life in obedient balance.

6. Jesus Christ's demands must be met before the Christ servant teacher is wisely able to meet the needs of others. Now with all that having been said, the serious truth seeker's spiritual progress within awareness is its own reward.

\+ +

LESSON: 156 — SEXUAL ENERGY

SEXUAL ENERGY IS the gross, dense, vibrating energy.

1. Sexual energy's prime purpose is procreation. "And God blessed them, and God said unto them, Be fruitful, and multiply, and replenish the earth, and subdue it: . . ." (Genesis 1: 28). Sexual energy in its broader use may be a force to be reckoned with.
2. Sexual energy in itself is neither negative nor positive. It is how the individual chooses to express it that determines its charge.
3. Sexual energy may influence behavior to the detriment of how sexual energy is expressed towards the individual and/or others. It may have the strength to break wills, good intentions, risk any loss of respect, dignity, or integrity.
4. Sexual energy is vibrating energy. It lacks a conscience. Its use, misuse, or abuse is solely dependent on the intention of the individual's state of consciousness.
5. An individual may attempt to contain or repress negative sexual activity. Societies may attempt to regulate what is or is not acceptable expression of sexual energy. There are no guarantees such containment or repression can be maintained. Cultural and societal values are subject to change and reinterpretation.
6. Because it is a lower heavy vibratory energy, sexual energy may affect an individual's emotional stability, thus interfering with decision making.
7. Sexual energy may overshadow common sense and extreme norms and lead an individual through a mire of offensive behaviors not ordinarily indulged in. It is a powerful energy which can override good intentions when left unchecked.
8. Sexual energy's strong pull toward an offensive activity may override all common sense, all good intent, and the love for a spiritual quest.
9. Selfish sexual activity possessively holds the individual's attention to the point of obscuring all that is reasonable and worthy.
10. A silent prayer practice over time may transmute, sublimate sexual energy into selfless service.

\+ +

LESSON: 157 — SIGN OF THE CROSS

MAKING THE SIGN of the cross is a Christian symbol of the Holy Trinity.

1. You honor and express your belief in the Holy Trinity whenever you make the sign of the cross — center of forehead saying, "In the name of the Father," center of chest, "and of the Son," left and then right shoulder, "and of the Holy Spirit. Amen."
2. If you would look into a mirror while making a sign of the cross, you may be aware that your form represents the appearance of a cross.
3. You are a living cross, the cross which you are instructed to take up and follow Jesus. "Then said Jesus unto his disciples, If any *man* will come after me, let him deny himself, and take up his cross, and follow me. For whosoever will save his life shall lose it: and whosoever will lose his life for my sake shall find it" (Matthew 16: 24 - 25).
4. The making of the sign of the cross is more than an outer symbol. It points directly to the straight

gate and narrow way — forehead, mental to the Spiritual Heart Center which you may enter, with the practice of the silent Christ Centered Prayer

5. Every time you touch the center of your forehead, the center of your chest, and say, "In the name of the Father, and of the Son," you are pointing to the straight gate and the narrow way. "Because strait *is* the gate, and narrow *is* the way, which leadeth unto life, and few there be that find it" (Matthew 7: 14). You have found it.

6. Every time you touch your center chest area and say, "And of the Son," you are pointing to the Spiritual Heart Center — the Christ Center.

7. And, every time you touch your shoulders and say, "And the Holy Spirit - Amen," you are acknowledging the power through which, in the name of Jesus Christ, you may become aware of the Father, Son, and Holy Spirit.

8. You have through the symbol of the sign of the cross, the way of the cross — the way of your spiritual journey. Every time you make the sign of the cross become aware of its inherent meaning, guidance, and blessing.

9. The Father, the Son, and the *Holy Spirit*. The Holy Trinity of the sign of the cross contains a sacred message. A message that is available at all times. One that is realized from the Father to the Son through the Holy Spirit within your Spiritual Heart Center.

10. With the practice of the Christ Centered Prayer, you may take up your cross through the purification/forgiveness process and be worthy to follow Jesus Christ. "And he that taketh not his cross, and followeth after me, is not worthy of me" (Matthew 10: 38).

+ +

LESSON: 158 — SILENCE - OUTER AND INNER

OUTER SILENCE:

1. The outer silence exists when there is less talk and more listening to the revelation of truth.

2. As you progress on a spiritual walk, there is less talk and more listening. You learn there are many times you can hold a peaceful silence and trust the Lord fights your battles. ". . . for the battle *is* not yours, but God's" (2 Chronicles 20: 15). When there is an appreciation of the outer silence, there is a greater longing for the inner silence.

3. On a spiritual walk, it is wise to practice outer silence whenever possible. "For by thy words thou shalt be justified, and by thy words thou shalt be condemned" (Matthew 12: 37).

4. Condense your paragraph speech into a sentence. Use your words economically and you may hear the silence between the sentences, between the words.

5. Idle talk allows the mind to stray from the things of a Godly nature and disturbs the mind and body.

6. It is best to refrain from idle talk and to keep the mind silently stayed on God. "Thou wilt keep him in perfect peace, whose mind is stayed on thee" (Isaiah 26: 3).

INNER SILENCE:

1. The inner silence is the still small voice of God. "And after the earthquake a fire; *but* the LORD *was* not in the fire: and after the fire a still small voice" (I Kings 19: 12).

2. In the stillness of awareness there is a silence so loud it can be heard. The "still small voice of God" is deafening beyond sound. It is in the deep, silence within awareness, you realize the voice of God.

3. God speaks without words, without sound and yet, you hear every word, you realize truth revealed. "Be still, and know that I *am* God . . ." (Psalm 46: 10).

4. As you progress in your silent Christ Centered Prayer practice, you may gradually experience moments of inner silence.

5. It is a silence that grants you peace beyond understanding. "And the peace of God, which passeth all understanding, shall keep your hearts and minds through Christ Jesus" (Philippians 4: 7).

6. In the silence of awareness, there is peace. It is not the peace the chatter of this world offers. "Peace I leave with you, my peace I give unto you: not as the world giveth, give I unto you. Let not your heart be troubled, neither let it be afraid" (John 14: 27).

7. The inner silence is beyond intelligence. It is not in a world of noise that you realize who or what you are, but from within comes the realization of awareness.

8. The Christ Centered Prayer method is a silent prayer practice guiding you to the straight gate and narrow way. It may guide you to become aware of the Spiritual Heart Center into the perfect inner silence of God's presence. When?

9. It is when there is room for God in your life. When the need for God is greater than all other needs. When the question of who am I? What am I? cannot be put aside. When the noise of this world has less of an attraction than the silence of your Being, the peaceful silence of God's presence is realized.

10. There is a silence within you the world knows not of. There is a presence within you the world cannot comprehend. There is a Kingdom of God within you. Seek it!

+ +

LESSON: 159 — SIN

SIN IS A false concept in thought, word, and deed that lacks the recognition for the truth of your being. To sin is to mistake something, someone, or some place for God.

1. Sin is the ignorance of not knowing or realizing all that you already are in the Kingdom of God. "That seeing they may see, and not perceive; and hearing they may hear, and not understand; lest at any time they should be converted, and *their* sins should be forgiven them" (Mark 4: 12).

2. As you awaken to the God of your being and are aware of your birthright, sinning becomes less and less possible. "Whosoever is born of God doth not commit sin; for his seed remaineth in him: and he cannot sin, because he is born of God" (1 John 3: 9).

3. Sin (ignorance) is the result in an activity that may move you further away from the knowing of your oneness. It is the belief in a separate and apart sense of being. Sin is relative, temporary, and fluid. It easily adapts to whatever you falsely want to believe. Thus it is short lived or may be held in place an entire lifetime.

4. Because sin is relative, it is subject to change. It is a creature of cultures and as cultures change, sin changes its identity and expression. Sin may be defined and punishment for sin meted out by religious or social institutions.

5. Sin appeals to your senses as a desire or temptation. Sin may express itself in an immoral thought, word, or deed according to your cultural orientation. It is always just there for the taking.

6. Sin may occur when you are growing in the Holy Spirit and you would deny the Holy Spirit's presence and return to a previous expression of consciousness. You have a responsibility to live out from and maintain what you have received/realized. "Afterward Jesus findeth him in the temple, and said unto him, Behold, thou art made whole: sin no more, lest a worse thing come unto thee" (John 5: 14).

7. Sin is a tormentor manifesting in the self-inflicting guilt you carry. Sin wears many disguises, walks in pretense, and appears to tempt you to succumb to the desires and temptations of this world.

8. Sin (ignorance) has no permanence and cannot hold you bound. Accept now you are in the bosom of the Lord and the Christ Consciousness. It is here you are cleansed in the love of forgiveness and purification of all that has gone before. "Come now, and let us reason together, saith the LORD: though your sins be as scarlet, they shall be as white as snow; though they be red like crimson, they shall be as wool" (Isaiah 1: 18).

+ +

LESSON: 160 — SITTING

SITTING IS THE position you are in during a silent prayer practice.

1. Sitting is a preferred position during a silent prayer practice.
2. Sit wearing loose comfortable clothing, remove eyeglasses, and use a shawl or blanket, if you wish.
3. Sitting may be on a chair or on the floor. Be comfortable.
4. Your spine should be upright but not ridged. The head and chin relaxed, and hands in your lap.
5. If you are practicing on a chair, you may choose to have arms on it for safety.
6. Sitting in the same area of your home or place of practice will facilitate comfort with your silent prayer practice. However, the prayer practice may be done anywhere.
7. Sit still during your practice. If discomfort rises, slowly and quietly adjust your posture.
8. Any movement while you are sitting should be performed in very slow motion. The less you disturb your vibrating energy, the better.
9. If you want to stop your prayer practice, stop. Don't force yourself to pray any particular length of time. Allow the time you pray to increase naturally. Be patient and gentle with your silent prayer practice.
10. Your determined purpose to sit will form the sitting habit and allow you more easily to practice your silent prayer.
11. At the end of your prayer practice, give yourself a moment to readjust to your immediate environment. Always get up carefully and slowly from your sitting position
12. You are always encouraged to practice your silent prayer in a sitting position. If for health reasons you are not able to sit, then of course, lie down. However, guard against falling asleep. Remember, a fool goes to sleep and a fool wakes up. You are practicing a silent prayer method to wake up, not to take a nap.

+ +

LESSON: 161 — SLEEP

SLEEP IS THE rest you may need less of as you commit to a silent prayer practice.

1. As you engage in a silent prayer practice, over time you may find your required sleep time may change.
2. Less sleep may be required. Do not become disturbed. This is not uncommon. The prayer practice may altar sleep time requirements, but does not substitute for sleep.

3. The change of sleep time may occur because during the moments you rest in the silence, the mind is resting and is refreshed.

4. If you find it difficult to fall asleep, lying on your back, put your right hand on your abdomen, breathe normally, and become aware of the rising and falling of your hand. This may allow you to fall asleep. This is not a silent prayer practice.

5. If you continue to find you cannot fall to sleep, don't struggle. Get up, read a book, or do something till you are ready to sleep.

6. Sleep time requirements are individual. Needs will vary from one person to another.

7. The need for sleep will adjust as your silent prayer practice develops. "Therefore let us not sleep, as *do* others; but let us watch and be sober" (I Thessalonians 5: 6).

8. During an intensive silent prayer practice in a retreat center, you may find you require less sleep than during your daily routines at home.

+ +

LESSON: 162 — SOUL

THE SOUL IS the light-breath of God. "Then the LORD God formed man of the dust of the ground, and breathed into his nostrils the breath of life; and man became a living soul" (Genesis 2: 7).

1. In the simplest of terms, the one God soul is the one manifesting as the many individual expressions of consciousness.

2. The soul is the substance of God's thought in action expressing from the formless to the form, animating human life.

3. The soul is the exhalation breath of its God-source and the breath of God is its eternal connection.

4. The soul possesses the innate inherent ability to know and to love its God-Self. "And thou shalt love the Lord thy God with all thy heart, and with all thy soul, and with all thy mind, and with all thy strength: this *is* the first commandment" (Mark 12: 30).

5. The soul is in the viable reflection from within awareness of each individual, unique expressions of consciousness. "So God created man in his *own* image, in the image of God he created he him; male and female created he them" (Genesis 1: 27).

6. The soul is differentiated into male - female, as it was in the beginning "But from the beginning of the creation God made them male and female" (Mark 10: 6).

7. The soul is the spark from within awareness that ignites the rhythm of the vibratory energy. It is the life force and time keeper determining the sojourn on the plane of opposites. The soul preserves and holds intact the vibratory energy memory of all necessary lessons in the individual expressions of consciousness.

8. The soul is the invisible fingerprint of God allowing God's own to be eternally known, identifiable.

+ +

LESSON: 163 — SOUL PAIN

SOUL PAIN IS the immersion of the soul in an illusion of total spiritual darkness. It is a cross bearing crucifixion in the name of Jesus Christ.

1. As a serious truth seeker, soul pain is the dark days and darker nights when you may feel totally disconnected from Jesus Christ.

2. These are times when silent prayer may bring inner torment. You may want to reach within your heart center and touch your soul it hurts so.

3. It is as if you were in a dark tunnel with no light at the end. You are bare foot, the tunnel floor is covered with cut glass, and every move you make causes excruciating pain — soul pain, but the light is upon you. "The people that walked in darkness have seen a great light: they that dwell in the land of the shadow of death, upon them hath the light shined" (Isaiah 9: 2).

4. It is an excruciating period of taking up your cross and continuing to walk a spiritual path. "Then said Jesus unto his disciples, If any *man* will come after me, let him deny himself, and take up his cross, and follow me" (Matthew 16: 24).

5. Soul pain is a time when you want to withdraw and at the same time strike out at anyone within reach. You are cast in an utter inner, dismal environment with a feeling of tumbling in a timeless, spaceless darkness. There seems no end to your soul pain, no cure.

6. You do not know exactly what to do, how to recover. You twist and turn in a whirlwind of shadows, doubts, and temptations. You may want to give up the spiritual walk but cannot. There is nowhere else you want to go. You just want to reestablish the inner realized connection with Jesus Christ.

7. In the darkness of confusion, you may question, "Is this penance? If so, I want to be finished with it." The temptation may be to want out. The feeling of total abandonment may cause you to fall on your knees and cry out, as Jesus did, ". . . My God, my God, why hast thou forsaken me?" (Mark 15: 34).

8. Soul pain may occur when you are well into your spiritual journey home and are steeped into the forgiveness and purification process. The surfacing of past hurts may cause an emotional turmoil of soul pain that cuts to the core of your existence.

9. Drifting from the spiritual path or trying to return to a previous expression of consciousness may plunge you deeper into the darkness of soul pain.

10. Don't give up. You are being made new, perfect, as your Father is perfect. The dark days and darker nights will pass. ". . . Behold, I am making all things new . . ." (Revelation 21: 5). "Be ye therefore perfect, even as your Father which is in heaven is perfect" (Matthew 5: 48).

11. Take comfort in knowing you may overcome the enemy of the dark days and darker nights. "Rejoice not against me, O mine enemy: when I fall, I shall arise; when I sit in darkness, the LORD *shall* be a light unto me" (Micah 7: 8).

12. If you are working with an outer teacher or guide, seek immediate help. If not, stay close to Jesus. No matter how remote or distant Jesus may seem during the darkest of times or the worst of the soul pain illusionary experiences, the Holy Spirit in the name of Jesus Christ is with you always. "Then spake Solomon, The LORD said that he would dwell in the thick darkness" (1 Kings 8: 12).

+ +

LESSON: 164 — SOUNDS

SOUNDS, INNER, ARE the result of the motion of vibrating energy.

1. As your silent Christ Centered Prayer practice deepens, you may hear inner sounds.
2. Because vibrating energy creates sound, you may hear several different sounds. It is possible to pass through the different frequencies and immediately hear a humming sound.
3. The humming sound is the deepest, purest sound. Once a humming sound is recognized, it is usu-

ally within inner hearing distance anytime you choose to listen whether in, or out of your silent prayer practice.

4. When the humming is strong during a silent prayer practice, it may be useful to listen to it for a time.

5. The humming sound may help support a calm restful mind. Placing your attention on the humming may quiet the mind during a restless silent prayer practice.

6. The humming sound may balance your vibrating energy supporting a stable silent prayer practice.

7. There is no reason for alarm. The Holy Spirit in the name of Jesus Christ is teaching you every step of the way on your spiritual walk.

8. Recognize the humming as the purest sound that it is and rest in the comfort of the Holy Spirit.

+ +

LESSON: 165 — SPIRITUAL DIRECTORS

SPIRITUAL DIRECTORS ARE the inner and/or outer guides you may encounter on a spiritual walk. You may receive spiritual direction from within and from without. When you are a serious truth seeker, many avenues of spiritual direction appear in the form of prayer practices, books, animals, and a teacher/guide. There are three different types of spiritual directors — intellectually trained, partially awakened, and fully awakened.

INTELLECTUALLY TRAINED - TYPE I:

A. The intellectually trained Spiritual Director is one who attends classes to attain psychological and spiritual knowledge about how to direct and counsel others who are seeking spiritual direction.

B. The intellectual spiritual director depends on academic training and book knowledge. Therefore the intellectual spiritual director's guidance to direct others is an outer intellectual one.

C. His or her guidance tends to lean on psychological understanding and comprehensive study of the Spiritual traditions of direction.

D. S/he may have a sincere desire to guide others and need the necessary credentials in a world which deems that a certificate guarantees qualification.

E. This level of a spiritual direction has its place in a society that believes everything, including spiritual direction, is possible through academic studies.

PARTIALLY AWAKEN - TYPE II:

A. This type of director has some experience with insights, realizations, and enlightenments.

B. The partially awakened spiritual director usually possesses both an intellectual understanding and spiritual realizations in a greater or lesser degree.

C. The Spiritual Director who has not realized the detachment enlightenment must remain ever alert to the pitfalls of an inflated ego.

D. The partially awakened Spiritual Director's gift of discernment may be just beginning to rise. Therefore, the director must be cautious when guiding others.

E. Although a partially awakened Spiritual Director has not completed his/her spiritual journey, whatever part that has been realized may be shared with students who are seeking truth at and below that level.

FULLY AWAKENED - TYPE III:

A. The fully awakened Christ Centered Spiritual Director of truth is one who has traveled the straight gate and narrow way through the Holy Spirit in the name of Jesus Christ. S/he possesses the necessary reality enlightenment and is prepared to assist others to realize the reality of their being.

B. The fully awakened Christ Centered Spiritual Director is credentialed by the Holy Spirit in the name of Jesus Christ. Ultimately, there are no intellectual credentials or degrees that convey the necessary spiritual realizations and enlightenments. Credentials may or may not accompany this type of Christ Centered Spiritual Director.

C. The fully awakened Christ Centered Spiritual Director maintains an opened Spiritual Heart Center in relationship with Jesus Christ.

D. Intellectual religious, psychological, and/or academic knowledge may be helpful, but the fully awakened Christ Centered Spiritual Director is one who has gone beyond the intellect and receives the teachings of Jesus Christ through direct inspiration and revelation of the Holy Spirit.

E. Through this Holy Divine connection, a Christ Centered Spiritual Director may teach and guide students to the necessary realizations and enlightenments.

F. The physical and spiritual well being of those who seek spiritual direction must always be first and foremost in the mind and heart of the Christ Centered Spiritual Director when offering guidance.

G. The fully awakened Christ Centered Spiritual Director's guidance is never guess work. It is through the Holy Spirit in the name of Jesus Christ that the fully awakened director knows at all times exactly what the seeker needs to hear and know in order to progress on his or her own individual spiritual journey.

H. The fully awakened Spiritual Director never pulls or pushes but rather guides with a gentle, loving sensitivity appropriate to each situation or challenge.

I. The fully awakened Christ Centered Spiritual Director is representing the Christ of his or her being and recognizes the Christ within all individual expressions of Consciousness.

J. The fully awakened Christ Centered Spiritual Director lives in the Jesus Christ model of humility and service. It is a humbling experience to have the responsibility of assisting others to turn within to the Christ of their being and the awareness of their reality.

1. You will seek spiritual direction from whom you are prepared to accept guidance. Nothing is written in stone. If any time you feel the need to change spiritual directors, you may do so. Your constant inner spiritual director is Jesus Christ.

2. There are teacher/guide directors of others on a chosen spiritual path. And, within the teacher/guide director there are different types of expression of consciousness. When you choose a spiritual truth director, you are selecting the spiritual direction you intend to travel. Truth is within all spiritual paths. Differences are found in what direction you will take to get to the truth you seek.

3. There are individuals who may falsely believe proof of enlightenment is in the outer manifestations. The manipulation of outer manifestations may be accomplished with a practice of a highly concentrated mental state. Elevating the body, walking through walls, etcetera are a few of the ways to demonstrate a highly concentrated mental state, not necessarily enlightenment.

4. The spiritual director you choose will direct your footsteps either to a straight gate and narrow way or one that may consist of many detours.

5. There are schools and organizations that may choose who will and who will not be a spiritual director. Their intention is a worthy one. The best any school or organization can do is to teach those who counsel or direct others to do it with the utmost care.

6. Spiritual Directors need to be aware that wisdom does not immediately follow realizations and enlightenments. Therefore, patience with their own spiritual journey is required.

7. The purpose of Spiritual Directors is to point the direction (within) where you go to awaken to the awareness reality of your being through the Holy Spirit in the name of Jesus Christ.

8. The spiritual directing of others on the spiritual walk is a sacred trust, one that is held close to the Spiritual Heart Center. It is from here the Spiritual Directors receive spiritual gifts through the Holy Spirit in the name of Jesus Christ that allows him or her to be a worthy servant.

9. All Spiritual Directors have their value according to the needs of the individual expressions of consciousness at any given moment in time and space.

10. The aware caring, compassionate disposition, and living example patterned through the Holy Spirit in the name of Jesus Christ are the most important qualifications any Spiritual Director may possess. "Wherefore by their fruits ye shall know them" (Matthew 7: 20).

+ +

LESSON: 166 — STRANGER

A STRANGER IS who you become in this world once you realize your true identity.

1. There may come a time on your spiritual walk when you experience being a stranger in this world.

2. The more you awaken to the reality of your true identity the more of a stranger you are in an imaginary world. "By faith he sojourned in the land of promise, as *in* a strange country, dwelling in tabernacles with Isaac and Jacob, the heirs with him of the same promise:" (Hebrews II: 9).

3. Habit may cause you to continue to want to relate your true identity to the false concept one you had believed in. How can you relate reality to an illusion?

4. You may try to return to the familiar, believing it somehow will calm the uneasiness with your new identity. It will not. In fact, it will only intensify the uneasiness and make it more acute.

5. You may disparately move outwardly while walking inwardly. Who you really are will not let go. It has you firmly in its grip. It does not play games, it does not give up, it loves you beyond understanding and will not allow those with a lesser love to draw you away. It will not allow you to draw "you" away. It is a jealous God.

6. What this world has to offer will never again match up to Christ's love and care for you. "Now therefore ye are no more strangers and foreigners, but fellow citizens with the saints, and of the house hold of God" (Ephesians 2: 19).

7. Do not overreact when your Christ realization occurs. You are realizing a different expression of consciousness between two worlds. In reality, it is the one appearing as the different expressions of consciousness.

8. You are familiar with the old false self, its habits, its false beliefs. Now you look in a mirror and you see the same reflection on the outside but are experiencing a new being on the inside. One whose eyes can see, ears can hear more clearly the Word of God.

9. As you slowly become familiar with your new identity, the adjustment occurs more smoothly and you accept what Jesus said, "They are not of the world, even as I am not of the world" (John 17: 16).

10. There is no going back to the false self in a world as you believed you once knew it, it is finished. You will adjust but it is not easy and it will take time, as you know it on this plane. Be patient, be kind to yourself, and know all is well.

+ +

LESSON: 167 — SUFFERING

SUFFERING IS THE attachment to emotional, personal, and/or physical sense of pain.

1. Suffering multiplies and intensifies through the attachment and improper use of the rising vibrating energy of past thought- memories of the false belief of a personal physical body.

2. An event, negative or positive, occurs once. With the rising vibrating energy of the memory of an event, you are able to reproduce the event many times by dialoguing or responding emotionally to the rising vibrating energy.

3. An attachment occurs when you react, dialogue, or attempt to hold to the rising of the memory of the event. The memory must be allowed to rise and fall freely without any dialogue or response of any kind.

4. With a physical sense body, you may feel pain but the suffering isn't necessary. It is with a false personal sense of, "My body, my pain," you become attached to the pain, creating intensified suffering.

5. A silent prayer practice may teach you how to detach from the personal sense of "my" and the rising thought-memory that causes suffering.

6. The habit of multiplying past harmful events and the attachment to them may be forgiven and purified during a silent Christ Centered Prayer practice.

7. It is during a "Holy Instant" moment of the forgiveness and purification process of a Christ Centered Prayer practice that detachment may occur. Your memory remains intact. However, once the attachment no longer exists, the memory rises and falls without any response.

8. You must stay alert to the temptation to become reattached to the appearances of physical or emotional pain, yours or others, whether it is during a silent prayer practice or in relationship to others in your daily practical activities.

9. Once you have overcome the attachment to the appearances of your suffering, it is easy to fall into the trap of being attached to the suffering of others.

10. Temptation is subtle and comes in many disguises. You may easily recognize the attachment to your own physical or emotional pain but be completely caught off guard when you are presented with the physical or emotional appearances of the pain and suffering of others.

11. Your inner response must always be realizing the Christ is where the appearance is. The pain and suffering of others is theirs to work through, not yours.

12. The greatest help you may ever give others is to realize the truth of yours and their reality within. Lift yourself up and you may be a greater help to others. "And I, if I be lifted up from the earth, will draw all *men* unto me" (John 12: 32).

13. Of course, do whatever is possible for them on the outer. Compassion meets the need in the moment. Be a good listener, ask questions of interest but remain centered within.

14. It is the freedom from the attachment of the appearances of physical or emotional pain, yours or others, that allows you to move on with your life and to progress on the spiritual journey within.

+ +

LESSON: 168 — SUPPLY

SUPPLY IS AN inherent spiritual source which already exists in un-manifested abundance. The power of its manifestation is within you. The Kingdom of God contains all that is necessary. "Seek ye first the kingdom of God, and his righteousness; and all these things shall be added unto you" (Matthew 6: 33).

1. Supply is infinitely limitless in its un-manifested source-state. It may manifest in various forms, shapes. Supply never is depleted.

2. Because you are your own source of all you need, all you will ever need, and all that is necessary for your spiritual progress, mental or physical care, supply is infinite in its manifestations.

3. Supply isn't a particular object, thing, or person. The forms and shapes supply manifest are a reflection of your spiritual consciousness. When a form appears in a mirror, the reflection is but an indication of what is appearing. The mirror reflects the appearance. The mirror may reflect various forms and shapes but the mirror "itself" never changes. So it is with supply. No matter how many forms or shapes supply reflects for your needs, the supply source remains untouched, never depleted.

4. Whether for the inner or outer spiritual progress, supply always exists. It is the lack of conscious realization of the spiritual supply source that interferes or prevents its manifestation,

5. The realization that is necessary to access and bring you into the full conscious awareness of your spiritual supply source is one of complete receptive surrender in realizing, "The Lord is my shepherd, I shall not want" (Psalm 23: 1).

6. Supply's manifestations appear in the moment of need. "Therefore I say unto you, Take no thought for your life, what ye shall eat, or what ye shall drink; nor yet for your body, what ye shall put on. Is not life more than meat, and the body than raiment?" (Matthew 6:25)

7. Supply is endless according to your need, not greed. When you lack faith in your source and fear what you have will be depleted or lost, you may hold back the materialization of any form of supply.

8. You of course are accountable for the proper use of all manifestations of supply. To hold back or not enjoy and share reasonably all that manifest is unnecessary.

9. Supply is an expression of consciousness. If you believe you are poor, you are poor. If what you have meets your present need and you use less in fear there may not be more, there will not be more.

10. You need not be foolish. To deprive yourself of the use of what you have is to create unnecessary stress, struggles, and hardships. "Which of you by taking thought can add one cubit unto his stature?" (Matthew 6: 27)

11. There is never a time when whatever or whoever you need does not already exist, nor is there ever a time when the God of your being does not know your needs. "(For after all these things do the Gentiles seek) for your heavenly Father knoweth that ye have need of all these things" (Matthew 6:32).

12. No one can take away what is yours and you can never lose what is not yours.

13. The problem is expecting a felt need to materialize a form of supply before the actual need arises. The deeper need may be for you to be without what is expected in order for you to come into a realization of supply.

14. To be momentarily without may help you to understand your lack of realization of your inherent spiritual supply source. Remember, supply meets need, not greed, and it meets need in the moment of need. Supply cannot be hedged or stored. "Behold the fowls of the air: for they sow not, neither do they reap, nor gather into barns; yet your heavenly Father feedeth them. Are ye not much better than they?" (Matthew 6: 26)

15. What is experienced as a form of supply being withheld is only a lesson not yet learned. Being without a form of supply *is* a form of supply meeting a need — the need to wake up and realize your spiritual supply source.

16. What you do not realize does not materialize. You are the creator of your forms of supply. When you have unwavering faith in your ability to draw from your infinite supply, it materializes without worry or effort.

17. There is a tendency to think of supply as the conditions, forms and shapes it takes. These are only the outer appearance. Your storehouse of un-manifested supply is without limit.

18. It is the outer form and shape supply manifests that causes you to mistake the appearance for the

reality, the impermanent for the permanent. Holdfast to that which you believe is possible, and it is. "But this *I say*, He which soweth sparingly shall reap also sparingly; and he which soweth bountifully shall reap also bountifully" (2 Corinthians 9: 6).

....

STUDENT'S STORY:

I have always been financially frugal to the point of even depriving myself when it was not necessary. Consequently, the spiritual principle and lesson of supply was not an easy one for me to realize. I read and studied this Lesson Paper but just didn't "get it."

I had an opportunity to travel with my teacher to Lourdes in France. I always wanted to visit a Christian shrine and had a particular longing to visit Lourdes. My spiritual journey contained the silent spacious unassuming presence of the Blessed Mother from its beginning.

As an eight year old, my first intentional spiritual journey steps were taken up the convent walk of Immaculate Heart of Mary Church in Scarsdale, New York. I knocked on the door and in response to Sister Peter's question, "Can I help you?" I answered, "Yes, I'd like to become a Catholic." Escorted in, given milk and cookies, made to feel an honored guest, the Blessed Mother Mary saw to my care and nurture.

Years later I would graduate from a Oblate School of Theology run by the Oblates of Mary Immaculate. I served as Director of Campus Ministry at Our Lady of the Lake University, and my ordination to the priesthood took place during Advent when the Gospel lesson preached was the Annunciation! I doubt this is mere coincidence! When the opportunity to visit Lourdes was presented, I was quick to accept.

A senior stewardess who worked for an Airlines, gifted me with a coach "Buddy Pass" to fly "stand by" anywhere in the world. My ticket cost forty-four dollars and my teacher's ticket cost $2,200 for a reserved round trip, first class ticket! I actually gloated to think that I could get by so cheaply. I was peach proud. I was also totally unaware of what this unnecessary decision would ultimately cost. I had plenty of money in my checking account for a reserved round trip first class ticket but I chose not to spend the money on myself. I had yet to learn the lesson of supply!

As the date for my trip to Lourdes approached, I made several inquiry calls to determine the availability of stand by status seats etc... it would be a "piece of cake" to get to France on July 4th out of Jackson Hole to Atlanta. I would meet my teacher in Atlanta and we would fly together to Charles DeGaulle Airport and then on to Orly near Lourdes. We would spend ten glorious days in prayer, sightseeing, walking, eating omelets, and drinking wonderful cafe-au-lait at the outdoor eateries. I had no trouble getting to France and was as pleased as I could be with myself. Until... the day came to get home. Bastille Day had just finished in France and everyone and their cousin was trying to fly around France on the fifteenth of July. My teacher and I returned to Paris and she calmly awaited her gate call while I anxiously sat hoping my "stand by" name would be called. What I did not know was that there were about fifteen more folks with greater airline seniority trying to do exactly the same thing!

After three planes took off each with only one or two seats for stand-bys, I began to get a taste of reality. Getting home to the USA was not going to be a "piece of cake." I watched my friend get on board and leave. I was alone now in the airport and it was only 1:00 pm and all the flights to the USA had taken off. It would be tomorrow morning before I could stand by for another flight. My enthusiasm was waning and my anxiety was rising.

I had to find a place to stay for the night and return at 6:00 am the next morning to repeat the stand by process. The next day the same thing happened. I could not get on any of the flights. It was another long day in the Paris airport. I was tired, discouraged, and rapidly running out of cash. I went to the ticket counter and asked about stand by availability for the next day only to find out all planes were booked full. I asked the attendant, "When does it look like I may get on a flight?" He replied after perusing the computer, "August!" Well, that was more than I could deal with.

It looked as if the only way to get home was to buy a ticket. At this point I didn't even care where in the States. I just needed to get back. I asked, "How much will it cost to get a one way ticket to the USA?" He paused, checked carefully, and said, "We do have an excursion ticket on the 2:00 pm flight to Dulles International and it will cost $2,550!" I did some quick calculating and realized it was going to cost me about the same to fly home one way excursion as it would have to fly with a reserved ticket round trip! Never mind. His news was music to my ears and anathema to my pocket book. I whipped out my credit card and walked away from the counter with a ticket in hand. Finally, I was going home.

After arriving in the states, there was more of the same. It was difficult getting a ticket to Jackson Hole, more time waiting, and more money spent. Exhausted and sitting in the rear of the plane after two days of trial, I let out a huge laugh. I remembered the lesson on supply I had studied with my teacher. I realized in a flash what I had done. I had the money. My need had been met abundantly and I had chosen to disregard and not accept that which had been prepared. I had no reason whatsoever to put myself through this struggle. In being too "big for my britches" and "thinking I could play the angles and get something for nothing" I ended up pinched in the pocket and totally humiliated.

Fortunately, I had a good sense of humor and on the flight back I realized how unnecessary and yet how necessary this lesson was for me. Poverty of Spirit has little to do with cash on hand and everything to do with gratitude and dependency on God for all things — including reserved airfares for a pilgrimage. It is the proud heart that reaps what it sows and in my case the principle of supply lesson could not have been clearer.

I am happy to say that my attitude towards the gift of money has changed. I am grateful for the opportunities I have been given to save money throughout my life and to share it. I realize money is only one of the many forms supply takes for my use. It is something to be earned, shared, saved, and not coveted. I realized clearly that it was never the money that was at issue, but rather the right relationship and right use of money. I realized my lesson. My spiritual economics are now in proper order. To reject a gift is as silly as coveting a gift. All is the gift of supply and it is gratitude and the proper use that is essential. I realized this the hard way, but I realized it!

+ +

LESSON: 169 — SURRENDER

SURRENDER IS AN instant of being at home in the Christ.

1. Surrender is to come to the Christ having no expectations and letting go. It is a, "Here I am Lord, thy will be done." This is followed by rest and trust..
2. There is nothing to get, nowhere to go. There is only being with what you really are within awareness.
3. Surrender is giving up the idea you are separate and apart from your God essence. It is not wanting to be anywhere but where you are at the present.
4. Surrender is not a giving up but rather a giving in. A giving in to that which you are in reality.
5. Surrender is cutting the strings attached to this world. When you let go of everything, you find you already have it all.
6. Surrender is giving up the false sense of a separate self and resting in the Holy Spirit in the name of Jesus Christ.
7. When you are unconditionally loving, you are in complete surrender. "And we have known and

believed the love that God hath to us. God is love; and he that dwelleth in love dwelleth in God, and God in him" (I John 4: 16).

8. Surrender to the Christ within. Come to Jesus empty, and let Him fill you.

+ +

LESSON: 170 — SYMBOLS AND RITUALS

SYMBOLS AND RITUALS are forms or outer actions reflecting an inner spiritual reality and/or intent.

1. Symbols and rituals, in and of themselves, have absolutely no power.
2. Symbols and rituals may be invested with power by individual expressions of consciousness or group consciousness.
3. Jesus made it clear that all power came from God when "Jesus answered, Thou couldest have no power *at all* against me, except it were given thee from above: . . ." (John 19: 11).
4. There is but one God, one power. You, as a vessel of the One God power, must invest this power in a symbol/ritual. ". . . I *am* the first, and I *am* the last; and beside me *there is* no god" (Isaiah 44: 6). "Let every soul be subject unto the higher powers. For there is no power but of God: the powers that be are ordained of God" (Romans 13: 1).
5. When individuals are unaware of the influence and conditioning that earthly institutions may exercise, symbols and rituals may be imbued with power "not from above." Religious, political, or social symbols may be co-opted by individuals exercising power over other individuals or groups.
6. This is why symbols and rituals are used or misused. They are great tools for the truth seekers, the initiate, and religious zealots alike. Discernment is of utmost importance.
7. It is your expression of consciousness that must invest the power from within, to make any symbol or ritual effective.
8. The more sacred you hold the symbol or ritual, the more effective it is. That is why generalizations about specific symbols or rituals cannot be made. What may affect you, may not affect another.
9. Symbols and rituals may appear powerful at one event and then seem to have lost their powers at another event. This is because the symbol or ritual never innately possessed any power in and of itself. Apart from you it has no power.
10. The most important thing to understand about symbols and rituals is that they may only possess the power you give them from within consciousness.

+ +

LESSON: 171 — TEACHER - TYPES

TEACHER IS AN individual who may influence you at different times during your spiritual journey on this plane. There are three major types of teachers.

PARENT, TEACHER - TYPE I:

A. A parent may be your biological or substitute parent.
B. A Parent Teacher or Guide may have the greatest impact on your physical and psychological growth.
C. Certain parental situations, events, and conditioning may expose you to the necessary lessons upon the plane of opposites.

EDUCATIONAL, TEACHER - TYPE II:

A. The educational teacher leads and guides you through your academic years.

B. This would include academic-teachers, peers, friends, animals, and enemies.

C. On the outer plane of opposites, you are constantly learning from just about everyone, or thing.

SPIRITUAL, TEACHER - TYPE III:

A. There may come a time when you may be ready for a spiritual teacher or guide.

B. Spiritual teachers may appear at different stages and at different times during your spiritual walk.

C. What dictates the stage and time a specific spiritual teacher may appear is your preparedness and readiness.

D. Your expression of consciousness is always attracted to that which you seek.

E. The more serious and committed you are on a spiritual walk, the more likely an outer spiritual teacher will appear when necessary.

F. Spiritual teachers are always available at every stage. It is your expression of consciousness that attracts you and the necessary spiritual teacher.

G. As Jesus Christ was an obedient son of God the Father, the Christ Centered teacher is the obedient child of the Holy Spirit in the name of Jesus Christ.

1. You need never search for a spiritual teacher. When you are prepared and ready one will appear. That is a spiritual principle/activity. All teachers have a purpose of service in your life. Each type meets a particular need when it is necessary.

2. Outer teachers may help guide and facilitate the ultimate realization. However, there is the constant inner spiritual teacher — the Holy Spirit in the name of Jesus Christ. "And if any man think that he knoweth any thing, he knoweth nothing yet as he ought to know" (I Corinthians 8: 2).

+ +

LESSON: 172 — TEACHER PRINCIPLES

TEACHER PRINCIPLES ARE the basic guidelines for a Christ Centered teacher.

1. A Christ Centered teacher is one who experiences more or less the expansiveness of the Christ Consciousness.

2. Be aware that you are the heart, intellect, and voice of the Christ Consciousness of your being on this plane.

3. Prepare, pray, study, know the materials, the steps and the lessons to be taught. Be concise, speak softly-firmly, and with conviction. Teach out of your own experiences, insights, and realizations.

4. The Christ is always teaching each individual. Trust that the Christ knows exactly what each student is to receive. Allow the Christ to be responsible for the teaching-giving and the acceptance-receiving.

5. Listen and hear what you are teaching. Listen to the feed back from students.

6. Always allow and encourage questions. Reassure the students; there are no foolish questions. Often questions provide the best lesson and teaching tool for the teacher and student alike.

7. The Christ Consciousness is not a role that the teacher assumes for a period of time but is an expression of your consciousness at all times.

8. Teaching truth automatically opens and expands the Spiritual Heart Center, causing a greater awareness of the Christ Consciousness.

9. There may be the experience of a "high" whenever you are teaching about truth. The Lessons' many topics may help you with the handling of your spiritual progress.

10. These are only basic principles. The necessary in-depth guidance comes within your own inner silent Christ Centered Prayer practice, the Holy Spirit in the name of Jesus Christ.

++++++++++++++++++++++++

LESSON: 173 — TEARS - CRYING

TEARS AND CRYING are what may occur at times on your spiritual walk.

1. A spiritual journey may present difficult times. Times when crying and shedding tears is all that you can do to maintain your sanity on a straight gate and narrow way.

2. As you become a more serious student, you may experience during a silent prayer practice the shedding of tears. Shedding tears and crying may occur in or out of a silent prayer practice. Periodical shedding of tears and crying is not uncommon.

3. You may cry when you are overcome by a realization or an enlightenment. You may also shed tears when you feel you are not making progress as you believe you should.

4. As memories rise and purification and forgiveness may take place during a silent prayer practice, you may respond with the overwhelming emotional release of tears. Tears - crying may be very therapeutic. Allow the tears to flow freely. Do not be embarrassed or ashamed of tears.

5. Shedding of tears and crying are part of the waking up process. They occur most often during or as a result of the forgiveness and purification process. Do not repress them.

6. There are times you may experience extreme loneliness because your experiences are held secret and sacred. If you do not have a teacher or guide, there may be no one to talk with and no one with whom to share. Your emotions may be raw. You may be overly sensitive to the loneliness of a straight gate and narrow way. Until loneliness is overcome, you may find shedding of tears your only response. It is not inappropriate.

7. The journey may at times test you, exhaust you, or bring you to your knees. Like Jesus, you too, may fall on your face and ask, "If it be possible, let this pass." "And he went a little further, and fell on his face and prayed, saying, O my Father, if it be possible let this cup pass from me: nevertheless not as I will, but as thou *wilt*" (Matthew 26: 39).

8. Be comforted in the knowledge that the Divine is with you in all of your trials through the Holy Spirit in the name of Jesus Christ.

++++++++++++++++++++++++

LESSON: 174 — THOUGHTS - EMOTIONS - FEELINGS

VIBRATING ENERGY TAKES the form of rising thoughts, emotions, and feelings. Emotions and feelings rise in response to any one or more of the conditioned thoughts or sense impressions.

1. Any thought or sense impression rising may initiate an experience of emotions or sensory feelings.

2. The emotional and feeling response, good or bad, depends on your personal attachment to the conditioning.

3. Thoughts rise in the form of plans, expectations, or memories. Thoughts are conditioned by family, friends, and culture.

4. Thoughts rising as expectations may hold you in a future that does not exist. You give concentrated thought the power to create constructive or destructive events and persons in your life. Be careful what you wish for.

5. Memories rising and engaged or dialogued with may recreate an emotion or feeling response from the past in the present.

6. Whether you are at peace or in total confusion when a memory rises, it matters not. Don't judge or dialogue with the emotions or feelings. Just witness them; as with everything else, they come and they go. They are just thoughts, just energy rising.

7. You do continue to express emotions and feelings as long as you are on this plane. You don't become a robot. You are more compassionate not less. God's nature, your nature, is a compassionate one. "But thou, O Lord, *art* a God full of compassion, and gracious, longsuffering, and plenteous in mercy and truth" (Psalm 86: 15).

8. On the plane of opposites, you may experience all of the rising senses and the impressions imprinted on them. As you become less attached, changes may take place in your response or non-response to the rising thought energy of emotions and feelings. In other words, you are free to respond or not. The distinction lies in your freedom to express emotions appropriately and let them go. There is no attachment.

9. As the rising energy of thoughts from the past or about the future attract less of your attention, they solicit less of an emotional or feeling response. The Christ love softens the rising of distracting emotions and feelings through the Holy Spirit in the name of Jesus Christ.

10. In this freedom you live fully in the present moment. Emotions faithfully, properly, and appropriately express themselves. You once again experience the peace of the present moment. This is the peace that indeed "Passes all understanding" it is your nature. "And the peace of God, which passeth all understanding, shall keep your hearts and minds through Christ Jesus" (Philippians 4: 7).

+ +

LESSON: 175 — TIME

TIME IS RELATIVE to this plane of opposites.

1. When you are first taught the silent Christ Centered Prayer practice, you begin with a few minutes twice a day.

2. During a silent prayer practice, you may go beyond time and times' duration may not be obvious.

3. It is not necessary to intentionally place strict time limits on your silent prayer practice. Allow your silent prayer practice to expand itself.

4. For many, this allows the mind and body to naturally adjust to sitting. Twenty - thirty minutes is the commonly chosen amount of time for any one prayer period. Usually the body wants to move about after sitting still for this amount of time in any one position.

5. There may be silent prayer periods of longer or shorter duration. There may be occurrences when the time of your practice will be shorter or longer.

6. You do not need to judge any prayer practice by its length of time. Longer is not better or shorter worse. The important issue is to do the silent prayer practice.

7. Your determined purpose to sit and practice will eventually become a habit. The time necessary will become established and comfortable.

8. There is no need to force a silent prayer time. If you are restless or uncomfortable, simply get up and return to the practice at another time when you are at ease. Your determined purpose to pray will find the proper time and space. Trust it.

9. The fruit of your prayer practice will be experienced in daily life as you are easily able to respond to the needs of others and your own legitimate needs.

10. Silent prayer time need not be dreaded nor should it be forced. Your prayer practice will meet your need in its own time through the Holy Spirit in the name of Jesus Christ.

+ +

LESSON: 176 — TOOLS

TOOLS ARE THE aids on this plane you may use to assist you on your spiritual walk. Books, tapes, teachings, stories, symbols/rituals, etcetera are tools.

1. There are many tools of various kinds. What is considered sacred to you may not be sacred to another. Although you may respect all tools that are available, it is your belief in any particular tool that matters.

2. The Bible scriptures are inspirational and may be of assistance. Within the scriptures are many Christian initiations. The Bible contains a road map along your spiritual walk.

3. Metaphysical books, tapes, and films may help guide you along the path. All tools serve to help wake you up.

4. Church services, pilgrimages, sermons, lectures, and metaphysical class lessons may all contribute to your spiritual progress. Some may be of greater or lesser use at different stages of your spiritual journey.

5. You may find some tools help prepare you to become aware more easily during a silent prayer practice.

6. Tools should be approached with contemplative reverence. However, tools are about truth, not truth itself. Truth is something you are. It is not outside of your reality.

7. It is as if you have taken a boat to cross a river; once there, you do not carry the boat around on your head. You leave it for someone else to use.

8. Use whatever you are drawn to and believe may help. Guard against becoming attached to a tool. Be grateful for its use, and when you are finished with any tool leave it behind and move on. The Holy Spirit in the name of Jesus Christ needs no tool and can teach you all things directly.

+ +

LESSON: 177 — TRANSITION

TRANSITION OCCURS WHEN you are ready to progress from one silent prayer practice to another.

1. You may come to the Christ Centered Prayer practice having practiced other silent prayer methods. You may be practicing a different method at the time you decide to learn the Christ Centered Prayer.

2. The transition from one method of silent prayer practice to another may not always be a smooth one. With a determined purpose and patience, a new practice may take hold.

3. If you find a previous practice rises to interfere with your new prayer practice, be gentle and allow the previous prayer practice to slowly recede.

4. Any silent prayer practice becomes a habit. The body and mind take time to transition from one habit to another. The transition is best supported in an atmosphere of patience.

5. You do not intentionally mix silent prayer practices. Each practice has its own methodology, theology, and integrity. These are to be respected and appreciated. It may also be time to say goodby to a practice when drawn by the Holy Spirit to a new practice. A Christ Centered Prayer teacher or *The Lessons* may assist you in making any necessary transition.

6. There is a readiness in coming to the awareness of the Spiritual Heart Center. This readiness moves you into action. "Now therefore perform the doing *of it*; that as *there was* a readiness to will, so *there may be* a performance also out of that which ye have" (II Corinthians 8: 11).

7. Being prepared to surrender all that has gone before brings you into the new readiness. "The preparations of the heart in man, and the answer of the tongue, *is* from the Lord" (Proverbs 16: 1).

8. All must be treated with respect and gratitude. All that was given before, prepared you, made you ready, and brought you here now for the natural transition into the awareness of the Spiritual Heart Center. "And because ye are sons, God hath sent forth the Spirit of his Son into your hearts, crying, Abba, Father." (Galatians 4: 6).

9. There is never any waste on the spiritual journey. All is used to move you along in a steady direction toward the Christ Consciousness. "Jesus saith unto him, I am the way, the truth, and the life: no one cometh unto the Father, but by me" (John 14: 6).

10. Never struggle or dialogue with a previous silent prayer practice rising during your Christ Centered Prayer practice. Allow it to rise and fall as you would any other thought and gently assume the new practice.

+ +

LESSON: 178 — TRUST I - THE CHRIST

TRUST IN THE Christ is the surrendering to the Will of God in all your ways. ". . . not my will, but thine be done" (Luke 22: 42).

1. When you begin silent Christ Centered Prayer practice, it is with a trust in the inner guidance of Jesus Christ.

2. You place trust in the Christ of your being for the shear joy of realizing the nature and activity of the Holy Spirit in the Name of Jesus Christ. Any other benefits are secondary.

3. Turning to the Christ of your being strengthens and accelerates your vibrating expression of consciousness.

4. As doubts and temptations rise in the prayer and are forgiven and purified, you may struggle to maintain a balance between your inner and outer life. Trust in the Christ of your being and continue your silent prayer practice. Trust and obey.

5. Your true life is in Christ. If your mental energies are focused on the things of this world, they may seem real and you may easily drift into a world of an illusion. "Those who find their life will lose it, and those who lose their life for my sake will find it" (Matthew 10: 39).

6. In times of chaos and confusion, you need to trust the Christ of your being. With fidelity to your silent prayer practice, trust in the Christ is gradually fortified. "No weapon that is formed against thee

shall prosper; and every tongue *that* shall rise against thee in judgment thou shalt condemn. This *is* the heritage of the servants of the LORD, and their righteousness *is* of me, saith the LORD" (Isaiah 54: 17).

7. As a realized being, your trust remains in the Christ under all circumstances. The temptation to become distracted by the things of the outer world is overcome. The truth of your fulfillment is in Christ and all other attractions may cease to sway you and draw you from this reality.

8. When you desire something/someone more than the Christ or trust anything other than the Christ to meet your needs, you are in the world of illusion. "It *is* better to trust in the LORD than to put confidence in princes" (Psalm 118: 9).

9. As a realized awakened being, you realize the Christ reality and must at all times trust the Christ is what meets all your needs regardless of the appearances. "And Jesus said unto them, I am the bread of life . . ." (John 6: 35).

10. Maintain your awareness in the Christ of your being and the candies of the world may never again fool you into believing they are the source of your fulfillment. Do not insult your attained spiritual integrity.

11. To sustain awareness of the Christ consists of more than a silent prayer practice. It requires living daily with conscious awareness of the Christ. Be alert, steadfast, and trust in the Christ. Such trust does not go unrewarded. "THEY that trust in the LORD *shall be* as Mount Zion, *which* cannot be moved, *but* abideth"(Psalm 125: 1).

12. Once, you have realized the Christ Consciousness and know the reality of your being in pure awareness, you have a greater capacity and responsibility to place your total reliance in the Christ and maintain it. "Cease ye from man, whose breath *is* in his nostrils: for wherein is he to be accounted of?" (Isaiah 2: 22)

STUDENT'S STORY:

Letting go and trusting more and more the inner voice, guidance and the Christ invitation, I find my work easier and the words flow. There is a strangeness about this type of life. It is not my own. It is God expressing Itself.

I remember the night I experienced the tremendous and profound love Jesus had for me and the fact of its truth in every cell of my body, mind, and soul. It was the same night Jesus kept asking me, "Will you trust me?" and I continually answered Jesus,

"It depends. What do you have in mind?"

The conversation went on and on throughout the night. I certainly wrestled with the "angel," and at the end of the evening I was wounded by loves's incessant question, and exhausted. It certainly was not piety that whispered the consent, "Yes" but the fact of Jesus' persistent questioning without anger or backing down one iota. Jesus was as determined to stay the course as I was to delay the course. Jesus won. As quietly as I could possibly consent, I did. I said, "Yes" and the deluge of hours was over.

I did not know specifically what I was consenting to other than to trust Jesus. The next day, I walked into the Bishop's office, made an appointment to let him know I had decided to ask permission to be received into the Episcopal Church and my desire to be ordained a priest. That was the day Jesus Christ began to lead my life and steps in places and ways I certainly would not have gone had I not consented to trust Him.

+ +

LESSON: 179 — TRUST II: TRUST IN A CHRIST CENTERED TEACHER

TRUST IN THE Christ within your Christ Centered teacher is necessary. If you have a teacher, your progress on your spiritual journey is effected by the trust or lack of trust you have in your teacher. There are many Christ Centered teacher signs.

1. A commitment to study spiritual principles with a Christ Centered truth teacher, involves trust, obedience, and surrender to the Christ within the teacher. It separates you from the masses as you begin the purification process. "Wherefore come out from among them, and be ye separate, saith the Lord, and touch not the unclean *thing*; and I will receive you" (2 Corinthians 6: 17).

2. Trust in the Christ gives the Holy Spirit permission to teach you all things in the name of Jesus Christ. Many expressions of consciousness manifest in the outer world of appearances. It is in the Christ that you trust.

3. When you have been prepared and are ready, your Christ Centered truth teacher will appear. It is the Holy Spirit in the name of Jesus Christ that selects the truth teacher.

4. Your trust is not given to personalities, things, supply, or those who would lead you other than to the inward path. When deciding to follow a Christ Centered truth teacher, the trust is in the Christ teaching, not the teacher. It is the Christ of your being resonating and responding to the Christ of the teacher's being.

5. A relationship of trust between student and teacher may develop over time. The teacher is a living example of truth teaching. "Even so hath the Lord ordained that they which preach the gospel should live of the gospel" (I Corinthians 9: 14).

6. A Christ Centered truth teacher would never guide you to follow what is seen, tasted, touched, smelled, or heard. This is the outer path, which may consist of mental tricks, magic, or a grandiosity of self. It is not the path that leads you to a realized Christ Consciousness. Have an alert and skeptical eye and mind for a teacher who would lead or direct you other than to the Christ within.

7. Total trust is reserved for the Christ Truth Teaching within. It is the Christ Consciousness a teacher has realized that you may also realize with the teacher's assistance. Be alert. A genuine truth teacher will be known by his or her fruits.

8. A Christ realized truth teacher will point you in an inward direction at all times. The teacher will guide you to the highest consciousness that the teacher has realized. So, choose wisely.

9. A truth teacher knows the Christ of your being, is aware of your reality, and at all times holds you in the Light of Truth.

10. The trust is always in the teaching not the person. It is the trust in the Christ of the teacher that allows your necessary spiritual progression.

11. You should consider carefully before a long-term commitment is made with a teacher. When considering a teacher, trust your inner guidance. Once a teacher - student relationship is established in trust, your sustaining trust and obedience will contribute largely to the speed of your progress.

12. When you and the teacher are placing trust in the highest expression of the Christ Consciousness, your progression is a natural result. The Holy Spirit in the name of Jesus Christ gifts you with every possible need at any given moment. Your seriousness and commitment attracts the necessary teacher when you are ready. Remember, you always have the greatest teacher within you — The Holy Spirit in the name of Jesus Christ.

CHRIST CENTERED TEACHER SIGNS:

A. First and foremost, a Christ Centered truth teacher points you to an inner direction, points you to an inner direction, and points you to an inner direction. There is no greater sign that distinguishes a truth teacher.

B. A truth teacher is one who directs you to the Divine presence of the Holy Spirit who is the teacher of all truth in the name of Jesus Christ.

C. Displays unconditional love, shares time, and is patient.

D. Cares for your physical, mental, and spiritual welfare.

E. Willingly gives of self and does not withhold knowledge when you are ready to receive it.

F. Forgives ten fold and is non-possessive.

G. Is firm but not dictatorial.

H. Answers questions in a timely manner.

I. Is willing to share a silent, Christ Centered Prayer practice, and guide you through all phases of your spiritual journey.

J. Knows the signs to watch for as you progress.

K. Is able to assist you through the relative highs and lows associated with the purification/forgiveness process, and its corresponding highs and lows. It is critical for your balance to be maintained and the teacher knows how to identify where and when a cautionary note is needed.

L. Carefully and gently guides you towards an ever more expansive consciousness.

M. Once you have awakened to the awareness of your being, the teacher nourishes, supports, and assists you in negotiating the complexities of this new way of living out from a realized expression of the Christ Consciousness.

N. Teaches you the subtleties of the unfolding of wisdom.

O. Identifies and validates realizations after you have realized them.

P. You are free at anytime to terminate the relationship. You may leave with the teacher's blessing.

....

STUDENT'S STORY:

As an addendum to this lesson paper, I must acknowledge that it is crucial to trust in the presence of the Christ of my own being, and trust that this *same* presence exists in the being of my teacher. Issues of trust have plagued my progress and I have tested that trust innumerable times. Just ask my teacher. Fortunately, a Christ teacher - student relationship once entered into cannot be severed by the naughtiness or haughtiness of the student. I can attest to the fact that the Christ of my teacher's being has consistently and persistently put my personal, physical, emotional, psychological, and spiritual well being ahead of any personal gain. It is a "servant teacher" model.

My teacher has always asked me to trust the Christ of my being who dwells in my Spiritual Heart Center. She has always encouraged me to "go within" for the truth. She has patiently listened to me prattle on for hours and hours. She has received my argument and protestations without interruption. When she agrees with me, she tells me. When she disagrees, she tells me and explains why. Decisions have always been mine to make. The choice to trust and obey, or not, has always been mine. I have always been free to "do as I wish," and I have. When I have made a mistake and acknowledged it we simply start over with a fresh slate. There are absolutely no grudges held.

My teacher maintains a lavish sense of humor that occasionally has gotten lost on me, especially when I have taken myself too seriously! What I have learned and seen demonstrated by my teacher is the fact of unconditional love, acceptance, and forgiveness. These are manifestations of the presence of Christ through the power of the Holy Spirit. I have been the recipient of these gifts many times. Gradually my conditioning of suspicion has been replaced by trust. With each reception I find myself less hesitant, more trusting, and obedient. "Trust and obey." There is no other way. I always remember that this trust and obedience is ultimately and necessarily to Christ who dwells in my Spiritual Heart Center and of my teacher's.

++++++++++++++++++++++++++

LESSON: 180 — TRUST III: TRUST REQUIRED OF A STUDENT

In Trust II, you were informed why and how you as a student may place trust in a Christ Centered truth teacher. In this Lesson Paper, you are informed about the trust and responsibilities a Christ Centered truth teacher requires of you, the student.

There are signs that alert the teacher to the readiness of a student to enter partial or total commitment

1. Trusting the Christ gives the Holy Spirit permission to teach all things in the name of Jesus Christ through a teacher. The Christ Centered truth teacher's trust and the student's trust must always reside in the Christ.

2. Teacher beware! Many students may want what you have realized. Few are ready and willing to walk in the necessary footsteps on a straight gate and narrow way to a realized Christ Consciousness and the reality of pure awareness.

3. As a Christ Centered truth teacher, be alert and watchful. Students come and go. You have a responsibility to listen but not necessarily to accept all who would command your attention. A Christ Centered Teacher must have the student's total trust. The teacher is not expected to accept a student if the student has doubts as to the ability of the teacher. Take your time. Be patient. Watch closely. Choose your students wisely!

4. A Christ Centered Truth Teacher should consider carefully the charge and responsibility before a possible long term commitment is made. There are many students seeking a truth teacher, but few serious truth seekers.

5. The teacher allows time and watches for a demonstration of serious commitment by the student before moving forward in a partial or total commitment with the student. This may mean working with a student for years before a serious commitment is forged.

6. Once a teacher - student relationship is established in trust, the student's trust and obedience contributes largely to the speed of the student's progress.

7. If the student, at any time, chooses to take another path and seeks a different teaching, the teacher - student commitment no longer exists. The student may end the commitment at anytime.

8. When the student comes to the stage of demonstrating sincere gratitude in his or her progress, the teacher knows the student is a seriously committed truth seeker and the student's progress may be accelerated.

9. Expressed, sincere gratitude is the sign that tells the teacher the student is seriously committed to the inner way. The sign reads, "This is my way, I will follow you to the Christ Consciousness and I will live the Christ of my Being."

10. Actually, it is the teacher who serves. The teacher and the student are in reality both Christ Servants. One is a fully awakened Being in the awareness of the Christ Consciousness and the other is not yet fully awakened.

11. The student has the responsibility to trust that the teacher knows the way and will carefully guide the student there. As the student fully awakens in awareness and realizes the Christ Consciousness, the differences fade. What is true of the teacher, is true of the student. All that the teacher is within the Christ Consciousness, the student is.

12. Along the way at times there are struggles, ups and downs in the teacher - student relationship; however, when established in total trust and obedience it is a joyous loving journey within.

STUDENT'S READINESS:

A. Listens to and trusts the teacher's guidance.
B. Guards and holds the teacher relationship as a sacred trust.
C. Is obedient to the guidance and teachings.
D. Gives willingly of his or her time.
E. Shows interest in the studies and asks questions.
F. Is eager and willing to spend time and money to travel, if necessary, to meet with the teacher.
G. Has a priority to observe, listen, and learn from the truth teacher.
H. Seeks the teacher's guidance in all phases of his or her life. The outer world is but a foggy reflection of the inner one.
I. May not always like what s/he hears but is willing to listen and consider the guidance.
J. Seeks more and more the gifts of the Holy Spirit in the name of Jesus Christ and less and less the things of this world.
K. Seeks to serve the teacher in any appropriate way.
L. Expresses sincere gratitude as part of his or her spiritual progress. An offering is never refused. An appropriate expression of affection is never rejected. The teacher always acknowledges the expressed sincere gratitude of the student.

+ +

LESSON: 181 — TRUTH

THERE IS ONE Truth. Truth is who and what you are. The teachings revealed by the Holy Spirit in the name of Jesus Christ, may help to wake you up to the reality of your being. "But the Comforter, *which is* the Holy Ghost, whom the Father will send in my name, he shall teach you all things, and bring all things to your remembrance, whatsoever I have said unto you" (John 14: 26).

1. Truth is everything real about your existence. It is awareness in God's nature and Its perfect work. "He *is* the Rock, his work *is* perfect: for all his ways *are* judgment: a God of truth and without iniquity, just and right *is* he just" (Deuteronomy 32: 4).

2. The Holy Spirit in the name of Jesus Christ stirs the remembrance of the teachings of the God - awareness. "Howbeit when he, the Spirit of truth, is come, he will guide you into all truth: for he shall not speak of himself; but whatsoever he shall hear, *that* shall he speak: and he will shew you things to come" (John 16: 13).

3. Truth is revealed through the purest vibrating energy of the Christ Consciousness within awareness. "Truth shall spring out of the earth; and righteousness shall look down from heaven" (Psalm 85:11).

4. Truth reveals the nature of its God Self, and the things of God. In truth, is life eternal, immortality, and perfection. "And this is life eternal, that they may know thee, the only true God, and Jesus Christ, whom thou hast sent" (John 17: 3).

5. Truth revealed has the ability to stir all expressions of consciousness throughout all generations. "For the LORD *is* good; his mercy *is* everlasting; and his truth *endureth* to all generations" (Psalm 100: 5). Because of truth's ability to stir all expressions of consciousness, it is subjected to distortion, misrepresentation, misuse, and impurities.

6. The silent Christ Centered Prayer practice in awareness of the Christ Consciousness may activate the forgiveness and purification process and rid impurities. This may allow you to love in deed and in truth. "My little children, let us not love in word neither in tongue; but in deed and in truth. And hereby we know that we are of the truth, and shall assure our hearts before him" (1 John 3: 18-19).

7. There is an infinity in truth. When you realize truth, it penetrates into all areas of your life. Do not be quick to brush aside an inner realization. Stay with it, ponder it, and it will expand its clarity and extensiveness infinitely.

8. Truth realized cannot be used against Itself. You will find honesty creeps into all your ways. The truth and the way are in your presence. "For we can do nothing against the truth, but for the truth" (2 Corinthians 13: 8).

9. Jesus presented the way, the truth, and life in His presence. "Jesus saith unto him, I am the way, the truth, and the life . . ." (John 14: 6).

10. Truth, once revealed and realized in its purest expression, frees you from the illusions of this world. "And ye shall know the truth, and the truth shall make you free" (John 8: 32).

++++++++++++++++++++++++++

LESSON: 182 — TRYING

TRYING IS THE attempt to succeed while building in failure.

1. To try is to invite failure. To do is to succeed. When you think or say, "I will try" you leave yourself a way out of doing.

2. Trying skirts the edges, while doing gets you into the thick of any venture.

3. The attitude of, "I will try" is the invitation to a half-hearted attempt at doing.

4. When you say you will try to do anything, including a silent prayer practice, you leave room for not accomplishing whatever you set out to try.

5. When you get caught up in trying and trying too hard, the necessary energy to complete a task gets scattered and mistakes and errors may occur. They are learning opportunities. Learn from them!

6. The attitude, "I can do it," "I will do it," is your moment of success — not the end result. You don't ask the Lord what He would have you "try." You ask the Lord what would He have you do. "And he trembling and astonished said, Lord, what wilt thou have me to do? . . ." (Acts 9: 6).

7. Your spiritual walk is always in the moment. There is no middle, no end. There is only where you always are in the present. There is no time for trying but all of the present for doing.

8. The attitude of doing is in the present regardless of the outcome. "For not the hearers of the law *are* just before God, but the doers of the law shall be justified" (Romans 2: 13). "And Jesus said unto him, No man, having put his hand to the plough, and looking back, is fit for the kingdom of God" (Luke 9: 62).

++++++++++++++++++++++++++

LESSON: 183 — TWO WORLDS

THERE IS A path that lies between two perceived worlds, the inner and the outer. Some call it the middle path. It is a path that requires you to maintain a balance.

MAINTAINING A BALANCE:

A. Be consciously aware of the two perceived different worlds. Know you can gradually learn to balance and live between them by living out from the awareness of your reality — the inner world. Be assured this is possible with patience and understanding.

B. Don't get caught up in the crazy mind games. Being judgmental, attacking yourself and others will not restore a balance.

C. Stay alert to the possible drift into other expressions of consciousness once previously experienced. To drift, is to create an imaginary move from your realized awareness. No imaginary move will cause a greater imbalance and send your head and heart spinning.

D. Realizing there are no right or wrong choices or decisions but only necessary ones will help you to keep a balance when under pressure.

E. Have the courage to respect your spiritual integrity. You can't abuse or misuse it. You have the responsibility to be the mind, body, and love of God expressed by the Holy Spirit in the name of Jesus Christ. It creates a balance in all you do. "But as for me, I will walk in mine integrity: redeem me, and be merciful unto me" (Psalm 26: 11).

F. Allow the purification/forgiveness process to clean house and help to maintain a balance. The outer becomes less as the inner becomes more — without a loss of balance.

G. With a determined purpose, walk slowly, steadily, and cautiously between the two worlds until you are aware the inner and outer are one. The outer is merely a reflection of an inner reality. "Judge me, O LORD; for I have walked in mine integrity: I have trusted also in the LORD; *therefore* I shall not slide" (Psalm 26: 1).

1. When you begin a spiritual journey, you are intentionally stepping upon the middle path, you are living between two worlds, and that requires a cautious balance. As you progress in a silent prayer practice, you gradually become aware you're living between two worlds. One, your reality — the other, your created layers of imaginary, relative, and temporary manifestations.

2. An inner world of greater awareness awakens you to insights, realizations, and revelations of reality. The outer world consists of conditioning, sense impressions, false concepts, and a temporary, relative existence — a world you are dream walking.

3. You must come to live from your inner world to the outer world. A reversal from the way you have lived — outer to the inner. It requires trust and a total reliance on the Lord. "Trust in the LORD with all thine heart; and lean not unto thine own understanding" (Proverbs 3: 5-6).

4. As you become more committed to your silent prayer practice, the inner world becomes more pronounced, thus requiring a conscious awareness of the least pull in either direction. The inner world may pull you away from the business of the outer world as it competes for your attention.

5. The difficulty for you may be in learning how to walk a middle path and maintain a balance. Living between two worlds may often be in conflict with the different demands on your time and energy. An extreme in either direction may cause a struggle and rising doubts. Unless you are living in a cave, and few are, you must establish a balance in order for the inner world to be practical in your daily life activities.

6. As a serious truth seeker, achieving a balance is both tricky and difficult. There is still this world of appearances and you may be taking it much too seriously. Yes, the outer daily activities must be handled

in an attentive and responsible manner. Realizing all outer activities are relative (temporary) allows you to approach all with a lighter, less serious nature.

7. You can do all things well in the service of the Lord without expecting a grade. The seriousness may come when you are grading yourself, or expecting others are grading you.

8. It may not be the goal for you to leave this world immediately. Whatever service you are given, you do as a Christ servant. This may allow you to achieve the necessary balance.

9. It may be the most difficult of paths to walk, the most difficult journey to travel and yet, it is a joyous walk in the presence of Jesus Christ. "Thou wilt shew me the path of life: in thy presence *is* fulness of joy; at thy right hand *there are* pleasures evermore" (Psalm 16: 11).

10. Keep a sense of humor when you teeter totter. So, trip, scrape your knees, tire, be tempted, doubt, struggle, cry, and complain. It matters naught. You are coming home within the awareness of the Christ Consciousness and because you have done all in His name, Jesus will love you in any condition you arrive.

+ +

LESSON: 184 — UNFORGETTABLE

UNFORGETTABLE IS THE permanent remembrance of realizations and enlightenments.

1. Realizations are unforgettable. Time will not erase the memory. In fact, what is unforgettable becomes more vivid over time.

2. You may be amazed how unforgettable a realization is.

3. The years do not dull the memory of an inner spiritual realization. Years cannot erase the realization because it occurs beyond the mind.

4. The more fully awakened you become, the more unforgettable are your journey's realization. Often you may find yourself astonished at how clearly you may recall an inner realization.

5. Events in life may tend to fade over time. These may become difficult to remember. A realization beyond the mind is unforgettable down to its most minute detail.

6. You are not reliving the realization, you are it. It is "being the realization" that is unforgettable. The reality of your being, once realized, is unforgettable.

+ +

LESSON: 185 — VALUING AND APPRECIATING

VALUING AND APPRECIATING is an inner acknowledging of the truth and maintaining all that you have realized.

1. As you practice the silent Christ Centered Prayer and the Holy Spirit in the name of Jesus Christ teaches truth, you may struggle for a time and experience doubts.

2. If you are faithful and practice with a devoted determined purpose, realizations and enlightenments naturally unfold and acceptance may follow.

3. Once the reality of truth is accepted and wisdom gradually deepens, your challenge is to continue the silent prayer practice and maintain a balance between your inner and outer world.

4. As the truth of your reality becomes first nature for you, it is easy to become complacent and take what you have realized for granted.

5. An alert awareness continuously knowing and honoring your God-self is required. What you constantly hold near and dear, you can value and appreciate.

6. The truths, realizations, and enlightenments are to be held in the highest honor. Truth most valued and appreciated continues to reveal itself in your daily life. "I will pay my vows unto the LORD now in the presence of all his people" (Psalms 116: 14).

7. The candies of the outer world may continue to plague you with doubts, desires, or temptations. You may find yourself questioning your realizations and comparing yourself with others.

8. Individuals may place their value and appreciation in appearances. They may recognize and acknowledge what they can taste, touch, smell, hear, and see. "Cease ye from man, whose breath *is* in his nostrils: for wherein is he to be accounted of? (Isaiah 2: 22).

9. Because the outer world cannot take note of a lifetime of inner devotion, it places its trust and belief in manmade paper credentials — certificates and degrees earned in weeks or a few years. "*It is* better to trust in the LORD than to put confidence in man" (Psalms 118: 8).

10. Unless you are able to value and appreciate your God-given reality, you may fall into the trap of mistaking the things of this world as having a greater value and more deserving of your appreciation.

11. A constant and unequivocal appreciation for all that you realize you are in truth may prevent you from being misled by appearances of this world. "And it came to pass, when they were come, that he looked on Eliab, and said, Surely the LORD's anointed *is* before him. But the LORD said unto Samuel, Look not on the height of his stature; because I have rejected him: for the *LORD seeth* not as man seeth; for man looketh on the outward appearance, but the LORD looketh on the heart" (1 Samuel 16: 6-7).

12. You cannot equate or evaluate the Christ Consciousness - pure awareness - God with or against its creations. The Creator is greater than its creations.

....

STUDENT'S STORY:

When I am overwhelmed, I have a tendency to get ahead of myself and have a lack of appreciation for the distance I have come on my spiritual journey. I even consider living out from the mind of doubts, fears, and questions. Then I get confused and it is down hill.

Like the disciples of Jesus, I struggled with many of the same doubts, fears, and questions. Some wanted to quit when they thought Jesus was just "too much for them and gone too far." I find myself questioning and contemplating "meaning of life" issues. As I gaze about, I get the gnawing feelings of disillusionment and entertain thoughts like "what's the use?" "It's all a sham." "Why bother?" Temptations rise to value the things of this world as more deserving of my attention than my relationship with Christ.

I have a sense of my nothingness in the midst of nothing. All the work and messing around on this planet, for what? A grand mental construct? Everything just seems such a sham and I wonder why I continue to be concerned and what the fuss is all about. I feel like no one, no where, doing no thing, and someone somewhere doing something at the same time. What difference in the big scheme of things does it make? What difference do I make, if any?

The mind's tricks and temptations certainly suggest doubts, fears, and criticisms until I realize, value, and appreciate the Christ of my being. Only then does my mind go to the edge of the universe and looks back on the cosmos and sighs. And, the wonder of the Christ within me stirs.

+ +

LESSON: 186 — VANITY

VANITY ON A spiritual walk is to give unnecessary attention to the appearance of the body's physical form. "Thou wilt keep *him* in perfect peace, *whose* mind *is* stayed *on thee:* because he trusteth in thee" (Isaiah 26: 3).

1. Vanity may be a stumbling block on your inner spiritual walk. It is easily overlooked and may trip you up with every step you take."Vanity of vanities, saith the Preacher, vanity of vanities; all *is* vanity" (Ecclesiastes l: 2).

2. Attachment to the body and the things of the body takes your attention away from the things of God. This world tempts you to hold fast to a form that deteriorates in time and space. There isn't anything under the sun that can give the body immortality. "I have seen all the works that are done under the sun; and, behold, all *is* vanity and vexation of spirits" (Ecclesiastes 1: 14)

3. "Who shall ascend into the hill of the LORD? or who shall stand in his holy place? He that hath clean hands, and a pure heart; who hath not lifted up his soul unto vanity, nor sworn deceitfully" (Psalm 24: 3-4).

4. Keep your mind stayed on the Lord and your eyes shall behold the wonders of an inner awareness of being. "Turn away mine eyes from beholding vanity; *and* quicken thou me in thy way" (Psalm 119: 37).

5. In the Kingdom of God, the earthly flesh counts for nothing. Your oneness is in the body of Christ, the spirit of Christ. "It is the spirit that quickeneth; the flesh profiteth nothing: the words that I speak unto you, *they* are spirit, and *they* are life" (John 6: 63).

6. The body has its purpose but it is not your reality. Give it what it needs but do not mistake it for your true reality as one in being with Christ Jesus in the Holy Spirit. "*There is* therefore now no condemnation to them which are in Christ Jesus, who walk not after the flesh, but after the Spirit" (Romans 8:1).

7. The body is a relative, temporary means of transportation upon this plane. As with all means of transportation, the body deteriorates and must be retired. The body is certainly to be given loving care. Avoid obsessive attachments to a body that rises and falls away.

8. The body changes — your life does not. You are not the body. In due time and in gratitude for its use, you will overcome the attachment to the body. "Him that overcometh will I make a pillar in the temple of my God, and he shall go no more out: and I will write upon him the name of my God, and the name of the city of my God, *which is* new Jerusalem, which cometh down out of heaven from my God: and I will write upon him my new name" (Revelation 3: 12).

9. When the mirror of vanity raises its glittering head to tempt you to judge what you see, remember the purpose the body serves in the awakening and overcoming process.

10. The body serves as a Holy temple at the service of the awakening process. With loving kindness, allow the body to slowly fade as its service is no longer needed. "What? Know ye not that your body is the temple of the Holy Ghost *which is* in you, which ye have of God, and ye are not your own? For ye are bought with a price: therefore glorify God in your body, and in your spirit, which are God's" (1 Corinthians 6: 19-20).

11. Gently and lovingly assist the body as it goes through its necessary changes. Accept, allow, respect, and appreciate the gradual body changes. These are signs of your progress as you draw near to the ultimate realization — that of a fully awakened, unattached Christ being in the Oneness of God.

12. Overcome the vain offerings of this world and seek to be clothed with the raiment that offers life eternal. "He that overcometh, the same shall be clothed in white raiment; and I will not blot out his name

out of the book of life, but I will confess his name before my Father, and before his angels" (Revelation 3: 5).

++++++++++++++++++++++++++

LESSON: 187 — VIRGINAL CONCEPTION

THE VIRGINAL CONCEPTION is the conception of Jesus by the power of the Holy Spirit. It is the angel Gabriel"s annunciation to Mary, foretelling Jesus' conception by the power of the Holy Spirit. ". . . Behold, a virgin shall conceive, and bear a son, and shall call his name Immanuel" (Isaiah 7:14).

1. Great and not so great scholars have debated, disagreed, and often declined to discuss the virginal conception of Jesus. It is not well to get caught up in an endless debate. Truth cannot be proven; it must be realized.

2. Because a virginal conception is beyond the human sense mind, the mind cannot comprehend it. The mind cannot grasp what is beyond it.

3. A mind that rises and falls, comes and goes, cannot grasp a reality that transcends its self. Jesus' conception originates in a vibration of pure consciousness.

4. In reality, there is but one power. This one God almighty power manifests at a slower vibratory energy speed as It enters the plane of opposites. "And the scribe said unto him. Well, Master, thou hast said the truth: for there is one God; and there is none other but he" (Mark 12: 32).

5. In the illusionary world of opposites, you believe in the power of opposites, two human, physical sense forms bring forth another human, physical sense form. You invest power in your belief. And as you believe, it is done unto you. You set the trap, you step into it. "And Jesus said unto the centurion, Go thy way; and as thou hast believed, *so* be it done unto thee. And his servant was healed in the selfsame hour" (Matthew 8: 13).

6. It was only necessary for Mother Mary to consent for Her energy to vibrate at the necessary rate that would attract the Holy Spirit and conceive. "And Mary said, 'Behold the handmaid of the Lord; be it unto me according to thy word. And the angel departed from her'" (Luke 1: 38).

7. With God, all things are possible. Why not a virginal conception? Jesus cautions it is hard for a rich man to enter the kingdom of God. Jesus is quick to add,"And said, The things which are impossible with men are possible with God" (Luke 18: 27).

8. Though conceived without sin Jesus, in his humanity, experienced all that exists on the illusionary plane of opposites. You also imitate the Christ energy of your being. It may not be a very good or perfect imitation, but one nevertheless. There is only one Christ and we who are the many are one in Christ.

9. Realize all conceptions at the moment of conception are of the Holy Spirit, the One, Holy, Almighty, Intelligent Power. No thing, no individual expression of consciousness exists separate and apart from that which created it. "All things were made by him; and without him was not anything made that was made" (John 1:3).

10. A virginal conception had a purpose and fulfilled a need. God's purpose is reveled and met in the conception of Jesus born of the virgin Mary by the power of the Holy Spirit. Such a powerful revelation imprints eternally on the memories of individual expressions of consciousness.

12. Yes, Mary's conception served its purpose. God is infinite and is infinitely unfolding in all ways possible, in all ways necessary. All your needs are constantly being met and that would include a Jesus to reveal the truth of the Kingdom of God and provide the means of realizing reality. "Jesus saith unto him, 'I am the way, the truth, and the life: no man cometh unto the Father, but by me" (John 14: 6).

STUDENT'S STORY:

This is the story that always brings tears to my eyes and expands love in my heart. Perhaps it is because I, too, am a woman. Although I cannot claim Mary's total trust in God, obedience to God's will, and gentle humility, I recognize and give thanks for her unique role in salvation history. Mary's story is the greatest example of an innocent trust and faith in God. Mary, of humble estate, chosen directly by God, credential-less by worldly standards and inquisitive by nature, gives her fiat to bear a son of the most high by the power of the Holy Spirit. Mary says, "Yes," "be it unto me according to thy word." (Luke 1: 38), without guarantees, without asking permission of any man and ultimately without hesitation,

The Annunciation story is about a woman greatly loved by God. It is also about Mary, a woman who greatly loved God more than her own life, more than her reputation, and more than anything else in the whole wide world. The ultimate request and the ultimate act of faith come together in the Gabriel's Annunciation proclamation, "fear not." And the angel said unto her, Fear not, Mary: for thou hast found favour with God" (Luke I: 30). Favored by God, Mary's humility and trust in God's promise, and obedience to his word allow her to be chosen and enable her to conceive. She believes, receives, conceives, and bears Christ into the world. A greater gift no woman has ever given. She is one who can truly say, "This is my body, this is my blood."

As Mother Mary gives hands, feet, ears, eyes, voice, taste, reason, intellect, and will to baby, Mary becomes the living temple of the living Jesus ushering in a new age of grace. Heaven and earth are indeed wed in the incarnation. All separation and alienation is overcome in and through the mystery of God made flesh. Emmanuel, God is with us.

Mary was not just a young courageous woman. She was a devotee of her Lord, God, and the Lord knew her well. Mary understood deeply Gabriel's words, "With God nothing shall be impossible." Did she wonder if the timing was right? Did she know she had found favor with God? She did not. She simply looked, listened, and obeyed. She gave full consent of her will to God's will and never looked back. We have in Mary a model to follow. Annunciations and consents presents themselves everyday in our lives. I believe we are all asked by God to believe, receive, conceive and bear Christ in our world. "Nothing is impossible with God." We, too, may choose to consent.

+ +

LESSON: 188 — VOCABULARY

VOCABULARY IS THE change in word usage that occurs on the spiritual journey.

1. As you awaken to realizations and enlightenments, some changes in your vocabulary may occur. The multitude of old tried and used words may no longer be suitable.

2. Realizations and enlightenments are beyond this world of words. You may struggle with words. "For a dream cometh through the multitude of business; and a fool's voice *is known* by multitude of words" (Ecclesiastes 5: 3).

3. The more words you attempt to use, the more likely you are apt to be misunderstood. Silence is golden. Wisdom teaches you to say less and listen more. A tongue that knows no pauses of silence is not a sign of enlightenment. "Be still, and know that I *am* God: . . ." (Psalm 46: 10).

4. In sharing truth, oral or written, economy of words is best. "Be not rash with thy mouth, and let not thine heart be hasty to utter *any* thing before God: for God *is* in heaven, and thou upon earth: therefore let thy words be few" (Ecclesiastes 5: 2)

5. There are words that may be eliminated from your vocabulary. For example: the words try, tired, and need, may fall away. You are no longer trying, you are doing. You are aware that you will always have the necessary energy to complete a task. All of your needs are being met. As you change so do the words you use to express yourself.

6. There are many times you may be lost for words! Words that would judge or condemn you, whether used by you or others, no longer have a home in your vibrating energy vocabulary. "Verily, verily, I say unto you, He that heareth my word, and believeth on him that sent me, hath everlasting life, and shall not come into condemnation; but is passed from death unto life" (John 5: 24).

7. Words and appearances are subject to change. The Word of God is the living truth that does not change. "The grass withereth, the flower fadeth: but the word of our God shall stand for ever" (Isaiah 40: 8).

8. You live by the Word of God through the Holy Spirit in the name of Jesus Christ. "But he answered and said, 'It is written, Man shall not live by bread alone, but by every word that proceedeth out of the mouth of God'" (Matthew 4: 4). Hear God's Word and live.

+ +

LESSON: 189 — VOICES - COMMENTS AND THOUGHTS - INTERNAL

VOICES, COMMENTS, AND thoughts - internal are the conditioned (negative or positive) internal chatter. They may rise, demanding attention. They attempt to create false concepts and beliefs about yourself or others.

1. Like a broken record conditioned internal voices, comments, and thoughts know only how to repeat and repeat. It does not matter if you or others originally put them in motion.

2. The conditioned internal chatter that was created by others who played dominant authority roles in your life, may have more of a believability content. "Cease ye from man, whose breath *is* in his nostrils: for wherein is he to be accounted of?" (Isaiah 2: 22).

3. As a young child and young adult, you are more vulnerable to the conditioning of others who would mold you in an image to their liking. As you awaken to your reality, you may shed any false image and all of the conditioned internal noise. Forgive yourself and those who "knew not what they did!"

4. As a child and as a young adult it may have been natural for you to internalize the positive or negative conditioned chatter. Regardless of origin, you have the responsibility to purify all conditioning and live faithfully from the Christ of your being.

5. If you have accepted the conditioned voices, comments, and thoughts, and made them your own by giving them a home and energy, you may be distracted, aggravated and tormented.

6. You may experience negative conditioned internal chatter as solid steel forms — impenetrable. This is the most difficult vibrating energy to purify. Accepting the false sense of belief in negative conditioned chatter creates a situation very difficult to change.

7. One way to overcome, penetrate, and alleviate the suffering from disturbing conditioned internal chatter is to divest the power you have given (continue to give) it. Allow the forgiveness and purification process to take place. Allow yourself to realize the love of a God that holds you dear. "The LORD hath appeared of old unto me, *saying*, Yea, I have loved thee with an everlasting love: therefore with loving kindness have I drawn thee" (Jeremiah 31: 3).

8. You may have personally identified with the self incriminating internal voices, comments, and

thoughts throughout a life of conditioning. When the invested power is finally withdrawn, your identification with and attachment to the rising internal chatter no longer exists. You are free.

9. The Power Prayer, Part I and Part II, may assist you in penetrating and divesting the disturbing conditioned internal chatter.

10. Realize you are a spiritual being created in the image of God. The rising chatter has no sustaining power of its own. The power is directly given to you from within and you decide to withhold, or continue investing it in the internal chatter. "The LORD thy God in midst of thee *is* mighty; he will save, he will rejoice over thee with joy; he will rest in his love, he will joy over thee with singing" (Zephaniah 3: 17).

....

STUDENT'S STORY:

When having to understand and confront my own internal conditioning, this Lesson Paper and the Power Prayer practice were of special value on my spiritual walk.

As an ordained Episcopal priest, my formal ministry life began in 1995 in Alta, Wyoming as Vicar of Saint Francis of the Tetons Episcopal Church and Director of the Alta Retreat Center. They were intended by the Bishop to share land, space, facilities, human resources, and finances. It was my job to figure out a way to do that. I spent my first eleven years as a priest doing just that . . . and a lot more!

Growing up my mother's voice resonated, "Sandy, darling, nothing is impossible. The impossible simply takes a little longer." Other competing voices, however, were not so encouraging. My father's German matter of fact bottom line philosophy was different. "So, who is going to pay for it!?"

I grew up (as many of you probably did) with conflicting and competing messages with layers of parental, familial and cultural conditioning. In my thirties, I became increasingly aware of the dilemma I had in living out of these two polar reference points. I often experienced myself as full of self doubts. I also had tremendous faith in the goodness and infinite possibilities of life and my abilities to live in and out of them. I struggled between encouragement and criticism. I struggled between the sky's the limit and the sky's limited.

I arrived at mid-life with mixed messages of optimism and pessimism that I had been taught, accepted, and interiorized. For better or worse, these values operate unconsciously until such time as they were brought into the light of day by some person or event. The spiritual journey, as many of you may know by now, has a way of allowing such illuminations to come forth for well or for woe! I had my share of events!

Preaching on Sundays in a parish with only one priest was demanding, relentless, challenging, sometimes fulfilling, sometimes discouraging, and always public! Preaching the Word of God is certainly ambitious if not inherently presumptuous. In any case, it can be humbling as well as humiliating. I have never been particularly shy; however, I don't think anything prepared me for the constant battle I encountered on Sunday afternoons.

When I finally arrived home alone after my celebrations of Holy Eucharist with sermon delivered, the inner comments of criticisms would play themselves out in my heart and mind. This inner conversation took place in the silence and solitude of my log cabin in the Teton woods. Snow, ice, and cold blanketed my home most months of the year. Jesus had his desert and Sandy had her log cabin!

We both encountered the tempter! The comments were all too familiar. The tempter was at work trying to raise suspicions and doubts. However, unlike Jesus' response of total and immediate fidelity to His Father, mine was too often one of resignation, restlessness, grief, self doubts, self criticism, fatigue and indigestion! I had accepted the internal chatter. It hooked me and I suffered the consequences.

Praise and blame, doubt and faith, pride and humility, success and failure were the all too familiar variations on the "you are not enough or you are too much" themes conditioned during my growing up years. Unable to find relief in face of my self doubts, I would call a friend, go for a walk, enact a gestalt conversation with Jesus in my living room, meditate, have a cup of tea, or get a log fire going.

All of this background is to illustrate the opportunity and necessity of moving through the apparent emotional turmoil. All caused by conditioned responses to the present events of life that are influenced by past conditioning. I was living out from the conditioned responses rather then live out of a place of serenity, peace, trust, and fidelity to the Christ.

Studying this Lesson, practicing the Power Prayer, and my regular silent prayer practice helped me to reach a place of relative calm and non-attachment to the conditioned comments whether they were of praise or blame, regardless of the day of the week they would arise. It has taken a long time to drop the temptation to blame my parental conditioning and take personal responsibility for my emotional responses. I have gradually come to know that if and when I choose not to identify with or empower comments and criticisms, self inflicted or delivered by others, and rest quietly and confidently in the Christ of my being, the storm quickly passes.

It has taken a long time to realize this truth and I have had numerous opportunities to practice. I continue to be grateful to God through the power of the Holy Spirit in the name of Jesus Christ. I continue to consciously be aware of these choices whenever the occasions rise — and there are lots of opportunities!

+ +

LESSON: 190 — VOID

THE VOID, FOR which there is no description. The Void that is not Void-less. The Void that many of you may have realized. The Void you may have realized and yet may have not been cognizant of.

1. Beyond the body, mind, consciousness, and awareness there is the Void. It is the indescribable almighty Void-God.

2. When you return to conscious awareness, you only know you know. It is the Almighty indescribable Void-God Being from which all exist. You can only be totally amazed at the wonder of It. "He stretcheth out the north over the empty place, *and* hangeth the earth upon nothing" (Job 26:7)

3. You may be surprised and confused that there is this Void-God that exists. Your first inclination is to describe it to yourself — not possible. You struggle to understand It; you cannot; you struggle to talk about It; you cannot.

4. As you return from being the Void, you know that you know the unknown, the Almighty Void-God Being none can describe. Once known, you know it will be for others to venture within, to know they know.

5. You are left with the knowing there are two types of individuals. The one who knows the Void-God and cannot describe It and one who does not know the Void-God and describes It. Those who can describe the Void-God do not know the Void-God.

6. The Almighty Void-God is truly all in all and beyond all. The Supreme Being is beyond words, thoughts, consciousness, and awareness.

7. Whatever you can imagine It is, It is not. Whatever you say It is, It is not.

8. Written here in this Lesson are over two hundred and fifty words about the Void-God and not one of them describes It. It is for you to know. "And this is life eternal, that they might know thee the only true God" (John 17: 3).

STUDENT'S STORY:

Oh, Oh, Oh how long I waited for the Void and the no-thing-ness. This is a strange, strange journey full of twists and turns. How many times I wondered what "pure transcendence" would be like and now I am told by my teacher not to get carried away with it to the point of desiring to go off into the Void.

I was not trying to let go and go there, I just went there. I was on a nine day private intensive retreat with a rigorous schedule of silent prayer and solitude. I was simply practicing the silent Christ Centered prayer as my teacher had instructed. As thoughts, emotions, and sensations rose, I simply again became aware of my spiritual heart center. Nothing more, nothing less. I returned and rested in awareness.

After three days of intense silence, I was just sitting there and without warning, without fanfare, without doing anything, it just happened. I just slipped from awareness into the Void. I was looking at the light of consciousness on the inner screen and the next thing I knew I was coming up from a deep place not knowing how I got there, how long I'd been there, or even remembering wanting to go there. Yes, the Void is indescribable.

The Void surely made an impact on my life. Coming off the retreat I noticed people were strangely beautiful. I found myself perceiving goodness in people in whom I previously saw nothing to commend. Now they seemed full of potential. Perhaps it was simply that my potential was expanding. I was amazed at myself. The sharp edge was not there, I was relating more kindly and the world seemed to be relating to me more kindly.

Returning to the hectic demands of a householder and priest, I carried with me a sense of awe and gratitude. Nothing had changed, but everything had changed. It would take years for the event to be integrated and to settle. It has taken years for me to put pen to paper about this retreat. I speak of it now simply to say the Void exists. I am now aware, in retrospect, that Its value is not in "Itself" an end, but rather, one means in more fully understanding and appreciating in this life some of the mystery of God. This mystery to be lived fully in each individual life as compassion, mercy, peace, justice, and unconditional love.

++++++++++++++++++++++++++++

LESSON: 191 — VULNERABLE

BEING VULNERABLE IS a fear of a false sense of feeling on your own. It is not knowing or realizing the truth of your oneness.

1. Vulnerable is a fear of being without the Holy Spirit armor and hung out to dry. It is a false sense of a person separate and apart from the Holy Spirit in the name of Jesus Christ. None of which is true. "For God hath not given us the spirit of fear; but of power, and of love, and of a sound mind" (II Timothy 1: 7).

2. Desires and temptations pave the way for vulnerability to deceive you into believing you are an individual separate and apart from the Christ consciousness of your being. You believe you could be harmed, hurt, or something can be taken away. In reality, there is no-thing this world could ever take away or add to your being. All that God has is already yours. "And he said unto him, Son thou art ever with me, and all that I have is thine" (Luke 15: 31).

3. Vulnerability usually rises when you have a false sense of abandonment by the Lord. A sense of loneliness creeps in and all matter of vulnerable scenarios rise to tempt and torment. The Christ would never abandon you. "Teaching them to observe all things whatsoever I have commanded you: and, lo, I am with you always, *even* unto the end of the world. Amen" (Matthew 28: 20).

4. Vulnerability is particularly strong when you have had a spiritual realization or have had a reasonable time of general "good feelings." You may be quick to forget you live on the plane of opposites. The false appearances of doubts, desires, and temptations constantly rise, causing exposure to feelings of rising vulnerability. Remember, temptations never cease and they may intensify.

5. The mind creates a false sense of vulnerability. Use the mind instead in the service of remembering the realized truth. Stand fast in the knowledge of your oneness in the one God. ". . . for there is one God; and there is none other but he" (Mark 12: 32).

6. Realize the truth, contemplate truth, and hold fast to the truth during the critical trials. God never denies you the Kingdom.

7. When feelings of being vulnerable rise, stand at the top of the mountain and say, "No" to the temptation of being vulnerable and, "Yes" to the Holy Spirit in the name of Jesus Christ.

8. "Yes, I am not alone. Yes, I am a spiritual being. Yes, my God knows my needs before I do. Yes, the Holy Spirit of Jesus Christ is within me, behind me, and goes before me. And, yes, the Holy Spirit knows exactly where I should be at all times."

9. Trust the Christ and the reality of being is never vulnerable and remember that the Holy Spirit in the name of Jesus Christ is an army of one that is constantly revealing its care and unconditional love when meeting your needs.

10. The sense of vulnerability does not make it reality. Vulnerability rises to fall and what remains before the rise, in between the rise, and after the fall is the reality of which no one or thing can ever harm, take away, destroy, or separate — a child of God. "The Spirit itself beareth witness with our spirit, that we are the children of God: and if children, then heirs; heirs of God and joint-heirs with Christ; if so be that we suffer with *him*, that we may be also glorified together" (Romans 8: 16-17).

....

STUDENT'S STORY:

I was feeling most vulnerable when this paper was written in response to my self-pity pot. It had been a long week of "poor me." I thought for sure Jesus Christ had decided I was too much to handle and had enough of my nonsense. I sent my teacher a long exaggerated email of just how deserted and lonely I felt. My teacher was quick to respond with this Lesson. Here is what I emailed my teacher after having received her email.

"I appreciate the vulnerable Lesson and it is true to my experience. I had some inkling about this pity feeling as 'temptation' and yet, I didn't know exactly how to respond to it. I am so glad to have had this experience in order to have this Lesson written so clearly and reassuringly and without hesitation. Reading it has been and is a total delight and renews my spirit. It is a *very* important Lesson. I express sincere gratitude for it big time."

+ +

LESSON: 192 — WAKING UP

WAKING UP IS the coming home to your reality.

1. Did you think that waking up would not hurt? It will.
2. Did you think that waking up would not humiliate you? It will.
3. Did you think waking up would not strip you of your outer armor and make you vulnerable? It will.
4. Did you think waking up would not expose you to the deceptions of this world? It will.

5. Did you think waking up would not exhaust and weaken you before it would make you strong? It will.

6. Did you think waking up would not come at a price? It does.

7. You can only pay the price by realizing that which is demanded of you. The price is waking up to the truth of this world and all of its deceits, desires, and wants.

8. Wake up and know you are not of this world. "And he said unto them, Ye are from beneath; I am from above: ye are of this world; I am not of this world" (John 8: 23).

9. Wake up and return to the place you never left.

10. You want God, Christ, Truth? Then be willing to pay the price. Be willing to wake up to the reality of your life. "Wherefore he saith, awake thou that sleepest, and arise from the dead, and Christ shall give thee light" (Ephesians 5: 14).

+ +

LESSON: 193 — WALKING ALONE

WALKING ALONE IS the experience of feeling abandoned by God.

1. Whenever you feel it necessary to have your existence confirmed by others, you experience the illusion of walking alone.

2. As you progress on your spiritual walk, the gate seems to become straighter and the way more narrow. You may have the false sense of being alone.

3. The sense of walking alone may, at times, weaken your faith. You may feel the need to share with others, "(For we walk by faith, not by sight)" (II Corinthians 5: 7).

4. When your attention is on a personal sense of self, separate and apart, you may feel the need to be complimented, supported, and validated by others.

5. You experience walking alone, when your attention is drawn outward to other personal sense Beings instead of inward to the oneness of God.

6. Looking to the outer appearances for confirmation or appreciation, turns your attention to the illusionary experience of walking alone.

7. Focusing outward upon another as a personal solitary, single separate self pulls you from your Christ Center where you may become aware of your spiritual support and spiritual companionship. This tactic creates the illusion of walking alone.

8. It is the self absorption in a personal separate sense that pricks at the fringes of your sense personality. It encourages you to indulge in the outer needy syndrome.

9. Everything that is necessary for your progress and any one who you will ever need to companionship with, is always available. If you are walking in truth, you never are walking alone. "Teach me thy way, O LORD; I will walk in thy truth: unite my heart to fear thy name" (Psalm 86: 11).

10. On the spiritual walk, the entire universe comes to assist. The Holy Spirit in the name of Jesus Christ, the Saints, and all previously attained realized individuals are walking every step of the way with you. You are truly a member in the "community of saints!"

+ +

LESSON: 194 — WALKING IN PLACE

WALKING IN PLACE is how you are traveling on your spiritual walk.

1. Although the spiritual journey may seem like a long one with many twists and turns, it is all happening where you began in consciousness.

2. In reality there is no time, no space. Everything and everyone is in consciousness.

3. Every category that rises and every step you express is taken in place. It is not that "you are in the world," rather it is, "the world is within you!"

4. Through the Holy Spirit in the name of Jesus Christ, there are three categories and ten steps within the categories you may encounter during your spiritual journey.

BEGINNER - CATEGORY I:

A. Turning within — Acknowledging a path
B. Discipline — Expressed sincerity
C. Obedience — Keeps you on the path

ADVANCE - CATEGORY II:

A. Acceptance — Surrender
B. Receptivity — Readiness
C. Devotion — Loyalty

AWAKENED - CATEGORY III:

A. Gratitude — Preparedness for the deepest mysteries
B. Realization — Communion
C. Resting - Wisdom — A state of full awareness
D. The Void — Indescribable.

++++++++++++++++++++++++

LESSON: 195 — WASTE

WASTE IS THE putting off of your spiritual practices.

1. It is a waste to argue truth. Truth must be realized.
2. Too much time is wasted on efforts to dispute truth.
3. Be a skeptic. That's fine. However, continue your spiritual practices.
4. Don't be so quick to give up because you believe your spiritual progress is not to your liking.
5. Too much time and effort are wasted in a commitment to the habit of constant stop-and-go.
6. It is a waste to give up because you believe you are wasting time. Often, the mistake is to give up just when a break through is on the horizon.
7. There will always be the temptation to walk away from your spiritual practices for worldly pursuits.
8. The inner journey may not be a quick or easy one, but it is never a waste to investigate who or what you are.
9. To put aside your spiritual practices for worldly priorities is the greatest waste of your sojourn upon this plane.
10. The relative time on this earth plane is precious. Use it wisely, don't waste it.

++++++++++++++++++++++++

LESSON: 196 — WHEN THE STUDENT IS READY

WHEN THE STUDENT is ready, the moment an inner linking with "the" outer teacher upon this plane of opposites occurs.

1. There is a saying, "When the student is ready, the teacher appears."
2. The readiness may have evolved over time preparation for the auspicious meeting.
3. You may have had many teachers who have helped to prepare you for "the" outer teacher who will teach and guide you to the realization of the Christ Consciousness and the awareness of your reality.
4. You cannot seek the outer "teacher." There isn't any search that will reveal to you the one who will appear in the right place at the right moment. The attraction simply occurs. It is a spiritual principle. You can count on it.
5. You and the teacher are mutually drawn to meet — no matter when or where you may be at the time. Your responsibility is to seek truth wherever it may lead you.
6. All will be in perfect alignment for the moment of the teacher's appearance and the inner connection. The moment of meeting "the teacher" is usually unexpected, unplanned, and may be in the most unlikely place.
7. You know this is the "one" because the Holy Spirit in the name of Jesus Christ, will validate your intuition..
8. Your life will be changed in a more intensive inward direction.
9. For a time, you may experience a resistance and disobey the inner pull this teacher may cause.
10. Eventually, you find yourself drawn to the teacher for spiritual direction. In time, the student - teacher relationship becomes one of surrender, obedience, and trust. The surrender and obedience are to the Christ of the teacher's being not the teacher's personality
11. Your inner spiritual teacher is the Holy Spirit in the name of Jesus Christ. The Holy Spirit knows the exact moment you are ready for the outer teacher to appear.
12. It is with the outer teacher the Holy Spirit in the name of Jesus Christ may intensify your spiritual progress within the awareness reality of your being.

+ +

LESSON: 197 — "WHY, GOD?"

OFTEN WHEN THERE is a disaster, the question arises, "Why, God?" Why do certain events occur? Why doesn't God interfere? You either blame or praise God. Neither apply. In God, there are no opposites.

1. In the Void/God there is no awareness, no consciousness. This is why God cannot be described with a rising mind in consciousness. The mind does not exist during the Void/God to witness it. Therefore, it cannot describe God.
2. The Void/God is that which you only know you have had when you return and you are once again in conscious awareness. You know, you know. That is all of it.
3. However, the Void is not Void-less. It is because of the Void/God that awareness exists. It consists of the purest, impersonal God love.
4. Within awareness rises Consciousness and within individual expression of consciousness rises mind — thinking, emotions. If you cause impurities by your misuse of this pure vibrating energy through your misdeeds in thought, word, and action, it is not, "Why, God?" It is, "Why, you?" Why do you choose to do great harm to yourself and others?

5. As an individual expression of consciousness, you have the choice to love or to do harm. You are using the free will of God and you may use it wisely or distort it. God can't interfere because God is always being God in the purest of be - ing. How can a God of pure love interfere with that which does not exist in Its nature? It cannot.

6. It is your option to interfere or not. You are the one to forgive, it is you who ultimately awakens to the Christ Consciousness and the awareness of your being. You, and individuals like you, may change negative actions. You are the one who has a false sense of separation from what you are in your reality. Thus, you and others with similar false sense are the ones causing the havoc on the plane of opposites.

7. It is not a God somewhere far away who must forgive, purify, but your personal sense of "I, Me, My" who must wake up to your Christ Self that possesses the attributes you attribute to God - love - mercy - forgiveness. They are in reality your attributes and you, and others like you, are the ones to be loving, caring, merciful, and forgiving of one another. You are the one to express the Christ/God in action by your words, thoughts, and deeds.

8. You cannot separate from yourself that which you call Christ/God. "I and *my* Father are one" (John 10: 30). Jesus taught us that His Father is your Father. You need only to wake up and you are once again in the pure state of Grace that is loving, forgiving and the old ways are finished, all things are new. It is in the fully awakened state that you are graced with detachment from the suffering of this world.

9. In the Christ of your being there are no broken pieces to put together. There is a whole unbroken Christ being. It is for you to give up that which you falsely have believed and accept the mercy and forgiveness of the impersonal Christ nature, which is your birthright.

10. Jesus came as a personal image of God and demonstrated the loving, caring, and healing one individual can give to another. He demonstrated the love, mercy, and forgiveness the impersonal Christ has for Itself, *you*. Jesus demonstrated you aren't separate and alone.

11. There is the Holy One, Christ within each of you, the One always awaiting the return of the many. The One who, if you allow, does the perfect personal works of an impersonal Christ through Jesus, through a Jane, a Tom, Dick, or Harry. Jesus demonstrated that the many have access to the One by right of being a child of man, a child of God, and ultimately the One of God. "For through him we both have access by one Spirit unto the Father" (Ephesians 2: 18).

12. You can turn to Jesus the personal and be healed of your hurts and then Jesus Christ guides you to the Christ, the impersonal awareness of His and your being. Once again you are an aware impersonal pure being.

13. It is not, "Why does God allow?" but rather, "Why do you choose to do what is opposite of your true graced nature?" Jesus came to show you the way, to example the way, and to be the way to the awareness of your Christ Consciousness.

14. This is the Christ Centered spiritual walk and the long journey home. The prodigal son returns home from the separate false personal sense to an aware impersonal being "BEHOLD, what manner of love the Father hath bestowed upon us, that we should be called the sons of God: therefore the world knoweth us not, because it knew him not" (I John 3: 1).

+ +

LESSON: 198 — WILL- FREE

FREE WILL IS exercise of concentrated mental, vibrating energy applied to any wish, desire, or temptation that grabs your attention.

1. Often referred to as "will power," concentrated mental vibrating energy possesses an extraordinary

strength and may accomplish difficult tasks when seeking to fulfill desires, overcoming temptations, or realizing the truth.

2. You have wishes, desires, and temptations. Most wishes and desires you don't necessarily fulfill, nor do you succumb to all temptations.

3. There are desires you plan to fulfill and temptations you may need to use your free will to overcome, as Jesus did. "Get thee behind me, Satan!"(Luke 4: 8)

4. When you are ardently intense about fulfilling a wish, desire, or responding to a temptation, free will moves you into a plan of action and helps to maintain your attention span until the desire is fulfilled or the temptation is overcome.

5. As an aware conscious spiritual being, you have the free will to choose to manifest desires and act, or not, on temptations. In progressively realizing the truth, your prayer becomes, ". . . nevertheless not my will, but thine be done" (Luke 22: 42).

6. Free will is the engine that drives the car. It takes you wherever it is you believe you want to go. However, you may not want to be there once you have arrived and achieved. So, be careful what you wish for! "For my thoughts *are* not your thoughts, neither *are* your ways my ways, saith the Lord" (Isaiah 55: 8).

7. It is the strength of your belief, faith, and your free will that may bring into fruition your wishes, desires, or plans. It is by sheer "will power" you may overcome adversities through the Holy Spirit in the name of Jesus Christ. Jesus gave you an example to follow. ". . . O my Father, if it be possible, let this cup pass from me: nevertheless not as I will, but as thou *wilt*" (Matthew 26: 39).

8. All that you are and ever will be is the nature of God. As you continue with the silent Christ Centered Prayer practice and realize the oneness of being, your aware free will *is* Divine will. "Thy Kingdom come. Thy will be done in earth, as *it is* in heaven" (Matthew 6: 10).

+ +

LESSON: 199 — WITHDRAW

WITHDRAW IS THE inner pull or temptation to leave this world that comes to all truth seekers sooner or later.

1. As you progress on the spiritual walk, there may be, at times, a strong inner pull to leave the business of world and seek the solace of the semblance of a cave.

2. The world may seem as if it is one gigantic disturbance. You may want to seek only the quiet and peace of your inner being.

3. Your interest in the things and individuals of this world may wane to the point of your wanting to withdraw and be alone with the inner silence of your being.

4. This may be a temporary condition. If you have responsibilities to family or position, you may find withdrawing is not possible.

5. Until you have overcome the temptation to entirely withdraw from the world, it is best you stay in it. You may satisfy this inner tugging for your complete attention by periodically withdrawing, as is appropriate to your state of life.

6. This is one of the values of retreat centers or working with a teacher. Visiting a retreat center, a teacher, or making a silent retreat when possible, may help to restore a more even balance between your inner and outer life.

7. All or any of the above may help to satisfy a momentary need to withdraw and, in time, you may realize the cave of silence is always within you.

8. There may come a time when you are able and wish to withdraw and live a solitary, silent life. When and if that time should come and you choose a life of silence, it is a draw to the silent awareness, not a withdrawal from this world.

++++++++++++++++++++++++++

LESSON: 200 — WISDOM

WISDOM IS RECOGNITION, God recognition. Wisdom does not necessarily come with age. It comes when you have been properly seasoned in the living out from the truth revealed.

1. Recognition of your God-Self is the beginning of wisdom. Wisdom may not immediately follow realizations or enlightenments. It takes time to mature, ripen, and rise in full awareness.

2. Because you have a great realization does not necessarily mean you are immediately wise. "Be not wise in thine own eyes: fear the LORD, and depart from evil" (Proverbs 3: 7).

3. Because realizations and enlightenments require time to expand and deepen, wisdom may seem to lag behind. Learn to hold your tongue and rest in the silence of what is given you instead of being quick to express your thoughts.

4. Wisdom does not rise in the mind. Say less and turn your hearing inward where wisdom expresses itself from the Holy Spirit in the name of Jesus Christ. "If any of you lack wisdom, let him ask of God, that giveth to all *men* liberally, and upbraideth not; and it shall be given him" (James I: 5).

5. Realizations and enlightenments cause life changes that are occurring through a mental state that is slow to acknowledge truth. An adjustment period may be necessary before you can experience the calm assurance of wisdom.

6. Ponder your realizations and live with them, allowing wisdom to slowly rise to the surface in its own time as the need requires it.

7. Nothing is ever applied to anything and nothing is ever added to anything. Wisdom cannot be applied because it exists within the appearance waiting to be recognized.

8. The getting of wisdom is the getting of understanding. Both of which are inherent within your patience of waiting on the Lord. "Wisdom *is* the principal thing; *therefore* get wisdom: and with all thy getting get understanding" (Proverbs 4: 7).

9. Wisdom is the unknowing of what seems to appear as a situation, problem, individual, or condition.

10. From the unknowing of all that is false comes God recognition of the truth. God in every situation and individual that presents itself.

11. The necessary answer, resolution, or conclusion (wisdom) exists within the present. You cannot dip into memories for wisdom. Wisdom's birth is a constant present.

12. Wisdom isn't knowledge that can be spread like peanut butter. Its value is greater than any man's wealth. "The gold and crystal cannot equal it: and the exchange of it *shall not be for* jewels of fine gold cannot equal it, nor can it be exchanged for jewels of fine gold. No mention shall be made of coral, or of pearls: for the price of wisdom *is* above rubies" (Job 28: 17-18).

13. Wisdom is not the application of the accumulation of acquired knowledge. Wisdom is an instant recognition of truth in a present moment when you are living out from realizations and enlightenments and are consistently able to turn within.

14. Wisdom isn't gleaned from acquired knowledge. It already exists, it's an inherent gift within all who awaken to the recognition of the God in Christ and the Christ awareness in all.

STUDENT'S STORY:

Perhaps there is a body wisdom so deep that alleviates fear. I have a mind, senses, intellect, reason, emotional body and, whether or not I like it, an ego and sense of self. My wisdom has more pathways to traverse before coming to be second nature and ultimately first nature. Wisdom for me has taken time to recognize. I find it rises slowly from a deep place within my core and heart. Uncensored, it is an impulse that rises in purity and is translated in truth. The "I am" able to live wisely. Wisdom has come after the natural progression from lived experience registered by the senses and reflected and interpreted by the intellect and mind and rising from realizations within the heart. This amalgam of impressions align in intelligent order and speak a language called wisdom. It is a silent language yet powerful beyond measure. Rooted in wisdom the ebb and flow of life's contingencies are rendered manageable.

I take neither credit nor apology for my wisdom or lack of. Wisdom simply is more or less operative in my life. As I journey further on this path towards wholeness in Christ through the power of the Holy Spirit I find wisdom quietly ingratiating itself in my every thought, feeling, emotion and action. Wherever I go, it goes. It is a sweet sound in my heart and the song it sings is the glory of God.

+ +

LESSON: 201 — WITNESS

THE WITNESS IS an aware individual expression of consciousness witnessing the rising of the vibrating energy.

1. During an intensive silent prayer practice, the witness is just there witnessing all that rises and falls.
2. The witness practice is used to realize the detachment enlightenment. There is no dialoguing, no labeling, no identifying any *thing*, nor any *one*.
3. No matter how tempting it is for the witness to get caught up in the rising vibrating energy of conscious expressions of thoughts, or images, the witness temporarily remains in place.
4. The witness stays alert and witnesses everything rising and falling in consciousness, until the witness *itself* falls away.
5. When the witness falls away, there is no "you" left to witness, no "I," no "me." Just the rising and falling of vibrating energy in pure awareness.
6. What remains once the witness falls away is the awareness of all that is going on: vibrating energy rising and falling. There is no you, no I, nor any me there at all.
7. There is pure awareness of the vibrating energy rising and falling. Total detachment. It is a realization of no person and no personal to attach: just a being in pure awareness.
8. Once total detachment is realized, the witness may be consciously re-created but the witness has no reality, no permanency.

+ +

LESSON: 202 — THE "WORD"

THE "WORD" IS the word made flesh. "And the Word was made flesh, and dwelt among us (and we beheld his glory, the glory as of the only begotten of the Father,) full of grace and truth" (John I: 14).

Jesus promised what was true of Him was true of us. "And the glory which thou gavest me I have given them; that they may be one, even as we are one" (John 17: 22).

1. All vibrating energy creates sound. All forms have an individual sound. The mind has its sound, as does the body. You live and move as the spiritual source of your God. "For in him we live, and move, and have our being; as certain also of your own poets have said, For we are also his offspring" (Acts 17: 28).

2. When you practice the silent Christ Centered Prayer, the straight gate and narrow way, all that you need is the "Word" and sound that *you are* to become aware of the Spiritual Heart Center and rest in awareness.

3. Although the "Word" is made flesh, it remains the Word of God and the Word of God *is* eternal. "The grass withereth, the flower fadeth: but the word of our God shall stand for ever" (Isaiah 40: 8).

4. You live and breathe as the image of your God source. It is like water frozen: when it melts it is again liquid water. Its source never changed. Although the Word is made flesh, its God source/spirit, never changed. "Hereby know we that we dwell in him, and he in us, because he hath given us of his Spirit" (I John 4: 13).

5. With the help of the Christ Centered Prayer practice, you may silently and directly enter into the recognition of the fullness of your God-nature. "In the beginning was the Word, and the Word was with God, and the Word was God" (John I:1).

6. The silent Christ Centered Prayer practice, with you as the "Word," may vibrate without hindrance of any kind to the ultimate awareness of the oneness — the nature of your Being. "One God and Father of all, who *is* above all, and through all, and in you all" (Ephesians 4: 6).

7. The "Word," that you are, is a powerful individual vibrating energy sound. You are unique and wonderfully made. There is only one exactly like you in the entire universe. How special you are, how loved by God you are! "I will praise thee; for I am fearfully *and* wonderfully made: marvelous *are* thy works; and *that* my soul knoweth right well" (Psalm 139: 14).

8. As the "Word" of God, you may consent and open directly to the awareness of the Divine presence within the Spiritual Heart Center. "And he *was* clothed with a vesture dipped in blood: and his name is called The Word of God" (Revelation 19: 13).

9. There is not any time that you are separate and apart from being the "Word" of God/Spirit. "He that dwelleth in the secret place of the most High shall abide under the shadow of the Almighty" (Psalm 91: 1).

10. Your spiritual nature is recorded in the heavens and exists in the Trinity of God's Being. "For there are three that bear record in heaven, the Father, the Word, and the Holy Ghost: and these three are one" (I John 5: 7).

+ +

LESSON: 203 — WORDS - WRITTEN - SPOKEN

Words - written - spoken are the outward accumulation of the manifestation of thoughts.

1. Written and spoken words continue to be translated about the truth. The written and spoken words may carry power invested by either messenger or the recipient.

2. Any language may carry an important truth message. Words may also be used to distort truth.

3. Words may also fail to convey the messenger's true intent. "For a dream cometh through the multitude of business; and a fool's voice *is known* by multitude of words" (Ecclesiastes 5: 3).

4. Words may have different meanings and definitions, depending on the particular conditioning of the culture. Translations may fail in their attempt to convey an exact meaning from one conditioned culture and language to another.

5. Words, no matter how fancy, small, or large are not in and of themselves truth. Words may have an influence and be about truth. In reality only truth *is*, and you are it.

6. On a spiritual walk during a spiritual journey, words may help explain and guide. Words may also be locks on the entrance door to realizing truth.

7. Do not get hung up and attached on the words themselves. Go beyond words to the truth within. Do not create false idols with words. "And the scribe said unto him, Well, Master, thou hast said the truth: for there is one God; and there is none other but he:" (Mark 12: 32).

8. Within the Spiritual Heart Center, the Holy Spirit in the name of Jesus Christ, silently speaks without words. Learn to listen.

+ +

LESSON: 204 — WORSHIP

WORSHIP IS COMING before God with an open surrendered posture to receive God in spirit and in truth. "God *is* a Spirit: and they that worship him must worship in spirit and in truth" (John 4: 24)

1. Worship is the opening to that place in consciousness where you are receptive to receive the gifts of God through the Holy Spirit in the name of Jesus Christ.

2. Worship is an inner spiritual falling to your knees with an opened heart to receive the things of God. "O come, let us worship and bow down: let us kneel before the LORD our Maker" (Psalm 95: 6).

3. Worship is that moment you willingly say, "Yes, Lord." In an aware Christ Consciousness, worship may exist every moment of your life. "Then saith Jesus unto him, Get thee hence, Satan: for it is written, Thou shalt worship the Lord thy God, and him only shalt thou serve" (Matthew 4: 10).

4. Worship is the acceptance of your true nature in Christ Jesus. It is a state of being.

5. Worship is being ever mindful of your true nature in the oneness of pure awareness and the Christ Consciousness.

6. Worship is an established relationship with Jesus Christ through the activity of the Holy Spirit.

7. Worship with others occurs in that moment when you share the revealed truth of your Christ Being with those who are also ready to receive.

8. Worshiping in the name of Jesus Christ may grace you with the presence of the Christ Consciousness and realized awareness.

+ +

LESSON: 205 — X-MAS - CHRISTMAS

X-MAS IS AN abbreviation for Christmas. Christmas is the name given for the day that Christians celebrate the birth of Jesus Christ.

1. The word X-mas for Christmas has become acceptable by many Christians.

2. Symbols may have sacred invested powers. X-mas as a word symbol, denigrates what it represents.

3. To intentionally, or unintentionally, remove the word Christ from Christmas X's out the opportunity to invest the sacred power connected with the vibratory energy of Jesus.

4. You do yourself an injustice and insult your spiritual integrity when you X out the Christ.

5. To deny the Christ in Christmas is to deny your Christ identity in the oneness of the Christ.

6. Christmas has been commercialized. The Christ of your being cannot be brought into the market place under the guise of X-mas. Celebrate Christmas in your religious sanctuaries of prayer and within your Spiritual Heart Center.

7. During Jesus' time, the market place was brought into God's house of prayer in Jerusalem. Is there a difference?

8. The sacredness of Christmas need not be profaned. Remove the stains of thievery and honor the day of remembrance. "And said unto them, It is written, My house shall be called the house of prayer; but ye have made it a den of thieves" (Matthew 21: 13).

9. You have been given the greatest gift of all gifts — the birth of Jesus Christ. Why would you want to remove the remembrance of this gift from the sacred word of Christmas?

10. Words may have an influence and may have a resounding impact on the mind.

11. The mind is in consciousness. Be cautious what you allow to enter.

12. Take back this sacred symbol and return it to its proper place within your conscious mind.

13 Celebrate the birth of Jesus Christ — not your parents, aunts, uncles, and friends. Give to them your warm greetings and the blessed reminder just whose birthday it is Christians celebrate on this day of remembrance.

14. Present your gift to Jesus Christ. And the greatest gift you may present to Him on the day of *His* birthday celebration is the one of *yourself*.

++++++++++++++++++++++++++

LESSON: 206 — YIELDING

YIELDING IS A moment of surrender to the inner Christ when there is a time of choice between the inner and the outer world. "I delight to do thy will, O my God: yea, thy law *is* within my heart"(Psalm 40: 8).

1. There are times on your spiritual walk when you are asked to yield to your inner life's commitment. It is a hard lesson and a demanding invitation. It is one you will be faced with as long as you are in this world and not of it.

2. A lifetime of resisting surrender to the demands of your inner life may challenge your demand to be in control rather than the Christ of your being. To yield, to surrender, to give in, to let go, and to willingly follow where Jesus leads *is* where your strength lies. "My flesh and my heart faileth: *but* God *is* the strength of my heart, and my portion for ever" (Psalm 73: 26).

3. When you come to a time-place of yielding, there may be a small part of you that still does not want to render to God that which belongs to God. ". . . Render therefore unto Caesar the things which are Caesar's; and unto God the things that are God's" (Matthew 22: 21).

4. You may struggle to holdout and not yield to that which you are. The mind sense is constantly trying to hold on to its false belief that it is in control and hesitates to yield to the inner guidance of the Holy Spirit in the name of Jesus Christ.

5. In this world of competition, you are conditioned to be strong in your resolve and yielding may be seen, or felt, to be a sign of weakness. This may cause an inner or outer struggle at moments of invitation from the Christ to yield. Yielding to the Christ's agenda may, at times, come in direct conflict with your outer life's preferences.

6. You may be asked to choose between an inner commitment and an outer choice. It may seem easier to accept the outer invitation and put off the inner commitment for another time. "O Timothy, keep that

which is committed to thy trust, avoiding profane *and* vain babblings, and oppositions of science falsely so called" (I Timothy 6: 20).

7. When you can walk away from an inner commitment for an outer invitation (not a necessary one) it is as good as saying, "Jesus you can wait, I have something better to do." Jesus will wait. That is what He does best, but you put your spiritual progress on hold. Ultimately, you are the one who will do the waiting.

8. Yielding to the inner demands of your spiritual life may be the most difficult lesson for you to learn. When a moment of temptation rises, "Choose ye who you shall serve," you either strengthen your inner connection or you weaken it. It is a lesson you meet or repeat.

9. It is a difficult lesson because it comes when least expected often in disguise. "Temptation" is not written across anyone's chest in large red letters nor in blazing red flames in any situation. You usually have a twinge (Ouch!) in consciousness when you are about to succumb to temptation of choice.

10. It is when you ignore the twinge and push ahead that you insult your spiritual integrity. To remain loyal to the Christ of your being requires a disciplined obedience to the warning twinge in consciousness. The flesh is weak and more easily yields to worldly temptations. "Watch and pray, that ye enter not into temptation: the spirit indeed *is* willing, but the flesh *is* weak" (Matthew 26: 41).

11. Once aware, there is no spigot for turning off or on at your convenience. You cannot separate your awakened state from the dream play. The flow is from within therefore, that twinge in consciousness is your caution light. You need take the time to pause before proceeding. It may prevent a head on crash.

12. The temptation to betray the Christ of your being comes in many disguises and degrees. Each is a betrayal. You are a living Bible and all of the lessons are there. Heed them or repeat them. ". . . Verily, verily, I say unto you, that one of you shall betray me" (John 13: 21).

13. As you do the will of God, the Christ Consciousness does not interfere with your daily responsibilities. The conflict of interest usually rises outside from your daily or job responsibilities. "Not with eye service, as men pleasers; but as the servants of Christ, doing the will of God from the heart;" (Ephesians 6: 6).

14. This is a journey of pure awareness. Pure in thought, word, and deed. With respect and reverence, this purity comes from the awareness of the Christ of your being. It is responsible living. "Wherefore we receiving a kingdom which cannot be moved, let us have grace, whereby we may serve God acceptably with reverence and godly fear: For our God *is* a consuming fire" (Hebrews 12: 28 - 29).

+ +

LESSON: 207 — ZONE — SPIRITUAL

Zone — spiritual, is a designated area for the Spiritual Heart Center where the Holy Spirit reveals the teaching of the Father in the name of Jesus Christ.

1. When you began your spiritual practices and studies of The Lessons, you entered the Spiritual Heart Center Zone. All of The Lessons were gifted from the Spiritual Heart Center.

2. Life upon this plane is a spiritual walk. If you are a follower of Jesus Christ, it is a Christ Centered Spiritual journey by way of the straight gate and narrow way. Within your Spiritual Heart Center, the Sacred Heart of Jesus Christ and the Immaculate Heart of the Blessed Mother Mary continuously touch your Spiritual Heart in the oneness of Their love.

3. It is a love that guides you home to your eternal awareness of being. The silent Christ Centered Prayer practice is in support of the journey that draws you directly into the Spiritual Heart Center Zone.

4. It is in the Spiritual Heart Zone that the Holy Spirit awaits your entrance and teaches you all that Jesus Christ promised. "But the comforter, which is the Holy Ghost, whom the Father will send in my name, he shall teach you all things, and bring all things to your remembrance, whatsoever I have said unto you" (John 14: 26).

5. When you are where you belong, continue your silent Christ Centered Prayer practice. Pray and read Holy Scripture.

6. God speed your journey home and God bless your secret and sacred determined purpose to awaken to that which you are.

PART III

EXERCISES

MAJOR POINTS

"NOW WHAT?"

CONCLUSION

EXERCISES

These are exercises you may wish to work with, practice, and/or ponder.

1. ATTENTION:

Place your thumb and index finger together. Place your attention on the thumb touching the index finger then shift your attention to the index finger touching the thumb.

2. BEYOND DIFFERENCES:

For one day, do any household chore as though it were a sacred ritual.

3. CONSCIOUSNESS WITHIN AWARENESS:

With paper and pencil, draw a cooking pot filled with water on a stove burner. Now, draw small round circles (bubbles) within the water. As the water (consciousness) boils within the pot (awareness), bubbles (individuals consciousness) rise. So it is in awareness, consciousness individually rises. All is within awareness, the pot.

4. EXPANDING CONSCIOUS AWARENESS:

Sitting on a chair, close your eyes, be aware of your body touching the chair seat, the chair feet touching the floor within the room, the foundation of the house touching the earth, the earth connected to the neighborhood block, the block within the city, the city within the state, the state within the nation, and the nation touching other nations.

5. FOCUSED ATTENTION:

Visit a friend. Allow the friend to converse without any interruption. Allow the entire conversation to be about your friend.

6. STAMINA THROUGH AWARENESS:

Stand up straight with arms folded over chest, relax, and be aware of your feet touching the ground. You may be able to stand for hours by staying aware of your feet touching the ground.

7. HANDS - AWARENESS EXPERIENCE:

Sitting, close your eyes, raise both hands chest high, and "very" slowly turn your hands with full awareness of each movement of your hands.

8. PERSONAL SENSE OF "I, ME, MY, MINE:"

For a half day, do not use the words "I, me, my, mine" in speech or writing. If not a half day, do an hour or whatever is possible.

9. JESUS:

If Jesus were standing before you right now, this moment, what would you do? Do it.

10. KNOWING:

On a bright morning, look out of a window and write down on paper everything you are seeing. Next, take each concept you have written down and write the nature of what you were seeing.

11. LIVING IN THE PRESENT:

Start a day without any plans. Do only what is given to you to do each moment. Do not plan your next moment — there is none. Stay only with the present moment.

12. MIND - RESTING:

Talk less and listen more. Practice talking when it is absolutely necessary. Be aware of thoughts having to rise less often, when you talk less. Idol talk helps create a restless mind.

13. NOT DISTINGUISHABLE:

The next time anyone praises you consider it criticism and the next time anyone criticizes you consider it praise. Eventually, they are not distinguishable.

14. ON AWAKENING:

On first awakening in the morning, note the "flash instant" of awareness before consciousness - mind rises. Note the sequence: awareness, self-consciousness, mind, and its contents. In that flash instant of awareness, there is no content.

15. PRESENT - PAST - FUTURE:

Imagine you are on a street corner watching a parade approaching. You can see and are aware of its beginnings (present). Imagine that you go to a second story window to watch the same parade. You are able to see and be aware of the passing (past) and more of the coming parade (future). Now, imagine you move to the roof of the house and can view the entire parade — present, past and future. All occurring at the same time, in the present, and you are aware of it.

16. QUALITY — Do this exercise only if you are permitted to use salt and pepper.

At a meal time, label the salt shaker good and the pepper shaker bad. For lunch use only what is labeled good. At dinnertime label the salt shaker bad and the pepper shaker good. Use only what is labeled good. What changed the shakers quality?

17. REALIZATIONS:

If you have never tasted chocolate ice-cream, can you realize what it tastes like from someone else talking about it? If you want the realization for yourself, what must you do? The same is true of realizing truth.

18. SILENCE:

Sit comfortably, eyes closed, and place your attention on listening to hear a phone ring.

19. SOUND:

Gently press your fingers over your left ear. Listen carefully and you may hear the "humming" sound. You may also do it with both ears closed.

20. TIMELESS DAY:

When you have a free day, remove your wrist watch, cover all clocks in the house, and live a day without time. If a day is too long, do it for a half day and experience the freedom without time.

21. WRITE:

Write on a piece of paper, "I am." now, draw a diagonal line through the "I." Ponder what you have left.

22. YES:

Review a day or week of how often you said, "No" and note if any "no" could have been a "yes." Would it have changed anything? How does it feel?

MAJOR POINTS

REVIEWING THE FOLLOWING major points from the 207 Lessons, may assist you in your zeal to wake up and dream walk no more.

1. The entire universe is consciousness. All that is, is consciousness.
2. All that is consciously created in the universe is relative to the universe.
3. Conscious mind-body are in conscious awareness. Consciousness is within awareness.
4. You are not the mind, body, nor anything in the universe.
5. You are not in the universe, the universe is in you.
6. As the universe disappears, the different and many usages of consciousness fade.
7. Consciousness changes and is limited. Awareness is changeless and limitless.
8. You may be aware of being conscious, but not conscious of awareness.
9. There is One Void - One God Aware Consciousness.
10. The One becomes the many. The many returns to the One.
11. This world, earth plane of opposites, is not your permanent home.
12. All of this world must deteriorate and die. The life you are is immortal, eternal.
13. Be aware, there isn't anything that can attach to what or who you are. Mind's identifying attachment to anything, causes suffering.
14. Constantly, constantly know, you are not that which you can taste, touch, smell, hear, think, and what is true of you is true of all.
15. You may become aware of your Spiritual Heart Center with the practice of the silent Christ Centered Prayer, the straight gate and narrow way.
16. Turn within to your Spiritual Heart Center and listen for your spiritual guidance directing your spiritual progress and practical living.
17. You are an aware, free being, coming and going in experiences of dimensions in consciousness within awareness. Wake up and live!
18. Jesus Christ is alive and well. Enter by the "straight gate and narrow way" and know Him as He *is* and you *are*.

"NOW WHAT?"

YOU HAVE SOARED to the heights of your reality and still you question, "Lord, here I am, your image, your light, and your way upon an earth of quicksand, now what?"

You have finally gone beyond this world of make believe. You have done all the necessary spiritual practices, learned all the necessary lessons, you *are* the necessary enlightenment, and still you may be left befuddled about what, where, how, and when.

All your work, all your struggle has finally paid off big time. You are an awakened being, ready and willing to leave this plane of opposites. Yet, here you are still among the sleep walkers, dream makers. Questions rise rapidly. You question yourself in reflection, "Did I think the world and its illusions of false concepts would disappear? Or did I think I would disappear?" Neither may happen. Instead, you are here, not of this world, but still in it. So, there may be a period of adjustment. Remember, wisdom is slow to rise.

All of your emotions are intact. All of your needs are met. All of the things of this world are at your disposal. You desire nothing, you have everything. You are a Contemplative among a world of sleep walkers and truth seekers. You know the truth and yet you may find yourself still in a world of illusion. A world you no longer call home. "Now What?" Where to go from here?" "What do you do, and how do you do it?"

Your first thought may be to hide in a cave or remote area — away from the hustle and bustle of this world. Perhaps, for a time you may be able to do just that and it may be the wise thing to do, for a time. Live in the silence and solitude with your realization of who and what you are. You may find like most enlightened beings you are called back into the thick of this world's activities.

At first, you may honestly put up a good fight — not wanting to be bothered by the time illusions created by false concepts, wanting to stay at the zenith of your aware being. You may find yourself slowly or abruptly dragged back into the center of it all. If you have a teacher, you are wise to continue to work closely with your teacher. A teacher will assist you to adjust to living between two worlds as smoothly as possible.

The, "Now what?" does not have to be earth shattering to be effective. Your work is to maintain your awakened state to the truth of your reality. You live quietly among the noise of this world. You are the expression of unconditional love, God's nature existing among those who may struggle with doubts and temptations to the contrary. You serve and do what is necessary in each and every moment.

You may or may not teach others. You may or may not be called upon to guide another to the place you are in. The, "What now? is your light among the darkness that may brighten someone's life, stir an awakened moment, or plant a fruitful spiritual seed. Your very presence among the many, who are the one, is a light you cannot hide, nor should you.

Although, you continue to walk in the dream, you are no longer a dreamer. Although, you are aware of the false appearances, concepts, and illusions, you are no longer creating them. Through the Holy Spirit in the name of Jesus Christ, you are here as a witness to all who see you — see the Father.

Now, you know you are the one of God, now you are an awakened being, now you are as you were in the beginning — with God before the world existed. "Now what?" There is no "what," there is only "now." Now, you are the living scriptures revealed in the lives of all you may see, pass, or touch. Like Jesus, you are a walking messenger creating the Father's footprints on this earth.

CONCLUSION - A CERTAINTY

"And this is life eternal, that they might know thee the only true God, and Jesus Christ, whom thou hast sent" (John 17: 3).

Jesus Christ is alive and well. He is a certainty, a living Being whom you may meet and embrace, during your lifetime upon this earth plane. Unfortunately, there may be more time spent dwelling on Jesus' death than on His life-living. His death teaches you that He lived. His life teaches you that *you* live. "Yet a little while, and the world seeth me no more; but ye see me: because I live, ye shall live also" (John 14: 19).

There is a spiritual and religious environment that may have brought confusion to the Christian reality of Jesus Christ. Jesus is more often than not thought of as an unreachable spiritual Being. One whom you may implore, pray to, and beg forgiveness. All of which you may do; however, the most important information about Jesus Christ is that you may meet Him. You may embrace Him. You may converse face to face with Him. The distance between you and Jesus is imaginary. "Jesus Christ the same yesterday, and to day, and for ever" (Hebrews 13: 8).

You may have the mistaken belief you must die to go to heaven and meet Jesus. In truth, heaven, Jesus, and the Father exist within you and you may enter that kingdom. No one can take you there. No one can give it to you. No one can take it away from you. No one can deny your entrance. No one can steal it from you. No one can buy it for you. No one can sell it to you. Through the Holy Spirit in the name of Jesus Christ, the kingdom of heaven and the presence of Jesus Christ is always yours free and clear. "For through him we both have access by one Spirit unto the Father" (Ephesians 2: 18).

Jesus' crucifixion was a necessary, one-time event but the resurrection and ascension is a constant ongoing celebration of His and your life eternal. Jesus Christ is not a myth, image, nor idol. Jesus is as real now, as He ever was or will be. There is not any time that Jesus does not stand and await your return to His and the Father's warm welcome home. "At that day ye shall know that I *am* in my Father, and ye in me, and I in you" (John 14: 20).

Jesus' availability need not be surrounded by mystery, symbolic rituals, nor religious institutions. The silent Christ Centered Prayer practice guides you to the straight gate and narrow way that may take you directly to His presence, in the Spiritual Heart Center within you. When Jesus walked the earth plane, He walked and talked directly to the Father within His being. Jesus came to teach you that you could do the same. The Father and Jesus are one and your life exists within that oneness. "That they all may be one; as thou, Father, *art* in me, and I in thee, that they also may be one in us: that the world may believe that thou hast sent me" (John 17: 21).

You do not have to travel a distance, pay large sums of money, perform mysterious rituals, nor undergo difficult initiations. Turn within and open your Spiritual Heart Center to the presence and reality of the Kingdom of God and Jesus Christ. Turn within and you are there where you never left and will always be. Come home to the source of your being without ever taking one step in any direction. ". . . The Kingdom of God cometh not with observation: Neither shall they say, Lo here! or, lo there! For, behold, the Kingdom of God is within you" (Luke 17: 20-21).

Jesus Christ brings to your daily practical outer living a greater dimension, as He accompanies you on your spiritual walk. Knowing and trusting Jesus Christ adds the necessary clarity, understanding, and guidance to your daily practical life. "Trust in the LORD with all thine heart; and lean not unto thine own understanding. In all thy ways acknowledge him, and he shall direct thy paths" (Proverbs 3: 5-6).

The silent Christ Centered Prayer practice will assist you to turn within. Your kingdom is not of this world. Your peace beyond understanding is not of this world. Your eternal life is not of this world. Turn within, turn within, turn within. "Behold, I stand at the door, and knock: if any man hear my voice, and open the door, I will come in to him and will sup with him, and he with me" (Revelation 3: 20). Jesus is knocking at the inner door of your Spiritual Heart Center, won't you open it?

NOTES

NOTES

NOTES

NOTES